Frommer's®

P9-BYM-797

Shanghai

3rd Edition

by Sharon Owyang

Shan Xi and Fuzhou
nar Shan Xi Subway

Here's what the critics say about Frommer's:

"Amazingly easy to use. Very portable, very complete."
—*Booklist*

"Detailed, accurate, and easy-to-read information for all price ranges."
—*Glamour Magazine*

"Hotel information is close to encyclopedic."
—*Des Moines Sunday Register*

"Frommer's Guides have a way of giving you a real feel for a place."
—*Knight Ridder Newspapers*

WILEY
Wiley Publishing, Inc.

About the Author

Sharon Owyang, born in Singapore and a graduate of Harvard University, divides her time between film and television projections in the U.S. and China, and free-lance travel writing. She was a contributor to *Frommer's China, 1st Edition,* and has also written about Shanghai, China, Vietnam, and San Diego for *Insight Guides, Compact Guides,* and the *Los Angeles Times.* She speaks Mandarin, Cantonese, and enough Shanghainese to be a curiosity to the locals. She would like to thank Tess Johnston, and Wu Zhude and his family for their various forms of help.

Published by:

Wiley Publishing, Inc.

111 River St.
Hoboken, NJ 07030-5774

ISBN 0-7645-7305-5

Editor: Caroline Sieg
Production Editor: Heather Wilcox
Cartographer: Roberta Stockwell
Photo Editor: Richard Fox
Production by Wiley Indianapolis Composition Services

Front cover photo: Large group doing Tai Chi
Back cover photo: Nanjing Dong Lu shopping area, night: elevated view

For information on our other products and services or to obtain technical support, please contact our Customer Care Department within the U.S. at 800/762-2974, outside the U.S. at 317/572-3993 or fax 317/572-4002.

Wiley also publishes its books in a variety of electronic formats. Some content that appears in print may not be available in electronic formats.

Manufactured in the United States of America

5   4   3

Contents

5 Where to Dine   90

6 What to See & Do in Shànghǎi   116

7 Shànghǎi Strolls   176

8 Shopping   198

List of Maps

An Invitation to the Reader

In researching this book, we discovered many wonderful places—hotels, restaurants, shops, and more. We're sure you'll find others. Please tell us about them, so we can share the information with your fellow travelers in upcoming editions. If you were disappointed with a recommendation, we'd love to know that, too. Please write to:

Frommer's Shanghai, 3rd Edition
Wiley Publishing, Inc. • 111 River St. • Hoboken, NJ 07030-5774

An Additional Note

Please be advised that travel information is subject to change at any time—and this is especially true of prices. We therefore suggest that you write or call ahead for confirmation when making your travel plans. The authors, editors, and publisher cannot be held responsible for the experiences of readers while traveling. Your safety is important to us, however, so we encourage you to stay alert and be aware of your surroundings. Keep a close eye on cameras, purses, and wallets, all favorite targets of thieves and pickpockets.

Other Great Guides for Your Trip:

Frommer's China

Frommer's China: The 50 Most Memorable Trips

Frommer's Beijing

Frommer's Hong Kong

Frommer's Portable Hong Kong

Suzy Gershman's Born to Shop Hong Kong, Shanghai & Beijing

Frommer's Star Ratings, Icons & Abbreviations

Every hotel, restaurant, and attraction listing in this guide has been ranked for quality, value, service, amenities, and special features using a **star-rating system.** In country, state, and regional guides, we also rate towns and regions to help you narrow down your choices and budget your time accordingly. Hotels and restaurants are rated on a scale of zero (recommended) to three stars (exceptional). Attractions, shopping, nightlife, towns, and regions are rated according to the following scale: zero stars (recommended), one star (highly recommended), two stars (very highly recommended), and three stars (must-see).

In addition to the star-rating system, we also use **seven feature icons** that point you to the great deals, in-the-know advice, and unique experiences that separate travelers from tourists. Throughout the book, look for:

Finds	Special finds—those places only insiders know about
Fun Fact	Fun facts—details that make travelers more informed and their trips more fun
Kids	Best bets for kids and advice for the whole family
Moments	Special moments—those experiences that memories are made of
Overrated	Places or experiences not worth your time or money
Tips	Insider tips—great ways to save time and money
Value	Great values—where to get the best deals

The following **abbreviations** are used for credit cards:

AE	American Express	DISC	Discover	V	Visa
DC	Diners Club	MC	MasterCard		

Frommers.com

Now that you have the guidebook to a great trip, visit our website at **www.frommers.com** for travel information on more than 3,000 destinations. With features updated regularly, we give you instant access to the most current trip-planning information available. At Frommers.com, you'll also find the best prices on airfares, accommodations, and car rentals—and you can even book travel online through our travel booking partners. At Frommers.com, you'll also find the following:

- Online updates to our most popular guidebooks
- Vacation sweepstakes and contest giveaways
- Newsletter highlighting the hottest travel trends
- Online travel message boards with featured travel discussions

What's New in Shànghǎi

With skyscrapers going up faster than old houses can be preserved, plus restaurants, bars, and shops opening and closing faster than the palate and wallet can keep up, Shànghǎi continues to change at warp speed. As the designated host of the 2010 World Expo, and a big beneficiary of China's recent accession to the World Trade Organization, Shànghǎi, pulsating with energy, vitality, and possibility, is once again attracting record numbers of foreigners and Chinese flocking here to stake out their share of the ever-expanding pie. Here are the latest changes, openings, and offerings in a city that is easily the most exciting in China, if not the world.

PLANNING A TRIP TO SHÀNGHǍI The formerly biennial **Shànghǎi International Film Festival** is now an annual affair moved up to June from its original fall dates.

GETTING TO KNOW SHÀNGHǍI The highly anticipated **Maglev** train is now running between Pǔdōng International Airport and Lóngyáng Lù Metro Station, where travelers can connect to the Metro Line 2 subway. However, few travelers actually use the new train to get to town—navigating Shànghǎi's crowded subway system with luggage and changes of train is more of a hassle and takes almost as long as a taxi or an **airport shuttle** (the latter recently expanded its service to a wide range of downtown hotels). Completion of the **Lúpǔ Bridge** west of the Nánpǔ Bridge now offers another, faster option of reaching downtown from

Pǔdōng Airport, reducing the journey to around 45 minutes in regular traffic. New higher-speed **trains,** some with soft-sleeper cars only, have now reduced the journey between Shànghǎi and Běijīng from 14 hours to 12 hours. There are special soft-sleeper ticket counters at the railway station and around the city. Shànghǎi's waterfront continues to undergo massive changes as the old **Shíliùpǔ Wharf** is no longer a working dock. It is currently being renovated into a marina, park, and commercial complex due to open sometime in the next 4 to 5 years (although projected dates by Chinese authorities are never realistic). However, the plan is to finish the Wharf in plenty of time to impress visitors when Shànghǎi hosts the 2010 World Expo. Boats serving the Yángzǐ River and Pǔtuó Shān now berth at **Wúsōng Passenger Terminal** (② 021/5657-5500), where the Huángpǔ River flows into the Yángzǐ.

Shànghǎi's preparation for the 2010 World Expo doesn't end here—related construction on subways, roadways, hotels, and museums continues unabated. Expect traffic delays and allow enough time to reach your destination. At least traffic assistants at major intersections now help control pedestrian and automobile traffic.

For complete information on getting to know Shànghǎi, see chapter 5.

WHERE TO STAY New four- and five-star hotels continue to open in Shànghǎi. While demand has ratcheted to unprecedented levels, the glut of high-end hotels continues to mean highly competitive discounts except during times when large conventions, expos, and, special events such as Formula One racing come to town, at which point hotel rates actually approach their published rack rates. Leading the way for the luxury hotels is the stunning **JW Marriott** (© 021/ 5359-4969), which finally opened at Tomorrow Square in late 2003 after many months of delay as tallest hotel west of the Huángpǔ River. Other new aspiring five-star hotels include the handsome and colorful **Renaissance Shànghǎi Pǔdōng Hotel** (© 021/3871-4888) in the Jīn Qiáo business area of Pǔdōng; the **Howard Johnson Plaza Hotel** (© 800/820- 2525 or 021/3313-4888) just off the Nánjīng Lù Pedestrian Mall; and the Hong Kong–run **Mayfair Hotel** (© 021/6240-8888) next to Zhōngshān Park in the developing area of northwestern Shànghǎi. Happily, Pǔdōng Airport now has the **Ramada Pǔdōng Airport Hotel** (© 021/3849-4949) located within a 10-minute walk.

The **Pǔdōng Shangri-La Hotel** (© 800/942-5050 or 021/6882- 8888), still boasting the best views of the Bund, is getting ready to open its new wing in 2005, which should bring the total number of rooms to around 1,000. The **Hilton Hotel** (© 800/ 445-8667 or 021/6248-0000) is in the middle of a long-term upgrade to its rooms, which, when complete, should feature such luxurious amenities as flatscreen televisions and bedside curtain controls.

Many other hotels took advantage of the SARS-related tourist lull in 2003 to upgrade their rooms and facilities, including the **Huá Tíng Hotel Towers** (© 021/6439-1000), and other four-star outfits such as the **Broadway Mansions Hotel** (© 021/ 6324-6260) just north of the Bund,

and the **Héngshān Hotel** (© 021/ 6437-7050) at the southern end of trendy Héngshān Lù.

Beyond the slick modern towers, an increasing number of hotels are now located inside restored colonial mansions and old Art Deco buildings: On the northwestern edge of the French Concession, the acid-trip that is the **Héngshān Moller Villa** (© 021/ 6247-8881), once firmly closed to the public as the headquarters of the Communist Youth League, is now an overpriced but still fascinating hotel worth a visit; the Art Deco **Yangtze Hotel** (© 021/6351-7880) is getting raves for its facilities, location (just east of People's Square and within walking distance of Nánjīng Lù and the Bund), and most of all its reasonable prices; and even the old backpacker standby, the **Pǔjiāng Hotel** (© 021/6324-6388) has upgraded and now rents out four "celebrity" rooms (including one in which Albert Einstein stayed). Budget travelers need no longer settle for hovels, not with the no-frills but totally charming **Jùyīng Bīnguǎn** (© 021/6466-7788, ext. 885/886) and the **Shànghǎi Conservatory of Music Guest House** (© 021/6437-2577), both located in the French Concession.

See chapter 4 for additional details on accommodations in Shànghǎi.

WHERE TO DINE   The dynamic Shànghǎi dining scene continues to bedazzle with new openings, led by the world-class restaurants at **Three On the Bund complex:** Jean-Georges Vongerichten's **Jean Georges** (© 021/ 6321-7733) may finally appease folks who complain about Shànghǎi's mediocre French fare; former executive chef of London's Mezzo restaurant, Australian David Laris, promises to serve up "new world" cuisines at **Laris,** while the **Whampoa Club** will test master chef Jerome Leung's ability to take traditional Shànghǎi recipes and make them all his own. Meanwhile, **Xīn Tiāndì** restaurants continue to proliferate; especially noteworthy is the Cantonese/Shànghǎi eatery **Crystal Jade Restaurant** (℃ **021/6385-8752**), out of Singapore, which churns out the best *xiǎolóng bāo* dumplings and hand-pulled noodles on either side of the Yángzǐ River. Shànghǎi cooking is more exciting than ever, headlined by the three branches of **Shànghǎi Uncle** (℃ **021/6339-1977**), which puts a delightfully modern and creative spin on old classics. Other Chinese cuisines are rapidly gaining popularity in Shànghǎi, with standouts including the Hú'nán **Dī Shuǐ Dòng** (℃ **021/ 6253-2689**); the Sìchuān **Bā Guó Bù Yī** (℃ **021/6270-6668**); and the utterly delightful Guìzhōu find, **Lǎo Tán** (℃ **021/6283-7843**).

Continental and fusion fare continue to sport exciting new faces: **Mesa** (℃ **021/6289-9108**), from the former chef of T8 and one of the former owners of the bar Face, boasts a chic French concession restaurant offering creative nouvelle cuisine, while lovely **La Villa Rouge** (℃ **021/ 6431-9811**), located in the restored red brick mansion that formerly housed EMI Recording Studios, serves up winning French-fusion cuisine from its team of Japanese chefs.

Chic, nouvelle Japanese dining has arrived with the post-modern Bauhaus-style **Shintori Null II** (℃ **021/ 5404-5252**). Thai and Indian cuisines continue to catch on with locals.

The SARS-driven downturn closed many restaurants, but one victim, **Le Garçon Chinois** (℃ **021/6445-7970**), happily reemerged as a Spanish restaurant (despite its French name which translates to "The Chinese Boy") tapping into the latest tapas craze.

For complete information on Shànghǎi's restaurants, see chapter 5.

WHAT TO SEE & DO IN SHÀNGHǍI With Shànghǎi's goal of housing 100 museums by the World Expo of 2010, museums continue to sprout. Two worthy mentions include the **Shànghǎi Music Conservatory Oriental Musical Instrument Museum** (℃ **021/6437-0137**, ext. 2132), with its range of rare and traditional Chinese and ethnic minority musical instruments; and the **Shànghǎi Bank Museum** (℃ **021/ 5878-8743**) in Pǔdōng, which traces the history of Chinese banking, especially apropos for this city, but at press time, the museum was inexplicably open only to tour groups. Most exciting is the new **Bibliotheca Zi-ka-wei** (℃ **021/6487-4095**) next to the Xújiāhuì Cathedral, the former library of the Jesuits, which has preserved remarkably well its collection of over 560,000 volumes. Due to high rents, the **Museum of Ancient Chinese Sex Culture** has been forced out of Shànghǎi to the neighboring village of Tónglǐ.

The Daoist temple **Báiyún Guàn** in the old Chinese city is apparently no match for a new Taiwanese development, and at press time, it was being relocated next to the **Dàjìng Gé,** the old city wall (℃ **021/6385-2443**), or at least what's left of it.

Alas, the **Jǐnj Jiāng Tourist Bus,** which used to stop at the major sights, has been discontinued.

Formula One racing now includes Shànghǎi. At press time, the suburb of Āntíng was in the midst of hosting the event, which promises to spawn a whole new Chinese spectator sport, if only the locals can afford the tickets or find some convenient way to get out there.

For complete information on exploring Shànghǎi, see chapter 6.

SHOPPING The biggest changes on the shopping front continue to be the turnover in retail stores. Two large new malls, **Super Brand Mall** (✆ 021/6887-7888) in Pǔdōng (*the mall to be seen at*) and **Raffles City** (✆ 021/6340-3600) at People's Square, do their part to make Shànghǎi even more of a consumer city than it already is. Shànghǎi's **Friendship Store** (✆ 021/6337-3555), meanwhile, has moved from its original Běijīng Lù glass house to a new address at Jīnlíng Dōng Lù 68. The **Xiāngyáng Clothing Market** continues to thrive despite WTO prohibitions forcing a number of vendors underground. These vendors without visible stalls will nevertheless find you the moment you approach the market, armed with laminated photos of all their knockoffs. Do not go with them. The **Dǒngjiādù Fabric Market** in the southern part of the old Chinese city sells silks, cashmere, and yards of every fabric imaginable at less than half the cost at retail stores, and there are even tailors on-site to turn your dream outfit into a reality. **Tàikàng Lù** in the southern part of the French concession is a trendy street of artists' lofts, stylish retail stores, and hip nightclubs, though there have been rumors of the street being developed for higher rent–paying establishments.

For complete information on shopping in Shànghǎi, see chapter 8.

SHÀNGHǍI AFTER DARK

Nightlife continues to flourish despite or perhaps because of the large turnover of bars and clubs. **Màomíng Lù** has replaced Jùlù as Shànghǎi's main bar and clubbing street. Hot new nightclubs include the ultrapopular **Guandii** (✆ 021/3308-0726) next to the still popular California

Club in Fùxīng Park; the ultrapretentious **Babyface** (✆ 021/6445-2330) on Màomíng Lù; and the too-eager **B.Boss** (✆ 021/6467-0031) off Tàikàng Lù. New bars worth mentioning include the chic **Manifesto** (✆ 021/6289-9108), by the same folks operating the new restaurant Mesa, and **Amber** (✆ 021/6466-5224) on Màomíng Lù. Shànghǎi's jazz and blues scene has a few more new venues to draw artists from around the world. **Club JZ** (✆ 021/6415-5255) in the western part of the French Concession is unpretentious with good acoustics, and is considered one of the best places in town to hear improvisational jazz. **CJW,** with one outlet in Xīn Tiāndì (✆ 021/6385-6677) and another with fabulous views on top of the Bund Center (✆ 021/6339-1777), attracts quality jazz acts from abroad, but its stiff drink prices tend to keep away all but those with expense accounts.

For complete information on Shànghǎi after dark, see chapter 9.

SIDE TRIPS FROM SHÀNGHǍI

The water village of Zhōuzhuāng, though pretty, has become such a tourist trap that we found two less commercial but no less charming water villages for you to explore instead. **Tǒnglǐ,** only 20km (12 miles) away from Sūzhōu, is a pretty water town that's now also home to China's first sex museum. The still-quiet town of **Nánxún,** located between Sūzhōu and Hángzhōu, is unique for its traditional gardens and houses that blend both Chinese and Western architectural characteristics.

1

The Best of Shànghǎi

If you simply count heads, Shànghǎi is the biggest city in the biggest country on Earth. If you simply scan statistics, this is China's capital of commerce, industry, and finance. But numbers don't tell the whole story. Shànghǎi has a colonial past more intense than that of any other city in China, save Hong Kong, and this legacy gives it a dramatic character, visible in the very facades of its buildings. But the city is not only a museum of East meeting West on Chinese soil. Overnight, Shànghǎi has become one of the world's great modern capitals, the one city that best shows where China is headed at the dawn of the 21st century.

Shànghǎi was not always much of a delight to tour, but that has changed. After the building boom of the 1990s tore the city apart, new roads, highways, tunnels, and bridges, not to mention new hotels, restaurants, and sights now make Shànghǎi a city that a visitor can once again comfortably enjoy and explore. Today there are large neighborhoods of foreign architecture, wonderful for a stroll, where Europeans, especially the French, once resided. Shànghǎi's great river of commerce, the Huángpǔ, a tributary of the mighty Yángzǐ River, is lined with a gallery of colonial architecture, known as the Bund, grander than any other in the East, much of it recently refurbished and beckoning the curious visitor. The mansions, garden estates, country clubs, and cathedrals of Westerners who made their fortunes here a century ago pepper the city. Even a synagogue exists, dating from the days of an unparalleled Jewish immigration to China. These are not the typical monuments of China, but they are typical of Shànghǎi.

At the same time, creations of a strictly Chinese culture prevail. A walk through the chaotic old Chinese city turns up traditional treasures: a teahouse epitomizing old China; a quintessential Southern-Chinese classical garden; active temples and ancient pagodas; and even a section of Shànghǎi's old city wall. If Shànghǎi's primary architecture and avenues recall 19th-century Europe rather than old Cathay, this is still a Chinese city to the core.

Shànghǎi is a haven for shoppers—Nánjīng Lù is the number-one shopping street in all of China—but perhaps even more importantly, Shànghǎi represents the future of China. Across the mighty Huángpǔ River, which served as old Shànghǎi's eastern border, Pǔdōng, serving as the face of new Shànghǎi, now boasts the tallest hotel in the world, Asia's largest shopping mall, China's largest stock exchange, and one of the highest observation decks in Asia, the Oriental Pearl TV Tower. Not to be outdone, old Shànghǎi has its own legions of new skyscrapers, too, and a booming collection of fine international restaurants, several of them taking over the rooftops of the colonial gems lining the Bund and the mansions that went to seed in Shànghǎi's French Quarter.

Shànghǎi is also reestablishing itself as a leading trendsetter for fashion, design, culture, and the arts. New theaters and cultural centers attract top performers from China and abroad, while designers of every stripe are taking

China

Legend:
- — · — · — International Boundary
- Provincial Boundary
- ⊛ National Capital
- ◉ Provincial Capital
- **The Silk Road**

RUSSIA

MONGOLIA

KAZAKHSTAN

Bishkek ⊛

KYRGYZSTAN

Ürümqi ◉

Turpan ○

TAJIKI-STAN

Kashgar ○

XĪNJIĀNG

GĀNSÙ

Jiāyùguān ○

PAKISTAN

Xīníng ◉

QĪNGHĂI

PLATEAU OF TIBET

TIBET

SÌCHUĀN

New Delhi ⊛

HIMALAYA

Lhasa ◉

NEPAL

Mt. Everest ▲

Kathmandu ⊛

Thimbu ⊛

BHUTAN

Lijiāng ○

INDIA

Ganges

BANGLADESH

Dàlĭ ○

Ěrhăi Lake

Kūnmíng

Dhaka ⊛

YÚNNÁN

NORTHEAST

Běijīng ★

CENTRAL

MYANMAR

LAOS

SOUTHWEST

MOUNTAIN CHINA

Bay of Bengal

SOUTHEAST

Salween

Rangoon ⊛

Vientiane ⊛

THAILAND

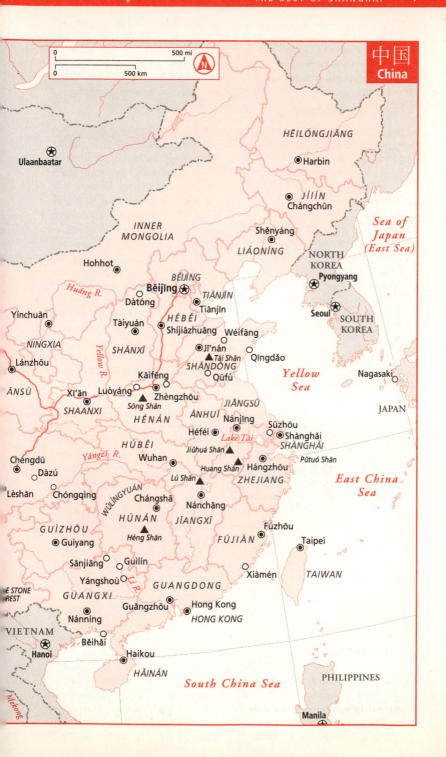

advantage of the mix of the East, West, past, and future by blazing their own unique styles.

Herewith I present a list of Shànghǎi's highlights, both the obvious and the more offbeat choices that make the most of all that is unique about the city. Shànghǎi is fast regaining its footing in a country in the midst of rediscovering its own. This sense of possibility imbues Shànghǎi with a palpable energy unmatched anywhere in the world, once again attracting legions of visitors to its shores.

1 Frommer's Favorite Shànghǎi Experiences

- **Strolling the Bund:** The most widely known street in Asia, with its gorgeous colonial buildings that were the banks, hotels, trading firms, and private clubs of foreign taipans (bosses of old Shànghǎi's trading firms) and adventurers past, deserves to be walked over and over again. See up close the exquisite architectural details of the **Peace Hotel,** the **Customs House,** the **former Hong Kong and Shànghǎi Bank,** and scores of other buildings, some lavishly restored, others closed awaiting development. Then head across the street to the **Bund Promenade,** where you mingle with the masses while admiring the splendor and grandeur of old Shànghǎi. See "Walking Tour" on p. 176.

- **Admiring the Collections in the Shànghǎi Museum:** China's finest, most modern, and most memorable museum of historic relics has disappointed almost no visitor since it opened in the heart of People's Square. Make it a top priority, and allow a few hours more than you planned on. See p. 144.

- **Surveying Shànghǎi from Up High:** After crossing the Huángpǔ River from old Shànghǎi to the new Shànghǎi (whether by taxi, subway, tunnel, or ferry), enjoy the ultimate panorama from either the sphere atop the **Oriental Pearl TV Tower** or the **Jīn Mào Tower,** two of Asia's tallest structures. On a clear day, you can see forever. See p. 166 for both.

- **Cruising the Huángpǔ River:** A 27km (17-mile) pleasure cruise from the Bund to the mouth of the mighty Yángzǐ River, past endless wharves, factories, and tankers at anchor, gives substance to Shànghǎi's claim as China's largest port and the fact that nearly half of China's trade with the outside world travels these same waters. A shorter 1-hour cruise, and an abbreviated 30-minute cruise from the Pǔdōng side, do not convey the full importance of the river, but they will suffice if you're pressed for time. See p. 147.

- **Drinking Tea in the Perfect Teahouse:** Shànghǎi's Húxīngtíng (Mid-Lake) Teahouse is the quintessential teahouse in China, often thought to be the original model for the one in the Blue Willow plate pattern. Here, at the center of Old Town Shànghǎi, is the place to pause for a refreshing cup of green tea, and count yourself on a par with Queen Elizabeth II, who was also a visitor. See p. 165.

- **Shopping Nánjīng Lù:** Even if you're the kind of person who only shops once a year, a visit to this "Number One Shopping Street in China" is practically required, if only to appreciate how the pre-Revolutionary era department stores, hotels, and silk shops are mixing it up with the glitzy, modern stores and international boutiques. Better yet, you'll get a chance to marvel (or shudder) at the sheer numbers of people, people, people everywhere! A pedestrian mall makes strolling and browsing that much easier and that much more crowded. See "Walking Tour 2: Nánjīng Lù" on p. 182.

- **Shopping 'til You Drop:** Nánjīng Lù is for the tourists, but savvy local shoppers know if you want greater choice and better deals, Huáihǎi Lù with its slew of international boutiques and large department stores is the place to shop. Branching off and parallel to Huáihǎi Lù, Màomíng Lù, Xìnglè Lù, and Chánglè Lù are also home to a number of delightful small shops. See chapter 8, "Shopping."

- **Bargaining for Fakes at the Fúyòu Market:** Shànghǎi has any number of antiques markets where you can hone your bargaining skills, but none more colorful than the **Fúyòu Market** in the old Chinese city (at the western end of Shànghǎi's restored old street, Shànghǎi Lǎo Jiē). On Sunday mornings, the third and fourth floors are where the interesting junk can be found, though visitors have walked away with some real finds. Half the fun is in rifling through all the personal collections of memorabilia and antiques that the vendors seem to have scavenged; the other half is in dramatically protesting the high prices quoted, walking away, then being called back by a vendor newly willing to deal. See p. 201.

- **Strolling the French Concession:** This is the most interesting of the colonial districts left in Shànghǎi, filled with the gorgeous villas, mansions, and apartment houses of the 1920s and 1930s when the French made their mark here. The avenues are being restored, the facades cleaned up, and the great houses with their balconies, private gardens, and carved paneling are opening their doors as upscale restaurants.

Plenty of Art Deco gems abound, hidden behind years of grime and buried beneath webs of laundry poles, awaiting discovery, so keep your head up. See "Walking Tour 4: French Concession " on p. 191.

- **Rediscovering Shànghǎi's Jewish Past at the Ohel Moshe Synagogue:** In the mid–19th century, SephardicJews from the Middle East helped make Shànghǎi a great city. In the mid–20th century, thousands of Jewish refugees flooded the International Settlement north of the Bund. Today, this history can be encountered at the Ohel Moshe Synagogue, where the curator, Mr. Wáng, has vivid accounts of this little-known but important Jewish ghetto. See p. 155.

- **Wandering the Old Chinese City:** The narrow winding alleys of the old Chinese city may strike some as mysterious and forbidding, but they are neither of these, and are worth exploring even beyond the walking tours in chapter 7. Here is a chance to come upon a wet market, or run into the increasingly rare sight of a night soil worker on his morning rounds (many houses in this part of town still lack indoor plumbing). See it before the bulldozer shows up. See Walking Tour 3 on p. 188.

- **Morning Exercises on the Bund:** There's no better way to greet the day than to join the thousands of Shànghǎi residents in their morning tai chi exercises (and occasionally Western ballroom dancing) on the Bund and in Shànghǎi's parks. The Bund is preferable: The first golden rays hitting the colonial facades are truly something to behold. See chapter 6 for details on the Bund and on Shànghǎi parks.

- **Dining on Hairy Crab:** The signature dish of Shànghǎi is absolutely scrumptious, but it is seasonal (autumn), and it is best enjoyed at a big local restaurant. See chapter 5 for recommended restaurants.

- **Watching the Acrobats:** This has "TOURIST" stamped all over it, but it's nevertheless a totally worthwhile pleasure, especially since Shànghăi's dazzling troupes are rightly considered China's very finest at this ancient craft. See chapter 9.

- **Sampling Shànghăi's Jazz Scene:** The **Peace Hotel Jazz Band**'s (p. 217) nightly performances of New Orleans–style jazz, with some members who have been playing here since before the Revolution (1949), are the ultimate piece of colonial nostalgia, but if this doesn't grab you, modern and more improvisational jazz can be heard at a number of true blue joints: the **Cotton Club** (p. 217), **Club JZ** (p. 217), and the **House of Blues and Jazz** (p. 217).

- **Rooftop Dining on the Bund:** Whether it's savoring world-class cuisine on the open-air balcony of Shànghăi's top international restaurant, **M on the Bund,** or lingering over a cappuccino on the rooftop of the new bistro, **New Heights,** dining high above Asia's most famous street is a heady experience not to be missed. See p. 94 and 95.

- **Exploring Shànghăi's New Heaven on Earth:** Downtown Shànghăi's most lavish redevelopment, Xīn Tiāndì (New Heaven and Earth) has become the prime place to see and be seen. The new restaurants here rank as Shànghăi's most sophisticated and expensive; the boutiques are pricey, too; and the architecture, an artful blend of native traditional and ultramodern Western, may mark a turning point in Shànghăi's redesign for the future. See p. 168.

- **Eating *Xiǎolón gbāo*:** Unless you're a vegetarian, not trying Shànghăi's favorite (pork) dumpling while you're here is tantamount in some circles to not having been to Shànghăi at all. The "little steamed breads" spill broth in your mouth when you bite into them. You can find them everywhere, but for a list of the best places, see **"Best *Xiǎolóng bāo* (Dumpling)"** on p. 13. For tips on how to eat it without scalding your tongue, see "Shànghăi's Favorite Dumpling" on p. 114.

- **Drifting in a Gondola through a Water Village in Tónglĭ or Nánxún:** There are any number of picturesque "water villages" near Shànghăi where you can be paddled in a gondola along streams and canals as you pass traditional arched bridges, quaint stone houses, and classical Chinese gardens. Two villages stand out: Tónglĭ and Nánxún Also, both have additional sights worth seeing and considerably smaller crowds than at tourist traps like Zhōu Zhuāng, but see them soon. See p. 240 and 238.

2 Best Hotel Bets

For complete hotel listings, see chapter 4, "Where to Stay."

- **Best Historic Hotel:** The legendary Cathay Hotel, now the **Peace Hotel,** Nánjīng Dōng Lù 20 (© **021/6321-6888**), located at Shànghăi's most fabled intersection (Nánjīng Lù and the Bund), is a living museum of Shànghăi's Art Deco and colonial past. See p. 72.

- **Best Hotel for Today:** The honor remains with the **Portman Ritz-Carlton,** Nánjīng Xī Lù 1376 (© **800/241-3333** or 021/6279-8888), owing to its tremendous business and shopping facilities, as well as a recent remodeling (though right on its heels are The Westin Shànghǎi and the Four Seasons). See p. 80.

- **Best Hotel for Tomorrow:** The highest hotel in the world, the **Grand Hyatt,** Shìjì Dà Dào 88 (© **800/233-1234** or 021/5049-1234), is also the highest in high-tech amenities and designs. This 21st-century pagoda has 60 elevators, 19 escalators, a 57th-floor skypool for "swimming in the sky," and a 360-degree panorama from the cloud tops. See p. 86.

- **Best Service:** An impossibly difficult category with fierce competition, but our vote goes to the *consistently* friendly and efficient service at the **Four Seasons Hotel Shànghǎi,** Wēihǎi Lù (© **800/819-5053** or 021/6256-8888). Staff is extremely discreet and anticipates your needs rather than reacts to requests. See p. 80. A close second is the **St. Regis Shànghǎi,** Dōngfāng Lù 889 (© **800/325-3589** or 021/5050-4567), where no request seems too frivolous or difficult for the hotel's butlers. See p. 87.

- **Best Business Hotel:** It seems unfair for one hotel to hog the limelight, but the **Portman Ritz-Carlton,** Nánjīng Xī Lù 1376 (© **800/241-3333** or 021/6279-8888), not only wins this category in Shànghǎi, as poll after poll of foreign business travelers consistently show, but it has been deemed by the same polls to be the "Best Business Hotel in Asia." **The Hilton,** Huáshān Lù 250 (© **800/445-8667** or 021/6248-0000), also consistently receives raves from foreign business travelers for its efficiency and location, as does **The Westin Shànghǎi,** Hénán Zhōng Lù 88, Bund Center (© **888/WESTIN-1** or 021/6335-1888). See p. 80 and 71.

- **Best Hotel Perks:** Perhaps to compensate for its less-than-ideal location in Pǔdōng, the **St. Regis Shànghǎi,** Dōngfāng Lù 889 (© **800/325-3589** or 021/5050-4567), throws in a host of perks like free broadband Internet in all rooms, and free happy hour cocktails and canapés for all in their executive lounge. They also have the largest rooms in town, fitted with Herman Miller Aeron chairs, BOSE CD wave radios, and some of the largest bathtubs in town. There's no reason to leave the hotel at all. See p. 87.

- **Best Hotel on the Bund:** Set back a block or two, but towering nonetheless over the Bund, is **The Westin Shànghǎi,** Hénán Zhōng Lù 88, Bund Center (© **888/WESTIN-1** or 021/6335-1888), opened in 2002 with heavenly beds and wonderful views. See p. 71.

- **Best View of the Bund:** The nearby Grand Hyatt is higher, but the 28-story **Pǔdōng Shangri-La,** Fùchéng Lù 33 (© **800/942-5050** or 021/6882-8888), is closer and at just the right elevation for a spectacular view of Shànghǎi's European architecture across the Huángpǔ River. The view is even better at night when this riverfront "colonial scroll" of banks and trading houses is lit up. See p. 86.

- **Best Value for Money:** At the Art Deco **Yangtze Hotel,** Hànkǒu Lù 740 (© **021/6351-7880**), ¥680 to ¥780 ($85–$98) before discounts will get you a comfortable, clean room with all the basic amenities including broadband Internet service. Rates are usually discounted by 30%. All this, and it's within walking distance of People's Square and Nánjīng Lù as well. See p. 73.

- **Best Undiscovered Budget Lodgings:** Who needs the extra frills when you can get a room in a French Concession mansion for under $50? The **Shànghǎi Conservatory of Music Guest House,** Fēnyáng Lù 20 (© **021 6437-2577**), has three charming doubles (¥300/$39) with en suite bathroom and balcony; while the **Jùyīng Bīnguǎn,** Jùlù Lù 889 (© **021/6466-7788,** ext. 885/ 886), has impeccably clean rooms overlooking a pleasant garden compound for around ¥450 ($56) before discount. See p. 79 and 82.

- **Best Celebrity Room:** Of all the famous visitors who have stayed in Shànghǎi's hotels through the years, perhaps no guest is more renowned than Albert Einstein, who stayed at the then-Astor House Hotel, now the decidedly no-frills **Pǔjiāng Hotel,** Huángpǔ Lù 15 (© **021/6324-6388**). His room is yours for the relatively cheap rate of ¥880 ($110) a night. See p. 75.

- **Best Setting:** The **Ruìjīn Hotel,** Ruìjīn Èr Lù 118 (© **021/6472- 5222**), located on the former Morriss Estate in the French Concession, boasts one of the loveliest colonial settings with four original villas (and several *faux* additions) amid sprawling manicured lawns that are lovely to stroll. To boot, there are several excellent restaurants and bars on the premises, which means you never have to leave the grounds of this block-long estate. See p. 77.

- **Best Newcomer:** The finally opened (Oct 2003) **JW Marriott,** Nánjīng Xī Lù 399 (© **800/ 228-9290** or 021/5359-4969), is staking out its new turf with the tallest hotel in Pǔxī, stunning views, luxurious in-room amenities, and a superb location close to People's Park and Xīn Tiāndì. See p. 70.

- **Best Health and Fitness Facilities:** The health and fitness facilities at the **Regal International East Asia Hotel,** Héngshān Lù 516 (© **800/222-8888** or 021/ 6415-5588), don't stop at just the 25m (82-ft.) lap pool, the aerobics gym, the simulated golf range, or the 12-lane bowling alley; add in the 10 world-class tennis courts (2 indoors), including a center court with viewer seating for 1,200. See p. 78.

3 Best Dining Bets

For complete restaurant listings, see chapter 5, "Where to Dine."

- **Best International Dining:** Shànghǎi's world-class Mediterranean restaurant, **M on the Bund,** Guǎngdōng Lù 20, 7th Floor (© **021/6350-9988**), not only serves impeccable Continental cuisine, but features a knockout view of the Bund and riverfront from atop a colonial-era trading house. See p. 94. The darling of many of Shànghǎi's gourmands, **T8** (© **021/6355-8999**), located downtown at Xīn Tiāndì, continues to garner international acclaim for its highly creative "new world" cooking. See p. 97.

- **Best Shànghǎi Dining:** The city abounds in restaurants serving tasty local fare, but the standout for contemporary Shànghǎi cuisine has to be newcomer **Shànghǎi Uncle,** Yán'ān Dōng Lù 222, Bund Center Basement (© **021/ 6339-1977**), featuring creative spins on old classics, focusing on tender and flavorful pork dishes that can turn even the most diehard vegetarians into carnivores. Three branches already pepper the city. See p. 112. Another stellar choice is long-standing expatriate-favorite **1221,** Yán'ān Xī Lù 1221 (© **021/6213-6585**), serving delicious Shànghǎi fare that's neither too sweet nor too oily. See p. 110. More traditional (sweeter and oilier) Shànghǎi cuisine is probably best sampled at **Shànghǎi Lǎo Fàndiàn,** Fúyòu Lù 242 (© **021/6355-2275**), with a history dating to 1875 and the most meltingly tender eight treasure duck you'll ever taste. See p. 114.

- **Best Dining in a Colonial Mansion:** These days it's easy to find an old mansion for dinner, but former favorite Sasha's has now been trumped by **La Villa Rouge,** Héngshān Lù 811 (© **021/6431-9811**), located in a gorgeous red brick mansion on the edge of Xújiāhuì Park that was the former EMI Recording Studio. The food is expensive French/fusion from award-winning Japanese chefs, but its grand staircase, antique wallpaper, and old gramophones are pure Shànghǎi nostalgia. See p. 101.

- **Best Hotel Dining:** No hotel gives more high-quality choices (or a better view) than the **Grand Hyatt** in Pǔdōng, Shìjì Dà Dào 88 (© **021/5049-1234,** ext. 8898), with its Grand Café's international buffets (54th floor), the Canton's gourmet Cantonese dishes (55th floor), or the Grill's seafood and steaks, Kobatchi's yakitori, and Cuchina's Tuscan pastas and pizzas (all on the 56th floor)—not to mention the 10 open kitchens that make up the Food Live "food street" on podium level 3. See p. 86.

- **Best Deli:** Stock up big time at the **Bauernstube** on the second floor of the **Sheraton Grand Tài Píng Yáng Hotel,** Zūnyì Nán Lù 5 (© **021/6275-8888**), with its huge selection of cheeses, sausages, Norwegian salmon, breads, cakes, and roast chicken. See p. 83.

- **Best Places to Eat & Be Seen:** Modern taipans, celebrities, and sophisticated locals can be found dining at the very chic restaurants in the French Concession's **Lan Kwai Fong at Park 97** complex, Gāolán Lù 2 (© **021/5383-2328**); or at downtown's **Xīn Tiāndì** mall on Tàicāng Lù; and, increasingly, at the trendy and perhaps still-a-little-too exclusive **Three on the Bund.** The food in the restaurants at each site is, for the most part, as superb as it is varied. See p. 97 and 95.

- **Best Burgers:** For big, authentic burgers with all the fixings, there's still no beating **Malone's,** Tóngrén Lù 255 near the Shànghǎi Centre (© **021/6247-2400**), a Canadian-owned sports bar that's as American as it gets. See p. 109.

- **Best Light Lunch:** Delicious fresh salads are now readily available in Shànghǎi at **Element Fresh** at the Shànghǎi Centre, Nánjīng Xī Lù 1376, no. 112 (© **021/6279-8682**). Wash it down with a fresh-squeezed carrot-apple-ginseng or your favorite smoothie. See p. 109.

- **Best Teahouse:** The most famous teahouse in China, its eaves soaring over the pond by Yù Yuán (Yù Garden), is Shànghǎi's own **Húxīngtíng** (© **021/6373-6950**), a welcome haven in the crunch of Old Town shopping and mass tourism. See p. 165.

- **Best *Xiǎolóng bāo* (Dumpling):** The traditional favorite establishment for Shànghǎi's favorite dumpling has always been **Nánxiáng Mántou Diàn,** Yùyuán Lù 85 (© **021/6355-4206**), near Yù Yuán in the old Chinese City. Patrons line up here for hours. But the new **Crystal Jade Restaurant** in Xīn Tiāndì, Xìnyè Lù 123,

Nánlǐ 6–7, 2nd Floor, 12A & B (☎ **021/6385-8752**), can now rightfully claim the crown with the thinnest dumpling wrapper in town, and perfect *xiǎolóng bāo* that are served at just the right temperature. Crystal Jade also serves an excellent *dān dān miàn* (noodles in spicy peanut sauce), not that you need another reason to head straight there. See p. 115 and 99.

- **Best Cantonese:** Any hotel worth its salt in Shànghǎi has a Cantonese restaurant (the second most popular Chinese regional cuisine in town after Shànghǎi's own), but the two top choices are the long-presiding **Dynasty,** Yán'ān Xī Lù 2099, in the Renaissance Yangtze Hotel (☎ **021/6275-0000**); and the 55th-floor **Canton** restaurant at the Grand Hyatt Hotel, Shìjì Dà Dào 88, in Pǔdōng (☎ **021/5049-1234,** ext. 8898; reserve 3 days in advance). These elegant restaurants feature top chefs from Hong Kong. See p. 110 and 112.
- **Best European: Danieli's,** at the St. Regis Shànghǎi, Dōngfāng Lù 877, 29th Floor, Pǔdōng (☎ **021/5050-4567**), is the best option, out of a crowded field and some fine competition, for Italian, with excellent pastas, panoramic views, and exquisite service. See p. 112. The purple-themed French restaurant **La Seine,** Jì'nán Lù 8 (☎ **021/6384-3722**), offers superb entrées and sinful desserts, and is a favorite with its international clientele. See p. 99. **Jean Georges,** Zhōngshān Dōng Yī Lù 3, 4th Floor (☎ **021/6321-7733**), opened at press time and promises to be a hit. See p. 95.
- **Best Asian (Non-Chinese): Simply Thai,** Dōngpíng Lù 5, Unit C (☎ **021/6445-9551**), in a quaint French Concession cottage, offers the most authentic Thai food in the most pleasing environment.

The best nouvelle Japanese cuisine comes by way of an über-hip Bauhaus bunker known as **Shintori Null II,** Jùlù Lù 803 (☎ **021/5404-5252**), while the best place for more traditional hearty Japanese favorites is **Itoya,** Nánjīng Xī Lù 1515, 1st Floor (☎ **021/5298-5777**). **Indian Kitchen,** Yǒngjiā Lù 572 (☎ **021/6473-1517**), is your best source for tasty Indian fare that is also easy on the wallet. See p. 103, 105, and 107.

- **Best Decor:** The trove of Asian artifacts, Buddha statues, and Míng Dynasty furniture inside the incense-filled loft of a Tudor-style mansion makes the fine food at **The Door,** Hóngqiáo Lù 1468, 3rd Floor (☎ **021/6295-3737**), secondary to its decor. See p. 110.
- **Best for Kids:** Overall, most Chinese restaurants are very child-friendly. The staff at **1221,** Yán'ān Xī Lù 1221 (☎ **021/6213-6585**), tends to dote on children and give families the private rooms. **O'Malley's,** Táojiāng Lù 42 (☎ **021/6437-0667**), has a children's playground on the front lawn that's a hit with both kids and parents. See p. 110 and 103.
- **Best Tongue Twister (Due to Spicy Food):** Two of the spiciest Chinese cuisines are well represented here: **Bā Guó Bù Yī,** Hóngqiáo Lù 1676 (☎ **021/6270-6668**), is one of the most authentic Sìchuān restaurants in town and will introduce neophytes to the Sìchuān peppercorn. At **Dī Shuǐ Dòng,** Màomíng Nán Lù 56 (☎ **021/6253-2689**), you'll get chilies straight up by way of Húnán Province. Either place will have your sweat glands working overtime. See p. 111 and 100.
- **Best Chinese Restaurant Undiscovered by the Masses: Lǎo Tán,** Xìngfú Lù 42, 2nd Floor (☎ **021/6283-7843**), squirreled away on

the western edge of the French Concession, serves the spicy and sour cuisine of Southwestern China's Guìzhōu Province. Its signature sour beans with smoked bacon and its fiery chicken dishes are probably not what you're used to, but they are definitely worth trying. Light on the wallet as well. See p. 111.

- **Best Crab: Wáng Bǎo Hé,** Fúzhōu Lù 603 (© **021/6322-3673**), a Shànghǎi institution that claims to be the oldest restaurant in town, brings political and business leaders and crab aficionados to their knees with its multitude of crab dishes,

but especially during hairy crab season (autumn). You'll be on your knees, too, when you see the bill. See p. 94.

- **Best Vegetarian:** The French Concession **Zǎo Zǐ Shù,** Sōngshān Lù 77, 1st Floor (© **021/6384-8000**), takes its mission seriously (its name is also a pun that exhorts diners to become vegetarians as soon as possible, *zǎo chī sù*). There's no smoking, no MSG, no alcohol, and no dairy, but plenty of organic tea, fruit appetizers, flavorful vegetables, mushrooms, and tofu doubling as meat. See p. 100.

2

Planning Your Trip to Shànghǎi

This chapter is intended to demystify traveling in China: It's not as hard as you think, and in Shànghǎi, it's even easier than that. Of all the cities in China, Shànghǎi is the easiest for an independent traveler to navigate. Tens of thousands of visitors arrive here every year, usually armed with nothing more than some solid pre-planning, a guidebook, and a sense of adventure. However you choose to visit and whatever your preconceptions about traveling to China, it is important that you read this chapter carefully. It contains all the basics for designing a trip to Shànghǎi and entering China with the right documents in hand.

1 Visitor Information

NATIONAL TOURIST OFFICES

China's travel industry, though ostensibly controlled by a central authority, is, in general, so mired in misinformation and obfuscation that it is often difficult for visitors to get truly reliable and accurate information either inside or outside the country. The all-controlling China National Tourism Administration has branches in foreign countries known as **China National Tourist Offices (CNTO)** whose purpose is ostensibly to provide tourist information and services, though traditionally, it has usually just funneled all visitors to the agency handling all travel within China, **China International Travel Service (CITS** or *guójì lǚxíngshè*). There are a few more tour operators inside China now, but don't expect the information CNTO provides to always be accurate or up-to-date. CNTO office addresses are listed below; the Internet address is **www.cnto.org**.

- In the **United States:** 350 Fifth Ave., Suite 6413, New York, NY 10118 (© **212/760-8218;** fax 212/760-8809; ny@cnta.gov.cn); 600 W. Broadway, Suite 320,

Glendale, CA 91204 (© **818/545-7505;** fax 818/545-7506; la@cnta.gov.cn).

- In the **U.K.:** 4 Glentworth St., London NW1 5PG (© **020/7935-9787;** fax 020/7487-4842; london@cnta.gov.cn).

- In **Australia:** Level 19, 44 Market St., Sydney NSW 2000 (© **02/9299-4057;** fax 02/9290-1958; sydney@cnta.gov.cn).

- In **Canada:** Suite 806, 480 University Ave., Toronto, ONT M5G 1V2 (© **416/599-6636;** fax 416/599-6382; www.tourismchina-ca.com).

SHÀNGHǍI ONLINE The best way to receive fairly up-to-date information on Shànghǎi before departure is on the Internet, though it's best to surf a variety of websites so you can compare information. Treat with some skepticism those that only sell travel services—they are a dime a dozen on the Web and there is no guarantee of reliability. The Shànghǎi Tourist Information Service Center (**www.shanghaitour.net**) offers an introductory overview to the city as well as links to accommodations, restaurants and sights (though at press time they were having problems with their English-language link). A Shànghǎi search engine with links to shopping, leisure, and other travel-related issues is at www.sh.com.

Shànghǎi's English-language newspaper, *Shanghai Daily* (**www.english.eastday.com**) offers both Shànghǎi and China news. The online edition of the glossy English-language monthly *that's Shanghai* (**www.thatsShanghai.com**), which has local restaurant and bar reviews and listings, is less useful than its hard copy version. In the same mold, *City Weekend* (**www.cityweekend.com.cn**) usually has some Shànghǎi news, and listings of what's going on in town. Another useful Shànghǎi website is **www.shanghai-ed.com**, where you can post Shànghǎi-related questions.

The Oriental-List offers an ad and spam-free discussion of issues relating to travel in China, and is a good place to ask questions that may not be addressed in this book. To subscribe, send a blank e-mail to subscribe-oriental-list@list.xianzai.com.

2 Entry Requirements & Customs

ENTRY REQUIREMENTS

PASSPORT   Visitors must have a valid **passport** with a 6-month validity beyond the date of arrival and two blank pages remaining.

VISAS   All visitors to mainland China (but not the Special Administrative Regions of Hong Kong and Macau) are required to have a **visa.** Tour groups are usually issued a group visa, with the paperwork handled by the travel agency (check with your agent). Individual travelers should apply for visas from your nearest Chinese embassy or consulate. Contact information for all Chinese embassies and consulates can be found at www.fmprc.gov.cn/eng. Some consulates require in-person applications while others allow applications by post or courier with extra charges. Visas are typically processed in 3 to 5 business days, though 1-day service is possible if you apply in person and pay extra fees.

The most common type of visa is the single-entry "L" tourist visa, usually good for 30 days, though you can request a longer validity period. Your request may not always be granted, and in some cases, you may be asked to produce supporting documentation (such as a travel agent–issued itinerary or an airline ticket with a return date).

If you're going to be leaving and then returning to mainland China, apply for a double-entry visa. There is also a multiple-entry 6-month visa, but these are significantly more difficult to come by (requiring mounds of documentation) in most countries except in Hong Kong. Visas are typically valid for 1 to 3 months after the date of issue.

To apply for a visa, you must complete an **application form,** which you can request by mail or download from the various consular websites. Also required is one **passport photo** per individual traveling (including for a child traveling on a parent's passport). Though the visa is valid for the entire country (with a few exceptions that may require special permits), in general, avoid mentioning Tibet or Xīnjiāng on your application.

Following is a list of embassy addresses and visa fees for some countries, along with their respective Web pages that link to the appropriate consular sites and downloadable visa application forms.

Warning: Visa fees listed are accurate as of press time, but are subject to change at any time.

- **United States:** Room 110, 2201 Wisconsin Ave., Washington, DC 20007 (© **202/338-6688;** fax

202/588-9760; www.china embassy.org). Single-entry visas are US$50; double-entry US$75. Applications must be delivered and collected by hand, or sent via a visa agency.

- **Canada:** 515 Patrick St., Ottawa, ON K1N 5H3 (© **613/789-3434;** fax 613/789-1911; www.chinaembassycanada.org). Single-entry visas are C$50; double-entry C$75. Applications must be delivered and collected by hand, or sent via a visa agency.
- **United Kingdom:** 31 Portland Place, London W1N 3AG (© **020/7631-1430;** fax 020/7588-2500; www.chinese-embassy.org.uk). Single-entry visas are £30; double-entry £45, with an extra charge of £20 for each package received through the mail.
- **Australia:** 15 Coronation Dr., Yarralumla, ACT 2600 Canberra (© **02/6273-4783;** fax 02/6273-5189; www.chinaembassy.org.au; www.chinaconsulatesyd.org). Single-entry visas are A$30; double-entry A$45, with an extra charge of A$10 for each package processed by mail or courier.
- **New Zealand:** 2–6 Glenmore St., Wellington (© **04/472-1382;** fax 04/499-0419; www.chinaembassy.org.nz; www.chinaconsulate.org.nz). Single-entry visas are NZ$60, double-entry NZ$90, with an extra charge of NZ$15 for each package processed by mail or courier.

GETTING A VISA IN HONG KONG Nationals of most developed nations require only a valid passport to enter Hong Kong, even though it's a part of China. Chinese visas can be easily secured at countless Hong Kong travel agencies, including the official branch of **China Travel Service (CTS)** at 27–33 Nathan Rd., Kowloon (© **852/2315-7188;** fax 852/2721-7757), second floor of the Alpha Building (entrance on Peking Rd.), but they're cheaper at **Grand Profit International Travel Agency,** 705AA, 7th Floor, New East Ocean Centre, 9 Science Museum Rd., Tsimshatsui; (© **852/2723-3288**), where citizens of most countries can get a same-day single-entry visa for HK$200 (US $26) if you bring in your passport before noon. U.S. citizens have to pay HK$780 (US $100).

VISA EXTENSIONS As a rule, visas may be extended once for a maximum of 30 days at the local PSB (Public Security Bureau, *gōng'ān jú*) in most cities. In Shànghǎi, head to the Foreign Affairs Section of the PSB located at Wúsōng Lù 333 (© **021/6357-7925,** ext. 2), several miles north of the Bund. Office hours are Monday to Saturday 9 to 11:30am and 1:30 to 4:30pm. Extensions usually require 3 business days, and extension fees are ¥160 ($20) for U.S., U.K., Canadian, and Australia citizens. Bring your passport and two passport photos.

CUSTOMS
WHAT YOU CAN BRING INTO CHINA

In general, you can bring in anything for personal use that you will take with you when you leave, including laptops, GPS devices, cameras, video recorders, and other electronic equipment. You're also allowed four bottles of alcoholic beverages and three cartons of cigarettes. Travelers are prohibited from bringing in firearms, drugs, plant material, animals, and food from diseased areas, as well as "printed matter, magnetic media, films, or photographs which are deemed to be detrimental to the political, economic, cultural and moral interests of China." This last section covers pornography, overtly political and religious material, and anything related to Tibet. In practice, however, small amounts of personal reading material in non-Chinese languages have yet to present a problem. Currency in excess of US$5,000 is supposed to be declared on Customs declaration forms, though most major points of entry seem to have dispensed with the Customs declaration form entirely.

WHAT YOU CAN TAKE HOME

Upon departure, antiques purchased in China, defined as any item created between 1795 and 1949, must be accompanied by an official red wax seal before being taken out of the country (see chapter 8, "Shopping," for more details). Any item created before 1795 is prohibited for export. Check with your country's Customs Service for what you may bring back home.

3 Money

CURRENCY

Though it's usually a good idea to change at least some money before you leave home, this scenario doesn't apply as readily to mainland China, as the Chinese RMB is not a commonly held currency. Where it's carried, it will most likely be exchanged at a highly unfavorable rate. This shouldn't present too much of a problem for most travelers arriving in Shànghǎi by plane, as airports all have money exchange facilities and ATMs. Those arriving by train from Hong Kong would do well to change a small amount of money in Hong Kong where the RMB *yuán* is readily obtainable.

Currency exchange in China is legal only if conducted at hotels, banks, and stores, at the official rate set by the central government through the Bank of China. This rate is the same at all nationwide outlets, saving travelers the hassle and stress of having to find the best rate. Besides at the airport, you can change money at hotel bank desks, at larger branches of the Bank of China, and occasionally at some major department stores, though the last is quickly going out of vogue in Shànghǎi. Hotel desks have the convenience of being open long hours 7 days a week, but their services are usually restricted to guests. For bank hours, see "Banks, Currency Exchange & ATMs" in the "Fast Facts" section in chapter 3. You'll have to provide your passport for any kind of currency exchange.

Keep all receipts when you change money; you will need them should you wish to reconvert any excess ¥RMB into your home currency.

Reject any attempts by private individuals or shops to change money at rates different from the official rate: Not only is this illegal, you may well end up with fake bills. Avoid especially the black-market money-changers who congregate outside branches of the Bank of China that are popular with tourists, such as the one on the Bund, and the one north of the JC Mandarin Hotel.

YUÁN NOTES & EXCHANGE RATES

Chinese currency is known as *rénmínbì* (RMB, literally "the people's money") or the *yuán* (¥). However, you'll mostly hear money referred to as *kuài qián,* literally "pieces of money," or *kuài* for short. Bills come in denominations of ¥100, ¥50, ¥20, ¥10, ¥5, ¥2, and ¥1, which also appears as a coin. The next unit down is the *jiǎo* (¥0.10), commonly referred to as *máo.* There are notes and coins for ¥0.50, ¥0.20, and ¥0.10. Beyond that is the *fēn* (¥0.01), but you'll hardly ever see or have use for it. China being primarily still a cash society, keep a good stock of smaller bills, especially ¥10 notes, for street stalls, convenience stores, and taxis, all of whom will balk if you offer a ¥100 bill first thing in the morning.

What Things Cost in Shànghăi	U.S.$	U.K.£	Yuán ¥
Taxi from Pŭdōng airport to city center	24.00	15.10	198.76
Airport bus (Pŭdōng) to city center	3.80	2.27	31.47
Taxi ride up to 5km (3 miles)	1.80	1.00	14.91
Subway ride	0.36	0.23	2.98
Local telephone call	0.06	0.04	0.50
Dinner for two in top hotel/international restaurants	80.00	49.00	662.54
Dinner for two in popular local restaurants	18.00	11.30	149.07
Steamer of dumplings at a basic local restaurant	1.00	0.50	8.28
Bottle of beer at a trendy Shànghăi bar or hotel	7.00	3.70	57.94
Bottle of beer at an ordinary restaurant or store	3.00	1.90	24.83
Bottle of beer at the 24-hour neighborhood store	1.00	0.50	8.28
Admission to Shànghăi Museum	2.40	1.50	19.86
Theater ticket to Shànghăi Acrobatics	7.20	4.56	59.59

The *yuán* is pegged to the U.S. dollar at the rate of about ¥8.27 to US$1 (though U.S. dollar rates given in this book have been rounded off to ¥8 to US$1). The strength of all other currencies is determined by their strength against the U.S. dollar, with the pound sterling trading around press time at ¥15.18 to £1, and the euro at ¥10 to 1 euro. For the latest exchange rates, consult www.xe.com/ucc.

TRAVELER'S CHECKS

Traveler's checks, still a popular way to bring money into China, are only accepted at major branches of the Bank of China, at foreign exchange desks in hotels, and occasionally at major department stores and shops targeted to foreign tourists. Bigger bank branches will accept checks in any hard currency from any major company, but smaller branches will only accept the currencies of larger economies. The exchange rate for traveler's checks is fractionally better than for cash, though the commission charged on checks (0.75%) usually offsets any gains. Most Chinese banks will change U.S. dollars cash into *yuán*, so it's a good idea to have some U.S. dollar notes on hand in case of emergencies. If you carry traveler's checks, be sure to keep a separate record of their serial numbers so you're ensured a refund in case of loss.

CREDIT CARDS

Despite the plethora of Visa and MasterCard signs throughout town, your international credit card (*guójì xìnyòng kǎ*) is usually accepted only at the top international hotels, and at restaurants and shops catering to foreigners. You can also obtain cash advances (in *yuán*) against your American Express, Visa, MasterCard, and Diners Club card at major branches of the Bank of China (bring your passport). This is an expensive way of getting cash as you'll have to pay a 4% commission plus whatever your card issuer charges you, so use it only as a last resort. Finally, you can use your card at ATMs where international cards are accepted, if you have a PIN and have properly set up your account for this service before leaving home. If you plan to use your credit cards in China, notify your issuer(s) beforehand, as many companies, to prevent fraud, often put a hold on cards that suddenly start registering foreign charges. Loss of credit cards should be reported immediately (see "Lost & Found" in the "Fast Facts" section of chapter 3).

ATMS

There are many ATMs in China, but only a handful that will accept your foreign issued card. Check the back of your ATM card to see which network your bank belongs to: **Cirrus**
(www.mastercard.com), **PLUS** (www.visa.com), or **AEON** (www.americanexpress.com). Before you leave home, you can contact the proper institutions to locate ATMs currently available in Shànghǎi or ask your bank for a list of ATMs in China and Shànghǎi. Also check for the daily withdrawal limit. In general, the ATMs at the major branches of the Bank of China will accept your card, as will a Citibank ATM at the Peace Hotel (Nánjīng Dōng Lù 20, Huángpǔ), and a Hong Kong and Shànghǎi Bank ATM at the Shànghǎi Centre (Nánjīng Xī Lù 1376, Jìng Ān).

4 When to Go

Except for the windy, chilly winter months, Shànghǎi teems with tourists and business travelers, most notably May through October. July and August are unpleasantly hot and humid as a rule; locals often sleep on cots on the sidewalks to escape the pent-up heat of the day in their small apartments. Shànghǎi's busiest tourist periods coincide with its mildest weather in the spring and fall. September and October are really the ideal times to visit, but they're also popular times for meetings and conventions, leading to high hotel occupancy and uncompetitive room rates. To avoid the big crowds and still enjoy decent weather, the ideal time to visit is in late March or late October/early November. Besides the climate, the other major consideration in the timing of your visit should be the domestic Chinese travel season (see "Holidays" below).

CLIMATE   Shànghǎi, located on the 31st parallel north, has a climate comparable to that of the southeastern coast of the United States, except that Shànghǎi's summer is hotter. Spring, from mid-March to mid-May, is mild but rainy. Summer, from mid-May to mid-September, is oppressively hot, and humid. Winter, from mid-November to mid-March, is damp and chilly, but there is seldom snow and the daytime temperatures are usually above freezing. Autumn (Sept–Oct) is the most comfortable season, being neither too hot nor too rainy, but typhoon-propelled rains can strike in September.

HOLIDAYS   National holidays observed in Shànghǎi with days off include **New Year's Day** (Jan 1), **Spring Festival/Chinese New Year** (first day of the lunar calendar: Feb 9, 2005; Jan 29, 2006; Feb 18, 2007; and Feb 7, 2008), **Labor Day** (May 1), and **National Day** (Oct 1). Domestic travel peaks during these last three holidays.

Shànghǎi's Average Temperatures & Rainfall

	Jan	Feb	Mar	Apr	May	June	July	Aug	Sept	Oct	Nov	Dec
Temp. (°F)	39.5	40.5	47.5	58.0	68.0	74.5	82.0	82.0	74.0	65.5	54.0	44.5
Temp. (°C)	4.0	4.5	8.5	14.5	20.0	23.5	27.5	27.5	23.5	18.5	12.0	7.0
Days of Rain	9.0	10.2	13.1	13.5	15.0	13.1	11.4	10.0	11.6	8.4	9.1	8.6

Spring Festival, the Chinese New Year, is the most important holiday. Officially, it is a 5-day national holiday (expanded to 7 days when you include the weekend), meaning that on the first 3 days banks, offices, and many workplaces are closed. In reality, the effects of this holiday are felt from 2 weeks before the date until 2 weeks after, as Chinese travel to and from their hometowns, which may be very far from their place of work. The 15th day of the New Year is marked by the Lantern Festival celebrations.

The other two busy periods for domestic travel are the weeks surrounding **Labor Day** (May 1), and **National Day** (Oct 1). Both holidays have been expanded to 7 days (including 1 weekend) to encourage Chinese to travel and shop. During these times, hundreds of millions of Chinese are on the move, especially at the beginning and end of the 7 days, taxing all transportation systems to the extreme. While offices, banks, smaller restaurants and some sights may be closed for part of each holiday period, you will find in Shànghăi that hotels that normally cater to business travelers will offer significant discounts during those times.

SHÀNGHĂI CALENDAR OF EVENTS

Festivals and celebrations are not numerous in Shànghăi, and many are family affairs, but there are some opportunities to mix with the locals at city parks and other locations at annual public events.

Winter

Lónghuá Temple Bell-Ringing. On New Year's Eve in the Gregorian calendar (Dec 31), crowds gather at Lónghuá Temple to pray for good fortune as the bell is struck 108 times during a special midnight Buddhist service. Fireworks, dragon and lion dances, folk art shows, and music go into the wee hours.

Spring Festival/Chinese New Year (Chūn Jié). This is the time when Chinese return to their hometowns for family get-togethers, to visit friends, to settle the year's debts, to visit temples to pray for prosperity in the coming year, and to decorate their homes with red paper (signifying health and prosperity). Parks and temples hold outdoor celebrations and put on markets, the best places for tourists to visit. Begins the first day of the lunar calendar: February 9, 2005; January 29, 2006; February 18, 2007; and February 7, 2008.

Lantern Festival (Dēng Jié, sometimes called Yuánxiāo Jié): On the 15th day after Chinese New Year, on the first full moon, people used to parade through town with paper lanterns, while parks and temples displayed more elaborate and fanciful lanterns, all accompanied by fireworks and folk dances. In Shànghăi in recent years, there's been a minor revival of sorts, especially around the Yù Yuán Old Town Bazaar, but Shanghainese mostly mark the occasion by eating *yuánxiāo* (glutinous rice balls with sweet stuffing). This always falls 15 days after the Spring Festival.

Guānyīn's Birthday. Held on the 19th day of the 2nd lunar month, about 50 days after Chinese New Year, in honor of the Goddess of Mercy, Guānyīn, this is a good opportunity to visit one of the Buddhist temples in Shànghăi and join in the celebrations.

Spring

Lónghuá Temple Fair (Lónghuá Miàohuì). Beginning on the third day of the third lunar month, this 10-day temple fair, featuring an array of vendors, Buddhist worshippers, and local opera performers, dates from the Míng Dynasty (1368–1644). Typically first or second week of April.

Western Holidays in Shànghǎi

Christmas has become an increasingly popular holiday in Shànghǎi, celebrated at hotels and restaurants with large dinner parties. As commercial a holiday as it is in the West, **Valentine's Day** has caught on with a vengeance, with hotels and international restaurants offering room and dining packages that would have Cupid working overtime. Western **New Year's** has not caught on to the same extent, although Lónghuá Temple has become *the* place to literally ring in the new year. **St. Patrick's Day** and **Halloween** are celebrated by locals and expatriates at the cafes, bars, and discos.

Tomb Sweeping Festival (Qīng Míng Jié). This day honors the dead, which in Chinese communities overseas and some rural counties usually entails the sweeping of ancestral graves and the offering of food and wine to the departed. In Shànghǎi it usually means a mass run on the parks, where kite flying goes into high gear. April 5 in the Gregorian calendar; April 4 in leap years.

Labor Day. There's little for the Shànghǎi tourist to do except shopping, shopping, and more shopping. May 1.

Shànghǎi Spring International Music Festival. One of many recent festivals instituted by Shànghǎi, this one usually runs for 2 weeks in mid-May and has attracted such performers as the Chicago Symphony Orchestra and the Vienna Choir. It's also when the "Golden Chime" award is given to China's best music DJs.

Summer

Shànghǎi International Film Festival. This formerly biennial film festival, usually held in the fall of odd-numbered years, is now an annual June affair. Scores of international films are screened, providing many Chinese with a chance to see films they would ordinarily not be able to. An international jury judges competition films. Early June.

Autumn

Mid-Autumn Festival (Zhōngqiū Jié). Traditionally the time to read poetry under the full moon, but this festival, also known as the "Mooncake Festival," is primarily celebrated by the eating of "mooncakes," pastries with extremely rich sweet bean filling. During the Yuán Dynasty (1206–1368), Chinese attempting to revolt against their Mongol rulers sent each other messages hidden inside these cakes. Held on the 15th day of the 8th lunar month (usually Sept).

Shànghǎi International Arts Festival. This wide-ranging annual festival (of quite recent origin) is expanding. The major shopping streets, parks, and tourist sites take turns hosting special events and performances, and rural areas put on various agricultural festivals. The venues and events change every year. Usually the month of November.

5 Travel Insurance

Check your existing insurance policies and credit card coverage before you buy travel insurance. You may already be covered for lost luggage, cancelled tickets, or medical expenses.

The cost of travel insurance varies widely, depending on the cost and length of your trip, your age, your health, and the type of trip you're taking, but expect to pay between 5% to 8% of the vacation itself.

If necessary, purchase insurance from a broker rather than travel agencies, credit card companies, or outlets at the airport, all of whom will charge you higher rates.

TRIP-CANCELLATION INSURANCE (TCI)

Trip-cancellation insurance helps you get your money back if you have to back out of a trip, if you have to go home early, or if your travel supplier goes bankrupt. Allowed reasons for cancellation can range from sickness to natural disasters to a government department declaring your destination unsafe for travel. Insurers usually won't cover vague fears, though, and in 2003, travelers were not given refunds for SARS-related cancellations.

Note: Many tour operators, including those catering to China, include insurance in the cost of the trip or can arrange insurance policies through a partnering provider, a convenient and often cost-effective way for the traveler to obtain insurance. Make sure the tour company is a reputable one, however: Some experts suggest you avoid buying insurance from the tour or cruise company you're traveling with, saying it's better to buy from a "third party" insurer than to put all your money in one place.

MEDICAL INSURANCE

Check with your individual health plan to see if it provides coverage for travel to China. In any event, consider purchasing travel insurance that includes an air ambulance or scheduled airline repatriation, but be clear as to the terms and conditions of repatriation. With several advanced clinics staffed by foreign doctors in Shànghǎi, travelers can expect a fairly high quality of healthcare, though avoid, if possible, regular Chinese hospitals. In the latter, you'll have to pay your (more than likely substantial) bill upfront and in cash, and then only submit your claim after you've returned home. Be sure you have adequate proof of payment.

LOST-LUGGAGE INSURANCE

On domestic U.S. flights, checked baggage is covered up to $2,500 per ticketed passenger. On international flights (including U.S. portions of international trips), baggage coverage is limited to approximately $9.07 per pound, up to approximately $635 per checked bag. If you plan to check items more valuable than the standard liability, see if your valuables are covered by your homeowner's policy, and get baggage insurance as part of your comprehensive travel-insurance package. Don't buy insurance at the airport, as it's usually overpriced. Be sure to take any valuables or irreplaceable items with you in your carry-on luggage, as many valuables (including books, money, and electronics) aren't covered by airline policies.

If your luggage is lost, immediately file a lost-luggage claim at the airport, detailing the luggage contents. For most airlines, you must report delayed, damaged, or lost baggage within 4 hours of arrival. The airlines are required to deliver luggage, once found, directly to your house or destination free of charge, though don't expect that necessarily to work with domestic Chinese airlines.

6 Health & Safety

STAYING HEALTHY

Hygiene standards in Shànghǎi are some of the highest in China, but even then, are in many places still not up to those in developed nations. Do take precautions here you may otherwise overlook at home, more so if you plan to travel outside of China's big cities.

Still, travelers shouldn't be unduly worried. The greatest risk to your enjoyment of traveling in China is probably that of **stomach upsets** caused by low hygienic standards. To minimize this risk, wash your hands frequently, and keep them away from your mouth and eyes; eat freshly cooked hot food, especially if away from the top international hotels; eat only fruit that you peel yourself; and only drink boiled or bottled water bought in supermarkets, larger shops, and convenience stores. *Never drink tap water.* Use bottled water to brush your teeth.

Another common ailment is respiratory illnesses of various kinds, from the **common cold** (which can be picked up anywhere from the long flight over, to the overcrowded subways, to the change in temperature and humidity) to **upper respiratory tract infection,** often mistaken for a cold, all of which are exacerbated by Shànghǎi's heavy pollution. Standard over-the-counter cold remedies are easily available at drugstores and supermarkets, though you may want to bring your own if you use any regular medications. More serious infections can be treated at any of the clinics that cater to foreigners. Especially during the **SARS** crises of 2003, some locals have taken to wearing cloth or gauze masks (some do this regularly because of the pollution), but this is not necessary as they often hinder breathing much more than they actually protect you. At press time, **SARS** was not a concern in Shànghǎi, but check the latest news before you leave (see "Before You Go," below).

In early 2004, **avian influenza** (or "bird flu") struck a chicken farm on the outskirts of Shànghǎi, but other than temporarily emptying Kentucky Fried Chicken outlets of their customers and causing restaurants to remove all fowl from their menu, it has since been brought under control and the traveler has little to be concerned about.

GENERAL AVAILABILITY OF HEALTHCARE

Shànghǎi has several clinics with the latest equipment and English-speaking, foreign-trained doctors who deliver international-caliber healthcare. Expect to pay rates comparable to those in the West. In general, Chinese hospitals should be avoided.

BEFORE YOU GO

No **vaccinations** are required for entry to China and Shànghǎi, but be sure your inoculations are up-to-date. The standard inoculations are for **polio, diphtheria,** and **tetanus,** while additional inoculations may be against **meningococcal meningitis, cholera, typhoid fever, hepatitis A and B,** and **Japanese B encephalitis.** Some of these vaccinations, such as against Hepatitis B, may require several shots over a span of several months, so allow enough time before your trip. Mosquito-borne **malaria,** while a cause for concern in more rural parts of China, is not a factor in Shànghǎi. Consult your doctor or a specialist travel clinic about your individual needs. For the latest information on infectious diseases and health-related travel risks (including the latest update on the ever-changing situation with malaria), consult the **World Health Organization** (www.who.int) and the **Centers for Disease Control and Prevention** (www.cdc.gov). You can also contact the **International Association for Medical Assistance to Travelers (IAMAT;** ✆ **716/754-4883** or, in Canada, 416/652-0137; www.iamat. org) for tips on travel and health concerns in China and lists of local, English-speaking doctors.

Standard over-the-counter remedies are easily available at drugstores and supermarkets, though you may want to bring your own if you use any regular medications. It's best to stock up on all your prescriptions before you leave, but prescriptions can also usually be filled (at least with a generic equivalent, if not the actual drug) at select Shànghǎi pharmacies if you're in a pinch. (See "Fast Facts: Shànghǎi" in chapter 3.) Carry the generic name of prescription medicines, in case a local pharmacist is unfamiliar with the brand name. Don't forget an extra pair of contact lenses or prescription glasses, though there are plenty of optometrists in Shànghǎi who can replace your glasses or lenses. Feminine hygiene products such as sanitary napkins are widely available, but tampons are usually sold only in international supermarkets and pharmacies like Watson's.

COMMON AILMENTS
Besides the common illnesses mentioned earlier, other ailments to guard against, especially in the summer months, include excessive sun exposure, heatstroke, and dehydration. Shànghǎi's pollution makes most days appear overcast, but the sun still has the power to burn. Shànghǎi's hot humidity during the summer can also cause those just coming from drier climes to fatigue quickly. Drink plenty of bottled water.

Led by AIDS, **sexually transmitted diseases** are also on the rise in China. The government denied the existence of AIDS for as long as it could, and while there are now a few public campaigns addressing the issue, there is still a lot of ignorance and silence surrounding AIDS and other sexually transmitted diseases. Condoms, including Western brands, are widely available in Shànghǎi.

WHAT TO DO IF YOU GET SICK AWAY FROM HOME
If you begin to feel unwell, contact your hotel reception first. The top hotels have in-house doctors or doctors on call who may be able to treat minor ailments and direct you to the best places should further treatment be required. See "Fast Facts: Shànghǎi" in chapter 3 for a list of the top clinics in Shànghǎi that cater to foreigners. Foreign consulates can provide a list of area doctors who speak English. In many cases, you'll be expected to pay the full medical costs upfront. Keep all proof of payment so you can submit your health insurance claim when you return home.

STAYING SAFE
China is one of Asia's safest destinations. Most likely the biggest potential threat you'll encounter will be the **pickpockets** who tend to congregate in crowded places like train, bus and subway stations, airports, popular tourist sights, and crowded markets. As always, the standard precautions apply: Leave as many of your valuables

---

Avoiding "Economy Class Syndrome"
Deep vein thrombosis, or as it's know in the world of flying, "economy-class syndrome," is a blood clot that develops in a deep vein. It's a potentially deadly condition that can be caused by sitting in cramped conditions—such as an airplane cabin—for too long. During a flight (especially a long-haul flight), get up, walk around, and stretch your legs every 60 to 90 minutes to keep your blood flowing. Other preventative measures include frequent flexing of the legs while sitting, drinking lots of water, and avoiding alcohol and sleeping pills. If you have a history of deep vein thrombosis, heart disease, or another condition that puts you at high risk, some experts recommend wearing compression stockings or taking anticoagulants when you fly; always ask your physician about the best course for you. Symptoms of deep vein thrombosis include leg pain or swelling, or even shortness of breath.

as you can in hotel safes; any other valuables should be distributed around your person, and not kept inside your purse or backpack which can be easily picked. Wear a money belt *inside* your clothes. Always leave one copy of your passport and traveler's check receipts at your hotel.

Visitors should also beware various **scam artists** who will use the pretext of practicing their English to try and befriend you, all with the goal of separating you from your money. As far as many Chinese are concerned, there's no such thing as a poor foreigner. These scams can range from "art students" taking you to special shops and pressuring you to buy paintings that are neither authentic, unique, or worth what's claimed, to the friendly face who'll offer to buy you a meal or a drink at a local haunt, where you'll find yourself with 12 opened bottles of warm beer you didn't order; and if you refuse to pay, several thuggish bouncers stand between you and the door.

Solicitations are also commonplace, whether in a bar, karaoke joint, or even your hotel room, where many a China visitor has been telephoned in the wee hours, with a voice on the other end inquiring "Massagee?" (The caller always hangs up when a woman answers.) Caveat emptor: Not only is there a higher than expected incidence of sexually transmitted diseases in China, but there have been reports of men, foolish enough in the first place to accept such invitations, being forced to pay huge sums for services not actually rendered.

If you find yourself a victim of theft, file a police report at the local PSB (Public Security Bureau; see "Visa Extensions" earlier in this chapter for the address). Don't expect any redress, necessarily, but at least you'll have the report for insurance claims back home.

In general, there's very little harassment of **solo female travelers,** in and of itself a rare sight among Chinese.

Another major hazard that tourists will have to contend with is **traffic.** Even if foreign visitors were allowed to drive (which you are not without a Chinese driver's license), you stand little chance against Chinese motorists who treat lane markings and traffic lights like so much fluffy roadside decoration. Seat belt and speed limits are consistently ignored. There really is only one rule on Chinese roads: Might is right, which kicks pedestrians down to the bottom of the traffic food chain. Still, if you look every which way before you cross, generally go with the flow, and take your cue from locals, there's little cause for concern. Paying greater attention in the streets will also prevent you from falling down open manholes or being hit by falling debris from any one of Shànghǎi's many construction projects.

DEALING WITH DISCRIMINATION

In general, there is little overt discrimination in China against non-Chinese, except perhaps for persistent overcharging. But then again, many Chinese have the attitude that *all* foreigners (including ethnic Chinese from Hong Kong, Táiwān, and Southeast Asia) are moneybags, and will simply overcharge anyone and everyone they can. Ethnic Chinese, on the other hand, can use the "We're all Chinese after all" appeal for better prices, which the *lǎowài* (the somewhat condescending "old foreigner" term applied to non-Chinese) cannot do. Darker-skinned visitors may also have a slightly more difficult time of it than whites, especially outside of the big cities.

On the other hand, once some sort of communication has been established, non-Chinese tend to receive better treatment from locals than the Chinese dole out to each other. Unfortunately, this situation sometimes even extends to Shànghǎi's top hotels.

7 Specialized Travel Resources

TRAVELERS WITH DISABILITIES

China has more citizens with disabilities than any nation on Earth. Despite the fact that some efforts have been made in addressing their needs (spearheaded for several decades by the son of former Supreme Leader Dèng Xiǎopíng, who is in a wheelchair as a result of persecution during the Cultural Revolution), Chinese with disabilities are still largely hidden from public view while specialized facilities for them range from sporadic to nonexistent. The situation is fractionally better in Shànghǎi: Sections of some major sidewalks are now equipped with "raised dots" to assist the blind; modern buildings and some major tourist sites have elevators; and a handful of top hotels have wheelchair-accessible rooms, but the bottom line is that Shànghǎi is a city of long stairways (even at most subway stations) and crowded, crumbling sidewalks. Even so, most disabilities haven't stopped travelers from making their way through the Shànghǎi obstacle course and enjoying its many sights.

To minimize the difficulties of navigating a place like China, it's best that you travel with a specialist group (such tours to China are rare but are slowly starting to catch on). One outlet offering such customized tours to China is **Flying Wheels Travel** (www.flyingwheelstravel.com), which organizes escorted private tours in minivans with lifts. **Access-Able Travel Source** (www.access-able.com) offers extensive access information and advice for traveling around the world with disabilities.

GAY & LESBIAN TRAVELERS

Shànghǎi is quite tolerant of gay and lesbian travelers, though there are no specialized resources catering to them. This is not all that unusual, given how puritanical Chinese society tends to be in sexual matters, gay or straight.

(Walking hand in hand with a same-sex partner won't raise any eyebrows because it is deemed a sign of friendship.) Shànghǎi does have a homosexual community, but it is not organized or sanctioned in any way. Because foreigners are perceived as "different" from Chinese in the first place, gay and lesbian travelers should experience no discrimination here. In recent years, a few nightspots have even become identified with a gay, lesbian, and transsexual clientele (see chapter 9). To date, the popular **International Gay & Lesbian Travel Association (IGLTA; ✆ 800/448-8550** or 954/776-2626; www.iglta.org) has no listings for gay-friendly organizations in China.

SENIOR TRAVEL

The Chinese generally respect age far more than do their Western counterparts, but don't expect to find a plethora of "senior discounts" at tourist attractions or in stores. A handful of outlets will have special rates for those over 70, but these are few and far between. If you book a hotel from an international hotel chain overseas, inquire about but don't expect senior discounts. In Shànghǎi, brace yourself for long stairways at some museums and temples, and impatient crowds everywhere you turn.

Elderhostel (✆ 877/426-8056; www.elderhostel.org) arranges study/travel programs for those aged 55 and over (and a spouse or companion of any age) in the U.S. and in more than 80 countries around the world, including China. **ElderTreks** (✆ 800/741-7956; www.eldertreks.com) also offers expensive small-group tours to China.

FAMILY TRAVEL

If you have enough trouble getting your kids out of the house in the morning, dragging them thousands of

The Ethnic Chinese Foreigner

Ethnic Chinese who are born and raised outside China, but who do not speak any Chinese (and that includes any number of second-generation-on-down Chinese-Americans, Chinese-Britons, Australian-Chinese, and more) usually find themselves in an awkward position when visiting China. Simply by virtue of the fact they look Chinese, they are expected to speak the language, and those who don't are often viewed with a mix of subtle derision and exasperation. At the same time, they are not given the same benefit of the doubt as non-Chinese foreigners (see above section on "Discrimination"). While the reasons for this unfortunate phenomenon are age-old and complex, ethnic Chinese foreigners, like any foreign visitor, can go a long way in endearing themselves to locals by learning some Chinese and displaying some knowledge of Chinese culture and history. Even if you speak with a funny accent, the effort is usually appreciated. Learn the words for "We're all Chinese!" (*Wǒmén dōushì zhōngguó rén!*), and you may well find yourself paying a little more than local but a little less than foreigner prices for that special scarf. Mainland Chinese also tend to look very favorably upon ethnic Chinese foreigners "returning" to the motherland to search for their roots, a process known in Mandarin as *xún gēn*.

miles away may seem like an insurmountable challenge, especially to a place as seemingly foreign as China. But the difficulties of family travel to China lie less in the "foreignness" of the environment than in the lack of services and entertainment geared towards children.

Hygiene, or rather the lack thereof, presents the other main challenge. Much of China is quite dirty, so young children who have the tendency of putting their hands in their mouths should be closely monitored, while older children should be reminded to wash their hands frequently and to follow the general health tips outlined in the "Staying Healthy" section earlier. Challenges notwithstanding, family travel to China can be immensely rewarding, and you shouldn't let the absence of children-friendly resources deter you from venturing here *en masse*.

The Chinese tend to dote on their children, and you may find your children given the same amount of attention, which usually takes the form of a lot of friendly touching, chatter, and photo-sessions with the young ones.

Children traveling on a parent's passport have to submit a separate photo per child during the visa application process.

Many hotels in Shànghǎi allow young children (usually under 12) to stay free with their parents, and some hotels provide babysitting service for a fee (though the caretakers are usually just culled from in-house staff).

Probably more so than anywhere else in China, Shànghǎi has plenty of sights to dazzle and distract your children. For Western kids, there are many familiar fast-food and foreign-style eateries, several amusement and theme parks, a natural history museum, a children's palace, the zoo, indoor playgrounds and toy stores in shopping centers, and plenty of parks for rowing, kite-flying, and in-line skating. As a rule, there are special discounts for children at museums and attractions, though discounts are given based on height, not age.

To locate accommodations, restaurants, and attractions that are particularly kid-friendly, refer to the "Kids" icon throughout this guide, and to the "Especially for Kids" section in chapter 6.

WOMEN TRAVELERS

Women travelers to China generally have a no more difficult time of it than their male counterparts. You should, however, be prepared for the inevitable questions, whenever casual communication has been established (and especially if you're traveling solo), of whether you are married and have children.

In general, there is very little discrimination against women travelers. If anything, women (who "hold up half the sky" as Máo Zédōng proclaimed) are expected to pull their own weight. Don't expect any help in lugging that heavy bag up and down trains, or for doors to be opened for you.

In response to the greater numbers of women business travelers, several top hotels in Shànghǎi like the St. Regis and the Novotel Atlantis have started to offer secure "women only" floors, complete with added perks like fine toiletries, women's magazines, and spa services.

SINGLE TRAVELERS

Single travelers on a group tour to China are often hit with a "single supplement" to the base price. Unfortunately, there is no real way to avoid it unless you agree to room with other single travelers on the trip. If you are traveling by yourself in China, however, you may find that you can sometimes get a smaller "single" room (with one twin or double bed, often called a *dānrén jiān*) for considerably less than the standard double *(biāozhǔn jiān)*.

STUDENT TRAVELERS

Student travelers, like visiting seniors, should not expect special rates or other discounts in Shànghǎi. There are a few attractions that offer discounts to students, but you'll have to produce a Chinese student identity card for that.

8 Planning Your Trip Online

SURFING FOR AIRFARES

The "big three" online travel agencies, **Expedia.com, Travelocity.com,** and **Orbitz.com,** sell most of the air tickets bought on the Internet. (Canadian travelers should try Expedia.ca and Travelocity.ca; U.K. residents can go for Expedia.co.uk and Opodo.co.uk.) Each has different business deals with the airlines and may offer different fares for the same flights, so it's wise to shop around.

Also remember to check **airline websites** for Web-only specials. For the websites of airlines that fly to and from Shànghǎi, go to "Getting There," p. 33. Whatever you do, *do not* buy China domestic plane tickets from online English-language websites; the mark-ups are exorbitant and you will do much better to purchase domestic tickets once you're in the country.

SURFING FOR HOTELS

For the pros and cons of online booking of hotels in China, see the "Booking Online" section in chapter 4. In general, online booking, whether done directly through the hotel's own website or through services like Hotels.com, Travelocity, and Expedia, provide convenience and but usually not the best prices. Unless you have to stay in a specific hotel at a particularly busy time of year, you'll usually, but not always, get a better rate if you show up in person. However, it does occur, especially during the low season months of January and February, that you may find some very competitive rates for Shànghǎi hotels on the hotels' own websites or on the big hotel-booking sites.

A random search on the Web will uncover a host of Chinese agencies that purport to book hotels and flights for you, but do not book with them because there are no safeguards you'll ever get your room or your money back. One exception incredibly popular with many Chinese is the consolidator **C-Trip** (http://english.ctrip.com), which offers discounts at hotels throughout China that range from minimal to significant. However, because they do not require pre-payment for the most part, your "reservation" may not always be honored when you show up, a confirmed reservation number notwithstanding (the hotel will simply claim they never received the reservation). Still, if you are shopping for your own hotel, it is worthwhile to consult this website if only to compare prices and to get an idea of what you can reasonably bargain for in person.

9 The 21st-Century Traveler

INTERNET ACCESS AWAY FROM HOME

Travelers in China should find it quite easy to check their e-mail and access the Internet on the road, despite periodic government attempts to block websites, control traffic, and shut down cybercafes. If you find yourself unable to access a popular website or search engine, try returning to it in a day or two; some shutdowns are temporary.

WITHOUT YOUR OWN COMPUTER

The comparative wealth of the Shanghainese (making personal computers more popular than ever), along with recent government crackdowns, has reduced the number of cybercafes, or *wǎngbā* (literally, net bar) in town. Where they still exist, charges range from ¥5 to ¥20 (60¢–$2.50) an hour. For a list of locations, see "Fast Facts: Shànghǎi" in chapter 3. Avoid hotel business centers if possible unless you want to pay significantly higher rates.

WITH YOUR OWN COMPUTER

In Shànghǎi, those using dial-up access no longer need the local access number for their ISP, but can connect directly by dialing the number 16300 and making that the account number and password. Cost is a little more than a local call. Mainland China uses the standard U.S. RJ11 telephone jack, easily available at any of Shànghǎi's major department stores and electrical shops. Electrical voltage in China is 220V, 50Mhz.

Those with on-board Ethernet can avail themselves of broadband services now available in many Shànghǎi hotels. The typical charge is around ¥100 ($13) for 24 hours. It's best to bring your own Ethernet cables, but hotels can usually provide them as well, either for free or for a small fee.

Digital Photography on the Road

Travelers toting their latest digital cameras to China would do well to bring enough memory cards from home, as getting additional cards may not be as easy outside the bigger cities. (Each camera model works with a specific type of card, whether memory sticks, flash cards, or secure digital cards, so you'll need to determine which storage card is compatible with your camera.) Also be sure to bring enough batteries or a battery re-charger with a built-in converter that can operate on 200V, 50 MHz. In Shànghǎi, you should be able to purchase memory cards, batteries, and other accessories without too much problem. If you can't wait to get home to print out your images, you can even have them developed and printed when you're here. See p.205 for more details.

Online Traveler's Toolbox

- **ATM Locators:** Visa ATM Locator (www.visa.com) provides locations of PLUS ATMs worldwide; MasterCard ATM Locator (www.mastercard.com), gives locations of Cirrus ATMs worldwide.
- **Cybercafes.com** (www.cybercafes.com) or **Net Café Guide** (www.netcafeguide.com/mapindex.htm) locates Internet cafes at hundreds of locations around the globe, including some in China and Shànghǎi, though the lists are hardly comprehensive and are not always up to date.
- **Frommers.com** (www.frommers.com), to toot our horn a bit, not only provides online versions of all its guidebooks, but also maintains popular message boards where travelers can post queries and share advice.
- **Online Chinese Tools** (www.mandarintools.com) has Chinese dictionaries for Mac and Windows users, and also provides conversions between the solar and lunar calendar.
- **The Oriental-List** is a spam- and ad-free moderated mailing list focusing only on travel in China, and is an excellent location to post questions not already covered in this guide. To subscribe, send a blank e-mail to subscribe-oriental-list@list.xianzai.com.
- **Travel Warnings** are available at www.travel.state.gov/travel_warnings.html, www.fco.gov.uk/travel, www.voyage.gc.ca, and www.dfat.gov.au/consular/advice.
- **Universal Currency Converter** (www.xe.net/currency) provides the latest exchange rates for any currency against the ¥RMB.
- **Weatherbase** (www.weatherbase.com) provides month-by-month temperatures and rainfalls for individual cities in China.
- **World Health Organization** (http://who.org) and the **Center for Disease Control** (http://cdc.org) both provide information on health concerns that may affect travelers around the world, including in China.
- **Xianzai.com** (www.xianzai.com) provides entertainment and restaurant listings for Běijīng, Shànghǎi, and Guǎngzhōu, as well as special offers for air tickets and hotels in China.

Wi-fi (wireless fidelity), the buzzword in computer access, has also caught on in Shànghǎi, with a number of the top business hotels (Westin, St. Regis, Sheraton) now offering wireless "hot spots" in their lobbies, executive lounges, and boardrooms, from where anyone can get high-speed connection without cable wires if you have a wireless card installed on your computer. Check with hotel reception to sign up for access, which averages around ¥100 ($13) for 24 hours.

USING A CELLPHONE IN CHINA

China's wireless capabilities function on the quasi-universal GSM (Global System for Mobiles) network, which is used by all Europeans, most Australians, many Asians (except in Japan and Korea), and many North Americans as well. If you're coming from North America and want to use your GSM phone in China, make sure it's a tri-band (900 Mhz/ 1800 Mhz/ 1900 Mhz) phone that's been "unlocked" to receive service in China. The roaming and international call charges will be predictably exorbitant, so consider buying a prepaid SIM card (known as *shénzhōuxíng*, about ¥100/$13) in China, which you can install in your GSM phone. Recharge cards *(chōngzhí kǎ)* are available at post offices and mobile phone stores. If you don't have a GSM phone, you can purchase an older Chinese model in any of Shànghǎi's department stores or phone shops for around ¥800 ($100).

Alternatively, it's easy to rent a phone in Shànghǎi. There are rental shops in the arrival hall of Pǔdōng Airport, and the city's largest phone company, China Mobile (www.china-mobile-phone.com), can deliver phones to your hotel. Rental costs range from $2 to $9 a day before airtime and long distance charges.

10 Getting There

BY PLANE

Chinese carriers serving international destinations include Air China (www.airchina.com), China Eastern Airlines (www.chinaeastern.com), and China Southern Airlines (www.china-southern.com). On direct nonstop flights, flying with one of the above is often cheaper than flying with your country's airline. Chinese airlines frequently "code share" with foreign airlines as well, which means you may end up flying on a Chinese airline jet even if you've purchased a foreign airline ticket, or vice versa.

FROM NORTH AMERICA

Of the North American airlines, **Air Canada** (www.aircanada.ca), **Northwest Airlines** (www.nwa.com), and **United Airlines** (www.ual.com) all fly to Shànghǎi. **American Airlines** (www.aa.com) appears to fly to Shànghǎi but it is actually a code-share flight on China Eastern.

Japan Airlines (www.jal.co.jp) and **All Nippon Airways** (www.ana.co.jp) fly to Shànghǎi via Tokyo. **Korean Air** (www.koreanair.com) and **Asiana Airlines** (us.flyasiana.com) fly via Seoul.

FROM THE UNITED KINGDOM & EUROPE

Shànghǎi is connected to the U.K. and Europe by **Virgin Atlantic** (www.virgin-atlantic.com), **Air France** (www.airfrance.com), **Austrian Airlines** (www.austrianair.com), **KLM Royal Dutch Airlines** (www.klm.com), **Lufthansa** (www.lufthansa.com), **Aeroflot** (www.aeroflot.com), **Finnair Airlines** (www.finnair.com), **Scandanavian Airlines** (www.scandanavian.net), and **Turkish Airlines** (www.turkishair.com).

FROM AUSTRALASIA

There are plans for **Qantas** (www.qantas.com) to fly nonstop to Shànghǎi from Sydney starting in December 2004. Alternatively, it may be cheaper to fly one of the other Asian carriers via their home country, such as **Singapore Airlines** (www.singaporeair.com), **Malaysian Airlines** (www.malaysiaairlines.com.my), **Garuda Indonesia** (www.garudaindonesia.com), **Philippine Airlines** (www.pal.com.ph), or **Thai Airways** (www.thaiairways.com). Other carriers serving Asia Pacific include **Dragonair** (www.dragonair.com), which flies from Hong Kong to Shànghǎi and is partly owned by Cathay Pacific, **Air Macau** (www.airmacau.com.mo), **Royal Brunei Airlines** (www.bruneiair.com), **Royal Nepal Airlines** (www.royalnepal.com), and **Emirates** (www.emirates.com).

FLYING FOR LESS: TIPS FOR GETTING THE BEST AIRFARE

Passengers sharing the same airplane cabin rarely pay the same fare. Travelers who need to purchase tickets at the last minute, change their itinerary at a moment's notice, or fly one-way often get stuck paying the premium rate. Here are some ways to keep your airfare costs down.

- Passengers who can book your ticket **long in advance,** who can **stay over Saturday night,** or who **fly midweek** or **at less-trafficked hours** may pay considerably less. If your schedule is flexible, say so, and ask if you can secure a cheaper fare by changing your flight plans.
- Fly with one of China's airlines like Air China, China Eastern, or China Southern, all of which will always charge less than your country's airline. These airlines often "code share" with Western carriers, so you may end up on the same plane anyway, but a little richer for it.
- Fly via an intermediate country rather than directly. From North America, you can save by flying Asian carriers that stop over in Tokyo, Seoul, or Taipei. From Europe, flying with smaller eastern European carriers via their home country often yields even greater savings.
- Keep an eye out in local newspapers for **promotional specials,** especially by Asian-based airlines during off-peak months (usually Nov–Feb for China destinations).
- Search the **Internet** for cheap fares (see "Planning Your Trip Online").

- **Consolidators,** also known as bucket shops, are great sources for international tickets. Start by looking in Sunday newspaper travel sections. Agents in local Chinatowns often have the best deals. *Beware:* Bucket shop tickets are usually nonrefundable or rigged with stiff cancellation penalties, often as high as 50% to 75% of the ticket price. Several reliable consolidators are worldwide and available on the Net. **STA Travel** (www.sta.com) offers competitive fares for travelers of all ages, while **Flight Centre** (www.flightcentre.com) guarantees they'll match or better the lowest written quotes you find elsewhere.

LONG-HAUL FLIGHTS: HOW TO STAY COMFORTABLE

With stuffy air and cramped seats, those 12-hour flights to Shànghǎi can certainly be trying. For international airlines, research firm Skytrax has posted a list of average seat pitches at www.airlinequality.com. Here are some tips to make the long flight more bearable:

- Request an emergency exit seat if possible, as these have the most legroom, followed by bulkhead seats. The latter is also where families with young children are often seated, so you may not want these if sleep is a priority.

Travel in the Age of Bankruptcy

Airlines go bankrupt, so protect yourself by **buying your tickets with a credit card,** as credit card companies in most countries guarantee that you can get your money back if a travel supplier goes under (and if you request the refund within a limited time of the bankruptcy). **Travel insurance** can also help, but make sure it covers against "carrier default" for your specific travel provider. And be aware that if a U.S. airline goes bust mid-trip, a 2001 federal law requires other carriers to take you to your destination (albeit on a space-available basis) for a fee of no more than $25, provided you rebook within 60 days of the cancellation.

- To have two seats for yourself in a three-seat row, try for an aisle seat in a center section toward the back of coach. If you're traveling with a companion, book an aisle and a window seat. Middle seats are usually booked last, so chances are good you'll end up with three seats to yourselves. And in the event that a third passenger is assigned the middle seat, he or she will probably be more than happy to trade for a window or an aisle.
- To sleep, avoid the last row of any section or a row in front of an emergency exit, as these seats are the least likely to recline. Avoid seats near highly trafficked toilet areas. Avoid seats in the back of many jets—these can be narrower than those in the rest of coach class. Reserve a window seat so that you can rest your head and avoid being bumped in the aisle.

- Get up, walk around, and stretch every 60 to 90 minutes to keep your blood flowing. This helps you avoid **deep vein thrombosis,** or "economy-class syndrome," a potentially deadly condition that can be caused by sitting in cramped conditions for too long. See the "Avoiding 'Economy Class Syndrome'" box under "Health & Safety," p. 26.
- Drink water before, during, and after your flight to combat the lack of humidity in airplane cabins. Bring a bottle of water on board. Avoid alcohol, which will dehydrate you.
- If you're flying with kids, don't forget to carry on toys, books, pacifiers, and chewing gum to help them relieve ear pressure buildup during ascent and descent.

11 Packages for the Independent Traveler

The single biggest decision first-time visitors to China often have to make is whether to travel independently, booking all accommodations and onward transportation on your own as you go; travel on a structured escorted group tour with a group leader, where everything from airfare to hotels, meals, tours, admission costs, and local transportation are included; or travel on an unescorted package tour, which straddles the two by having the basic elements such as airfare, accommodations, and transfers taken care of but leaving you the freedom to visit sights, shops, and restaurants at your will. Your decision will of course depend on your experience and goals. Shànghǎi itself can be comfortably explored on your own (especially armed with this guide!) and any package tour, escorted or otherwise, is really just a waste of money. The rest of China is possible to see on your own, even if you don't speak the language, but it will require a lot of patience, energy, resourcefulness, time, goodwill, and not a little luck.

The unescorted package tour provides convenience, but while it may make economical sense for many destinations in the world because the package ends up being cheaper than buying the individual elements yourself, in China you usually end up paying more for the convenience. The reason is that any foreign tour operators you may purchase your package from are required to use Chinese state-registered travel agencies to act as local handlers. These local agencies usually quote unconscionably high rates, which become even more exorbitant when your tour operator tacks on the middleman fee. The lack of competition—the Chinese travel agency scene has been dominated since the 1980s by CITS, and to a lesser extent, CTS and CYTS—has only served to keep prices high. In recent years, more private operators have been allowed to compete but their comparative lack of experience and size still drive most travelers, however grudgingly, to CITS, which is at least established and has some experience with foreigners' whims and fancies. Of course you can book directly with CITS, but there is no guarantee of redress or compensation should something go wrong.

If convenience is paramount and money no object, consider booking with one of the agencies listed in the next section that can also book unescorted tour packages. You can also check with the China National Tourism Office (see earlier) for a list of registered Chinese agencies that can help. In each case, always comparison-shop, as package tours vary widely with regard to choice of airlines, hotels, and other hidden expenses; never go with the first company on the list. Do not under any circumstances book with private Chinese tour agencies or guides online, as many of them are not licensed.

12 Escorted General-Interest Tours

Escorted tours are structured group tours, with a group leader. The price usually includes everything from airfare to hotels, meals, tours, admission costs, and local transportation, but not usually domestic or international departures. Most require you to pay upfront. Many, but not all, escorted China tours include Shànghăi (1–2 nights), but do not really cover it in any kind of depth (as with any escorted tour, you'll get little opportunity for serendipitous interactions with locals and you'll likely miss out on some lesser-known gems).

As noted previously, it is possible to travel through China on your own even if you don't speak the language (even more so through an increasingly international city like Shànghăi), but time, energy, and resourcefulness are required to arrange your own way. For those short on time and who want the security and ease that come from knowing all you have to do is show up, escorted tours have traditionally been and continue to be the preferred way to see China.

Unfortunately, however, China package tours, escorted or otherwise, are usually unbridled attempts at gross profiteering, all at your expense. Foreign tour operators are required to work with, and essentially cede control to, a handful of Chinese travel agencies on the ground (historically the cabal of CITS, CTS or CYTS), where there is every attempt to pad every pocket (except yours) at every possible level. From the number and location of shopping stops, to the strong suggestions of tipping, to the extra "must-see" sight the guide tries to fob upon you, no attempt to fleece you will be bypassed. Of course, most visitors never realize the full extent to which they are being taken.

While this situation will likely not change without some larger structural changes in the Chinese tourism industry, there are several precautions you can take to ensure you get as much value for your money as possible should you decide to join an escorted tour.

EVALUATING TOURS
In evaluating tour companies for China, besides the usual considerations of price, itinerary, schedule, size, and demographics of the group, physical ability required, types of hotels you're likely to stay at, existence of single supplements if you're traveling alone, and payment and cancellation policies (especially as they pertain to

health-related issues like SARS), here are some other questions to ask your tour operator:

- **Shopping Stops:** This is how tour guides, drivers, tour operators, and all their kith and kin make money: by ferrying you to as many shopping outlets as possible in between the sights, and then collecting commissions on every item purchased. (Equal opportunity fleecers, they do this to *all* tourists, not just foreigners.) The better foreign tour operators try as much as possible to design their own itineraries, keeping shopping stops to a minimum, but it is difficult to avoid the stops entirely. Ask your tour operator how many of these stops are included, and if they don't know, find another company. This is as sure a sign as any that your company is not a China specialist and is only cobbling together a package without much concern for their clients. If you're stuck at one of these stops, sit them out if possible, as prices are astronomically marked up to begin with, so any discounts promised are no big deal.

- **Additional Costs:** You cannot be too clear on what *exactly* is included in the price of the tour. Watch out especially for additional **tips** that may be asked of you. For what it's worth, there is officially *no* tipping in China. Taxi drivers, your average restaurant waitstaff, and the staff at most hotels do not expect tips and will usually return any change. However, where escorted tours are concerned, there invariably ends up being some form of tipping of guides and drivers. In general, payment for the tour guides and drivers, including reasonable tips, should be included in the initial cost quoted by your tour operator; if your tour operator tells you that tips are not included, you will need to add the anticipated tips onto the initial cost quoted you. As a general rule, despite the non-stop pressure you'll get to tip and tip well, only tip for truly excellent or exceptional service, and then pull together a reasonable (by Chinese standards, not the West's) sum from the group. Some guides claim they would not be making a living wage were it not for tips and shopping commissions, but it's also true that many tour guides make many times more than what an ordinary factory worker makes. Any excessive or misguided tipping merely makes it more difficult on the travelers that follow you.

- **Guides:** The quality of guides in China varies widely, from genuinely knowledgeable and critically thinking guides to those who merely repeat verbatim every bit of propaganda they've had to study to become licensed, to those whose grasp of the English language makes it all sound like Chinese to you. Your chances of encountering the first are considerably greater, though hardly assured, in the big cities where competition has forced the better guides to a level of proficiency and accountability not demanded of guides in smaller towns and areas. Many guides, though, still tend to err on the side of telling foreigners what they want to hear; others don't have much experience beyond their limited purview. Ask your tour company if they will be sending an accompanying guide or tour manager from home to oversee the trip and supplement the local guides. This person, who should be knowledgeable about not only Chinese history and culture, but also the workings of Chinese tourism, is worth paying more for as they can help ensure a smoother trip. Depending on your itinerary and tour operator, you may get a Chinese tour guide who will accompany you throughout China (called a *quánpéi*) as well as local guides in the different cities, or simply local guides at every destination. As noted above, make sure *all* the guides and drivers' fees are included in the tour cost, or factor in the accurate number of guides along the way if you have to prepare for tips.

TOUR COMPANIES

The following is but a short list of companies offering packages to China that span different interests and budgets. While they are located in North America, the U.K., and Australia, they have representatives around the world, and it's usually possible to fly in on your own and join only the land portion of the tour.

- **Abercrombie and Kent** (U.S.): Classy top-of-the-line luxury-travel company that specializes in tailor-made private tours and escorted small group travel. ☎ 800/323-7308, fax 630/954-3324, www.abercrombiekent.com (U.S.); ☎ 08450/700610, fax 08450/700608,www.abercrombiekent.co.uk (U.K.); ☎ 1300/851-800, www.abercrombiekent.com.au (Australia); ☎ 0800/441-638 (New Zealand).

- **Academic Travel Abroad** (U.S.): Arranges all the tours for The Smithsonian (educational, cultural) and National Geographic Expeditions (adventure, natural history). ☎ 877/EDU-TOUR, fax 202/633-9250, www.smithsonianjourneys.org; ☎ 888/966-8687, fax 202/342-0317, www.nationalgeographic.org/ngexpeditions.

- **Adventure Center** (U.S.): Touts a plethora of China trips that offer a more adventurous twist on the standard itineraries; activities can include walking, cycling, and even staying at a Hángzhōu farm. ☎ 800/227-8747 (U.S.); ☎ 888/456-3522 (Canada); www.adventurecenter.com.

- **China Focus** (U.S.): Its large mainstream tours have received good reviews from travelers on Frommer's message boards; they have been described by an enthusiastic client as "champagne tours at beer prices." Watch out for additional costs to cover extras. ☎ 800/868-8660 or 415/788-8660; fax 415/788-8665; www.chinafocustravel.com.

- **Elderhostel** (U.S.): Popular educational tours for those 55 and older. ☎ 877/426-8056; www.elderhostel.org.

- **Gecko's Adventures** (Australia): Budget adventures aimed at 20- to 40-year-old travelers who normally journey independently. Uses local accommodations and transport. ☎ 03/9662-2700; fax 03/9662-2422; with branches worldwide; www.geckosadventures.com.

- **Helen Wong's Tours** (Australia): Experienced group offering longer stays to savor the "local" experience. ☎ 02/9267-7833; fax 02/9267-7717; www.helenwongstours.com.

- **Intrepid Travel** (Australia): As its name suggests, adventurous trips with competent guides; good value for money. ☎ 613/9478-2626, fax 613/9419-4426, www.intrepidtravel.com (Australia); ☎ 877/448-1616 (U.S.).

- **Laurus Travel** (Canada): A small China-only specialist that runs well-received small group tours. ☎ 604/438-7718; fax 604/438-7715; www.laurustravel.com.

- **Pacific Delight** (U.S.): Popular outfit offering a wide range of mainstream tours, many economical. Expect many shopping stops:

Company uses local operators that rake in massive commissions on the back end. ✆ 800/221-7179; www.pacificdelighttours.com.

- **Peregrine Adventures** (Australia): Upmarket counterpart to Gecko's Adventures; emphasizes soft adventure and new angles on standard experiences such as visiting an untouristed part of the Great Wall or checking out Shànghǎi's local food stalls. ✆ 03/9663-8611, fax 03/9663-8618; www.peregrine adventures.com (Australia); ✆ 800/227-8747 (U.S.).

- **Ritz Tours** (U.S.): The largest China tour operator in the U.S., with over 20,000 visitors in 2002;

after some complaints of lack of service and attention, now limits its China tour group size to 24; varying ages, popular with families; expect many shopping stops and pressure to tip. ✆ 800/900-2446; www.ritztours.com.

Another option is to visit Shànghǎi on a **themed escorted tour,** such as one on Chinese cooking, shopping, architecture, tai chi, traditional medicine, art, or another topic. Such tours are usually one-time offerings, however, led by experts in the field, so finding them requires research and some luck. Search magazines, newspapers, and the Internet for groups that specialize in your interest.

13 Recommended Books & Films

RECOMMENDED BOOKS

At the top of the list on Shànghǎi history is Pan Ling's nostalgic, romantic, easy-to-read history of the city and its characters, *In Search of Old Shanghai* (Joint Publishing [H.K.] Co., Ltd., 1982). Many accounts of Shànghǎi's history tend to focus on the lurid, the sensational, and the exotic, including Stella Dong's spicy, reasonably well researched history of colonial Shànghǎi, *Shanghai: The Rise and Fall of a Decadent City, 1842-1949* (William Morrow, 2000). It suffers, as any general book on Shànghǎi must, from a lack of depth, but it at least summarizes the main events and personalities that came to define the time. Harriet Sergeant's equally entertaining *Shanghai* (Jonathan Cape, 1991) focuses on a shorter period (1920s and 1930s) and uses stories and anecdotes to bring to life Shànghǎi in its heyday. Considerably more academic but still fascinating, *Beyond the Neon Lights: Everyday Shanghai in the Early Twentieth Century* (University of California Press, 1999) by Hanchao Lu gets past the myth and the hype to examine the daily lives of ordinary Shanghainese in

their *shíkù mén* (stone frame) lane housing.

For a mostly fascinating and detailed narrative of contemporary Shànghǎi, warts and all, Pamela Yatsko's *New Shanghai: The Rocky Rebirth of China's Legendary City* (Wiley Publishing, Inc., 2001) provides a wider perspective on Shànghǎi now and in the future.

As biographies and memoirs go, only the first section of colorful American journalist Emily Hahn's *China to Me* (Blakiston Co., 1946) is set in Shànghǎi, but it offers a vivid and entertaining account of life amongst the Shànghǎi elite in the 1930s, including her encounters with members of the Soong family, who are themselves profiled in great, highly readable detail in Sterling Seagrave's *The Soong Dynasty* (Harper & Row, 1985).

Old Shànghǎi comes alive in Vickie Baum's novel *Shanghai '37*, in which different characters' lives collide at the Cathay (Peace) Hotel just before the Sino-Japanese War. No literary masterpiece, it nevertheless succeeds in bringing a tumultuous bygone era to life.

Far darker visions of Shànghăi are powerfully evoked in J. G. Ballard's personal novel, *Empire of the Sun* (V. Gollancz, 1984), based on his imprisonment as a child during the Japanese occupation; and in Nien Cheng's *Life and Death in Shanghai* (Grove Press, 1986), a memoir of her imprisonment during the Cultural Revolution. Anchee Min's *Red Azalea* (Pantheon Books, 1994) recounts her extraordinary journey from revolutionary Red Guard to film star in Shànghăi under the watchful eye of Madame Máo.

A welcome antidote to the dark and heavy survival stories is the light and fun detective novel *Death of a Red Heroine* (Soho Press, 2000) by Chinese author Qiū Xiǎolóng, featuring a poetry-writing Shànghăi police inspector who investigates the death of a model former Red Guard.

Finally, for a pictorial memoir on Shànghăi's colonial architecture, there's no topping Tess Johnston and Deke Erh's *A Last Look: Western Architecture in Old Shanghai* (Old China Hand Press, 1993), which is more widely available in Shànghăi than in the West. The two have also released a series of books on Western colonial architecture in other parts of China.

RECOMMENDED FILMS

Films about Shànghăi, at least those familiar to Western audiences, trade heavily on the nostalgia of the mysterious and romantic 1930s. For Western audiences, the classic is Josef von Sternberg's 1932 film *Shanghai Express,* starring Marlene Dietrich. The Shànghăi underworld of 1930s gangsters and their molls is also stylishly evoked in Zhāng Yìmóu's 1995 film *Shanghai Triad (Yáo a yáo yáo dào wàipó qiáo),* starring China's then and probably still best known actress (at least to Western audiences), Gŏng Lì. Steven Spielberg's 1987 film *Empire of the Sun,* based on English author J. G.

Ballard's autobiographical novel, takes a look inside the concentration camps of Shànghăi during the Japanese occupation; some of the most gripping scenes were filmed in the streets of Shànghăi (using 15,000 local extras) and at the Peace Hotel on the Bund.

Although Hong Kong director Wong Kar-Wai's 2000 award-winning film *In the Mood For Love (Huā Yàng Nián Huá)* is set in Hong Kong, it evokes the lives of displaced Shanghainese in the former British colony during the 1960s. Everything in this wonderfully moody movie oozes nostalgia, and the lead actress Maggie Cheung's slim, figure-hugging *qípáo* outfits even sparked a fashion craze in Shànghăi in 2001 when old-time tailors were forced out of retirement to churn out once again this quintessentially traditional Chinese dress which had fallen so out of fashion until then.

For those who like a little more challenging fare, Taiwanese director Hou Hsiao-hsien's beautiful chamber piece *Flowers of Shanghai (Hăi Shàng Huā,* 1998) takes place entirely inside four turn-of-the-century opium-filled Shànghăi brothels, as madams, servants, and courtesans (called *huā* or flowers) despair and connive for the attentions of their patrons. There's nothing lurid or sensational here, only a slow-moving existential meditation that grows increasingly claustrophobic as the evening wears on. Not for those with short attention spans.

The darker side of modern Shànghăi as seen through the failed dreams and bleak hopes of a lonely Shànghăi youth is depicted in the stylized low-budget *Sūzhōu River (Sūzhōu Hé,* 2000) directed by Ye Lou.

Finally, a 1998 Austrian documentary by Joan Grossman and Paul Rosdy, *The Port of Last Resort,* tells the story of the Jews who fled Nazi Europe for Shànghăi from 1937 to 1941.

3

Getting to Know Shànghǎi

This chapter deals with the practical matters you'll need to know to get around the city. After the building boom of the 1990s, Shànghǎi is now relatively easy to navigate by taxi, subway, bus, ferry, and on your own two feet. In anticipation of the 2010 World Expo, the face of the city will continue to change as roads are ripped by, subway lines are added, and new skyscrapers are built, but the basic infrastructure and tourist services in place should serve most visitors quite well.

ARRIVING

BY PLANE

Shànghǎi has an older airport to the west, **Hóngqiáo International Airport (Hóngqiáo Jīchǎng);** and a newer airport to the east, **Pǔdōng International Airport (Pǔdōng Jīchǎng),** which began operations late in 1999. Virtually all of the international carriers use the Pǔdōng airport.

The Pǔdōng International Airport (☎ **021/3848-4500**), your likely point of arrival, is located about 45km (28 miles) east of downtown Shànghǎi. Transportation on the new highway to hotels in Pǔdōng and downtown Shànghǎi run between 45 minutes to 1½ hours depending on traffic. The new stunningly high-tech airport, designed by French architect Paul Andreu, has two departure halls (international and domestic) on the upper level and arrivals on the lower level. Moving walkways and escalators link the terminals, making transfers easy and quick (less than a 15-min. walk).

Arrival procedures are straightforward. Depending on the severity of health issues like SARS, you may be required to fill out a **health declaration form** and be subjected to a **health check** (involving the reading of your temperature) as you approach immigration. **Immigration forms** are usually distributed in-flight but are also available just before the immigration counters. Depending on your time of arrival, it should take 15 to 30 minutes to clear immigration. Have your passport and completed form(s) ready. Baggage claim is followed by Customs. Foreigners are no longer required to fill in Customs declaration forms and are seldom stopped.

The international arrival hall has hotel counters, bank counters for **money exchange** (directly across from the baggage area exits), and, just outside the arrival doors, several ATMs. There is a Tourist Information Center (TIC) counter, as well as a branch of China International Travel Service (CITS) in the international arrival hall.

The older **Hóngqiáo Airport** (☎ **021/6268-8899**), now largely reserved for flights within China, is located 19km (12 miles) west of the city center. Arrival procedures here are fairly routine, and it usually takes about 20 minutes to retrieve your luggage. There are two arrival halls, A and B, both somewhat

Shànghǎi Orientation

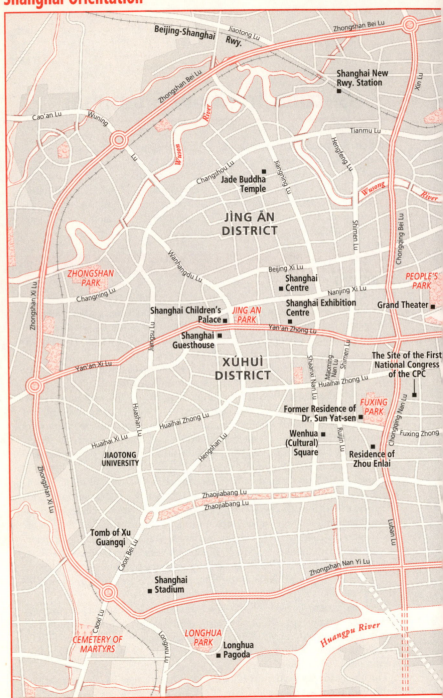

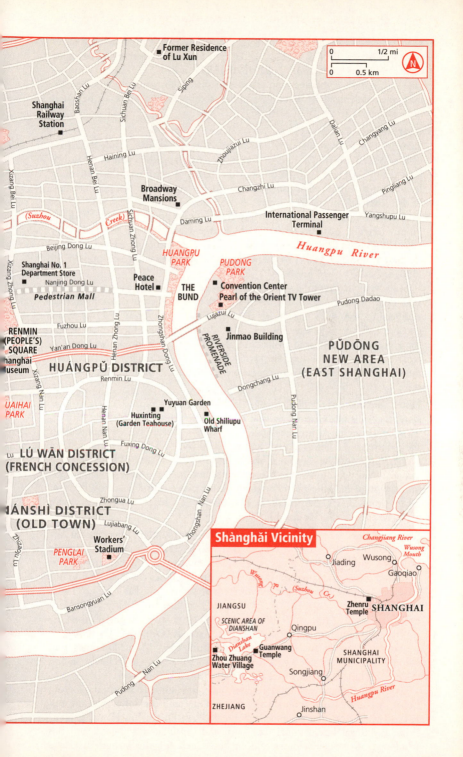

Former Residence
of Lu Xun

Shanghai
Railway
Station

Baoshan Lu
Sichuan Bei Lu
Siping
Zhoujiazui Lu
Dalian Lu
Changyang Lu

Haining Lu

Xizang Bei Lu
Henan Bei Lu
Changzhi Lu
Pingliang Lu

Broadway
Mansions

(Suzhou
Creek)

Daming Lu

Sichuan Zhong Lu

International Passenger
Terminal

Yangshupu Lu

Huangpu River

Beijing Dong Lu

HUANGPU
PARK

PUDONG
PARK

Shanghai No. 1
Department Store

Nanjing Dong Lu

Peace
Hotel

THE
BUND

Convention Center
Pearl of the Orient TV Tower

Pudong Dadao

Pedestrian Mall

Xizang Zhong Lu

Fuzhou Lu

Henan Zhong Lu

Zhongshan Dong Lu

Lujiazui Lu

Jinmao Building

RENMIN
(PEOPLE'S)
SQUARE

Shanghai
Museum

Yan'an Dong Lu

RIVERSIDE
PROMENADE

PŮDŎNG
NEW AREA
(EAST SHANGHAI)

HUÁNGPŮ DISTRICT

Renmin Lu

Dongchang Lu

Pudong Nan Lu

UAIHAI
PARK

Henan Nan Lu

Yuyuan Garden

Huxinting
(Garden Teahouse)

Old Shiliupu
Wharf

Fuxing Dong Lu

LÚ WĀN DISTRICT
(FRENCH CONCESSION)

Zhongua Lu

Zhongshan Nan Lu

ÁNSHÌ DISTRICT
(OLD TOWN)

Lujiabang Lu

Workers'
Stadium

PENGLAI
PARK

Bansongyuan Lu

Pudong Nan Lu

0   1/2 mi
0   0.5 km

Shànghǎi Vicinity

Changjiang River

*Wusong
Mouth*

Jiading

Wusong

Gaoqiao

Wusong R.

(Suzhou Cr.)

JIANGSU

Zhenru
Temple

SHANGHAI

*SCENIC AREA OF
DIANSHAN*

Qingpu

*Dianshan
Lake*

Guanwang
Temple

Zhou Zhuang
Water Village

SHANGHAI
MUNICIPALITY

Songjiang

ZHEJIANG

Jinshan

Huangpu River

chaotic, each with hotel counters, though the majority of the hotels are represented in Arrival Hall B. Also in the latter is a **Tourist Service Center,** open daily from 10am to 9:30pm ((©) **021/6268-8899** or 021/5115-1692), that provides maps and information, and can also help with hotel reservations. There is no money exchange here, but an ATM that accepts foreign cards can be found in Arrival Hall A.

Getting into Town

Taxis The legitimate taxis are lined up in a long queue just outside the arrival halls of both airports. *Never* go with taxi touts who approach you in the arrival halls with "Take taxi?," which is about the extent of their English. At Pǔdōng International Airport, taxis using the new highways and the Nánpǔ and Lúpǔ bridges charge ¥160 ($20) and up for the 1-hour (or longer) trip to hotels in downtown Shànghǎi, and only slightly less for the nearer hotels in Pǔdōng. From Hóngqiáo Airport, taxis should charge from ¥40 to ¥80 ($5–$10), depending on traffic and the location of your hotel, and require from 20 to 40 minutes to transport you. Taxis between the two airports will cost around ¥240 ($30) and take 1 to 1½ hours.

Most Shànghǎi taxi drivers are honest, but be sure the meter is on; if not, say *"Dǎ biǎo!;"* if that doesn't work, select another taxi. All legitimate taximeters are equipped to print out a receipt, which you can ask for by saying "*Fā piào.*" It's a good idea always to get a receipt, which will have the phone number of the taxi company and numerical identification of the driver, should you ever need to recover any lost items. Flagfall for taxis is ¥10 ($1.25) for the first 3km (2miles), then ¥2 (25¢) for every subsequent kilometer (⅔ miles). For more tips on taking the taxi, see p. 56.

Hotel Shuttles Many of Shànghǎi's hotels maintain service counters situated along the walls in the arrival halls in both airports, though at Pǔdōng Airport, it's a bit of a mystery why, since none of the hotels offer shuttle bus service from there. Instead, the hotel's airport staff will help you find a taxi or arrange for a very expensive private car to take you to the hotel in the city. Alternatively, you can take an airport bus (see below) to selected hotels. In the older Hóngqiáo Airport, many of the hotels *do* offer free or inexpensive shuttlebuses. (When you make advance hotel reservations, be sure to include a request for shuttle service from the airport, if it is offered.)

Airport Buses The most economical transfer from Pǔdōng International Airport is via the official Airport Bus ((©) **021/6834-6912**). There are a multitude of routes, with numbered buses (1, 2, 3, and so on) traveling between the airports and other transportation stops, while lettered buses (A, B, C, and so on) travel between Pǔdōng Airport and different hotels. Airport Bus Line no. 1 goes from Pǔdōng to Hóngqiáo Airport; Airport Bus Line no. 2 (Jīchǎng Èrxiàn) goes from Pǔdōng (every 15–20 min. from 7:20am to last flight) to the City Air-Terminal Building (Chéngshì Hángzhàn Lóu) at Nánjīng Xī Lù 1600 (just west of the Shànghǎi Center), with buses departing every 15 to 20 minutes from 6am to 7pm; and bus no. 5 goes from Pǔdōng to the Shànghǎi Railway Station (Shànghǎi Huǒchē Zhàn). Prices range from ¥17 to ¥25 ($2–$3).

Bus A serves the City, and the Jǐnjiāng and Garden hotels; Bus B, the Hilton, Equatorial, and Shànghǎi hotels; Bus C, the Peace and the Sofitel Hyland; Bus F, the YMCA, the Yangtze, and the Ramada Plaza hotels; Bus H, the Crowne Plaza, the Regal International East Asia, and the Héngshān hotels; and Bus "Pǔdōng A" makes a loop of the Pǔdōng hotels including the Shangri-La, Grand Hyatt, Novotel Atlantis, and Intercontinental hotels. Hotel bus tickets are ¥30

($3.60). These buses usually depart hourly between 6am and 8pm, although schedules can vary; they require about 1 hour to reach the far side (the west side) of downtown Shànghǎi; trips to hotels nearer the airport require slightly less time. Check at the Airport Bus counter in the arrival hall for the number and exact schedule of the bus that stops at your hotel or at the nearest hotel.

From Hóngqiáo Airport, several buses make the run into town: a CAAC shuttle, Mínháng Zhuānxiàn (Airport Special Line) departs for the Chéngshì Hángzhàn Lóu (City Air-Terminal Building) at Nánjīng Xī Lù 1600 every 20 minutes from 6am to 8:30pm. Tickets cost ¥4 (50¢). Airport Bus Line no. 1 (Jīchǎng Yīxiàn) connects Hóngqiáo (buses depart every 20 min. 6am–9pm) with Pǔdōng Airport (every 20 min. from 7:20am to last flight). Public bus no. 941 goes to the railway station while bus no. 925 runs to People's Square (Rénmín Guǎngchǎng).

Subway   The good news is that the highly anticipated magnetic levitation (Maglev) train is now up and running. The bad news is that unless you're staying in the eastern reaches of Pǔdōng, it's not much faster or more convenient than a taxi or airport bus in getting you to your destination. Covering some 30km (19 miles) in 8 minutes, this ultra high-speed train (¥50/$6 regular ticket; ¥100/$13 VIP ticket) connects Pǔdōng International Airport to the Lóngyáng Lù metro stop, the eastern terminus of Shànghǎi Metro Line 2, where you transfer to the subway. Depending on your hotel's location, you may have to change subways once more at Rénmín Guǎngchǎng, and possibly even hail a taxi before you arrive at your hotel's door, all of which makes it highly inconvenient for travelers with any kind of luggage. Maglev trains run every 20 minutes between 8:30am and 12:30pm on weekdays, and between 8:30am and 5:30pm on weekends. There is currently no subway service to Hóngqiáo Airport, though plans have been in the works for several years now to connect it to Metro Line 2.

BY TRAIN

If you are arriving by train from Hong Kong (via the 29-hr. deluxe train, no. 99), you will have completed your immigration and Customs procedures before disembarking. If you're arriving from any other Chinese city, there're no Customs procedures but you will have to produce your train ticket to attendants at the station exits in order to leave the terminal. The massive **Shànghǎi Train Station** (**Shànghǎi Huǒchē Zhàn;** © 021/6354-3193 or 021/6317-9090) is located in the northern part of town in Zháběi District. You will have to walk a block to the Metro Line 1 station (Shànghǎi Huǒchē Zhàn) by following the signs, or hail a taxi (¥2/25¢ surcharge) on the lower level of the terminal. There are no currency exchange facilities or ATMs here, though if you're really in a pinch, you might head for the Holiday Inn Downtown, just a block south across the shopping plaza, and politely beg them to exchange some money (a service normally reserved for guests only).

BY SHIP

International arrivals from Japan are at the **International Passenger Terminal** (**Guójì Kèyùn Mǎtóu**) at Yángshùpǔ Lù 100 (© **021/6595-9529**), not far north of the Bund. Domestic ships arriving from Dàlián, the Yángzǐ River, and Pǔtuó Shān now arrive at the **Wúsōng Passenger Terminal** (Shànghǎi Gǎng Wúsōng Kèyùn Zhōngxīn, Sōngbǎo Lù 251; © **021/5657-5500**), at the intersection of the Huángpǔ and Yángzǐ rivers. If you arrive here as an independent traveler, you will have to hail a taxi at the passenger terminal to reach your hotel, which is likely another 30 to 45 minutes away.

Mass Levitation

Shànghǎi's much-hyped mass transit showpiece, the magnetic levitation (**Maglev**) train, finally started running in late 2003, with trains now connecting the 30km (19 miles) between Pǔdōng International Airport and Pǔdōng's Lóngyáng Lù Station of Metro Line 2 in no more than 8 minutes. "While the wheel-track link—which is run on mechanical technology—works like a propeller-driven aircraft, the Maglev line—motored by electrical technology—is like a jet," crowed Xú Kuāngdí, the former Shànghǎi mayor who got the project off the ground during his tenure. Traveling at up to 430kmph (266 mph), Maglev (a Sino-German joint-venture) has cost Shànghǎi upwards of ¥8.9 billion ($1.07 billion), making this the most expensive subway spur in the world. In addition to showing off, Shànghǎi is using Maglev as the guinea pig for far bigger projects, which, depending on the success of the airport link, may include a long-distance line between Shànghǎi and Běijīng, and more recently talk of a link between Shànghǎi and Hángzhōu. Unfortunately, Maglev in its current form is not very practical for most travelers (see above), so the government has taken to promoting this as a tourist attraction, Shànghǎi's latest must-ride. Thus far, the public response has been underwhelming at best, with many complaining of its poor value for money (¥50/$6 for an 8-min. ride), especially considering that a round-trip journey is often required.

DEPARTING SHÀNGHĂI
BY PLANE

Shànghǎi has air connections with all of China's main cities and many international destinations as well. All international departures and some domestic flights as well leave from Pǔdōng International Airport. If you're leaving on a domestic flight, be sure to confirm in advance which airport serves your flight. Arrive at the airport at least 1½ hours before departure for international flights and 1 hour before departure for domestic flights (more if there's a current SARS or other health alert in force, as you'll be required to fill in a health form and have your temperature taken). Note that check-in for international flights officially closes 30 minutes before departure, so budget plenty of time. Also have enough ¥RMB in hand to pay the **international departure tax** (¥90/$11) or the **domestic departure tax** (¥50/$6.25). Credit cards and foreign currencies are not accepted. At Pǔdōng Airport, the departure-tax counters and dispensers are behind the check-in counters just before the entrance to emigration. In Hóngqiáo Airport, the counters are just inside the departure hall. Remember to fill out a departure card then proceed to emigration with passport, boarding card, departure card, and departure tax receipt all in hand. At Pǔdōng Airport, there are exchange counters just inside the departure hall to convert your remaining ¥RMB to your home currency, but you'll often have to show proof of the initial exchange (either the exchange receipt from the bank or hotel desk, or the ATM withdrawal receipt).

Airport-bound passengers not wanting to splurge on a taxi can take the airport bus from the Shànghǎi Airport City Terminal (Shànghǎi Jīchǎng Chéngshì Hángzhàn) at Nánjīng Xī Lù 1600. Buses (¥19/$2.50) leave for Pǔdōng Airport every 15 minutes between 6am and 7:30pm. Buy your ticket on the bus. Buses for Hóngqiáo Airport (¥4/50¢) leave just to the east at the intersection of Nánjīng Xī Lù and Chángdé Lù with departures every 20 to 30 minutes between 6am and 8pm.

Tickets for domestic flights (and international flights) on Chinese airlines can be purchased at the airport, through travel agencies such as CITS (at either Běijīng Xī Lù 1277, Guólǚ Dàshà, ℂ 021/6289-4510 or 021/6289-8899, ext. 263; or the branch at the Bund at Jīnlíng Dōng Lù 2, ℂ 021/6323-8770); or at the Shànghǎi Spring International Travel Service, Dīngxī Lù 1558 (ℂ 021/6251-5777), though there will be a service charge. There are a plethora of other travel agencies all over town offering discounted airline tickets, but you'll usually need some Chinese to get the best deals from them. Whatever you do, shop around. You can also go directly to the airlines and specifically ask for the lowest discounted (dǎzhé piào) ticket (they may not automatically give you the lowest rate, so you have to ask). Besides having ticket booths at both airports, Shànghǎi Airlines has an office in town at Jiāngníng Lù 212 (ℂ 021/6255-8888; www.shanghai-air.com), and China Eastern has offices in town at Yán'ān Xī Lù 200 (ℂ 021/6247-5953 or 021/6247-2255).

BY TRAIN

Shànghǎi is well connected by train to many major Chinese destinations, including Běijīng (12–14 hr.), Guǎngzhōu (12 hr.), Hong Kong (12 hr., Train K100), and the nearby towns of Hángzhōu (2 hr.) and Sūzhōu (45 min.). At press time, brand-new trains, some of them dedicated soft-sleeper trains, were being rolled out; they are scheduled to make the journey between Shànghǎi and Běijīng in 12 hours. There are currently no plans to increase the cost of soft sleeper tickets (¥448 – ¥499/$56–$62) but there are plans to offer free food in the soft-sleeper sections. Watch for the dedicated soft-sleeper ticket counters in the main ticket hall of the main train station, Shànghǎi Huǒchē Zhàn (ℂ 021/6317-9090, ext. 4), which is located north of the Sūzhōu Creek in Zhábĕi District and is accessible by taxi or the subway's Metro Line 1. Train tickets can be purchased up to 10 days in advance at the train station or at any number of satellite ticket offices around town, including at Běijīng Dōng Lù 230. Soft seat and soft sleeper tickets only can be purchased at Xīzàng Nánlù 121, just north of the YMCA Hotel. You can also now purchase round-trip tickets for Shànghǎi–Běijīng (return trip within 3–20 days), Shànghǎi–Sūzhōu (return trip within 3–8 days), and Shànghǎi–Hángzhōu (return trip within 3–8 days), but only at the main train station. If you have any queries or problems, someone at Counter 9 should be able to speak some English. Tickets can also be bought through CITS (see "By Plane" above), through any other travel agency, or through your hotel ticket desk, though fees will of course accrue, ranging from ¥5 (60¢) at CITS if you purchase it yourself to ¥50 ($6) from some hotel ticket desks. As well, tickets can be bought at the Lóngmén Hotel, Héngfēng Lǚ 777 (ℂ 021/6317-0000), just southwest of the train station.

Warning: Larger bags will be x-rayed when you enter the train station departure hall, so keep any film in your hand luggage.

BY SHIP

The Shànghǎi Ferry Co. Ltd (ℂ 021/6537-5111; www.shanghai-ferry.co.jp) has a weekly sailing to Osaka on Tuesday at noon, while the Japan-China International Ferry Co. (Chinajif; ℂ 021/6325-7642; www.fune.co.jp/chinjif/jikoku.html) operates a ship bound for either Osaka or Kobe every Saturday at

1pm. Ships depart from the **International Passenger Terminal (Guójì Kèyùn Mǎtóu)** at Yángshùpǔ Lù 100 (☏ **021/6595-9529**), not far north of the Bund. Tickets are available at the terminal or at travel agencies such as CITS.

Domestic boats bound for Níngbō (12 hr.), Dàlián (36 hr.), Wǔhàn (4 days), Chóngqìng (7 days), and Pǔtuó Shān (13 hr.) now depart from the **Wúsōng Passenger Terminal** (Shànghǎi Gǎng Wúsōng Kèyùn Zhōngxīn, Sōngbǎo Lù 251; ☏ **021/5657-5500**), about a 30- to 45-minute taxi ride northeast of the Bund at the mouth of the Yángzǐ River. Tickets can be bought at the terminal or at travel agencies such as CITS. For general inquiries about ships, call ☏ **021/6326-0050.**

VISITOR INFORMATION

Shànghǎi has an official **Tourism Hot Line** (☏ **021/6439-8947** or 021/6439-0630) with the occasional English speaker who can be helpful on occasion. You'll get slightly better service at the 24-hour **Tourist Information Line** maintained by Spring Travel Service (☏ **021/6252-0000**). Hotel staff and concierges can be a font of information as well, though even the most friendly and knowledgeable guest relations officers at the top hotels are still often in the dark about any options off the beaten path. Beware also those who would try to sell you expensive tours or outings.

There are about a dozen **Tourist Information Service Centers (Lǚyóu Zīxún Fúwù Zhōngxīn)** around Shànghǎi. They appear to exist mainly to sell various city tours and to book hotels but, depending on who is sitting behind the desk, they may be able to offer some guidance. You can also pick up city maps, postcards, brochures, and information on local sights, shopping, and restaurants here. The main office is at Zhōngshān Xī Lù 2525, Room 410, Chángníng District (☏ **021/6439-9806;** www.shanghaitour.net), with smaller branch offices at Nánjīng Xī Lù 1699, Jìng Ān District (☏ **021/6248-3259**); Nánjīng Dōng Lù 561, Huángpǔ District (☏ **021/5353-1117**); Chéngdū Nán Lù 127, Lúwān District (☏ **021/6372-8330**); and Lùjiāzuǐ Xī Lù 168, Zhèngdà Guǎngchǎng 1st Floor, Pǔdōng (☏ **021/6887-7888**).

The best sources for **current information** about Shànghǎi events, shopping, restaurants, and nightlife are the free English-language newspapers and magazines distributed to hotels, shops, and cafes around town. The glossy monthly *that's Shanghai* (www.thatsshanghai.com), featuring an extensive events calendar, restaurant and bar reviews, local features, and consumer ads, is the best of the lot. *Shanghai Talk* (monthly) and *City Weekend* (twice-monthly; www.city weekend.com.cn) with its Shànghǎi pullout section will suffice in a pinch though their listings are often several months behind.

CITY LAYOUT

Shànghǎi, with one of the largest urban populations on Earth (almost 14 million permanent residents, plus 3 million registered migrants), is divided by the Huángpǔ River into Pǔdōng (east of the river) and Pǔxī (west of the river). For the traveler, the majority of Shànghǎi's sights are still concentrated **downtown** in Pǔxī, whose layout bears a distinct Western imprint. After the First Opium War in 1842 opened Shànghǎi up to foreign powers, the British, French, Germans, Americans, and others moved in, carving for themselves their own "concessions" where they were subject not to the laws of the Chinese government but to those established by their own governing councils.

Today, the city is divided into districts *(qū)*, according to which listings in this book are organized. Today's districts hew fairly close to but do not follow exactly the original concession borders. For the traveler, the two most important geographical markers are the **Bund (Wàitān)** and **People's Square (Rénmín Guǎngchǎng)** about a mile to the west. Since the days of the International Settlement, established in 1863 with the melding of the British Concession and the American Concession, the **Bund,** with its signature colonial-era banks and trading houses, has been and still is the symbolic center of the city; from here, **downtown Shànghǎi** opens to the west like a fan. Today's practical and logistical center, however, is **People's Square (Rénmín Guǎngchǎng),** about a mile to the west of the Bund. This is the meeting point of Shànghǎi's two main subway lines, as well as the location of some major attractions, including the Shànghǎi Museum, Shànghǎi Art Museum, and Shànghǎi Grand Theatre. The Bund and People's Square are linked by several streets, none more famous than **Nánjīng Lù,** historically China's number-one shopping street.

Southwest of the Bund is historic **Nánshì,** Shànghǎi's old Chinese city, which was the first part of Shànghǎi to be settled (and one of the last to be developed, though building is certainly proceeding apace these days). Nánshì used to have a city wall, which followed today's Rénmín Lù and Zhōnghuá Lù circle. As its name suggests, the old Chinese city has retained the greatest number of typically Chinese sights, such as the quintessential Southern-Chinese Garden, Yù Yuán, the famous Húxīng Tíng teahouse, several temples, and even part of the old city wall.

A mile or so west of the Bund and the old Chinese city, Shànghǎi's former **French Concession,** established in 1849 and straddling both today's Lúwān and northern Xúhuì districts, is still one of Shànghǎi's trendiest neighborhoods. Chock-full of colonial architecture and attractions, it is home to some of the city's priciest real estate and to its most glamorous shops and restaurants, as seen in the mega-development Xīn Tiāndì.

Farther west still, beyond the Inner Ring Road that wraps around downtown Shànghǎi and the French Concession, is the **Hóngqiáo Development Zone,** where modern commercial and industrial development was concentrated beginning in the 1980s.

While sightseeing is concentrated in downtown Shànghǎi and the French Concession, **north Shànghǎi** has a scattering of interesting sights, including the Jade Buddha Temple, the Lǔ Xùn Museum, and the Ohel Moshe Synagogue; and **south Shànghǎi** has the Lónghuá Pagoda, Xújiāhuì Cathedral, Shànghǎi Botanical Garden, and the trendy cafes and shops of Héngshān Lù.

In contrast to the colonial and historical sights of Pǔxī, the district of **Pǔdōng,** lying east of the Huángpǔ River, is all about Shànghǎi's future. Mere farmland before 1990 when then-President Dèng Xiǎopíng designated it as the engine of China's new economic growth, Pǔdōng has sprouted in just a decade to become the city's financial center, and a high-tech and free trade zone, home to Asia's largest shopping centers, longest bridges, and tallest buildings. Modern skyscrapers like the Oriental Pearl TV Tower and the Jīn Mào Building, which houses the world's highest hotel, the Grand Hyatt, and a new slew of swanky international hotels, restaurants, and shopping malls, are attempts to attract the visitor over to the eastern shore of the Huángpǔ. With considerably less choice in the matter, many Shànghǎi residents were also displaced here in the last decade by the destruction of old neighborhoods in Pǔxī.

Traveling throughout town used to consume hours, but the completion of two important arteries—the elevated Yán'ān Expressway and the subway's Metro Line 2—has drastically reduced commuting time. Even Pǔdōng is directly connected to downtown Shànghǎi by a subway line, three huge bridges, and two tunnels (one for cars, one for pedestrians).

MAIN STREETS   In downtown Shànghǎi, the general rule is that east-west streets are named for Chinese cities, while north-south streets are named for provinces and regions. The main east-west street through downtown Shànghǎi is **Nánjīng Lù,** historically China's number-one shopping street. The portion running west from the Bund, through the pedestrian mall, to People's Park (Rénmín Gōngyuǎn) is known officially as **Nánjīng Dōng Lù;** it continues west as **Nánjīng Xī Lù.** Parallel to Nánjīng Lù in the south is **Yán'ān Lù** (originally a creek dividing the International Settlement from the French Concession to the south), which runs west through the downtown corridor all the way to the Hóngqiáo airport (changing its name in the western segment to Hóngqiáo Lù). Running above Yán'ān Lù is the elevated expressway **Yán'ān Gāojià,** the quickest way to traverse downtown Shànghǎi; near the Bund, this leads to the underground tunnel **Yán'ān Dōng Lù Suìdào** that resurfaces on the east side of the river in Pǔdōng. It used to take an hour to drive from the Hóngqiáo District through downtown to Pǔdōng, but the Yán'ān Expressway has cut the travel time to 20 minutes without traffic.

The major north-south thoroughfares include the **Bund,** on the west shore of the Huángpǔ River (the avenue along the Bund is known as **Zhōngshān Dōng Yī Lù**); and **Xīzàng Lù,** which divides Nánjīng Lù into its east and west sectors, and Yán'ān Lù and Huáihǎi Lù into their east and middle (zhōng) sectors. Xīzàng Lù also borders People's Square (Rénmín Guǎngchǎng), the site of the Shànghǎi Museum, the Grand Theater, and the central subway station for both Metro lines.

In the French Concession, the two big avenues are **Huáihǎi Zhōng Lù** (Shànghǎi's second most famous shopping street) and **Fùxīng Zhōng Lù,** both extensions of the east-west streets that begin downtown at the southern Bund (Zhōngshān Dōng Èr Lù). Crossing them are a number of smaller scenic streets, the liveliest of which are **Ruìjīn Lù** and **Màomíng Lù** (Shànghǎi's top bar street) near the historic Jǐn Jiāng Hotel. At the western end of the French Concession, the graceful and trendy avenue of **Héngshān Lù** runs south toward the Xújiāhuì shopping area.

Downtown Shànghǎi, the French Concession, large portions of north and south Shànghǎi, as well as the Pǔdōng New Area, are surrounded by the **Inner**

Making Sense of Shànghǎi Street Names

Shànghǎi's main streets, as well as some smaller streets that intersect them, are often mouthfuls to pronounce and difficult to remember at first, but after a few trips through the city, they begin to sort themselves out. One reason that the street names in **pīnyīn** (see appendix B) seem so long is that they incorporate the characters for north or south, street or avenue, all running together in the street name. Zhōngshān East First Road is written in pīnyīn as Zhōngshān Dōng Yī Lù. Common items in street names and their English translations are as follows:

Běi = North	*Jiē* = Street	*Yī* = First
Nán = South	*Dà Dào* = Avenue	*Èr* = Second
Dōng = East	*Lù* = Road	*Sān* = Third
Xī = West	*Nòng* = Lane	
Zhōng = Central		

The Streets of Old Shànghǎi

Up until the establishment of the People's Republic of China in 1949, many of Shànghǎi's streets bore foreign names, bequeathed to the city by colonial overlords. Here's a partial list of old and new:

Current street name . . . once known as
Fùxīng Zhōng Lù . . . Route Lafayette
Hénán Lù . . . Homan Road
Héngshān Lù . . . Avenue Petain
Huáihǎi Zhōng Lù . . . Avenue Joffre
Màomíng Běi Lù . . . Moulmien Road
Màomíng Nán Lù . . . Route Cardinal Mercier
Nánjīng Xī Lù . . . Bubbling Well Road
Nánjīng Dōng Lù . . . Nanking Road
Rénmín Lù . . . Boulevard des Deux Republiques
Ruìjīn Èr Lù . . . Route Pere Robert
Ruìjīn Yī Lù . . . Route des Soeurs
Sīnán Lù . . . Rue Masenet
Tiānshān Lù . . . Lincoln Avenue
Xīzàng Nán Lù . . . Boulevard de Montiguy
Yán'ān Dōng Lù . . . Avenue Edward VII
Yán'ān Xī Lù . . . Great Western Road
Yán'ān Zhōng Lù . . . Avenue Foch West
Zhōngshān Dōng Yī Lù . . . The Bund

Ring Road (Nèihuán Gāojià), an elevated expressway that bears the road name **Zhōngshān** along most of its route. This Inner Ring Road is bisected by the **North-South Elevated Road (Nánběi Gāojià),** which runs above **Chéngdū Běi Lù,** the first major street west of People's Square, a rough dividing line between downtown Shànghǎi and the French Concession. A second, even larger ring road is under construction; it will join the airports of east and west Shànghǎi.

FINDING AN ADDRESS

Nearly all of Shànghǎi's big streets have signs on poles near intersections that give the names in Chinese characters and in *pīnyīn,* which is the alphabetical rendering of those characters (used on maps and throughout this book). Though street numbers are given, few locals pay any attention to them, as navigation is usually by street name, landmarks, and nearby intersections. The only exception is in the case of Shànghǎi's many smaller lanes (*nòngtáng, nòng* for short) branching off the main streets and the smaller intersecting streets. An address sometimes given as Héngshān Lù 9, no. 3 means it's house no. 3 *(sānhào)* situated in Lane 9 *(jiǔ nòng)* off Héngshān Lù; Lane no. 9 could well be found between House no. 7 and Lane no. 11; taxi drivers and locals are quite familiar with this system should you need to locate such an address.

The maps in this book cannot fully capture the details of any given area, so it's highly recommended that you buy a map (p. 48) or get one from your hotel concierge. Between the Chinese characters provided in this book's map keys and a second (preferably trilingual) map with English, *pīnyīn* and characters, you should have no problems comparing the characters with the road signs as you make your way. It's always helpful to have your hotel staff mark your hotel and destination on your map before you set off so that you can show it to taxi drivers or passers-by should you get lost. There is, however, no question of truly getting lost even if you wander off the main paths indicated on the maps. Given Shànghăi's Western influence, it's not difficult these days to find even a marginal English speaker to help you, even if it's just to locate an address on the map and point you in the right direction. Though their daily attitudes may not reflect it, Shànghăi residents can be quite friendly and helpful to beleaguered foreigners.

NEIGHBORHOODS IN BRIEF

The Shànghăi municipality consists of 15 districts, four counties, and the Pǔdōng New Area, and covers an area of 6,341 sq. km (2,448 sq. miles), with its urban area measuring 2,643 sq. km (1,020 sq. miles). The eight main urban districts, running from east to west, are identified here.

Pǔdōng Located across the Huángpǔ River from the Bund, Pǔdōng (literally "east of the Huángpǔ") was formerly backwater farmland before 1990 when it was targeted by then-Chinese President Dèng Xiǎopíng to lead Shànghăi and the rest of China into a new age of economic growth. Today it is home to the Lùjiāzuǐ Financial with its many modern economic monuments (Oriental Pearl TV Tower, Jīn Mào Tower), the Shànghăi stock exchange, Asia's largest department store, a riverside promenade, and the new Pǔdōng International Airport.

Huángpǔ (Downtown Shànghăi) The city center of old Shànghăi lies in a compact sector west of the Huángpǔ River and south of Sūzhōu Creek. It extends west to Chéngdū Běi Lù (the North-South Elevated Hwy.), and encompasses the Bund, People's Square (Rénmín Guǎngchǎng), and the Shànghăi Museum.

Nánshì (Old Chinese City) Though officially part of Huángpǔ District, this area immediately south of downtown and the Bund, between the Huángpǔ River and Xīzàng Nán Lù, is often considered its own neighborhood because as the old Chinese city, it was different

in every way from the western concessions. Today's old Chinese city (or Old Town) includes the Old Town Bazaar with its traditional shopping, Yù Yuán (Yù Garden), Shànghăi's old city wall, and the Confucian Temple.

Hóngkǒu (Northeast Shànghăi) Immediately north of downtown Shànghăi, across Sūzhōu Creek, this residential sector along the upper Huángpǔ River was originally the American concession before it became part of the International Settlement in colonial days. Today it's a developing neighborhood with a few sights: the Ohel Moshe Synagogue, the Lǔ Xùn Museum, and the Duōlún Lù Commercial Street.

Lúwān (French Concession) Beginning at People's Square (Xīzàng Lù) and continuing west to Shǎnxī Nán Lù, this historic district was the domain of the French colonial community up until 1949. The French left their mark on the residential architecture, which boasts such tourist sights as Fùxīng Park, the historic Jǐn Jiāng Hotel, the shops along Huáihǎi Zhōng Lù, the new Xīn Tiāndì development, and the former residences of Sun Yat-sen and Zhōu Ēnlái.

Jìng Ān (Northwest Shànghǎi)
North of the French Concession
and part of the former International Settlement, this district has
its share of colonial architecture, as
well as the modern Shànghǎi Centre. Two of the city's top Buddhist
shrines, Jìng Ān Sì and Yù Fó Sì
(Jade Buddha Temple), are located
here, as are a number of Shànghǎi's
top hotels and restaurants.

Xúhuì (Southwest Shànghǎi)
West of the French Concession and
south along Héngshān Lù, this area
is one of Shànghǎi's top addresses

for cafes, bars, and shops. Sights
include the Xújiāhuì Cathedral,
Lónghuá Pagoda, the Shànghǎi
Botanical Garden, and the former
residence of Soong Chingling.

**Chángníng (Hóngqiáo Develop-
ment Zone)** Starting at Huáihǎi
Xī Lù, directly west of the Xúhuì
and Jìng Ān districts, this corridor
of new international economic ventures extends far west of downtown, past Gǔběi New Town and
the Shànghǎi Zoo, to the Hóngqiáo
Airport.

2 Getting Around

Given the size of Shànghǎi and the overcrowded condition of its public buses,
taxis and the subway become indispensable for any sightseer. Fortunately, both
are relatively inexpensive. An adventurous alternative is to travel as many
Shànghǎi residents do, by bicycle.

BY SUBWAY

The Shànghǎi subway *(dìtiě)* system, an inexpensive and fast way to cover longer
distances, is currently undergoing some much-needed expansion (from three—
including the existing light rail line—to eight lines), which accounts for some of
the above-ground traffic snarls in the middle of which you may find yourself
caught. During morning and evening rush hours and on weekend afternoons,
the system is so overburdened (Metro Line 1 handles around half a million passengers a day) that unless you like being elbowed and pushed, and generally
being swept along by a giant wave of humanity, it's best to avoid riding the subway at those times. Operating from 5:30am to 11pm daily, the subway currently
has two lines. **Metro Line 1,** the red line with 16 stops that opened in 1994,
winds in a roughly north-south direction from the Shànghǎi Railway Station in
the north through the French Concession and on down Héngshān Lù to the
southwest districts well past Shànghǎi Stadium. Metro Line 1 connects with
Metro Line 2, the green line with 12 stations, at People's Square (Rénmín
Guǎngchǎng) near Nánjīng Xī Lù. The still incomplete Metro Line 2 runs in an
east-west direction from Zhōngshān Gōngyuán across downtown Shànghǎi,
under the Huángpǔ River, and through Pǔdōng's most developed areas to
Lóngyáng Lù, where Maglev connections can be made to Pǔdōng Airport.
When it is up to steam, this line will provide service in both directions as often
as every 2 minutes (vs. every 6 min. on Metro Line 1) during peak hours. There
are plans in the future to extend the line eastward and westward to connect to
Shànghǎi's two airports, but there's no telling when this will be ready, as
resources seem to have been redirected into the construction of other lines.

Navigating the subway is relatively easy. To locate subway entrances, look for
the large signs with a jagged letter "M" that looks like a cluster of mountain
peaks. Subway platform signs in Chinese and *pīnyīn* indicate the station name
and the name of the next station in each direction, and maps of the complete

Metro system are posted in each station and inside the subway cars as well. In addition, English announcements of upcoming stops are made on trains. To determine your fare, consult the fare map posted near the ticket counters and on ticket vending kiosks. Fares range from ¥2 (24¢) for the first few stops to ¥4 (48¢) for the most distant ones. **Hang onto your electronic ticket, which you have to insert into the exit barrier when you leave.**

If you are going to be riding the subway a fair amount, consider purchasing a rechargeable **Jiāotōng Card (Jiāotōng Kǎ),** which costs ¥30 ($3.80), onto which you can then add ¥50 ($6) or ¥100 ($12) denominations. Instead of inserting your ticket into the slot, simply hold your card over the sensor on the barriers. The card can also be used to pay for bus, ferry, and taxi rides, with your fare being automatically deducted from the amount remaining on the card.

Unfortunately, most stations are not equipped to handle travelers with limited mobility. Metro Line 2 does have elevator access, but escalators at most other stations are up only and stairs are often quite long.

LIGHT RAIL   By 2001 Shànghǎi had opened the first phase of its Pearl Mass Transit Light Rail line, which it plans eventually to incorporate into its metro system. Currently, its 19 stations encircle the western outskirts of the city, with stops at Shànghǎi Stadium to the south and at Shànghǎi Railway Station to the north of downtown. Phase two of the Light Rail will complete what's started of this vast rail circle, extending the tracks across the river, through Pǔdōng, and then back across the river into downtown Shànghǎi's southern precincts. The aboveground Light Rail is clean, modern, and not heavily traveled except during rush hours. Ticketing is nearly identical to the Metro system's, with fares running ¥3 to ¥6 (36¢–75¢) depending on distance traveled. The Light Rail is seldom helpful for sightseeing, although it does stop near Lǔ Xùn Gōngyuán (Hóngkǒu Stadium Station) and Duōlún Lù cultural street (Bǎoxìn Lù Station) north of downtown, where the Metro lines do not extend. The Metro does usefully intersect with the Light Rail at the stations serving Shànghǎi Stadium, Zhōngshān Park, and the Shànghǎi Railway Station.

BY TAXI

With over 40,000 taxis in the streets, this is the most common means visitors use to get around Shànghǎi. Taxis congregate at leading hotels but can just as easily, and indeed, should preferably be hailed from street corners. The large majority of vehicles are fairly clean, air-conditioned, and reasonably comfortable Passat or Santana sedans (both built in the local Shànghǎi factory by Volkswagen). In recent years overall service has improved noticeably (at least at the top companies), and drivers more often than not will greet you and remind you to take all your items when you leave. All of this is in Chinese, of course, as few drivers speak English. Most taxis now post a passenger's "bill of rights" along the back of the front seat. Some of the "rights" include a smoke-free taxi and a driver not distracted by the lure of the mobile phone, though sometimes these "regulations" remain what most regulations are in China: not worth much more than the piece of paper they're laminated on.

By and large, most Shànghǎi taxi drivers are honest. If there's a commonly heard complaint, it's less about the dishonesty of taxi drivers than about their inexperience (some drivers may have arrived in town around the same time as you), and their lack of familiarity with local streets. I've sometimes had drivers ask me how to get to my destination, though that is unlikely to happen to you. Instead you'll just be driven around in circles, the driver unwilling to admit to a foreigner he or she doesn't know the way. To minimize the chances of this happening to you, stick with the top taxi companies, though it must be said that even then, such an experience may sometimes be simply unavoidable. In general, follow the advice in the box "Taxi Tips."

Your best bets for service and comfort are the turquoise blue taxis of **Dà Zhòng Taxi** (© 800/6200-1688 or 021/6258-1688), the yellow taxis of **Qiáng Shēng Taxi** (© 021/6258-0000), and the blue taxis of **Jín Jiāng Taxi** (© 021/6275-8800). Regardless of the company, the fare is ¥10 ($1.25) for the first 3km (1¾ miles) and ¥2 (25¢) for each additional kilometer. There is a surcharge for trips after 11pm (about 30% more) and for bridge and tunnel tolls between Pǔdōng and downtown Shànghǎi (¥15 ($1.80) for the tunnels, ¥10 ($1.25) for the bridges). Expect to pay about ¥15 to ¥25 ($1.90–$3) for most excursions in the city and up to ¥60 ($7.20) for longer crosstown jaunts. Carry smaller bills (no larger than ¥50) to pay the fare. If you anticipate a fair amount of taxi travel and don't want to be burdened with cash, you can purchase a taxi/subway card (Jiāotōng Kǎ) at ticket counters in subway stations. Cards come in denominations of ¥50 ($6) or ¥100 ($12), and are easily rechargeable, though you'll have to pay an extra ¥30 ($3.80) for the card itself. The fare is automatically deducted from the balance on your card. You can also use this card on the subway. Finally, for taxi service complaints, call © **021/6323-2150;** you may not get your money back, but you might be helping future riders.

BY BUS

Public buses (*gōng gòng qì chē*) charge just ¥1 (12¢) per ride (¥2/24¢ if air-conditioned), but they are considerably more difficult to use, less comfortable than taxis or the Metro, and for the truly intrepid only. Some buses have conductors but others only have money slots in the front of the bus with no change given. To figure out which bus number will get you to your destination, ask for help in your hotel. Bus nos. 20 and 37, for example, run between People's Square and the Bund; bus no. 16 connects the Jade Buddha Temple to Old Town; bus no. 65 travels from the Bund to the Shànghǎi Railway Station. Be prepared to stand and be cramped during your expedition, and take care with backpacks and purses, as these are inviting targets for thieves, who frequently target foreign visitors on public buses.

For more adventurous travelers, the **Shànghǎi Sightseeing Bus Center,** located under the no. 5 staircase at Gate 12 of the Shànghǎi Stadium (Tiānyáo-qiáo Lù 666; © **021/6426-5555**) runs 10 no-frills sightseeing bus lines, mostly to places on the outskirts of town, such as to Shéshān (Rte. 1B), the Shànghǎi Wildlife Zoo (Rte. 2), and the Formula 1 racetrack in Āntíng (Rte. 6B), but Route 10 makes a loop of Huáihǎi Lù, Xīzàng Lù, Nánjīng Lù, and Sìchuān Běi Lù to the Qūyáng business district in the north. Tickets cost ¥3 (40¢).

Alas, the **Jín Jiāng Tourist Bus,** which used to stop at targeted tourist sights, is no longer in operation.

BY BICYCLE

If you've always dreamed of joining in the dance that is millions of Chinese riding their bicycles, Shànghǎi is not the ideal place to fulfill that dream. The huge economic wealth generated in the last decade has resulted, predictably, in an exponential increase in the number of cars on the road and the concomitant decline in popularity of the bicycle (since 1990, sales have dropped from one million to 500,000 bikes per year). Wide avenues and small streets these days are much more likely to be taken up by honking vehicles spewing exhaust, making bicycle-riding appear even more hazardous and intimidating. That said, the

Tips   **Taxi Tips**

- Never go with taxi touts or individual drivers who approach you at airports, train stations, tourist sights, or even outside your hotel. The general rule is never go with a driver who asks you your destination before you even get into the cab.
- In general, always hail a passing cab if possible, as opposed to waiting for taxis that have been waiting for you. Opinions differ on the following point, but if you're staying at an upmarket hotel in Shànghăi, it is generally safe to go with the taxis called by the doormen, usually from a line of waiting cabs. It sometimes occurs that drivers give kickbacks to the doormen for being allowed to the head of the queue, but in my experience, I have not had nor have I heard of problems with hotel-hailed taxis. Some top hotels will give you a piece of paper with the taxi's registration number on it in case of complaints, though there's no guarantee of redress, of course. There are also hotels that restrict their waiting taxis to those from the Dà Zhòng Taxi Company, which has the best reputation in Shànghăi for honest and efficient service.
- Always have your destination marked on a map or written down in Chinese, as well as a business card from your hotel with the address in Chinese so you can show it to the taxi driver when you want to get back.
- Check to see that the supervision card, which includes the driver's photo and identification number, is prominently displayed, as required by law. If not, find another cab.
- If the driver's identification number is over 200,000, there's a good chance that the driver is newly arrived in town and may not be familiar with the streets, which is reason enough to find yourself another cab. Caveat emptor: This is not a fool-proof way of weeding out inexperienced drivers since a number of new arrivals actually "share" the taxis of more experienced drivers, even if this is against the law.

bicycle is still the main form of transportation for millions of Shànghăi's residents (recent rumored plans to prohibit bicycles on Shànghăi's main streets met with significant protest and uproar, and have been quietly shelved) and is not so difficult for the visitor to manage if you stick to a few general principles, namely: Ride at a leisurely pace, stay with the flow, and use the designated bike lanes on the big streets. A bicycle remains one of the best ways to cover larger portions of Shànghăi, especially its back streets, at your own pace. Unfortunately, most hotels don't rent bikes (you may get some daft looks if you inquire), but **Richard's Bar** at the **Pŭjiāng Hotel** (Pŭjiāng Fàndiàn, Huángpŭ Lù 15; ✆ **021/ 6324-6388**) does at ¥30 ($3.75) for 24 hours for a mountain bike. If you plan on doing a significant amount of cycling, consider buying a bicycle (average cost is around ¥300/$36) for a very basic bike without flashy accessories. One of the better places to purchase bicycles is a supermall like Carrefour (see chapter 8).

- Make sure the meter is visible, and that you see the driver reset it by pushing down the flag, which should happen *after* the taxi has moved off. You should also hear at that time a voice recording in Chinese and English welcoming you to take the taxi. If the driver fails to reset the meter, say, *"Qǐng dǎbiǎo,"* and if that fails, find yourself another cab.
- If traveling by yourself, sit up front and take out your map so you can follow (or at least pretend to follow) the taxi's route.
- If, on the rare occasion that the taxi driver refuses to honor your request after you're en route, make a big show of taking down the driver's identification number and suggesting, by any means available, that you intend to file a complaint. This can sometimes scare the otherwise recalcitrant driver into complying.
- If you're unwittingly riding with a driver who doesn't know the way (and you only realize this after you've been driving in circles or if the driver has had to stop to ask directions), it's best to find yourself another cab. Unfortunately, even if you have every "right" to not pay the fare, this can sometimes lead to more inconvenience than it's worth (the driver will likely complain loudly or create a scene). At such times, it may be more practical to pay the fare or a portion of it, but, as in the previous example, make a show of taking down the driver's identification number and notifying him/her of your decision to lodge a complaint.
- At the end of the trip, pay the indicated meter fare and no more. Tips are not expected. It's a good idea to carry smaller bills (¥100 notes can sometimes be changed, but don't count on it) to pay your fare.
- Be sure to get a receipt *(fā piào)* with the phone number of the taxi company and the taxi driver's numerical identification, should you need to file a complaint or retrieve lost items. All the legitimate taxis are now equipped with meters that can print receipts.

Whether you rent or buy, be sure the brakes and tires are in good working order. You'll also need a bicycle lock. Helmets are not required in Shànghǎi—few use them—but they are advised for the neophyte China bike rider. Should you have a flat or need a repair, there are sidewalk bicycle mechanics every few blocks, and they charge ridiculously low rates (¥1/12¢ or ¥2/24¢). Always park your bike in marked lots (identifiable by the forest of bikes outside a park, attraction, or major store) watched over by an attendant and lock your bike or it will be gone by the time you get back. Parking usually costs ¥.5 (6¢).

BY BRIDGE, BOAT & TUNNEL

Crossing the Huángpǔ River has become an increasingly frequent occurrence for Shànghǎi visitors as the Pǔdōng New Area on the east side of the river flexes its financial and touristic muscle. To shift the thousands of daily visitors between east and west Shànghǎi, there are seven basic routes. Three are by bridge, each handling around 45,000 vehicles a day: the 3.7km-long (2⅓-mile), harp-string-shaped **Nánpǔ Dàqiáo** (built 1991), and the **Lúpǔ Dàqiáo,** both in the southern part of town; and the 7.65km-long (4¾-mile) **Yángpǔ Dàqiáo** (built 1993) northeast of the Bund. A fourth route (and the cheapest) is by water, via the **passenger ferry** that ordinary workers favor. The ferry terminal is at the southern end of the Bund on the west shore (ticket price: ¥2/25¢), and at the southern end of Riverside Avenue at Dōngchāng Lù on the east shore. Three more routes across the river make use of tunnels. The Yán'ān Dōng Lù Tunnel is plied by motor vehicles (though taxis are barred 8–9:30am and 5–6:30pm); the new Metro Line 2 is filled with German-made subway cars; and the very new **Bund Sight-Seeing Tunnel (Wàitān Guānguāng Suìdào)** is equipped with glassy tram cars that glide through a subterranean 3-minute light show with music and narrative (daily 9am–9:30pm; ¥20/$2.40 one-way, children half-price).

BY FOOT

The best way to see Shànghǎi's sights and experience life at street-level is on foot. Much like downtown New York or Tokyo, Shànghǎi's streets can be almost impossibly crowded at times, but they are always fascinating to stroll. Doing so requires a bit of vigilance, of course, as Shànghǎi pedestrians are distinctly second-class citizens to the motorists who rule the road. Shànghǎi drivers, who drive on the right side of the road, have never been known to give pedestrians the right-of-way; at red lights, vehicles seldom stop when making a right turn, whether pedestrians are in the crosswalk or not. Drivers don't pay much attention to lane markings and will always rush to fill an empty space wherever they can find one, even if it's where you happen to be walking. Besides a sea of humanity, Shànghǎi pedestrians also have to contend with bicycles, scooters, and motorcycles on sidewalks. Happily, there are now surly brown-clad, whistle-blowing traffic assistants at the major roads and intersections to make sure both pedestrians and motorists obey the traffic lights. Jaywalk and you'll be yelled at, though it may just be a matter of time before the traffic authorities discover the power (and the potential wealth) of the jaywalking fine. In general, whether crossing large avenues or small lanes, look every which way before you cross, take your cues from locals, and you should be just fine.

FAST FACTS: Shànghǎi

Airport See "Arriving" under "Orientation" at the beginning of this chapter.

American Express Holders of an American Express card can make inquiries about currency exchange, emergency card replacement, and personal check cashing at Nánjīng Xī Lù 1376, Shànghǎi Centre, Room 206 (℃ **021/6279-8082;** fax 021/6279-7183; Mon–Fri 9am–5:30pm). Tickets, bookings, and tours are not handled directly by American Express in their Shànghǎi office.

Area Codes Shànghǎi's area code is 021. In mainland China, all area codes begin with a zero, which is dropped when calling China from abroad. The entire area code can be dropped when making local calls.

Babysitters Most government-rated four- and five-star hotels can provide babysitting service if you give them advance notice. Prices vary but average about ¥50 ($6) per hour; service is usually provided by hotel staff.

Banks, Currency Exchange & ATMs The most convenient place to exchange currency is your hotel, where the rates are similar to those at the Bank of China and exchange desks are often open 24 hours. Convenient **Bank of China** locations for currency exchange and credit card cash withdrawals are located on the Bund at the Bank of China building, Zhōngshān Dōng Yī Lù 23 (© 021/6329-1979); on the north side of the JC Mandarin Hotel at Nánjīng Xī Lù 1221 (© 021/6247-1700); at Yán'ān Xī Lù 2168 (© 021/6278-5060); at Huáihăi Zhōng Lù 1207 (© 021/6437-8753); and at Hóngqiáo Lù 2550 (© 021/6268-8866). The Bank of China's business hours are Monday through Friday from 9am to noon and 1:30 to 4:30pm, and Saturday from 9am to noon.

ATMs that accept international cards are available at all the above branches, as well as at People's Square (Rénmín Guăngchăng) north of the Park Hotel at the intersection of Huánghé Lù and Gŭlín Lù. The **Hong Kong and Shanghai Bank ATM** at the City Supermarket at Shànghăi Centre (Nánjīng Xī Lù 1376) is one of the most reliable in town. Another HSBC ATM is located at Huáihăi Zhōng Lù 282 on the ground floor of Hong Kong Plaza. **Citibank** has a branch at the Peace Hotel on the Bund (Zhōngshān Dōng Yī Lù 19; © 021/6329-8383; Mon–Fri 9am–4:30pm, Sat 10am–3pm) that can change American Express U.S. dollar traveler's checks (maximum $250 per day) and U.S. dollar cash. There is also an ATM here that accepts international cards.

Bookstores The biggest and best selection of English-language books in Shànghăi can be found at the **Shànghăi Foreign Language Bookstore (Shànghăi Wàiwén Shūdiàn),** Fúzhōu Lù 390 (© 021/6322-3200; 9:30am–6pm). You can find China-related books, including glossy photo books, travel guides, local histories, English translations of Chinese classics, and maps on the left side of the first floor, and classic and contemporary novels and magazines on the fourth floor. The **Shànghăi Museum,** Rénmín Dà Dào 201 (© 021/6372-3500), has selections of books on Shànghăi and Chinese art and culture, as do the gift shops and kiosks in major hotels, such as the Hilton and the Jǐnjiāng (which carry foreign newspapers as well). For a list of other bookstores, see "Bookstores" in chapter 8.

Business Hours Offices are open Monday through Friday from 9am to 5pm, although some still close at the lunch hour (about noon–1:30pm); a few maintain limited Saturday hours. Bank opening hours vary (see "Banks, Currency Exchanges & ATMs" above). Sights, shops, restaurants, and transportation systems offer the same service 7 days a week. Department stores are typically open from 10am to 10pm. Restaurants outside of hotels are generally open from 11:30am to 2pm and 5 to 9:30pm, while those catering to foreign visitors usually stay open later. The official closing time for bars is 2am, though some stay open later on weekends.

Car Rentals There is no shortage of car rental outlets in Shànghăi, but don't plan on picking your SUV up at the airport or anywhere else. Tourists are forbidden to rent self-drive cars (or motorcycles or scooters) in China because a Chinese driver's license is required (available only to foreigners with an official residency permit). Of course, major hotels are only too happy to rent chauffeured sedans to their foreign guests by the hour, day, or week, at rates that will make you never complain about car rental prices back home again.

Currency   See "Money" in chapter 2.

Doctors & Dentists   Shànghăi has the most advanced medical treatment and facilities in China. The higher-end hotels usually have in-house or on-call doctors, but almost all hotels can refer foreign guests to dentists and doctors versed in Western medicine. The following medical clinics and hospitals specialize in treating foreigners and provide international-standard services: **World Link Medical and Dental Centers,** Nánjīng Xī Lù 1376, Shànghăi Centre, Suite 203 (✆ **021/6279-7688**); and Unit 30, Mandarine City, Hóngxŭ Lù 788, Hóngqiáo District (✆ **021/6405-5788**), have 24-hour emergency services, offer Western dental care, offer OB-GYN services, and maintain a website (www.worldlink-shanghai.com); walk-in hours at both branches are from 9am to 7pm Monday through Friday, from 9am to 4pm Saturday, and from 9am to 3pm Sunday. In addition, World Link has a Specialty and Inpatient Center at Dànshuĭ Lù 170, 3rd floor (✆ **021/6385-9889**). The **Huá Shān Hospital,** Wūlŭmùqí Zhōng Lù 12, Jìng Ān District (✆ **021/6248-9999**, ext. 1921), has a special Foreigner's Clinic on the 19th floor, and a 24-hour hot line (✆ **021/6248-3986**). The **First People's Hospital International Medical Care Center (IMCC),** Jiŭlóng Lù 585 (✆ **021/6306-9480**), is located near the Bund and offers 24-hour medical emergency assistance. A representative office of **AEA International (SOS Alarm Centre),** Zūnyì Nán Lù 88, Shartex Plaza 2606 (✆ **021/6295-8277**), provides medical evacuation and repatriation throughout China on a 24-hour basis; for emergency medical evacuation, call ✆ **021/6295-0099.**

Dental care to foreign visitors and expatriates is provided by **World Link** Monday to Saturday (see above); by **Dr. Harriet Jin's Dental Surgery,** Huái-hăi Xī Lù 55, Sun Tong Infoport Plaza, Room 17C (✆ **021/5298-9799**), open from 9am to 6pm Monday through Friday, from 9am to 1pm Saturday; by the Canadian-managed **Sino-Canadian Shànghăi Dental Center** on the seventh floor of the Ninth People's Hospital, Zhìzàojú Lù 639 (✆ **021/6313-3174**), which is closed Sunday; and by **DDS Dental Care,** Táojiāng Lù 1, 2nd Floor (✆ **021/6466-0928**; www.ddsdentalcare.com). DDS Dental Care has multilingual Western-trained dentists, a lab, and a 24-hour emergency number (✆ **1301-288-1288**).

Driving Rules   Though foreign visitors are not allowed to drive in China (a Chinese driving license is required), they still need to be aware of local driving rules for their own safety as pedestrians. And the rules are as follows: Vehicles trump pedestrians, and Shànghăi drivers abhor empty space. Cars, driven on the right side of the road in Shànghăi, have the right of way even when they do not, so always yield. See "Getting Around: By Foot" above.

Drugstores   In general, bring any and all of your own prescription medicines, and your favorite over-the-counter pain and cold remedies. A limited selection of Western amenities like cough drops, toothpaste, shampoo, and beauty aids are available in international hotel kiosks, and most reliably, at **Watson's Drug Store,** which has branches throughout town, including at Huáihăi Zhōng Lù 787–789 (✆ **021/6474-4775;** 9:30am–10pm). If necessary, prescriptions can be filled at the **World Link Medical Center,** Nánjīng Xī Lù 1376, Shànghăi Centre, Suite 203 (✆ **021/6279-7688**). Chinese medicines (as well as some Western remedies) are dispensed at the **Shànghǎi No. 1 Pharmacy,** Nánjīng Dōng Lù 616 (© 021/ 6322-4567, ext. 0; 9am–10pm).

Electricity The electricity used throughout China is 220 volts, alternating current (AC), 50 cycles. Except for laptop computers and most mobile phone chargers, other North American electrical devices will require the use of a transformer. Outlets come in a variety of configurations, the most common being the flat two-pin (but not the three-pin or the two-pin where one is wider than the other), and also the round two-pin, the slanted two-prong and slanted three-prong types. Most hotels have a variety of outlets and can supply a range of adapters. Transformers and adapters can be purchased in department stores.

Embassies & Consulates The consulates of many countries are located in the French Concession and Jìng Ān districts several miles west of downtown. Visa and passport sections are open only at certain times of the day, so call in advance. The consulates are open from Monday to Friday only, and are often closed for lunch (noon–1pm). The Consulate General of the **United States** is at Huáihǎi Zhōng Lù 1469 (© 021/6433-6880; fax 021/6433-4122; www.usembassy-china.org.cn/shanghai). The **Canadian** Consulate General is in the Shànghǎi Centre at Nánjīng Xī Lù 1376, West Tower, Suites 604 and 668 (visa section, © 021/6279-8400; fax 021/6279-8401; www.shanghai.gc.ca). The **New Zealand** Consulate General is at Huáihǎi Zhōng Lù 1375, Suite 15A (© 021/6471-1108; fax 021/6431-0226; www.nzembassy.com). The Consulate General of **Australia** is in CITIC Square at Nánjīng Xī Lù 1168, 22nd Floor (© 021/5292-5500; fax 021/5292-5511; www.aus-in-shanghai.com). The **British** Consulate General is in the Shànghǎi Centre, Nánjīng Xī Lù 1376, Suite 301 (© 021/ 6279-8400; fax 021/6279-7651; www.britishconsulate.sh.cn).

Emergencies The emergency phone numbers in Shànghǎi are © 110 for police (English operators available), © 119 for fire, and © 120 for ambulance, though no English is spoken at the last two.

Etiquette & Customs **Appropriate attire:** The Shanghainese have a long-held reputation for being fashion conscious and are, on the whole, a comparatively well-dressed bunch. For the worldly Shanghainese who've seen it all, foreigners tend to get a pass when it comes to attire anyway, so wear whatever you find comfortable. Chances are you'll be out-dressed (or underdressed in some cases) by the trendy fashion plates. When in doubt, err on the side of modesty even if some of the younger locals don't. Business attire is similar to that in the West.

Greetings and gestures: The handshake is now commonplace, as is the exchange of business cards *(míng piàn),* so bring some along if you have them. Cards and gifts should be presented and received with both hands. Speaking a few words of Mandarin will go a long way in pleasing your host; you'll be told you speak very well, to which the proper reply should be a self-effacing denial, even if you are fluent. When invited to someone's house, never go empty-handed; always bring a small gift, even if it's just some fruit picked up at the last minute at the corner store.

Avoiding offense: Causing someone to lose face is the surest way to offend, and should be avoided as much as possible. This means not losing your temper and yelling at someone in public, not calling public attention to their mistakes, and not publicly contradicting them, no matter how great the grievance. Instead, take up the matter privately or complain to a superior, when appropriate.

Eating and drinking: If possible, master the use of chopsticks before you go. Chinese food is eaten family style with everyone serving themselves from several main dishes. As the guest, you'll be served first; accept graciously then reciprocate the gesture by serving your host in return. Use the communal serving spoon(s) or chopsticks provided. Eat with your chopsticks, but don't leave them sticking out of the bowl. Never criticize the food in front of your host. Your cup of tea will be constantly topped up. A Cantonese custom that has started to catch on in Shànghǎi is to acknowledge the pour by tapping your fingers lightly on the table. Feel free to top up other people's cups of tea every now and then, though it's likely that after the first time, your host will remove the teapot from your reach. If you're invited to eat at someone's home, never arrive empty-handed (fruit is always a fail-safe gift if you're stuck for options), and take off your shoes at the entrance even if your host demurs. They're merely being polite. If you're invited to a banquet, expect a great deal of drinking. Toasts are usually made with *báijiǔ* (potent Chinese spirits), often to the tunes of *"gān bēi"* (literally dry glass, the equivalent of "bottoms up"). If you can't keep up, don't drain your glass (for it will be filled up again quickly, sparking another round of drinking), but do return the toast, if necessary with beer, mineral water, or tea.

Holidays See "When to Go" in chapter 2.

Hot Lines Spring International Travel Service maintains a 24-hour hot line for tourist inquiries (in English and Chinese), ℂ 021/6252-0000.

Information See "Visitor Information," earlier in this chapter.

Internet Access Business centers at most three-star and up Shànghǎi hotels now provide online access and e-mail services, including PC rentals employing familiar English-language software programs. Dial-up Internet access (**16300,** with the same user name and password) is available in any hotel room with a phone, but broadband Internet access is now commonplace in Shànghǎi's top luxury hotels, some of which even offer wireless Internet access in their lobbies and executive lounges. (See "The 21st-Century Traveler" in chapter 2.) Internet cafes are subject to periodic government crackdown. The most reliable and the cheapest Internet access can be found at the **Shànghǎi Library (Shànghǎi Túshūguǎn),** Huái-hǎi Zhōng Lù 1557 (ℂ 021/6445-2001), in a small office on the ground floor underneath the main entrance staircase. It's open from 9am to 8:30pm daily (¥4/50¢ per hour), and is always packed with Chinese students. **Richard's Bar** at the Pǔjiāng Hotel (Pǔjiāng Fàndiàn, Huángpǔ Lù 15; ℂ 021/6324-6388; daily 8am–2am) charges ¥5 (60¢) for a half-hour of broadband access.

Language Mandarin is the official language throughout China. However, while many Shanghainese speak Mandarin, you're just as likely to hear locals conversing everywhere (shops, businesses, restaurants) in Shanghainese, which is as different from Mandarin as Cantonese is from English. Written Chinese, however, follows one standard script. Outside of international hotels, restaurants, and shops, English is still rarely spoken, though compulsory English tuition from primary grade one was implemented in local schools in 2003. Many younger urbanites should recognize at least a smattering of English words and phrases.

Legal Aid If you end up on the wrong side of the "still evolving" law in China, call your consulate immediately.

Liquor Laws There are no liquor laws in Shànghăi worth worrying about (in other words, no legal drinking age). Bars keep irregular closing hours, some not shutting down until well after the official 2am closing time. Supermarkets, hotel shops, and international restaurants sell imported and domestic beer, wine, and spirits. Inexpensive domestic beer and liquor can be bought any time at the 24-hour neighborhood convenience stores.

Lost & Found The loss of your passport should be immediately reported to your consulate, while the loss of credit cards should be immediately reported to your credit card company, some of which may require a police report. Contact the PSB (see "Police" below) for this. In China, the emergency toll-free numbers for lost or stolen credit cards are as follows: Visa (© 010/800-440-0027 or 021/6374-4418); American Express, which will also replace lost or stolen traveler's checks (© 021/6279-8082 or 010/800-610-0277); and MasterCard (© 010/800-110-7309). Diners Club members should call Hong Kong at © 852/2860-1800 or call the U.S. collect at © 1/416/369-6313. For other lost personal items, contact the site where you think you lost it, then report the loss to your hotel staff or the police if you want, though don't expect much sympathy, let alone results.

Mail Sending mail from China is remarkably reliable. Most hotels sell postage stamps and will mail your letters and parcels, the latter at a hefty fee, so take your parcels to the post office yourself, if possible. Overseas letters and postcards require 5 to 10 days for delivery. Current costs are as follows: overseas airmail: **postcard** ¥4.20 (50¢); **aerogramme** ¥5.20 (62¢); **letter under 10g** (.35 oz.) ¥5.40 (70¢); **letter under 20g** (.70 oz.) ¥6.50 (80¢). Domestic letters are ¥0.50 (6¢). EMS (**express parcels** under 500g/18 oz.): to the U.S. ¥180 to ¥240 ($23–$30); to Europe ¥220 to ¥280 ($28–$35); to Australia ¥160 to ¥210 ($20–$26). **Normal parcels** up to 1km (2.2 lb.): to the U.S. by air ¥95 to ¥159 ($12–$20), by sea ¥20 to ¥84 ($2.50–$14); to the U.K. by air ¥77 to ¥162 ($10–$20), by sea ¥22 to ¥108 ($11–$13); to Australia by air ¥70 to ¥144 ($8.75–$18), by sea ¥15 to ¥89 ($1.90–$11). Custom declaration forms in Chinese and French are available at post offices. When sending parcels, bring your package to the post office unsealed, as packages are often subject to inspection. Large post offices will sell packaging material.

The main Post Office (*yóuzhèng jú*; open 7am–10pm daily) is located at Běi Sūzhōu Lù 276 (© 021/6324-0069), at the intersection of Sìchuān Běi Lù, in downtown Shànghăi just north of Sūzhōu Creek; international parcels are sent from a desk in the same building, but its entrance is actually around the corner at Tiāntóng Lù 395. Other post offices where employees can speak some English are located at Shànghăi Centre, Nánjīng Xī Lù 1376, lower level (© 021/6279-8044); and at Huáihăi Lù 1337.

International parcel and courier services in Shànghăi include **FedEx,** Zūnyì Lù 107, Aetna Building, 10th floor (© 021/6275-0808); **DHL-Sinotrans,** Jìniàn Lù 303 (© 800/810-8000); and **UPS,** Huáihăi Zhōng Lù 381,

Shànghǎi Central Plaza, Suite 1318–1338 (© **021/6391-5555**). Pickup and delivery can usually be arranged by your hotel.

Maps City maps *(dìtú)* are indispensable and are available from most hotel desks. Chinese-only maps are available at train stations, bus stations and street vendors for around ¥5 (60¢). If you end up with one of these, have your hotel concierge circle your hotel and the places you'd like to visit so you can show it to the taxi driver. It's a good idea to always have a map out so you can follow (as best you can) the taxi route. The best tri-lingual map (with street and place names in English, *pīnyīn,* and Chinese characters), the *Shànghǎi Tourist Map,* issued by the Shànghǎi Municipal Tourism Administration, is available in bookstores for ¥10 ($1.25).

Newspapers & Magazines Foreign magazines and newspapers, including *USA Today, International Herald Tribune, South China Morning Post,* and Asian editions of the *Wall Street Journal, Newsweek,* and *Time,* are sold at kiosks in international hotels. For the world according to China's Communist party, there's the English-language *China Daily,* distributed free at many hotels. The local version, *Shanghai Daily* (www.shanghaidaily.com), a free 6-day-a-week newspaper, covers the city with the same propagandistic outlook, but has an occasionally helpful arts and entertainment section appearing on Saturday. Several free, once- or twice-monthly English-language magazines and newspapers produced expressly for travelers and expatriates in Shànghǎi such as *that's Shanghai, City Weekend, Shanghai Talk,* and *Metrozine* can be useful for entertainment listings (not always accurate) and restaurant reviews. See "Visitor Information" earlier in this chapter.

Passports See "Entry Requirements and Customs" in chapter 2.

Police Known as the **PSB (Public Security Bureau,** *gōng'ān jú*), the Shànghǎi police force has its headquarters at Hànkǒu Lù 210 (© **021/ 6357-6666** for English-speaking attendant, or 021/6321-5380). The police are identifiable by their navy blue parkas emblazoned with the Roman letters "Jing Cha" (meaning police or *jǐng chá*), though you wonder why, if they bothered with Roman lettering, they didn't simply write "Police" instead. Ideally, any interaction with them should be limited to visa extensions. These are handled at Wúsōng Lù 333 (© **021/6321-1997**), several miles north of the Bund. The emergency telephone number for the police is © **110.**

Post Office See "Mail," above.

Restrooms For hygienic restrooms, rely on the big hotels, restaurants catering to foreigners, new malls, and fast-food outlets, in that order. There are, of course, hundreds of public restrooms in the streets, parks, cafes, department stores, and tourist sites of Shànghǎi, but most of these consist primarily of squat toilets (a trough in the ground), are not particularly clean, and do not provide tissues or soap as a rule, though some public restrooms charge a small fee (¥0.5/6¢ or less) and will give you a rough sheet of what passes for toilet paper. Look for wc or TOILET signs at intersections pointing the way to all public facilities.

Safety Shànghǎi is one of the safest cities in the world for foreign travelers, but as in any major city, pickpockets and thieves exist. At crowded public tourist sites, keep an eye on purses, wallets, and cameras. Always store valuables in a concealed safety pouch. Backpacks and fanny packs are targets in buses, the subway, and markets. Use hotel safety-deposit boxes or room safes, and do not open your door to strangers. Violent crimes and cases of sexual harassment against foreign visitors are quite rare but do occur, so use common sense. Travel with others when possible, rebuff strangers in the streets, and avoid unlighted streets after dark. Beggars can sometimes be seen on Shànghãi streets. Idlers who speak a little English may pose as "friends" or art students and try to engage you in conversation in the street. While they are not thieves, as a rule, they are after more than friendship (usually some of your money, often turned over in the form of an outrageously expensive restaurant bill); they should be rebuffed quickly. Don't give strangers your hotel name or phone number unless you want to be bothered later.

Smoking China has more smokers than any other nation, an estimated 350 million, accounting for one of every three cigarettes consumed worldwide. About 70% of the men smoke. Recent antismoking campaigns have led to laws banning smoking on all forms of public transport (including taxis) and in waiting rooms and terminals, a ban, which has, surprisingly, been largely observed (except on long-distance buses). Top hotels provide nonsmoking rooms and floors, and a few restaurants have begun to set aside nonsmoking tables and sections. Still, expect to encounter more smoking in public places in China than in most Western countries.

Taxes Most four- and five-star hotels levy a 10% to 15% tax on rooms (including a city tax), while a few restaurants and bars have taken to placing a similar service charge on bills. In the case of the latter, you can almost be assured that the service will not justify the charge. There is no sales tax. Departure taxes must be paid in Chinese currency at the airport (¥90/$11 for international flights including to Hong Kong and Macau; ¥50/$6 domestic).

Telephone The international **country code** for China is **86**. The **city code** for Shànghãi is **021**. If you are calling a Shànghãi number from outside the city but within China, dial the city code (021) and then the number. If you are calling Shànghãi from abroad, drop the first zero.

Local calls in Shànghãi require no city code; just dial the eight-digit Shànghãi number (or the three-digit emergency numbers for fire, police, and ambulance). Calls from Shànghãi to other locations in China require that you dial the full domestic city code (which always starts with **0**). Public pay phones require either a deposit of a ¥1 coin or an IC card (*"àicēi" kǎ*) available from post offices, most convenience stores, and street stalls. Card values begin at ¥20 ($2.50).

To call Shànghãi from the United States, dial 011 (the international access code) + 86 (the country code for China) + 21 (the city code for Shànghãi minus the initial zero) + the eight-digit Shànghãi number.

To make an international direct dial (IDD) call from Shànghãi (which you can do from most Shànghãi hotel rooms), dial the international access code **(00)** + the country code for the country you are calling + the area code and the local phone number. The country code for the U.S. and Canada is **1,** for the United Kingdom **44,** for Australia **61,** and for New

Zealand **64.** To call the U.S. from Shànghǎi, for example, dial 00 + 1 + U.S. area code + U.S. phone number. If you have questions, speak with the hotel operator or an international operator (☏ **116**). You can also use your calling card (AT&T, MCI, or Sprint, for example) to make international (but not domestic) calls from Shànghǎi. The local access number for **AT&T** is ☏ **10-811;** for **MCI** ☏ **10-812;** for **Sprint** ☏ **10-813.** Check with your hotel for the local access numbers for other companies. The directions for placing an international calling-card call vary from company to company, so check with your long-distance carrier before you leave home. To save money, however, use an **IP card** *(àipì kǎ),* available from post offices, most convenience stores, and street stalls, but bargain for less than the face value of the card (in other words, you should bargain to pay around ¥80/$1 for a ¥100 card). Depending on where you call, a ¥50/$6 card can yield you up to an hour's talk time. Instructions in English should be on the back of the card.

Time Zone Shànghǎi (and all of China) is on Běijīng time, which is 8 hours ahead of Greenwich Mean Time (GMT + 8), 13 hours ahead of New York, 14 hours ahead of Chicago, and 16 hours ahead of Los Angeles. There's no daylight saving time, so subtract 1 hour in the summer. For the current time in Shànghǎi, dial ☏ **117.**

Tipping There is officially *no* tipping in China, but the reality is that it has become quite commonplace in Shànghǎi's hospitality industry, especially where bellhops (four- and five-star hotels), tour guides, and tour bus drivers are concerned. Though you may feel pressured to do so, only tip if you feel truly inclined to or for exceptional service. Restaurant waitstaff and taxi drivers usually do not expect tips, and will return any change due you.

Water Tap water throughout China is not safe for drinking (or for brushing teeth). Use only bottled water, widely available almost everywhere (supermarkets, convenience stores, neighborhood shops, vendors' stalls), and also provided in most hotel rooms.

Weather The *China Daily* newspaper, CCTV 9 (China Central Television's English language channel), and some hotel bulletin boards furnish the next day's forecast. You can also dial Shànghǎi's weather number, ☏ **121.**

Where to Stay

4

There are two types of hotels in China: **Sino-foreign joint venture hotels,** which are Chinese-owned properties with foreign management; and wholly **Chinese-owned and -managed hotels.** The former tend to be four- and five-star hotels (see below for more on the rating system) with familiar brand names, while the latter can range from five-star outfits to unrated hovels. Two of the biggest Chinese hotel management groups are the Jǐn_Jiāng chain and the Héngshān chain, both of which started with flagship hotels in Shànghǎi but have now extended their management to hotels around China.

The Chinese government ranks hotels on an almost meaningless star system whereby five-star accreditation is handed out by a central authority while four-star and below ranks are determined by local authorities, none of whom are beyond a little (or a lot of) wining, dining, and palm-greasing. **Five-star hotels** have the complete facilities and services of any international luxury hotel, but even among its ranks, quality varies more than it should. **Four-star hotels** come close, often lacking only a few technical requirements (such as a swimming pool or other facility). Both levels are popular choices for Western travelers, providing English-speaking staff and clean, comfortable, even luxurious accommodations. Foreign-managed hotels have foreign staff at the top levels, though increasingly the Chinese are filling more of these positions even in joint venture hotels. For Western travelers, your first choice should be foreign-managed hotels followed by the top Chinese-managed outfits. In general, four- and five-star Chinese-managed hotels do not match their foreign-managed counterparts in service or maintenance of facilities.

Three-star hotels are almost always Chinese-managed and provide less consistent services, fewer amenities, and more basic rooms, with almost no dedication to upkeep and maintenance. Few of them have English-speaking staff. In the bigger cities, three-star hotels are adequate for the budget traveler who merely needs a decent place to spend the night. In many parts of China, however, the three-star hotel is the best you'll find.

Due to the comparative lack of cleanliness (rather than safety issues), **two-** and **one-star hotels,** as well as unrated hotels and basic guesthouses catering to the rugged backpacking traveler are generally best avoided, if possible. In many parts of China, these hotels are not even allowed to accept foreign travelers. *Note:* The zero- to three-star rating system we use in the following reviews does not correspond to the Chinese star-rating system. For details on Frommer's Star Rating system, see p. viii.

In general, most hotel rooms, no matter how basic, have the following: a telephone whose line you can plug into your laptop computer; air-conditioning, either centrally or individually controlled, which often doubles as a heater; a television which usually receives only local Chinese channels, if that; and some sort of potable water, either in the form of hot water thermoses which are delivered to your room after you check in, or bottled water and an electric kettle. Except for the top hotels, most hotels do not have exclusively nonsmoking rooms. If they tell you they do, but put you in a room that reeks of every previous smoker, they mean the room is a nonsmoking room *for the moment!*

Note: It's quite common to receive telephone calls in the middle of the night (even in four- and five-star hotels, alas) inquiring if you would like *ànmó* (literally "massage," but in this case, a not-so-subtle euphemism for sexual services). The caller usually hangs up if a woman answers, or occasionally if a man answers in a non-Chinese language. However, bolder callers have learned enough to say "Massagee?" when they hear a foreign male's voice. If you are not amused, and complaining to the hotel staff doesn't work (much of this calling actually comes from in-house), unplug your phone.

In general, payment for your room is made upfront; many, but not all of the three-star and up hotels catering to foreigners accept foreign credit cards. Asked how long you're staying, always just say 1 day (or you'll be asked to pay for however many days you plan on staying). You can then pay as you go. Keep all receipts, from proof of your room payment to any room key deposits you might have had to make. The top hotels usually levy a service charge of 10% to 15%, though this is usually waived or included in the final negotiated price at smaller hotels. Children under 12 usually get to stay free in their parent's room.

With practically every international hotel chain and brand name represented in Shànghǎi, some of them exclusively (the Four Seasons and the JW Marriott are the first and only hotels of their brand in China), the visitor is spoiled for choice when it comes to high-end accommodations. Even more appealing, and unique to Shànghǎi, these luxury accommodations come in a range of styles, from modern luxury towers to restored Art Deco hotels to elegant colonial mansions. Prices are high but the fierce competition from the glut of hotels has led to significant discounts during parts of the year. These discounts disappear almost entirely during big conventions, meetings, and special citywide events, however. Mid-range accommodations are plentiful in Shànghǎi, but few foreigners choose these mostly three-star hotels when big discounts are available from the top hotels. Shànghǎi's budget hotels, few and far between, charge more than elsewhere in China, with the exception, perhaps, of Hong Kong and Běijīng.

Shànghǎi being more of a financial, commercial, and industrial city than a tourism-driven one, hoteliers like to claim that they have no low season. In reality, you can get the biggest discounts between December and February, while rates are highest May through October.

HOW TO GET THE BEST ROOM FOR THE BEST RATE

The room rates listed in this guide are **rack rates,** which is the maximum rate that a hotel charges for a room. Shànghǎi frequently hosts international conventions and large special events, so the top hotels will charge rack rates during these occasions. During all other times, however, almost no one pays more than 90%. On average, you can usually expect a discount of 20% to 40%, and occasionally even up to 60% to 70% during the low season. While this is true for most hotels in China at any given time, there are exceptions, of course: Some hotels in wildly popular cities like Guìlín will charge double the rack rate during the National

Day holidays in October. In general, to lower the cost of your room, consider the following:

- **Booking ahead vs. over-the-counter bargaining:** As a general rule, you can get the best rates by simply showing up at a hotel and bargaining, assuming of course, that there is room. For much of the year, most Chinese hotels are never full and your chances of getting a lower rate are much better on the spot than if you booked months in advance (perhaps paying double what you might in person). In addition, there is no guarantee that the booking you make will be honored, especially at local Chinese hotels. That said, most travelers to China (especially first-timers) who are not familiar with the language tend to find the prospect of negotiating on the spot daunting, not to mention highly inconvenient if you have to drag your luggage around until you find a suitable hotel. Those who want to get the best deal but also be assured of a place to stay can book a hotel for the first night, and then bargain in person once you've reached your destination. To bargain in person, it's helpful to keep in mind the general discounting structure mentioned above, as well as the discounted rates offered by various websites (see below).

- **Booking online:** If you have to stay at a specific joint-venture hotel during a particularly busy time, the best rates are usually offered on the **hotel's website.** Beware that these rates fluctuate constantly according to inventory. Unless there's a major event going on, the farther in advance you book, the smaller the discount you'll likely receive. Hotel prices quoted by services like Travelocity and Expedia can occasionally be quite competitive, especially closer to the time, but such rates can usually be matched by the hotels themselves. Several top international hotels such as the Marriott chain also have a "look no further" policy whereby they will match the lowest rates offered on any non-hotel-affiliated websites. As a general rule, do not book with any online Chinese travel agencies and hotel-booking sites, as many of them are not licensed and you have no guarantee of getting a room or your money back. That said, there's no harm consulting hugely popular Chinese travel websites such as C-Trip (www.english.ctrip.com), if only to get a sense of your beginning price for negotiation.

- **Dialing a central booking number:** With the better hotels, you can sometimes get better rates with their toll-free central booking number than by calling the hotel directly.

HOW TO CHOOSE THE LOCATION THAT'S RIGHT FOR YOU

No district has a complete lock on convenience for the traveler because the main tourist sites are scattered around the sprawling city, and shuttling by taxi and Metro is cheap and efficient. In general, hotels in Huángpǔ, Lúwān, and Jìng Ān districts have the most to see in their immediate neighborhoods.

Tips **Look before You Buy**

When bargaining for a room at a hotel, always ask to see the room first to avoid any rude surprises after you've put your money down. This is standard practice at all Chinese hotels, and any receptionist who would tell you otherwise is merely being lazy. Most of the top hotels will be more reluctant to show their rooms, but politely insist if it's important enough to you.

For the average visitor on a short stay, the downtown district of **Huángpǔ,** which encompasses the city center, the Bund, and the eastern half of Nánjīng Lù, and which has a number of top hotels like the Westin, JW Marriott, and a slew of hotels along or just off the Nánjīng Lù Pedestrian Mall, offers the convenience of being able to walk to central sites such as the Bund, People's Square, Shànghǎi Museum, and Shànghǎi Grand Theatre. However, the streets here tend to be smaller and considerably more congested, and taxis often have a harder time getting in and out of the city. Also, this downtown area tends to shut down by 10pm.

Those looking for a more exciting nightlife would do well to be based in the **Lúwān District** just southwest of the Bund, or the northeastern part of the Xúhuì District just to the west of Lúwān. This former French Concession area is one of the most pleasant areas to stay, whether as a tourist or resident. There is a good sprinkling of international-caliber hotels here, but even more attractive are the wide, tree-lined streets, hundreds of colonial mansions and Art Deco apartments hidden inside narrow lanes ripe for exploring, excellent restaurants in colonial settings, and colorful nightlife around Xīn Tiāndì and Héngshān Lù. Some of the best shopping in town is also found here along Huáihǎi Lù and Màomíng Lù.

North of Lúwān and west of Huángpǔ district, **Jìng Ān District (Northwest Shànghǎi)** has its share of colonial mansions (more of the British than of the French variety), some fine restaurants, and many top hotels including The Four Seasons, The Portman Ritz Carlton, and the Hilton.

To the west, the sprawling western district of **Chángníng** and the Hóngqiáo Development Zone is primarily a foreign investment and residential area, most easily accessible by taxi, as there is no subway service out here yet. A handful of top international hotels based here, such as the Sheraton and Marriott, cater mostly to business travelers, but there are some excellent restaurants in the district worth checking out.

To the east of city center, just across the Huángpǔ River, the **Pǔdōng New Area** has less to offer sightseers, as it's still primarily a business district. With several of Shànghǎi's best new hotels, and a subway link to downtown (Metro Line 2), however, it can now serve as a base for tourists as well.

The following hotel listings are arranged first by location, then by price. The **Very Expensive** category lists hotels with rack rates over $250 per night; the **Expensive** category lists hotels with rack rates of $150 to $250 per night; the **Moderate** category, rack rates of $100 to $150 per night; and the **Inexpensive** category, rack rates of under $100. Each listing also includes the average discount you can expect at that establishment.

Note: Maps for accommodations are in chapter 6—see the information following each review for specific page numbers.

1 Huángpǔ (Downtown)

VERY EXPENSIVE

JW Marriott (Wànháo Jiǔdiàn) ★★ Finally opened in October 2003 after several delays, China's first JW Marriott is a handsome five-star hotel for the new millennium. Lodged primarily on the 37th to 60th floors of the aptly named Tomorrow Square (Míntiān Guǎngchǎng), a fascinating futuristic tower that can look top or bottom heavy depending on the angle of approach, this is technically the tallest hotel in Pǔxī and has stunning panoramic views to show for it. The bottom half of the building is taken up by Marriott service apartments, retail shops, and the first Mandara spa in China. The luxury associated with Marriott's top brand is on ample display in the guest rooms which are spacious and furnished with three telephones, large work desk, CD radio, laptop safe, thick bathrobes, thin *yukatas* (cotton kimonos), and brilliant city views. Marble bathrooms have tubs, separate showers with power massage jets, and anti-fog mirrors. Service is coming along nicely, and facilities are extensive though a little too scattered (the gym, swimming pool, spa, and conference rooms are on the fifth and sixth floors). At press time, the hotel was still working on ways to clear up the confusion around its labyrinthine elevators. What is indisputably perfect, however, is the hotel's superb location: a short walk from both subway lines and attractions including the Shànghǎi Museum, Shànghǎi Art Museum, Grand Theatre, Nánjīng Lù Pedestrian Mall, and Xīntiāndì.

Nánjīng Xī Lù 399 (at Huángpí Běi Lù, west side of Rénmín Gōngyuán); see map p. 118. ✆ 800/228-9290 or 021/5359-4969. Fax 021/6375-5988. www.marriott.com. 342 units. ¥2,646 ($320) double; ¥3,143 ($380) executive level; from ¥4,052 ($490) suite (regular 40% discounts, up to 60% pending occupancy). AE, DC, MC, V. Metro: Rénmín Guǎngchǎng. **Amenities:** 3 restaurants; 2 lounges; indoor/outdoor pool; health club with Jacuzzi and sauna; Mandara spa; concierge; business center; salon; 24-hr. room service; babysitting; same-day dry cleaning/laundry; nonsmoking rooms; executive-level rooms. *In room:* A/C, satellite TV, broadband, minibar, coffeemaker, hair dryer, iron, safe.

The Westin Shànghǎi (Shànghǎi Wēisītīng Dàfàndiàn) ★★★ *Kids*
Located within the Bund Center (Wàitān Zhōngxīn), a corporate, residential, and hotel complex 5 minutes' walk from the Bund, the 26-story Westin brings a welcome dose of modern five-star luxury to the neighborhood. A bold tone is set in the lobby by the sweeping blue-tinted cantilevered glass staircase and pieces of modern artwork, but throw in some palm trees and red chairs and it all has the unfortunate effect of making a busy atrium look even more crowded and gaudy. Thankfully, the large guest rooms fare much better and show Westin at its best with its patented Heavenly Bed, plush furnishings, large work desk, fax machine, high-speed Internet access, and deluxe bathroom that includes a separate stall with a rainforest shower. The Westin Kids Club is nearly unique in Shànghǎi, consisting of a separate area with adjoining outdoor terrace and paddle pool. Adults meanwhile can avail themselves of the sybaritic experience at the hotel's Banyan Tree Spa. Service throughout is impeccable. Besides the Bund, the old Chinese city (Nánshì) can also be reached on foot (20 min.).

Hénán Zhōng Lù 88, Wàitān Zhōngxīn (3 blocks west of the Huángpǔ River); see map p. 118. ✆ 888/WESTIN-1 or 021/6335-1888. Fax 021/6335-2888. www.westin.com. 301 units. ¥2,464 ($320) double; ¥3,266 ($395) executive level; from ¥2,853 ($345) suite (40%–50% discount). AE, DC, MC, V. Metro: Hénán Zhōng Lù. **Amenities:** 3 restaurants; deli; 2 lounges; juice bar; 20m (66-ft.) indoor/outdoor pool; state-of-the-art health club and spa with Jacuzzi and sauna; children's programs; concierge; 24-hr. business center; salon; 24-hr. room service; babysitting; same-day dry cleaning/laundry; executive-level rooms; 3 rooms for those w/limited mobility. *In room:* A/C, satellite TV, broadband, minibar, coffeemaker, hair dryer, safe.

EXPENSIVE

Howard Johnson Plaza Hotel (Gǔ Xiàng Dàjiǔdiàn) *
Even Howard Johnson's has now gotten into the Shànghǎi luxury hotel scene with this newly opened (2003) 27-story tower just south of the new (and at press time unfinished) Century Square (Shìjì Guǎngchǎng) on the Nánjīng Lù pedestrian mall. A fully modern if somewhat unexciting hotel, this five-star aspirant has rooms furnished with redwood furniture, comfortable beds with down bedding, robes, and full amenities. Guests are also treated to two complimentary laundry washes per room. Marble bathrooms are large and clean. Service is friendly enough, if a little tentative. Attractive introductory discounts and an excellent location with easy access to the Bund and People's Square make this a competitive option in the Nánjīng Lù area.

Jiǔjiāng Lù 595 (south of Nánjīng Dōng Lù, west of Húběi Lù); see map p. 118. © **800/820-2525** or 021/3313-4888. Fax 021/3313-4880. www.hojochina.com. 360 units. ¥1,902 ($230) double; ¥2,315 ($280) club room; from ¥2,315 ($280) suite (40%–50% discounts). AE, DC, MC, V. Metro: **Amenities:** 3 restaurants; lounge; bar; indoor pool; health club and spa with Jacuzzi and sauna; concierge; business center; salon; 24-hr. room service; dry cleaning/laundry; nonsmoking rooms; executive-level rooms. *In room:* A/C, satellite TV, broadband, minibar, coffeemaker, hair dryer, safe.

Peace Hotel (Hépíng Fàndiàn) ★ (Overrated)

The best known of Shànghǎi's historic hotels, the Peace was built in 1929 by colonial millionaire Victor Sassoon. Known in its heyday as the Cathay Hotel, it was famous throughout Asia. Noel Coward wrote *Private Lives* while staying here in 1930, and Steven Spielberg filmed scenes for *Empire of the Sun* from inside the hotel. The hotel's restored Art Deco decor is most fully realized in its stunning lobby. Rooms, some most recently renovated in 2003, are spacious, with large closets and high ceilings, and some retain their old furnishings and trim. For the full effect, splurge on a "Nine Nations" deluxe suite (¥4,300/$520), each decorated in the style of a particular country (Chinese, British, American, French, Indian, and others). For all the Peace's renown and ideal location on Nánjīng Lù and the Bund, its amenities and service, which is inefficient and uninspired, barely rise to the four-star level (even though the hotel is rated a full five stars).

Across the street, the former Renaissance Mansion–style Peace Palace Hotel (Nánjīng Dōng Lù 23), also built by Victor Sassoon, but earlier in 1906, has now become the Peace Hotel's South Building. Extensively renovated in 1998, the guest rooms are furnished in nostalgic Victorian reproductions, complete with curtains and carpets, but the bathrooms are modernized. This south building is not as glamorous as the Peace, but the ornate lobby with chandeliers, original moldings, and carved wooden columns is still lovely to behold.

Nánjīng Dōng Lù 20 (on the Bund); see map p. 118. © **021/6321-6888.** Fax 021/6329-0300. www.shanghai peacehotel.com. 260 units (103 units in south building). ¥1,320 – ¥1,820 ($160–$220) double; ¥2,077 ($250) executive level; from ¥2,460 ($320) suite (up to 40% discount). AE, DC, MC, V. Metro: Hénán Zhōng Lù. **Amenities:** 3 restaurants; 2 lounges (jazz bar, rooftop bar); tiny health club with sauna; concierge; tour desk; small business center; salon; 24-hr. room service; babysitting; same-day dry cleaning/laundry; nonsmoking rooms; executive-level rooms. *In room:* A/C, satellite TV, dataport, minibar, coffeemaker, hair dryer, safe.

Ramada Plaza Shànghǎi (Nán Xīnyǎ Huáměidá Dàjiǔdiàn)

Opened on the Nánjīng Lù Pedestrian Mall in 1998 by a local millionaire who fell in love with European art, the block-deep, 20-story former Grand Nation Hotel is now under Ramada management. The hotel's cavernous, brightly lit lobby tries very hard for an Old World elegance, with Italian and Spanish marbles, stained-glass skylights, and wainscoting, but it all just seems a bit cold and empty. The staff is efficient enough but don't appear very happy to be there. Competitive discounts and an excellent location right on the pedestrian mall seem to please most guests, however. Rooms, all facing an enormous atrium festooned with Greek statuary and fake palm trees, are unremarkably decorated but comfortable, with firm beds and all the usual four-star amenities.

Nánjīng Dōng Lù 719 (1 block east of Xīzàng Zhōng Lù between Nánjīng Dōng Lù and Jiǔjiāng Lù); see map p. 118. © **800/854-7854** or 021/6350-0000. Fax 021/6350-6666. www.ramadahotels.com. 376 units. ¥1,240 – ¥1,320 ($150–$160) double; ¥1,650 ($200) club room; from ¥1,650 ($200) suite (40% discounts). AE, DC, MC, V. Metro: Rénmín Guǎngchǎng. **Amenities:** 3 restaurants; fitness center with sauna; concierge; business center; salon; 24-hr. room service; same-day dry cleaning/laundry; executive-level rooms. *In room:* A/C, TV, dataport, minibar, coffeemaker, hair dryer, safe.

Sofitel Hyland Hotel (Hǎilún Bīnguǎn) ★

This Accor-managed four-star, 30-story tower in the heart of the pedestrian sector of Nánjīng Lù has a superb downtown location. Opened in 1993, its rooms were renovated in 1998. The rooms themselves are quite small, furnished in light brown tones, with two phones and robes and slippers. Sofitel Club rooms are slightly larger and include a Western buffet breakfast. Entrance from Nánjīng Lù is via stairs and an elevator to the second-floor lobby. There's a European, even French feel to the hotel. Service is mostly efficient, if brusque at times.

Nánjīng Dōng Lù 505 (on Nánjīng Lù Pedestrian Mall); see map p. 118. 🕿 **800/221-4542** or 021/6351-5888. Fax 021/6351-4088. www.accorhotels.com. 389 units. ¥1,640 ($200) double; ¥2,130 ($260) executive level; from ¥1,880 ($230) suite. AE, DC, MC, V. Metro: Hénán Zhōng Lù. **Amenities:** 4 restaurants; deli; 2 lounges; health club with Jacuzzi and sauna; concierge; tour desk; business center; salon; 24-hr. room service; same-day dry cleaning/laundry. *In room:* A/C, satellite TV, dataport, minibar, coffeemaker, hair dryer, safe.

MODERATE

Pacific Hotel (Jīnmén Dàjiǔdiàn)   Just east of the Park Hotel, the three-star, nine-story Pacific Hotel began as the China United Assurance Company in 1926, before becoming the Overseas Chinese Hotel (Huáqiáo Fàndiàn). Changing its name once again to Pacific, it underwent renovation in the late 1990s, preserving its striking colonial portico and small but ornate lobby with coffered ceilings and carved columns in early Italian Renaissance style. It's a fine building but there's a whiff of staleness about the place and the staff appears a little forlorn, though they try their best. Guest rooms facing Nánjīng Lù (¥1,000/$125) have wooden floors and old furniture, while those in the ugly modern annex in the back (¥800/$100) sport carpets and the same dull wooden furniture. Satellite television appears limited to Chinese stations. While services and amenities are just average, the location is great, as are room rates if you bargain hard.

Nánjīng Xī Lù 108 (north of People's Park, west of Xīzàng Lù); see map p. 118. 🕿 **021/6327-6226.** Fax 021/6372-3634. 166 units. ¥800–¥1,000 ($100–$125) double; from ¥1,544 ($193) suite (40% discount). AE, DC, MC, V. Metro: Rénmín Gōngyuán. **Amenities:** 5 restaurants; bar; concierge; tour desk; small business center; room service; dry cleaning/laundry. *In room:* A/C, TV, dataport, minibar.

Park Hotel (Guójì Fàndiàn)   One of the swankiest hotels in old Shànghǎi, the historic Park Hotel was the tallest building in Asia when it opened in 1934 at the north end of what was then Shànghǎi's race course (today's People's Square/Rénmín Guǎngchǎng). A pale version of yesteryear's glory, today's hotel nevertheless retains some of its past elegance in a nicely restored Art Deco lobby. For a four-star hotel, rooms, modernized in 1997, are unexciting but functional, and the marble bathrooms are compact but clean. The service level is adequate at best, but its restaurants (which serve many tour groups) are well regarded, including a 24-hour international buffet on the 14th floor. Ask for a room with a view of Nánjīng Lù (south).

Nánjīng Xī Lù 170 (north of People's Park, west of Xīzàng Lù); see map p. 118. 🕿 **021/6327-5225.** Fax 021/6327-6958. www.parkhotel.com.cn. 250 units. ¥1,245 ($150) double; ¥1,245–¥1,360 ($150–$170) executive level; from ¥1,440 ($180) suite (40% discount). AE, DC, MC, V. Metro: Rénmín Gōngyuán or Rénmín Guǎngchǎng. **Amenities:** 2 restaurants; small health club with sauna; concierge; tour desk; business center; salon; 24-hr. room service; babysitting; dry cleaning/laundry; executive-level rooms. *In room:* A/C, satellite TV, broadband, minibar, hair dryer, safe.

INEXPENSIVE

Yángzǐ Fàndiàn (Yangtze Hotel) ⭐ *Finds*   Conveniently located a block south of the Nánjīng Lù pedestrian mall and a block east of People's Square, this striking Art Deco hotel with white-washed walls and black grill balconies, originally built in 1934 and at that time the third biggest hotel in the Far East, has undergone a complete refurbishment and is today a very popular mid-range choice amongst Chinese business travelers. Rated only three stars, the hotel offers in-room amenities that rival those at four-star outfits further down

Airport Hotels

There are plenty of hotels with free shuttle service near Hóngqiáo Airport. The closest five-star hotel is the **Marriott Hotel Hóng Qiáo** (p. 83), which is still about 6.4km (4 miles) to the east. The **Cypress Hotel** (p. 85) with its manicured lawns and colonial-style houses is nearer (1km/⅔ miles away), but for those who want to be even closer, the highly efficient, Japanese-managed, 308-unit **Shànghǎi International Airport Hotel** (*Shànghǎi* **Guójì Jīchǎng Bīnguǎn,** Hóngqiáo Lù 2550; *①* **021/6268-8866;** fax 021/6268-8393) is the nearest major hotel within a 10-minute walk from the airport. Rooms (¥880/$110 double, 10% service charge) are cozy, modern, and clean, and flight schedule monitors are mounted in the cheery lobby. A free shuttle is available to Hóngqiáo and Pǔdōng airports.

The only hotel currently serving Pǔdōng Airport is the newly opened (Aug 2003) **Ramada Pǔdōng Airport** (Shànghǎi Jīchǎng Huáměidá Dàjiǔdiàn, Qǐháng Lù 1100; *①* **021/3849-4949;** fax 021/6885-2889; www.ramadaairportpd.com), a 2- to 3-minute free shuttle ride or a 10-minute walk from the airport. The hotel has 370 units. Rooms (¥830/$100 double; 15% service charge, 40% discount) are clean and comfortable with the usual amenities, including safe and in-room movies. Both Western and Chinese dining are available.

Nánjīng Lù. Rooms, a portion of which were renovated in 2002, are spacious and come with thick drapes, perfectly comfortable beds, and broadband access. The majority of the staff tries to be helpful though the receptionists are occasionally lackadaisical.

Hànkǒu Lù 740 (east of Xīzàng Zhōng Lù, 1 block south of Nánjīng Dōng Lù); see map p. 118. *①* **021/6351-7880.** Fax 021/6351-6974. www.e-yangtze.com. 183 units. ¥680–¥780 ($85–$98) double; ¥880 ($110) executive; ¥1,280 –¥1,480 ($160–$185) suite (discounts 20%–30% pending occupancy; 10% service charge). AE, DC, MC, V. Metro: Rénmín Guǎngchǎng. **Amenities:** 2 restaurants; lounge; bar; business center; salon; room service; laundry service. *In room:* A/C, TV, broadband, dataport, minibar, hair dryer, safe.

YMCA Hotel (Qīngnián Huì Bīnguǎn)   This historic 11-story brick building, built in 1929, really was the YMCA in colonial times; now it's one of the most popular budget hotels in town, with a slightly dilapidated air but a great location right in the heart of old Shànghǎi. Rooms are drab and not well maintained, and the beds occasionally lumpy, but the bathrooms are at least fairly clean. A small TV on the desk and a hot water thermos constitute your basic amenities. Dorm rooms with shared bathroom facilities are also available though these are spartan at best. A cafe that serves Western food is a big draw for international backpackers. Front desk staff speaks a little English and can be helpful when pressed.

Xīzàng Nán Lú 123 (southeast of Rénmín Guǎngchǎng, north of Huáihǎi Zhōng Lù); see map p. 118. *①* **021/6326-1040.** Fax 021/6320-1957. www.ymcahotel.com. 150 units. ¥531 –¥565 ($64–$68) double; ¥680 ($82) executive; ¥1,204 –¥2,490 ($145–$300) suite (with 10% rather than 15% service charge). AE, DC, MC, V. Metro: Rénmín Guǎngchǎng. **Amenities:** Restaurant; cafe; health club; small business center; salon; room service; next-day dry cleaning/laundry. *In room:* A/C, TV, minibar.

2 Hóngkǒu (Northeast Shànghǎi)

MODERATE

Broadway Mansions Hotel (Shànghǎi Dàshà)   The Art Deco "Shànghǎi Mansions," as it's named in Chinese, has reverted to its original name, the Broadway Mansions, originally built in 1934 as an exclusive residential hotel by the British. Partially renovated in 2003, the 19-floor four-star hotel is now hoping to capitalize on its storied history (the building was sold to the Japanese in 1937 but later housed the Foreign Correspondents' Club of China after World War II) and is eagerly embracing foreign guests. The spacious rooms have high ceilings, firm beds, and central air, though individual old-style heaters remain as a nice touch. Renovated rooms on the fifth and sixth floors are much nicer and even have overhead bedside reading lights. The ¥1,080 ($135) rooms facing the Sūzhōu Creek are absolutely worth splurging on, as there are few other places where you can wake up to the creek, the Bund, *and* Pǔdōng outside your window.

Běi Sūzhōu Lù 20 (north of the Bund across the Sūzhōu River, just west of the Wàibáidù Bridge); see map p. 118. ☏ **021/6324-6260.** Fax 021/6306-5147. www.broadwaymansions.com. 233 units. ¥960 – ¥1,080 ($120–$135) double; ¥1,280 – ¥1,380 ($160–$173) executive level; from ¥1,300 ($163) suite (discounts up to 50% in low season). AE, DC, MC, V. No Metro. **Amenities:** 3 restaurants; bakery; lounge, bar; health club; sauna; concierge; business center; salon; 24-hr. room service; same-day dry cleaning/laundry; executive-level rooms. *In room:* A/C, satellite TV, broadband (executive rooms only), minibar, hair dryer, safe.

Holiday Inn Downtown Shànghǎi (Shànghǎi Guǎngchǎng Chángchéng Jiàrì Jiǔdiàn)   Except for those who need to catch early morning trains, few Western individual travelers stay at this Holiday Inn located just south of the Shànghǎi Railway Station. Even though there's a Metro entrance a mere block away, making access to downtown Shànghǎi relatively easy, the perception remains that it's inconvenient. The neighborhood is also a bit chaotic and there's not much within walking distance. Still, the hotel gamely musters on, relying mostly on business travelers, and offering attractive discounts (Internet rates have sometimes dipped below $50). There are two separate towers: The eastern Plaza Wing is quieter and slightly more upscale than the western Great Wall Wing, though room rates are virtually the same at both. Both wings have elegant lobbies and sparkling modern rooms (fourth- and fifth-floor Plaza Wing rooms were renovated in early 2004) with all the expected four-star amenities. Unfortunately, service is hit-or-miss.

Héngfēng Lù 585 (south side of Shànghǎi Railway Station). ☏ **800/830-6368** or 021/6353-8008. Fax 021/6354-3019. www.holiday-inn.com. 481 units. ¥1,180 ($140) double; ¥1,500 ($180) executive level; from ¥1,660 ($200) suite (30% discounts). AE, DC, MC, V. Metro: Shànghǎi Huǒchē Zhàn. **Amenities:** 3 restaurants; 2 lounges; health club with sauna; bowling alley; concierge; business center; salon; 24-hr. room service; same-day dry cleaning/laundry; nonsmoking rooms; executive-level rooms; rooms for those w/limited mobility. *In room:* A/C, satellite TV, dataport, minibar, coffeemaker, hair dryer, safe.

INEXPENSIVE

Pǔjiāng Fàndiàn (Pǔjiāng Hotel) ✿ *Value*   A backpackers' favorite, this two-star hotel north of the Bund just over the Wàibáidù bridge is loaded with history and colonial atmosphere. Built in 1860 and reconstructed in late Renaissance style on its present site in 1910, it was once known as the Astor House, Shànghǎi's top turn-of-the-century hotel. From 1990 to 1997, part of it even served as the Shànghǎi Stock Exchange. In 2003, the Pǔjiāng underwent the first phase of a much-needed renovation and so far, the results are heartening: the brick-enclosed inner courtyard on the third floor now leads to rooms that have been refurbished and stripped down to accentuate the building's original highlights (high ceilings, carved moldings, and wooden floors). Beds are firm and comfortable, bathrooms large and clean, and there are even little flourishes like old-fashioned dial telephones. Visitors can also choose from four restored "celebrity rooms," once occupied by famous visitors such as U.S. President Ulysses S. Grant in 1879 (Room 410), Scott Joplin in 1931 and 1936 (Room 404), Bertrand Russell in 1920 (Room 310), and Albert Einstein in 1922 (Room 304).

Huángpǔ Lù 15 (northeast side of Sūzhōu Creek, north of the Bund); see map p. 118. ✆ **021/6324-6388.** Fax 021/6324-3179. 116 units. ¥420–¥680 ($53–$85) double; ¥880 ($110) celebrity room; ¥55 ($7) dorm (20%–40% discount on doubles, 10% service charge). AE, DC, MC, V. Metro: Hénán Zhōng Lù (about a mile away). **Amenities:** Restaurant; Internet cafe; spa; bike rental; tour desk; self-service laundry. *In room:* A/C, TV, fridge (select rooms).

3 Lúwān (French Concession)

VERY EXPENSIVE

Okura Garden Hotel Shànghǎi (Huāyuán Fàndiàn) ★★   The top hotel in the French Concession, the five-star Japanese-managed Okura was built in 1990 on the site of the 1920s French Club and Cercle Sportif. The Art Deco features of the original structure have been preserved in its east lobby and grand ballroom with its gorgeous elliptical stained glass ceiling. Out front, the sprawling lawns with the gazebo were once the strolling grounds for Máo Zédōng. The 34-story tower that now rises above the original building is impeccably maintained and elegant throughout. The rooms are of average size, with white marble bathrooms that contain phones and potable tap water. Room renovations started in 2004 will continue for the next few years. With extensive and first-rate facilities and highly efficient service, there's little to complain of here. Japanese visitors dominate.

Màomíng Nán Lù 58 (1 block north of Huáihǎi Zhōng Lù); see map p. 122. ✆ **021/6415-1111.** Fax 021/ 6415-8866. www.gardenhotelshanghai.com. 500 units. ¥2,240–¥2,560 ($270–$310) double; ¥2,970– ¥3,200 ($360–$400) executive level; from ¥4,400 ($550) suite (40% discount). AE, DC, MC, V. Metro: Shǎnxī Nán Lù. **Amenities:** 4 restaurants; cafe; 3 bars; 25m (82-ft.) indoor swimming pool; 2 lighted outdoor tennis courts; health club with Jacuzzi and sauna; concierge; tour desk; business center; salon; 24-hr. room service; same-day dry cleaning/laundry; nonsmoking rooms; executive-level rooms. *In room:* A/C, satellite TV, dataport, minibar, hot water maker, hair dryer, safe.

EXPENSIVE

Jǐn Jiāng Hotel (Jǐn Jiāng Fàndiàn) ★   The most famous hotel in the French Concession, the Jǐn Jiāng Hotel opened its doors in 1929 as the Cathay Mansions but is best remembered as the location for the signing of the Shànghǎi Communique by President Nixon and Zhōu Ēnlái in 1972, re-establishing U.S.–China relations. Today's complex includes three major edifices: the 1929 North Building (Běilóu), remodeled as a five-star hotel; the central Grosvenor House (1931), with its facade an imitation of the Barclay-Vessey Building in New York City, recently redone as a five-star all-suite deluxe hotel; and the old South Building, which is closed for renovation until 2005 when it will be a four-star hotel catering mostly to tour groups. The Grosvenor House, reserved for long-term business guests, contains 28 suites with kitchens, and a Presidential suite containing Chairman Máo's desk and easy chair (with a concealed compartment on the right side for a pistol). Rooms in the North Building, where most guests are quartered, were remodeled in 1999 and have high ceilings, brown shutters, somewhat worn carpets, and separate tubs and showers in the marble bathrooms. Everything's just a little bit worn here for a five-star outfit, and the service, still lagging behind the international chains, is adequate though hardly exemplary. However, its excellent location in the very heart of the French Concession puts you just steps from some fine restaurants and shops.

Màomíng Nán Lù 59 (1 block north of Huáihǎi Zhōng Lù); see map p. 122. ⓒ 021/6258-2582. Fax 021/6472-5588. www.jinjianghotelshanghai.com. 515 units. ¥1,640–¥1,960 ($205–$245) double (North Building); from ¥2,400 ($300) suite (30% discount). AE, DC, MC, V. Metro: Shǎnxī Nán Lù. **Amenities:** 23 restaurants; food street on hotel grounds; 20m (66-ft.) indoor swimming pool; health club with Jacuzzi and sauna; 6-lane bowling alley; concierge; tour desk; business center; shopping street; salon; 24-hr. room service; same-day dry cleaning/laundry; nonsmoking rooms; executive-level rooms. *In room:* A/C, satellite TV, dataport, minibar, coffeemaker, hair dryer, safe.

Jǐn Jiāng Tower (Xīn Jǐn Jiāng Dàjiǔdiàn) ⚞
When it opened in 1988, this 43-story circular tower was the first Chinese-managed international luxury hotel in Shànghǎi. Renovations, most recently in 2002, have kept it in the five-star echelon. Whereas the Jǐn Jiāng Hotel is historic, everything about the Tower is modern and glossy, starting with its three-story marble lobby with plenty of colored glass. Guest rooms are rather small but well equipped. Service is fairly good, and the hotel has a prime location in the French Concession, but with so many Chinese and Western tour groups traipsing through, you're unlikely to get much personal attention. The best feature of the hotel is its sightseeing elevators that whisk guests to the rooftop revolving restaurant. Even if you don't stay or dine here, it's worth taking a ride up for the free views of Shànghǎi.

Chánglè Lù 161 (corner of Ruìjīn Yī Lù); see map p. 122. ⓒ 021/6415-1188. Fax 021/6415-0045. www.jjtcn.com. 728 units. ¥1,520–¥1,660 ($190–$200) double; from ¥3,200 ($400) suite. AE, DC, MC, V. Metro: Shǎnxī Nán Lù. **Amenities:** 3 restaurants; outdoor swimming pool; health club with Jacuzzi and sauna; concierge; tour desk; business center; shopping arcade; salon; 24-hr. room service; same-day dry cleaning/laundry. *In room:* A/C, satellite TV, dataport, minibar, coffeemaker, hair dryer, safe.

MODERATE

City Hotel (Chéngshì Jiǔdiàn)
Formerly a basic three-star business hotel catering mostly to Chinese business guests, the 26-story City Hotel has been renovated (2003) into a nicer, more professional four-star outfit attracting some international clientele as well. The modern guest rooms are still fairly plain and simple, and superior rooms run small, but are otherwise comfortable enough with firm beds and clean bathrooms. The staff seems to have improved their English but communication remains basic. Unfortunately, what is usually standard practice at equivalent four-star hotels (such as the free use of the hotel gym, swimming pool, and sauna for all guests) is touted here as extra benefits (except for guests in superior rooms who have to pay a use fee) and comes across as ungenerous at best. Still this centrally located hotel's chief appeal is its lower room rates, which, pending occupancy, can be up to 60% off on online hotel booking sites.

Shǎnxī Nán Lù 5–7 (south of Yán'ān Zhōng Lù); see map p. 122. ⓒ 021/6255-1133. Fax 021/6255-0211. www.cityhotelshanghai.com. 272 units. ¥1,300–¥1,500 ($163–$188) double; ¥1,800 ($225) executive level (40% discount). AE, DC, MC, V. Metro: Shǎnxī Nán Lù (5 blocks). **Amenities:** 3 restaurants; bar; indoor pool; fitness center with sauna; business center; 24-hr. room service; same-day dry cleaning/laundry. *In room:* A/C, satellite TV, dataport, minibar, coffeemaker, hair dryer, safe (in deluxe rooms).

Ruìjīn Bīnguǎn (Ruìjīn Hotel) ⚞
Right in the heart of the French concession, this pleasing 1930s colonial-style hotel is located on the grounds of the former Morris Estate. Owner of the *North China Daily News*, the oldest English-language newspaper in China, Morris also bred greyhounds, which he would race at the dog track located just behind his compound. Today, a number

of faux "old" houses have been added to the four original villas, and this grand estate occupying a whole city block is now home to offices, long-term rental villas, and a number of top restaurants and bars including Face, Lan Na Thai, and Hazarra. Clutter and traffic notwithstanding, it's still delightful to stroll the well-manicured lawns, though you'll likely have to share it with scads of wedding couples posing for photographs. Guest rooms, located in the largest of the original villas and renovated around 3 years ago, are comfortable enough with firm beds with fresh soft linens. Be sure to ask for a garden-view room. The facilities and the service may not be the finest for what you're paying, but the overall atmosphere of colonial Shànghǎi, at least the refined version of it, is unbeatable.

Ruìjīn Èr Lù 118 (south of Fùxīng Zhōng Lù); see map p. 122. ℂ **021/6472-5222.** Fax 021/6473-2277. www.shedi.net.cn/outEDI/Ruijin. 62 units. ¥1,200 ($150) double; from ¥2,400 ($300) suite (30% discount). AE, DC, MC, V. Metro: Shǎnxī Nán Lù. **Amenities:** Restaurant; bar; concierge; business center; salon; room service; next-day dry cleaning/laundry. *In room:* A/C, satellite TV, dataport, minibar, safe (select rooms).

4 Xúhuì (Southwest Shànghǎi)

EXPENSIVE

Huá Tíng Hotel & Towers (Huá Tíng Bīnguǎn)   Opened in 1986 as the first foreign-managed luxury hotel in Shànghǎi, the former Sheraton Huá Tíng reverted to local management in 1996. A couple of renovations since then have kept its five-star facilities in reasonably good repair. Rooms vary in size depending on where they're located in the "S" shaped building. Deluxe rooms, most recently renovated in July 2003 (and larger and considerably nicer than the unrenovated superior rooms), sport modern furniture, thick carpets, and comfortable beds. Marble bathrooms are simple but clean and come with full amenities. This is the nicest hotel in the Shànghǎi Stadium area, but service is just average, so stay here only if you can arrange a substantial savings on room rates.

Cáo Xī Běi Lù 1200 (west of Shànghǎi Stadium/Shànghǎi Tǐyùguǎn); see map p. 122. ℂ **021/6439-1000.** Fax 021/6255-0830. www.huating-hotel.com. 1,008 units. ¥1,880 – ¥1,960 ($235–$245) double; from ¥2,440 ($305) suite (30%–50% discounts). AE, DC, MC, V. Metro: Shànghǎi Tǐyùguǎn. **Amenities:** 3 restaurants; deli; 2 bars; indoor pool; outdoor lighted tennis courts; health club with Jacuzzi and sauna; bowling alley; concierge; tour desk; business center; salon; 24-hr. room service; same-day dry cleaning/laundry; nonsmoking rooms; executive-level rooms. *In room:* A/C, satellite TV, dataport, minibar, coffeemaker, hair dryer, safe.

Regal International East Asia Hotel (Fùháo Huánqiú Dōngyà Jiǔdiàn) ⓐ
The best luxury hotel in the district, the Regal has all the trappings of a grand hotel, from its expansive white marble lobby to superb health and fitness facilities. Opened in 1997, this 22-story hotel, managed by an international team, has bright, modern guest rooms with bedside electronic controls, robes, slippers, and all the amenities of a five-star establishment. Its Shànghǎi International Tennis Center offers Shànghǎi's best facilities, including a center court that seats 1,200 spectators. It's located along trendy Héngshān Lù, and the Metro is just a block away. Service is efficient enough, but drops off when it gets busy. *Tip:* Request a room number that ends in "9"—these are significantly larger than the rest.

Héngshān Lù 516 (west of Wúxìng Lù); see map p. 122. ℂ **800/222-8888** or 021/6415-5588. Fax 021/6445-8899. www.regal-eastasia.com. 300 units. ¥2,480 – ¥2,640 ($310–$330) double; ¥3,280 ($410) executive level (30%–40% discount in low season, otherwise 10%–20%). AE, DC, MC, V. Metro: Héngshān Lù. **Amenities:** 3 restaurants; lounge; 25m (82-ft.) indoor pool; 10 championship tennis courts; indoor squash court; extensive health club and spa with Jacuzzi and sauna; game room; 12-lane bowling alley; concierge; tour desk; business center; salon; 24-hr. room service; babysitting; same-day dry cleaning/laundry; nonsmoking rooms; 4 executive-level floors. *In room:* A/C, satellite TV, broadband, minibar, coffeemaker, hair dryer, safe.

MODERATE

Héngshān Bīnguǎn (Héngshān Hotel)   Located just south of the Regal International Hotel, this four-star French modern hotel, formerly the Picardie Apartments built in 1934, still looks rather old and wan on the outside, but the inside was thoroughly renovated in 2002 and now offers a comfortable stay at reasonable prices. Rooms are spacious and equipped with modern furniture and full amenities. Another good sign: The carpets are still relatively stain-free. If all the double rooms are being discounted to the same rate (as they often are), be sure to ask for the higher-end doubles (known as Superior Room A), as these have large bathrooms that come with separate tub and shower and even a television set. Service is on a par with your average Chinese-managed four-star hotel, which is to say, adequate for basic needs. It's a short walk to the subway, shops, and restaurants just up Héngshān Lù, and only a slightly longer walk to the Xújiāhuì area to the south.

Héngshān Lù 534 (south of Huáihǎi Lù at the intersection with Wǎnpíng Lù); see map p. 122. © 021/6437-7050. Fax 021/6433-5732. hshs@81890.net. 238 units. ¥828–¥952 ($100–$115) double; ¥1,127–¥1,252 ($136–$151) executive level; from ¥1,518 ($183) suite (discount 20%–30%). AE, DC, MC, V. Metro: Héngshān Lù. **Amenities:** 3 restaurants; lounge; bar; sauna; concierge; airline ticket office; business center; salon; 24-hr. room service; dry cleaning/laundry. *In room:* A/C, satellite TV, dataport, minibar, hair dryer, safe.

Tàiyuán Biéshù (Tàiyuán Villa) ★ *Finds*   Run by the same folks at the Ruìjīn Hotel, this villa is a more peaceful and possibly nicer option than the Ruìjīn. Also known as the Marshall House for American general George Marshall who stayed here between 1945 and 1949 when he was mediating between Máo Zédōng and Chiang Kai-shek, this magnificent mansion, originally built in 1920, was also one of many homes of Jiāng Qīng (also known as Mme. Máo) between 1949 and 1976. Dining options and facilities are fewer than at the Ruìjīn, though guests can use the pool and business center in the brand-new wing built in 2002 and currently catering only to long-term guests. No loss considering that the old mansion, with its dark wood paneling, grand circular stairwell, and large and comfortable rooms (now carpeted and adorned with modern furniture), is where you want to be. The grounds are some of the quietest you'll find in central Shànghǎi.

Tàiyuán Lù 160 (south of Yǒngjiā Lù, east of Yuèyáng Lù); see map p. 122. © 021/6471-6688. Fax 021/6471-2618. 19 units. ¥1,200 ($150) double; ¥2,400 ($300) master suite (20% discount). AE, DC, MC, V. Metro: Héngshān Lù. **Amenities:** Restaurant; indoor pool; fitness center; business center; room service (30% service charge); dry cleaning/laundry. *In room:* A/C, TV, dataport, fridge.

INEXPENSIVE

Shànghǎi Conservatory of Music Guest House (Shànghǎi Yīnyuè Xuéyuàn) *Finds*   Located on the lovely grounds of the Shànghǎi Music Conservatory are some of the cheapest accommodations you'll find in the former French Concession, if not in all of Shànghǎi. There are dorm beds and doubles with shared bathrooms in ugly concrete bunkers, but the hidden gem is the three double rooms (¥300/$38) with en suite bathroom on the second floor of the considerably more beautiful Zhuānjiā Lóu (Experts' Building). This three-story stucco colonial mansion, its beauty unfortunately somewhat marred by a recent coat of green paint, was once the old Brazilian consulate. The rooms here are large and have intact their original fireplaces and wooden floors, while bathrooms have blue-and-white porcelain sinks. The rooms also open onto gloriously spacious balconies where you can while away many a peaceful, lethargic afternoon. On the ground floor is the conservatory's restaurant, which serves decent and inexpensive *jiācháng cài* (home-style cooking).

Fēnyáng Lù 20 (east of Chángshú Lù, south of Huáihǎi Zhōng Lù); see map p. 122. © 021/6437-2577. Fax 021/6437-2577. 60 units. ¥100–¥300 ($13–$38) double; ¥50 ($6.25) dorm. No credit cards. Metro: Chángshú Lù. **Amenities:** Restaurant; laundry.

5 Jìng Ān (Northwest Shànghǎi)

VERY EXPENSIVE

Four Seasons Hotel Shànghǎi (Shànghǎi Sìjì Jiǔdiàn) ★★★   This relative newcomer (2002) to the Shànghǎi luxury hotel scene introduces the signature Four Seasons service and pampering to China. Well located right in the thick of Pǔxī (Nánjīng Lù is a 5-min. walk and the Shànghǎi Museum a 10-min. stroll), this modern 37-story tower boasts an elegant white and gold Italian marble lobby, tropical palm trees in the three-story atrium lounge, and alabaster chandeliers from Spain. No less lavish, rooms and suites are spacious and warmly decorated in gold and beige with red and blue trims. The furniture is classical and the patented Four Seasons bed alone is worth the stay. Each room is also equipped with three telephones, high-speed Internet access, *yukatas* (thin, unlined kimonos), and safes large enough for laptop computers. Marble bathrooms have separate shower and tub. Best of all, this hotel delivers impeccable service, from their 24-hour butler service for each guest to the highly efficient and friendly multilingual staff throughout the hotel.

Wēihǎi Lù 500 (at Shímén Yī Lù, between Nánjīng Xī Lù and Yán'ān Zhōng Lù); see map p. 126. ℂ **800/819-5053** or 021/6256-8888. Fax 021/6256-5678. www.fourseasons.com. 439 units. ¥2,500–¥2,900 ($312–$362) double; from ¥3,300 ($412) suite; ¥400–¥900 ($50–$110) extra for executive lounge benefits. AE, DC, MC, V. Metro: Shímén Yī Lù. **Amenities:** 4 restaurants; lounge; jazz bar; 20m (66-ft.) indoor pool; state-of-the-art health club and spa with Jacuzzi and sauna; concierge; 24-hr. business center; salon; 24-hr. room service; babysitting; same-day dry cleaning/laundry; nonsmoking floors; rooms for those w/limited mobility. *In room:* A/C, satellite TV, broadband, minibar, coffeemaker, hair dryer, safe, butler service.

Hilton Hotel (Jìng Ān Xīěrdùn Dàjiǔdiàn) ★★★ *Value*   Shànghǎi's first foreign-owned hotel (1987), the comparatively low-profile 43-story Hilton still rates among the very best of the city's hotels, even as it's been buffeted in recent years by an increasing number of ever-more-opulent five-star luxury hotels. In 2003, the hotel began some much-needed renovations and upgrades, which will continue well into 2005. Standard guest rooms, spacious and bright with firm beds and classic furniture, are a bit fatigued, but when fully renovated, they will eventually include flatscreen televisions, bedside controlled lighting, and broadband connection. There are also plans to make the lobby—among the most bustling in Shànghǎi—a wireless zone. Besides a slew of fine international restaurants, the hotel also boasts the fully renovated Spa at the Hilton (with reflexology, seaweed treatments, acupuncture, and more), which has few rivals. Above all, however, it's the hotel's top-notch service and highly competent staff that makes it a favorite of Western business travelers. Its prime location—within walking distance of the attractions of Héngshān Lù and the French Concession—doesn't hurt either.

Huáshān Lù 250 (1 block south of Yán'ān Zhōng Lù); see map p. 126. ℂ **800/445-8667** or 021/6248-0000. Fax 021/6248-3848. www.hilton.com. 720 units. ¥2,183 ($264) double; ¥2,638 ($319) executive level; from ¥4,300 ($520) suite (up to 60% discount pending occupancy). AE, DC, MC, V. Metro: Jìng Ān Sì. **Amenities:** 6 restaurants; deli; 2 lounges; indoor swimming pool; outdoor tennis court; squash court; state-of-the-art health club and spa with Jacuzzi and sauna; concierge; business center; 24-hr. room service; babysitting; same-day dry cleaning/laundry; nonsmoking rooms; executive-level rooms. *In room:* A/C, satellite TV, broadband, minibar, coffeemaker, hair dryer, safe.

Portman Ritz-Carlton Hotel (Shànghǎi Bōtèmàn Lìjiā Dàjiǔdiàn) ★★★
Despite some heavy competition, this is still Shànghǎi's top choice for many business travelers and world leaders (George W. Bush stayed here during the APEC Conference in 2001). Fully renovated in 2000 to the tune of $30 million,

the 50-story Portman offers all the luxury and service associated with the Ritz-Carlton brand. The elegance extends from the two-story lobby, with its fiber-optic lighting, laminated stacked-glass sculptures, Indonesian ebony columns, and marble and limestone walls, to rooms that are large, plush, and well fitted with writing desks, sofas, three phones, thick duvets, and all the amenities you could want. Service is as you'd expect—professional and excellent. The adjacent Shànghăi Centre provides one-stop shopping with airline offices, a medical clinic, a supermarket, a post office, automatic teller machines, an American Express office, a performing arts theater, upscale boutiques, and a little-known cafe called Starbucks.

Nánjīng Xī Lù 1376 (Shànghăi Centre); see map p. 126. © **800/241-3333** or 021/6279-8888. Fax 021/6279-8800. www.ritzcarlton.com. 564 units. ¥2,075 ($250) double. AE, DC, MC, V. Metro: Jìng Ān Sì. **Amenities:** 3 restaurants; 2 lounges; indoor/outdoor 20m (66-ft.) swimming pool; indoor tennis court; 2 indoor squash courts; indoor racquetball court; 3-story health club; Jacuzzi; sauna; concierge; 24-hr. business center; shopping arcade; grocery; salon; 24-hr. room service; babysitting; same-day dry cleaning/laundry; non-smoking rooms; executive-level rooms; World Link Medical Center; rooms for those w/limited mobility. *In room:* A/C, satellite TV, broadband, minibar, coffeemaker, hair dryer, safe.

Shànghăi JC Mandarin (Jìncāng Wénhuá Dàjiŭdiàn) ✦ *Kids*   This five-star, 30-story luxury hotel with management from the Singapore Meritus group seems perpetually consigned to the shadow of the neighboring Portman Ritz-Carlton, but manages to hold its own with big tour group bookings from Southeast Asia. It also boasts a special play area for children (a rarity in Shànghăi). The lobby has a glorious hand-painted mural of Míng Dynasty admiral Zhèng Hé (China's Columbus). Rooms, most recently renovated in 2002, are large and plush and have all the expected amenities. Overall service is efficient, though if the reception staff has a sense of humor, they're careful not to show it.

Nánjīng Xī Lù 1225 (1 block east of Shànghăi Centre); see map p. 126. © **021/6279-1888.** Fax 021/6279-1822. www.jcmandarin.com. 510 units. ¥1,945 ($243) double; ¥2,445 ($305) executive level (40% discount). AE, DC, MC, V. Metro: Jìng Ān Sì. **Amenities:** 2 restaurants; deli; 2 lounges; large swimming pool; 2 outdoor tennis courts and 1 indoor squash court; health club with Jacuzzi and sauna; game room; concierge; tour desk; 24-hr. business center; salon; 24-hr. room service; babysitting; same-day dry cleaning/laundry; non-smoking rooms; executive-level rooms. *In room:* A/C, satellite TV, broadband, minibar, coffeemaker, hair dryer, iron, safe.

EXPENSIVE

Hotel Equatorial (Guójì Guìdū Dàjiŭdiàn) ✦   This four-star hotel, located just north of the Hilton, has resuscitated its reputation from the late 1990s when it was perceived as a somewhat sordid hotel where solicitations were common-place. International management of the 27-story tower, provided by a Singapore group, now seems determined to maintain a squeaky clean image. Guest rooms, renovated in 2000, are bright and airy, with just enough room for a work desk, coffee table, and two chairs. Fitness facilities, refurbished in 2002 at a cost of $1.5 million, are extensive, as are the dining options. Guests hail from Singapore, Southeast Asia, North America, and Europe, giving the generally helpful staff plenty of opportunities to practice their English, which is quite good.

Yán'ān Xī Lù 65 (south of Jìng Ān Gōngyuán); see map p. 126. © **021/6248-1688.** Fax 021/6248-1773. www.equatorial.com. 509 units. ¥1,760 ($220) double; ¥2,000 ($250) executive floor (up to 60% discount pending occupancy). Children 18 and under stay free in parent's room. AE, DC, MC, V. Metro: Jìng Ān Sì. **Amenities:** 5 restaurants; deli; 2 lounges; 20m (66-ft.) indoor swimming pool; lighted outdoor tennis court; squash court; health club with Jacuzzi and sauna; 6-lane bowling alley; concierge; tour desk; business center; shopping arcade; salon; 24-hr. room service; babysitting; same-day dry cleaning/laundry; nonsmoking rooms; executive-level rooms. *In room:* A/C, satellite TV, dataport, minibar, coffeemaker, hair dryer, safe.

MODERATE

Héngshān Moller Villa (Héngshān Mǎlè Biéshù Fàndiàn)   The best way to approach and appreciate this eye-catching hotel is in the same state of mind that first conceived it: hallucinatory. A famous curiosity around town (p. 160), this Gothic/Tudor fantasia of brown-tiled steeples, gables, and spires was constructed by a Swedish shipping magnate, Eric Moller, in 1936. From 1949 until 2001, it was used as the headquarters of the Shànghǎi Communist Youth League. In 2001, the Héngshān Group restored the original mansion, added several hideous imitation buildings in the back, and reopened it all as a hotel. Inside the lobby of the original house, chandeliers and gilded furniture clash loudly with marble pillars, parquet floors, and a Chinese moon gate. Rooms here (all "superior business rooms" priced at ¥1,500/$180), with high ceilings, dark wood paneling, and thick drapes, are comfortable enough but overpriced; cheaper standard rooms in the back annex are dull. Despite a prime location at the northwestern edge of the French Concession, this hotel delivers poor value for money, trading heavily instead on its bizarre history and eclectic architecture.

Shǎnxī Nán Lù 30 (south side of Yán'ān Zhōng Lù); see map p. 126. ℂ 021/6247-8881. Fax 021/6289-1020. www.mollervilla.com. 45 units. ¥650 – ¥780 ($80–$95) double; ¥850 – ¥5,000 ($105–$602); 10% discount. AE, DC, MC, V. Metro: Shǎnxī Nán Lù. **Amenities:** Restaurant; bar; access to health club, pool, sauna and tennis court at the Shànghǎi Grand Club next door; business center; room service; dry cleaning/laundry. *In room:* A/C, satellite TV, dataport, minibar, hair dryer (select rooms).

Shànghǎi Hotel (Shànghǎi Bīnguǎn)   Formerly a three-star hotel, this 30-story tower under local management was partially renovated in early 2004 and is now aiming for four-star status. Most guests are Chinese, but the staff can handle non-Chinese guests as well. Guest rooms are fully modernized, with blue-tone decor, a work desk, and room for two chairs and a coffee table. If you want to be near the French Concession with convenient access to the trendy cafes of Héngshān Lù, but the prices at the adjacent Hilton and Equatorial hotels are too steep, the Shànghǎi will work.

Wǔlǔmùqí Běi Lù 505 (west of the Hilton, south of Yán'ān Zhōng Lù); see map p. 126. ℂ 021/6248-0088. Fax 021/6248-1056. 543 units. ¥988 ($123) double; ¥1,888 ($236) executive level; from ¥2,588 ($323) suite (10% service charge, 20%–30% discount). AE, DC, MC, V. Metro: Jìng Ān Sì. **Amenities:** 3 restaurants; small health club with Jacuzzi and sauna; tour desk; business center; shopping arcade; 24-hr. room service; next-day dry cleaning/laundry. *In room:* A/C, TV, minibar, hot pot, hair dryer.

INEXPENSIVE

Jùyīng Hotel (Jùyīng Bīnguǎn) ★ *Finds*   One of Shànghǎi's best-kept secrets for inexpensive, no frills, but perfectly charming accommodations, the Jùyīng, once restricted to members of the Chinese air force, is located just inside a large breezy compound of colonial villas. For those who don't need the full facilities and services of a hotel (the small guesthouse doesn't even have its own dining room, but there are three restaurants on the premises including the Vietnamese restaurant Cochinchina), this is an excellent opportunity to stay in a French Concession villa for a relative pittance. Wood-paneled rooms are decorated with somewhat scuffed-up old furniture, but are otherwise spacious and immaculate, and beds are comfortable. The charming attic rooms with sloping dormer windows that overlook the garden should be your first request (they're also cheaper at ¥400/$50 before discounts). The staff speaks no English but they're used to handling foreigners who are usually referred here by expatriate friends in the know.

Jùlù Lù 889 (east of Chángshú Lù, 1 block south of Yán'ān Lù); see map p. 126. ℂ 021/6466-7788, ext. 885/886. Fax 021/6445-9228. 12 units. ¥450 ($56) double (discounts 20%–30%). AE, DC, MC, V. Metro: Chángshú Lù. **Amenities:** 3 restaurants; business center. *In room:* A/C, TV.

6 Chángníng/Hóngqiáo Development Zone (West Shànghăi)

VERY EXPENSIVE

Shànghăi Marriott Hotel Hóng Qiáo (Shànghăi Wànháo Hóng Qiáo Dàjiŭdiàn) ★★ This grand five-star, eight-story Marriott is the top hotel address in the Hóngqiáo Airport neighborhood and appeals primarily to upscale conference delegates and travelers whose business takes them to western Shànghăi. (Microsoft's Bill Gates and Hewlett-Packard's Carly Fiorina have already dropped by.) Among its high-tech features is wireless broadband Internet access, available from rooms, restaurants, and the lobby. The guest rooms themselves are large and gracefully appointed with comfortable beds and DVD players. The zoo is a short walk away, but other attractions require a short taxi ride to town. The hotel is often sold out during weekdays but offers substantial discounts on weekends.

Hóngqiáo Lù 2270 (6.4km/4 miles east of Hóngqiáo Airport); see map p. 134. ✆ 800/228-9290 or 021/6237-6000. Fax 021/6237-6222. www.marriott.com. 315 units. ¥1,900 ($237) double; ¥2,500 ($312) executive level; from ¥3,300 ($412) suite (up to 50% discount pending occupancy). AE, DC, MC, V. No Metro. **Amenities:** 3 restaurants; deli; lounge; sports bar; indoor pool; outdoor tennis court; health club with Jacuzzi and sauna; concierge; business center; salon; 24-hr. room service; same-day dry cleaning/laundry; executive-level rooms. *In room:* A/C, satellite TV, dataport, minibar, coffeemaker, hair dryer, safe.

Sheraton Grand Tài Píng Yáng (Xĭ Lái Dēng Háo Dá Tài Píng Yáng Dà Fàndiàn) ★★★ The switch from the Westin brand to the Sheraton brand in early 2002 saw the complete renovation of guest rooms (followed by a furbished lobby in early 2004), but otherwise, little that matters has changed at this 27-story five-star outfit, which remains the best hotel in a cluster of good hotels in the heart of the Hóngqiáo Development Zone. Business travelers love it, not just for the location (halfway between the old Hóngqiáo Airport and downtown), but for the highly efficient service and the lush yet homey atmosphere. Rooms are still on the small side but are now decorated in a plush mix of Chinese and Western styles, with rich carpeting, overstuffed chairs, and a classical rollout desk top right under Chinese artwork. Bathrooms are sleek and modern with glass sinks, but rubber duckies in the bathtubs add a little touch of home. The hotel has a full range of dining, entertainment, and business-related facilities and can also arrange tee times and transportation to the Shànghăi International Golf and Country Club. Its deli, Bauernstube, is the best.

Zūnyì Nán Lù 5 (1 block north of Yán'ān Xī Lù); see map p. 134. ✆ 800/325-3535 or 021/6275-8888. Fax 021/6275-5420. www.sheratongrand-shanghai.com. 496 units. ¥1,909 – ¥2,324 ($230–$280) double; ¥2,614 ($315) executive-level double; from ¥3,884 ($468) suite. AE, DC, MC, V. No Metro station. **Amenities:** 5 restaurants; deli; 3 lounges; indoor swimming pool; health club with Jacuzzi and sauna; concierge; business center; salon; 24-hr. room service; babysitting; same-day dry cleaning/laundry; nonsmoking rooms; executive-level rooms; rooms for those w/limited mobility. *In room:* A/C, satellite TV, broadband, dataport, minibar, coffeemaker, hair dryer, iron, safe.

EXPENSIVE

Crowne Plaza Shànghăi (Shànghăi Yínxīng Huángguān Jiŭdiàn) ★ This 26-story, four-star hotel was upgraded to a deluxe Holiday Inn Crowne Plaza in 1993, but has dropped the Holiday Inn name. It is a fine hotel that enjoys a less than perfect location (too far to walk to much, including the Metro), unless you're in town for the Shànghăi International Film Festival that is held next door at the Shànghăi Film City (Shànghăi Yĭngchéng). Renovations in the last 2 years have ensured a consistent maintenance of facilities, and service remains friendly and attentive. Rooms are large, comfortable, and fully functional if not terribly luxurious, though the higher-level deluxe rooms are considerably warmer. Bathrooms run small throughout.

Pānyú Lù 400 (north of Huáihǎi Xī Lù, off Xīnhuá Lù); see map p. 134. ✆ **800/465-4329** or 021/6280-8888. Fax 021/6280-3353. www.shanghai.crowneplaza.com. 496 units. ¥1,909 ($230) superior; ¥2,075 ($250) deluxe; ¥2,573 ($310) executive level (seasonal discounts up to 45%). Children under 12 stay free in parent's room. AE, DC, MC, V. No Metro station. **Amenities:** 5 restaurants; deli; lounge; bar; indoor swimming pool; health club with sauna; concierge; tour desk; business center; salon; 24-hr. room service; babysitting; same-day dry cleaning/laundry; nonsmoking rooms; 8 executive-level floors; rooms for those w/limited mobility. *In room:* A/C, satellite TV, broadband, minibar, coffeemaker, hair dryer, safe.

Mayfair Hotel (Bālí Chūntiān Dàjiǔdiàn) ✰ The newest addition (Sept 2003) to the already crowded Shànghǎi luxury hotel scene, the Mayfair also claims to be the largest. Managed by the Hong Kong New World Group, the hotel is actually part of a giant complex comprising service apartments and a massive shopping mall. Located on the southern edge of Zhōngshān Park in a newly developing area, the hotel attracts mostly business travelers, but a nearby Metro station makes it accessible enough for the average tourist. The 60% discount introductory promotions tend to be a lure as well. Rooms are located in two wings, though the nicer deluxe rooms (¥1,388/$173) are all in the main wing, and are spacious and appointed with all the expected five-star luxuries. Marble bathrooms are a little small but immaculate. Request a room with a view of the park. Regular rooms in the "new" wing are considerably smaller and a bit inconvenient, as access to restaurants and facilities in the main wing require an additional change of elevators. The staff tries hard to please, but at press time, the hotel was still battling the usual teething problems.

Dingxī Lù 1555 (south of Zhōngshān Gōngyuán); see map p. 134. ✆ **021/6240-8888.** Fax 021/6240-7777. www.mayfairshanghai.com. 860 units. ¥988 – ¥1,388 ($123–$173) double; ¥2,000 ($250) executive room (promotions to 60% discount). AE, DC, MC, V. Metro: Zhōngshān Gōngyuán. **Amenities:** 3 restaurants; 2 bars; outdoor swimming pool; squash court; health club with Jacuzzi and sauna; concierge; tour desk; business center; shopping arcade; salon; 24-hr. room service; same-day dry cleaning/laundry; nonsmoking rooms; executive-level rooms. *In room:* A/C, satellite TV, broadband, minibar, coffeemaker, hair dryer, safe.

Radisson Plaza Xīng Guó Hotel (Shànghǎi Xīng Guó Bīnguǎn) ✰ The new Radisson in Shànghǎi (2002) has a sense of colonial history: Its pretty 70,000 sq. m. (752,773 sq. ft.) of old gardens and bungalows date to the 1920s when the John Swire Company had offices here. Today, a brand-new 16-story, five-star hotel tower offers state-of-the-art facilities and plush modern rooms with large work desks and full amenities. Individual travelers can also stay in the three-star Bungalow Number One, which may lack all the modern touches but offers plenty of Old World charm with its arched ceilings, wooden paneling, and grand winding staircase. (Máo Zédōng was a frequent guest in the days when this was the Xīng Guó Hotel.) The spacious rooms come with old brown furniture, new beds with soft linens, and hot water thermoses. Service is very friendly throughout, but the Radisson's main drawback could be its location in the serene but somewhat remote diplomatic precinct, a long walk to the nearest Metro station, tourist attraction, or entertainment district (but within minutes by taxi).

Xīngguó Lù 78 (junction of Xīngguó, Jiāngsū, and Huáshān Lù at western end of French Concession); see map p. 134. ✆ **021/6212-9998.** Fax 021/6212-9996. www.radisson.com/shanghaicn_plaza. 190 units. ¥1,990 – ¥2,160 ($248–$270) double; from ¥2,740 ($340) suite; ¥620 – ¥990 ($75–$120) double in 3-star building (20%–40% discount). AE, DC, MC, V. No Metro station. **Amenities:** 2 restaurants; lounge; bar; indoor pool; squash court; health club and spa with sauna; 8-lane bowling alley; concierge; business center; salon; 24-hr. room service; same-day dry cleaning/laundry; executive-level rooms. *In room:* A/C, satellite TV, broadband, minibar, coffeemaker, hair dryer, safe.

> ### (Kids) Family-Friendly Hotels
>
> Most of Shànghăi's international hotels offer free stays for children under 12 in their parent's room, and many can provide babysitting services with 4- to 6-hours' notice, but very few have any special programs or facilities for kids. Three exceptions are the **Shànghăi JC Mandarin** (p. 81), which in addition to its gym, tennis and squash courts, and year-round swimming pool, has a special children's playroom; the **Westin Shànghăi** (p. 71), which has a terrace paddle pool as part of its Westin Kids Club; and the **Novotel Atlantis** (p. 89), with its Dolfi Kid's Club and its special kids' buffet on Sundays.

Renaissance Yangtze Shànghăi Hotel (Shànghăi Yángzĭ Jiāng Dàjiŭdiàn) *Rebranded* Rebranded as the first Renaissance hotel in Mainland China in 2001, the Marriott-managed 33-story Yangtze was completely renovated into a five-star luxury hotel and is now comfortably holding its own against next-door rival the Sheraton Grand. Guest rooms are large, bright, and tastefully decorated with all the usual in-room amenities, including work desks with desktop-level controls. The Yangtze has long held a high reputation in Shànghăi for its catering, often preparing dinners for visiting heads of state; and its restaurants, especially the Cantonese Dynasty Restaurant, are well regarded. A large business center complete with a library, and a cigar bar with its own humidor, are popular as well with guests, many of them business travelers from North America and Europe.

Yán'ān Xī Lù 2099 (intersection with Zūnyì Lù); see map p. 134. ℂ 800/228-9290 or 021/6275-0000. Fax 021/6275-0750. www.renaissancehotels.com. 544 units. ¥1,240 ($150) double; ¥1,695 ($205) executive floor; from ¥2,150 ($260) suite (30% discount). AE, DC, MC, V. No Metro station. **Amenities:** 5 restaurants; deli; lounge; small outdoor swimming pool; health club with Jacuzzi and sauna; concierge; tour desk; business center; salon; 24-hr. room service; babysitting; same-day dry cleaning/laundry; executive-level rooms. *In room:* A/C, satellite TV, broadband, minibar, coffeemaker, hair dryer, safe.

MODERATE

Cypress Hotel (Lóngbăi Fàndiàn) *Set* Set on a large, historic garden estate that once partially belonged to Sir Victor Sassoon (of the Peace Hotel fame), and that has doubled as the Shànghăi Gold Course, the Cypress is one of the few airport hotels in the world that offers fishing (in ponds). Its unofficial four-star rating applies more to the facilities than the service staff who try but are inconsistent at times. Guest rooms, renovated in 2003, are compact, modern, and clean. The grounds are the key feature, with mature forest groves, arched bridges, streams, and areas for barbecues, strolling, and jogging. There's a free shuttle to take you downtown (10km/6¼ miles) and to the Hóngqiáo Airport (1km/⅗ miles).

Hóngqiáo Lù 2419 (west of the zoo, about ⅗ miles east of Hóngqiáo Airport); see map p. 134. ℂ 800/223-5652 or 021/6268-8868. Fax 021/6268-1878. www.cypresshotel.com. 149 units. ¥1,330 ($160) double; ¥1,992 ($240) executive level. AE, MC, V. No Metro. **Amenities:** 3 restaurants; 2 bars; large indoor pool; 4 lighted outdoor tennis courts; health club with sauna; bike rental; recreation club with bowling; concierge; tour desk; business center; salon; 24-hr. room service; babysitting; next-day dry cleaning/laundry; executive-level rooms. *In room:* A/C, satellite TV, dataport, minibar, fridge, coffeemaker, hair dryer, safe.

7 Pǔdōng (East of River)

VERY EXPENSIVE

Grand Hyatt Shànghǎi (Shànghǎi JīnMào Jūnyuè Dàjiǔdiàn) ★★★

Since its opening in 1999, this much-ballyhooed hotel has gotten a lot of attention for having some of the highest and grandest hotel rooms in the world (from the 54th to the 88th floor of the architecturally perfect Jīn Mào Tower). In truth, this is more of a novelty hotel than a practical one. As promised, the rooms, arrayed around a vertiginous 33-story cylindrical atrium, are like no other, offering a lush, postmodern mix of East and West with contemporary furniture against dark wood walls inscribed with Chinese poetry. Walls of glass afford stupendous views of Shànghǎi (on the rare smogless day, that is), while bathrooms are brazenly modern with all-glass washbasins, heated mirrors, and separate tub and shower. All this headiness, however, can also feel a little claustrophobic, and the burden of renown, not to mention one of the highest hotel occupancy rates in town, has occasionally made the staff a bit standoffish. Another trade-off to being so far above everyone else is convenience: Allow extra time to get to your destination, as you'll have to navigate some bewildering phalanxes of elevators. Still, with six international restaurants offering fine dining high above Shànghǎi and a cascading "sky pool" that stretches from window to window, this ultraluxurious hotel will continue to attract those looking for a unique stay.

Shìjì Dà Dào 88, 54th Floor, Jīn Mào Tower (southeast of the Oriental Pearl TV Tower); see map p. 130. ☎ **800/233-1234** or 021/5049-1234. Fax 021/5049-1111. www.hyatt.com. 555 units. ¥2,656–¥2,780 ($320–$335) double; ¥3,029–¥3,154 ($365–$380) executive-level room; from ¥3,969 ($480) suite. AE, DC, MC, V. Metro: Lùjiāzuǐ. **Amenities:** 6 restaurants; food pavilion; 2 lounges; nightclub; indoor "skypool" (world's highest swimming pool); health club with Jacuzzi and sauna; concierge; tour desk; 24-hr. business center; salon; 24-hr. room service; same-day dry cleaning/laundry; executive-level rooms. *In room:* A/C, satellite TV, dataport, minibar, coffeemaker, hair dryer, safe.

Hotel Inter-Continental Pǔdōng Shànghǎi (Shànghǎi Xīnyà Tāngchén Zhōujì Dàjiǔdiàn) ★

Formerly known as the New Asia Tomson Hotel, Pǔdōng's first international five-star hotel (1996), this property was taken over by Inter-Continental in 2002 and given an extensive remodeling. The large, elegant rooms encircle a handsome 21-story atrium lobby, now a wireless hot spot. Guest rooms, furnished in a contemporary classic style, are spacious and comfortable and contain separate showers and tubs. Guests can book tee-times at the members-only 18-hole Tomson Golf Course 15 minutes away, and Club Floor guests are treated to a free 15-minute neck and shoulder massage in addition to the usual perks. Service is professional and discounts (up to 50%) highly attractive.

Zhāngyáng Lù 777 (at intersection of Dōngfāng Lù, in the heart of downtown Pǔdōng); see map p. 130. ☎ **800/327-0200** or 021/5831-8888. Fax 021/5831-7777. www.intercontinental.com. 400 units. ¥2,282–¥2,465 ($275–$297) double; ¥3,012 ($363) executive floor; from ¥3,286 ($396) suite (discounts up to 50%). Children under 18 stay free in parent's room. AE, DC, MC, V. Metro: Dōngfāng Lù. **Amenities:** 2 restaurants; 2 lounges; small indoor pool; nearby golf course; health club with Jacuzzi and sauna; concierge; tour desk; 24-hr. business center; salon; 24-hr. room service; same-day dry cleaning/laundry; executive-level rooms. *In room:* A/C, satellite TV, dataport, minibar, coffeemaker, hair dryer, safe.

Pǔdōng Shangri-La Hotel (Pǔdōng Xiānggélǐlā Fàndiàn) ★★★

Boasting the best location in Pǔdōng, and a gorgeous view of the Bund across the river, the 28-story five-star Shangri-La couldn't be more convenient. Within walking distance of the subway, it's easily accessible to the heart of old Shànghǎi as well. There is a relaxed elegance to this comparatively older (1998) but still handsome hotel. Guest rooms are very spacious with generous counter and closet space, and while they may not have the latest gadgets, they are more than adequately equipped with large work desks, comfortable furniture, separate shower and tub, and an array of amenities. Bund-view rooms are worth the extra $20. Staff is exceedingly friendly and the service is of a high international caliber. In the never-ending quest to be the biggest and boldest in Shànghǎi, the hotel is building a tower annex and new convention facilities which, when complete in 2005, should mark it as the largest hotel in town with around 1,000 rooms.

Fùchéng Lù 33 (southwest of the Oriental Pearl TV Tower/Dōngfāng Míngzhū, adjacent to Riverside Ave/Bīnjiāng Dà Dào); see map p. 130. (C) **800/942-5050** or 021/6882-8888. Fax 021/6882-6688. www.shangri-la.com. 606 units. ¥2,729 – ¥2,894 ($330–$350) double; ¥3,060 – ¥3,225 ($370–$390) executive level; from ¥4,316 ($520) suite (40% discount). AE, DC, MC, V. Metro: Lùjiāzuǐ. **Amenities:** 3 restaurants; deli; lounge; nightclub; indoor lap pool; tennis court; health club with Jacuzzi and sauna; concierge; tour desk; large business center; 24-hr. room service; babysitting; same-day dry cleaning/laundry; executive-level rooms. *In room:* A/C, satellite TV, dataport, minibar, fridge, coffeemaker, hair dryer, safe.

Renaissance Shànghǎi Pǔdōng Hotel (Shànghǎi Chúndà Wànlì Jiǔdiàn) ★★

Located on the southeastern edges of the Lùjiāzuǐ financial district and just minutes from the Science and Technology Museum and the Shànghǎi New International Expo Center, this new (2003) five-star hotel attracts primarily business travelers and the occasional North American tour group, which is a shame considering it is one of the more colorful hotels around that would no doubt also appeal to the individual traveler. Formerly a three-star hotel owned by the police department, this 27-floor building has been completely refurbished to the Renaissance brand and now sports its own unique vibe, from the funky and loud orange color palette in the lobby and bar area to the tasteful mix of Chinese calligraphy and Chinese-style bedspreads in the otherwise modern and luxurious rooms. French doors open onto beautiful bathrooms, which come with separate shower and tub. But the Renaissance's attempt to distinguish itself really lies in the details, like the gifts (handicraft grasshoppers or Chinese orchids) that greet arriving guests, and its friendly and efficient service, all of which make the hotel poised to take off as Pǔdōng continues to develop.

Chángliǔ Lù 100 (2 blocks north of Shìjì Gōngyuán, 1 block east of Mínshēng Lù); see map p. 130. (C) **021/3871-4888.** Fax 021/6854-0888. www.renaissancehotels.com. 369 units. ¥2,324 ($280) double; ¥2,739 ($330) club floor; from ¥3,320 ($400) suite (30% discount Mar–June and Sept–Nov; up to 50% discount otherwise). AE, DC, MC, V. Metro: Shànghǎi Kējìguǎn (15-min. walk). **Amenities:** 2 restaurants; bar; lounge; gourmet deli; indoor pool; health club with sauna; concierge; business center; salon; 24-hr. room service; same-day dry cleaning/laundry; nonsmoking floor; club-level rooms. *In room:* A/C, satellite TV, broadband, minibar, coffeemaker, hair dryer, safe.

St. Regis Shànghǎi (Shànghǎi Ruìjí Hóngtǎ Dàjiǔdiàn) ★★★

As the second St. Regis hotel to open in China in 2001, the Shànghǎi version is a handsome robust hotel that has been quietly garnering a loyal following. Were it not for its less convenient location in the still emerging business district of Pǔdōng, it may well be *the* luxury hotel to stay at in town. Standard rooms, the largest in the city (48 sq. m/157 sq. ft.), are gorgeously furnished with comfortable sofas, large desks, ergonomic Herman Miller "Aeron" chairs, and Bose CD radios. The marble bathrooms are spacious and fitted with decadent "Rainforest" showers, separate larger-than-average bathtubs, and a flurry of amenities. But the St. Regis truly distinguishes itself with its signature 24-hour butler service. St. Regis butlers will not only press clothing and serve free in-room coffee and tea, they can also help with any Internet hook-up problems and make dinner reservations. Recently, the St. Regis has taken to offering free broadband Internet in all guest rooms, complimentary happy hour cocktails for all in the Executive Lounge, and a ladies-only floor featuring women butlers and a host of special in-room amenities including toiletries by Bulgari. The hotel spa offers treatments such as aromatherapy and a jet lag massage. With such luxurious pampering and *savoir-vivre* at your fingertips, you may not want to leave the hotel at all.

Dōngfāng Lù 889 (south central Pǔdōng); see map p. 130. ℂ **800/325-3589** or 021/5050-4567. Fax 021/6875-6789. www.stregis.com. 318 units. ¥2,656 – ¥2,819 ($320–$340) double; from ¥3,071 ($370) suite (up to 60% discount pending occupancy). AE, DC, MC, V. Metro: Dōngfāng Lù. **Amenities:** 3 restaurants; 2 lounges; indoor pool; tennis court; state-of-the-art health club and full-service spa with Jacuzzi and sauna; concierge; tour desk; business center; salon; 24-hr. room service; babysitting; same-day dry cleaning/laundry; 24-hr. butler service; 1 room for those w/limited mobility. *In room:* A/C, satellite TV, broadband, minibar, coffeemaker, hair dryer, safe.

EXPENSIVE

Holiday Inn Pǔdōng (Shànghǎi Pǔdōng Jiàrì Jiǔdiàn) ★ *Value*   This thoroughly western 32-story Holiday Inn offers excellent value, after discounts, among four-star hotels in Pǔdōng. Guest rooms are spacious and bright, with bird's-eye maple furniture, comfortable beds, and all the amenities you're likely to need. The white tile bathrooms are spotless, and service is efficient and professional. Given the hotel's tourist-unfriendly location in the middle of the business district of south central Pǔdōng, little wonder most of its guests are business travelers, but individual tourists occasionally find their way here as well. The nearby Metro 2 subway station, which is within walking distance, allows easier access to the rest of Shànghǎi.

Dōngfāng Lù 899 (south central Pǔdōng); see map p. 130. ℂ **800/465-4329** or 021/5830-6666. Fax 021/5830-5555. www.holiday-inn.com. 318 units. ¥1,500 ($187) double; ¥2,000 ($250) executive level; from ¥2,000 ($250) suite (discounts up to 50% during low season). AE, DC, MC, V. Metro: Dōngfāng Lù. **Amenities:** 4 restaurants; deli; pub; bar; indoor pool; large health club with Jacuzzi and sauna; game room; concierge; tour desk; business center; salon; 24-hr. room service; babysitting; same-day dry cleaning/laundry; nonsmoking rooms; executive-level rooms; rooms for those w/limited mobility. *In room:* A/C, satellite TV, dataport, minibar, coffeemaker, hair dryer, safe.

Oriental Riverside Hotel Shànghǎi (Dōngfāng Bīnjiāng Dàjiǔdiàn)
This locally managed five-star hotel built in 1999 and connected to the Pǔdōng International Convention Center is designed for delegations, convention groups, and business travelers, with tour groups moving in during slower times. It has views across the river to the Bund, and the relatively large discounts offered during non-convention times can be a lure to independent travelers, but the service can be painfully languorous. Rooms, with their somewhat scuffed furniture and stained carpets, also show wear. A welcome feature is that room windows can be opened (allowing you a chance to air out some of the mustiness and smoke if a nonsmoking room is not available). Bathrooms also have separate showers and tubs. Bund-view rooms are bigger and nicer than garden-view rooms, and are worth the extra $20.

Bīnjiāng Dàdào 2727 (1 block west of Oriental Pearl TV Tower, connected to Pǔdōng's International Conference Center); see map p. 130. ℂ **021/5037-0000.** Fax 021/5037-0999. www.shicc.net. 260 units. ¥2,240 – ¥2,480 ($280–$310) double; from ¥3,600 ($450) suite (discounts up to 50%). AE, DC, MC, V. Metro: Lùjiāzuǐ. **Amenities:** 4 restaurants; bar; indoor pool; health club with Jacuzzi and sauna; bowling alley; concierge; tour desk; business center; salon; 24-hr. room service; same-day dry cleaning/laundry; nonsmoking rooms. *In room:* A/C, satellite TV, dataport, minibar, coffeemaker, hair dryer, safe.

MODERATE

Courtyard by Marriott Hotel Pǔdōng (Shànghǎi Qílǔ Wànyì Dàjiǔdiàn) ★
Opened in 2002, the Courtyard is a thoroughly modern and busy four-star hotel catering to business travelers, most of whom are Asian. The government of wealthy Shāndōng Province owns the building, sparing no expense in maintaining its handsome facilities. The lobby lounge boasts a striking lattice wood and

glass partition. The comfortable rooms are of average size, with modern furniture and the Courtyard's signature floral bedspreads. The subway is just 2 blocks away, meaning a nonbusiness traveler could stay here comfortably, especially if a bargain room rate can be secured.

Dōngfāng Lù 838 (at intersection with Wéifáng Lù); see map p. 130. ☎ 021/6886-7886. Fax 021/6886-7889. www.courtyard.com. 218 units. ¥1,495 ($180) double; ¥1,985 ($240) executive level; from ¥2,315 ($280) suite (up to 50% discount). AE, DC, MC, V. Metro: Dōngfāng Lù. **Amenities:** 2 restaurants; lounge; fitness center with sauna; concierge; business center; salon; 24-hr. room service; babysitting; same-day dry cleaning/laundry; executive-level rooms. *In room:* A/C, satellite TV, dataport, minibar, coffeemaker, hair dryer, safe.

Novotel Atlantis Shànghǎi (Hǎishén Nuòfùtè Dàjiǔdiàn) ★ (Kids)

This glittering hotel offers a fresh, high-tech touch to the Pǔdōng scene, with a full-service Internet cafe dominating the entrance lobby. In addition to six executive floors and an elegant cigar bar, there's a separate "Ladies Floor." Rooms are filled with amenities, including interactive Web TVs. Bright, jazzy, and thoroughly contemporary, the Novotel Atlantis suffers a bit from its location (too far east to walk to Pǔdōng's attractions), making taxis a necessity. The Pǔdōng Airport shuttle bus (¥30/$3.60) is handy and fairly quick. There's a Dolfi Kid's Club to distract the young ones as well, and a Sunday brunch with magic acts and face painting for the young and the young-at-heart.

Pǔdōng Dà Dào 728 (east of Oriental Pearl TV Tower, at Fúshān Lù); see map p. 130. ☎ 800/221-4542 or 021/5036-6666. Fax 021/5036-6677. www.accorhotels.com. 303 units. ¥1,300 – ¥1,500 ($162–$187) double; ¥1,800 – ¥2,000 ($225–$250) executive level and "Lady Floor"; from ¥2,600 ($325) suite (30% discount). AE, DC, MC, V. No Metro. **Amenities:** 4 restaurants; deli; lounge; bar; Internet cafe; indoor pool; health club and spa with Jacuzzi and sauna; concierge; business center; 24-hr. room service; babysitting; same-day dry cleaning/laundry; executive-level rooms. *In room:* A/C, satellite TV, dataport, minibar, coffeemaker, hair dryer, safe.

5

Where to Dine

Gastronomes never had it so good in Shànghǎi. With restaurants serving a mind-boggling variety of Chinese cuisines, as well as a wide range of top-notch international fare, Shànghǎi is arguably mainland China's best city for eating. Běijīng boosters will disagree, of course, and it was not always so a decade, even 5 years ago, but the prosperous 1990s that saw Shànghǎi once again take to the world stage have reawakened the demand for *la bella vita,* as seen in the explosion of dining establishments in the last few years. For Shànghǎi residents, ever attuned to the latest trends and tastes, eating out and trying new restaurants is now a pastime rivaling shopping.

For the tourist, this means you no longer have to stick to safe hotel dining. While some of Shànghǎi's top restaurants can be found in hotels, there are scores of well-run private establishments that rival if not surpass the quality of hotel food, and usually at lower prices. Significantly improved hygiene standards should also allay any concerns you may have of eating out. Shànghǎi offers the unusual opportunity of dining one moment in a traditional teahouse and another in a restored colonial mansion; missing out would be a shame.

Don't expect the Chinese food here to taste the same as that at home; expect it to be light years better. While you can eat your way through China by sampling all the regional Chinese restaurants in Shànghǎi, the emphasis is on Shànghǎi's own renowned cuisine, commonly referred to as *běnbāng cài.* Usually considered a branch of Huáiyáng cuisine (see following box on "China's Cuisines"), Shànghǎi cooking has traditionally relied on soy sauce, sugar, and oil. The most celebrated Shànghǎi dish is hairy crab, a freshwater delicacy that reaches its prime every fall. Also popular are any number of "drunken" dishes (crab, chicken) marinated in local Shàoxīng wine, and braised meat dishes such as Lion's Head Meatballs and braised pork knuckle. Shànghǎi dim sum and snacks include a variety of dumplings, headlined by the local favorite *xiǎolóng bāo,* as well as onion pancakes and leek pies, all of which deserve to be tried. For more on Shànghǎi cuisine, see "Appendix A: Shànghǎi in Depth."

Those hankering for a taste of home will also find that Shànghǎi is the most foreign-belly-friendly city in China. From the trendiest Continental cuisine to the most recognizable fast-food chains, there is a staggering range of options that are guaranteed to take the edge off any homesick cravings. Many Asian and European cuisines are well represented, with Italian, Spanish, French, Japanese, Thai, and Indian cuisines of good enough quality to satisfy an overseas palate. World-renowned chefs like Jean-Georges Vongerichten have also chosen to launch their China flagship restaurants here. Where Shànghǎi particularly excels is in the bold new tastes that are arising from the mix of East and West.

At the other end of the dining scale, the American fast-food chains of McDonald's and Kentucky Fried Chicken are ubiquitous. So are Starbucks, Häagen-Dazs, and Pizza Hut.

China's Cuisines

China has a vast number of regional cuisines, which have traditionally been classified according to four main cooking styles. Below is a summary of the four styles and their various sub-branches:

Běijīng/Northern Běijīng or Northern cuisine is typically characterized by strong, robust flavors and hearty ingredients; pork and lamb dominate, the latter also due to the Muslim influence in the northwestern part of the country. Staples are heavy noodles and breads instead of rice. **Uighur** or **Xīnjiāng** cuisine falls under this rubric. *Jiǎozi*, small chunks of meat and vegetables wrapped in dough and boiled, are popular snacks also eaten during the Chinese New Year.

Huáiyáng/Shànghǎi Huáiyáng cuisine, encompassing the coastal areas of eastern China, and said to require the most skill, aims to preserve the basic flavor of each ingredient in order to achieve balance and freshness. River fish, farm animals, birds, and vegetables feature prominently, and braising and stewing are more common than stir-frying. Red sauces (from soy sauce, sugar, and oil) are popular. **Shànghǎi, Hángzhōu, Sūzhōu,** and **Yángzhōu**-style cooking are all minor variations on the same theme.

Cantonese Considered the most refined and sophisticated of the cuisines, the emphasis here is on freshness and lightness, with steaming and stir-frying the cooking methods of choice. Seafood dominates, but just about anything edible is fair game—the Cantonese are known for being the most adventurous eaters. Top hotels all have Cantonese restaurants, which are always the first choice for Chinese if they're trying to impress a guest. Cantonese dim sum, featuring little morsels of food like shrimp dumplings, barbecue pork crisps, and egg tarts, is widely popular.

Sìchuān Sìchuān cooking, born in the damp interior of Southwestern China, relies heavily on chilies, peppers, peppercorns, and garlic; spicy and pungent flavors are the result. Popular dishes include *gōngbǎo jīdīng* (diced chicken with chili and peanuts) and *mápó dòfu* (spicy tofu with minced pork). Sìchuān hotpot *(huǒguō)* is also a favorite. Although popular in Shànghǎi, Sìchuān cooking has seldom made it here intact: The local preference for sweet and salty is readily apparent on many a Sìchuān menu in town. Other southwestern cuisines, such as **Guìzhōu** and **Yúnnán,** which are themselves sub-divided into various ethnic minority cuisines, tend to be spicy and sour.

Subway is in the mix, and Tony Roma's and the Hard Rock Cafe have been longtime Shànghǎi residents. Check the local expatriate magazines for location details.

According to the corporate travel index published by *Business Travel News*, the corporate dining tab in Shànghǎi (said to lag behind London's but to exceed San Francisco's) averages around $110 per person per day, but most travelers can get by well below that amount. While Shànghǎi's top international restaurants tend to charge Western prices, you can have an excellent meal for two at a relatively upscale Chinese restaurant for ¥100 to ¥200 ($13–$25). Some of the best local foods can be had for less than that. (Prices quoted for a Chinese meal are for two bowls of rice and between two and four dishes.) The key is to mix it up with a combination of local and international dining. If you want to try Shànghǎi's more famous Western restaurants, consider going at lunchtime, when lunch specials and set menus can cost less than half of what you would spend at dinner. Hotel restaurants frequently levy a 15% service charge, but few private restaurants do. There is no tipping in restaurants, and the waitstaff will usually run after you to return your change.

The Shanghainese love affair with eating has spawned a dizzying number of restaurant openings (and closings) on any given week, a vexing matter not only for restaurant owners, but travel writers as well. What follows is a list of mostly established restaurants (with an emphasis on those outside of the big hotels) that should, barring any unforeseen health-related crisis (like SARS), still be thriving by the time you read this. Consult the local English-language weeklies for new restaurant listings.

The widest variety of dining options is in the Lúwān (French Concession), Jìng Ān, and Xúhuì districts. This is also where you'll find some of the most ambient restaurants located inside colonial mansions on large sprawling estates. With some of the city's top international restaurants and unimprovable views, the Bund is also another prime dining spot.

As well, Shànghǎi has five **food streets** (*měishí jiē*) lined with Chinese restaurants of every ilk, though few of them have English menus or English-speaking staff. They are: **Huáng Hé Lù,** northwest of the Park Hotel (Huángpǔ); **Wújiāng Lù,** just off Nánjīng Xī Lù by the Shímén Yī Lù Metro station (Huángpǔ); **Yúnnán Lù,** east of Xīzàng Lù and south of Yán'ān Dōng Lù (Huángpǔ); **Yùyuán Zhī Lù,** northwest of Jìng Ān Temple (Jìng Ān); and **Zhápǔ Lù,** north of Sūzhōu Creek and east of Sìchuān Běi Lù (Hóngkǒu).

Note: For tips on dining etiquette, see "Fast Facts: Shànghǎi" in chapter 3. For more tips and a menu guide to the city's most popular dishes, see "Appendix A: Shànghǎi in Depth."

1 Restaurants by Cuisine

AMERICAN
Element Fresh 🎖 (Jìng Ān, $, p. 109)
KABB 🎖 (Lúwān, $$, p. 98)
Malone's (Jìng Ān, $$, p. 109)

CANTONESE
Bì Fēng Táng (Jìng Ān, $$, p. 108)
Canton 🎖🎖🎖 (Pǔdōng, $$$$, p. 112)
Cū Cài Guǎn 🎖🎖 (Jìng Ān, $$, p. 109)
Crystal Jade Restaurant 🎖🎖🎖 (Lúwān, $$, p. 99)
Dynasty 🎖🎖 (Chángníng, $$$, p. 110)

Star East (Lúwān, $$$, p. 97)
Xien Yue Hien (Xúhuì, $$, p. 105)
Zen 🎖 (Lúwān, $$$, p. 98)

CONTINENTAL/FUSION
The Door 🎖🎖 (Chángníng, $$$$, p. 110)
La Villa Rouge 🎖🎖🎖 (Xúhuì, $$$$, p.101)
Luna 🎖 (Lúwān, $$$, p. 98)
M on the Bund 🎖🎖🎖 (Huángpǔ, $$$$, p. 94)
Mesa 🎖🎖 (Jìng Ān, $$$, p. 107)
T8 🎖🎖🎖 (Lúwān, $$$, p. 97)

Key to Abbreviations: $$$$ = Very Expensive $$$ = Expensive $$ = Moderate $ = Inexpensive

DIM SUM

Bì Fēng Táng (Jìng Ān, $$, p. 108)

Canton ★★★ (Pǔdōng, $$$$, p. 112)

Crystal Jade Restaurant ★★★ (Lúwān, $$, p. 99)

Dynasty ★★ (Chángníng, $$$, p. 110)

Xien Yue Hien (Xúhuì, $$, p. 105)

Zen ★ (Lúwān, $$$, p. 98)

DUMPLINGS

Cháng Ān Dumplings (Pǔdōng, $, p. 113)

Nánxiáng Mántou Diàn (Nánshì, $, p. 115)

Wáng Jiā Shā (Jìng Ān, $, p. 109)

FRENCH

Jean Georges (Huángpǔ, $$$$, p. 95)

La Maison (Lúwān, $$$, p. 98)

La Seine ★★ (Lúwān, $$$, p. 99)

GERMAN

Paulaner Brauhaus ★ (Xúhuì, $$$, p. 102)

GUÌZHŌU

Lǎo Tán ★ (Chángníng, $, p. 111)

HONG KONG

Xīn Wàng (Huángpǔ, Lúwān, $, p. 100)

HOT POT

Lái Fú Lóu ★ (Xúhuì, $$, p. 103)

HÚNÁN

Dī Shuǐ Dòng ★★ (Lúwān, $$, p. 100)

INDIAN

Hazara ★ (Lúwān, $$$, p. 98)

Indian Kitchen ★★ (Xúhuì, $$, p. 103)

Kaveen's Kitchen ★ (Jìng Ān, $$$, p. 107)

INDONESIAN

Bali Laguna ★ (Jìng Ān, $$$, p. 106)

INTERNATIONAL

Lan Kwai Fong at Park 97 ★★ (Lúwān, $$$$, p. 97)

Xīn Tiāndì Restaurant Mall ★★★ (Lúwān, $$$$, p. 97)

IRISH

O'Malley's ★ (Xúhuì, $$, p. 103)

ITALIAN

Danieli's ★★★ (Pǔdōng, $$$$, p. 112)

Trattoria Isabelle ★ (Lúwān, $$, p. 100)

Va Bene ★★ (Lúwān, $$$, p. 98)

JAPANESE

Dà Jiāng Hù ★ (Xúhuì, $$$, p. 102)

Itoya ★ (Jìng Ān, $$$, p. 107)

Shintori Null II ★★ (Jìng Ān, $$$$, p. 105)

KOREAN

Hánpǔ Yuán ★ (Pǔdōng, $$, p. 113)

SEAFOOD

Really Good Seafood ★ (Lúwān, $$$$, p. 98)

Wáng Bǎo Hé ★★ (Huángpǔ, $$$$, p. 94)

SHÀNGHǍI

Bǎoluó ★ (Jìng Ān, $$, p. 108)

Crystal Jade Restaurant ★★★ (Lúwān, $$, p. 99)

The Grape (Xúhuì, $, p. 105)

Lù Bō Láng ★ (Nánshì, $$$, p. 113)

Méilóngzhèn ★ (Jìng Ān, $$$, p. 107)

1931 Bar and Restaurant (Lúwān, $$, p. 99)

Shànghǎi Lǎo Fàndiàn ★ (Nánshì, $$, p. 114)

Shànghǎi Lǎo Zhàn ★ (Xúhuì, $$, p. 104)

Sū Zhè Huì ★ (Pǔdōng, $$, p. 113)

Shànghǎi Uncle ★★★ (Huángpǔ, Pǔdōng, Xúhuì, $$$, p. 96 and 112)

1221 ★★ (Chángníng, $$, p. 110)

Wáng Bǎo Hé ★★ (Huángpǔ, $$$$, p. 94)

Wáng Jiā Shā (Jìng Ān, $, p. 109)

Yè Shànghǎi ★★ (Luwan, $$$, p. 98)

SÌCHUĀN

Bā Guó Bù Yī ★★ (Chángníng, $$, p. 111)

Sìchuān Court ★★ (Jìng Ān, $$$$, p. 106)

SINGAPOREAN

Frankie's Place ★ (Chángníng, $$, p. 111)

SPANISH

Le Garçon Chinois ★★ (Xúhuì, $$$, p. 102)

THAI

Lan Na Thai ★★ (Lúwān, $$$, p. 98)

Simply Thai ★★ (Xúhuì, $$$, p. 103)

UIGHUR

Shànghǎi Xīnjiāng Fēngwèi Fàndiàn (Xúhuì, $$, p. 104)

VEGETARIAN

Chūnfēng Sōngyuè Lóu (Nánshì, $, p. 114)

Gōngdélín (Huángpǔ, $$, p. 96)

Zǎo Zǐ Shù ★ (Lúwān, $$, p. 100)

VIETNAMESE

Cochinchina ★ (Jìng Ān, $$$, p. 106)

YÚNNÁN

Yúnnán Měishí Yuán (Huángpǔ, $, p. 96)

2 Huángpǔ (Downtown)

VERY EXPENSIVE

M on the Bund (Mǐshì Xīcāntīng) ★★★ CONTINENTAL   The restaurant that put Shànghǎi dining on the world map, M on the Bund has drawn top international reviews for its gourmet Continental cooking. Lodged atop a handsome seven-story colonial building on the Bund, M, now going on its sixth year, is all Art Deco elegance with a recently renovated terrace that affords unsurpassed views of the Bund, the Huángpǔ River, and Pǔdōng's skyscrapers. In 2001, to complement its main dining room, M opened the "Glamour Room" for nightly dinners and drinks. The very fine menu changes frequently to take advantage of fresh local ingredients, but signature dishes include the slow-baked leg of lamb and the exquisitely sublime Pavlova dessert. M's wine list is also one of Shànghǎi's best. The waitstaff is mostly professional, though there have been complaints of poor service, especially during busy times. Now that M, spoiled for so long by being the only major restaurant on the Bund, has some competition from the neighboring Three on the Bund restaurants, look for the service to improve even more. The weekday set lunches (two courses ¥108/$15; three courses ¥138/$17) are excellent value for money.

Zhōngshān Dōng Yī Lù 5, 7th Floor (entrance on side street at Guǎngdōng Lù 20); see map p. 118. © **021/6350-9988.** Reservations required. Main courses ¥150–¥280 ($18–$35). AE, DC, MC, V. Daily 6–10:30pm; Tues–Fri 11:30am–2:30pm; Sat–Sun brunch 11:30am–3pm; Sun tea 3:30–5:30pm. Metro: Hénán Zhōng Lù.

Wáng Bǎo Hé ★★ SHÀNGHǍI/SEAFOOD   With an opening date stretching back to 1744, this restaurant claims to be Shànghǎi's oldest. It also claims to be the best place to feast on Shànghǎi's famous hairy crab, though you're just as likely to lose some hair when you see the final tab (a kilo/2¼ lb. of crab will cost

Three on the Bund (Wài Tān Sān Hào)

The latest and splashiest development to hit Shànghǎi, **Three on the Bund** ★★★ is Chinese-American businessman Handel Lee's attempt to bring a little world class swank to the Bund. Built in 1922, this former Union Insurance Company Building now houses an art gallery, exclusive fashion outlets (including a Giorgio Armani store), and a luxurious Evian spa, but it's the restaurants that should distinguish this "lifestyle destination." At press time several restaurants had yet to open. Still, if previous reputation counts for anything, look for the following restaurants, headlined by a few of the world's best-known chefs, to provide some of Shànghǎi's finest dining. *Note:* Reservations required at Jean-Georges, Laris, and Whampoa Club; reservations recommended at New Heights.

Jean Georges (fourth floor; ✆ 021/6321-7733; daily 11:30am–2:30pm and 5:30–10pm). From *amuse-bouche* to dessert, you can expect the finest contemporary French fare from world-renowned chef Jean-Georges Vongerichten. There are 2,500 bottles of wine to choose from, and a 30-seater wine cellar private dining room. Expect a dinner for two to hover immodestly around ¥2,000 ($250).

Whampoa Club (fifth floor; ✆ 021/6321-3737; daily 11:30am–2:30pm and 5:30–10pm). Modern Shànghǎi cuisine is brought to you by Chef Jerome Leung, who is putting a creative spin on classics learned from a passel of old-time Shànghǎi master chefs.

Laris (sixth floor; ✆ 021/6321-9922; daily 11:30am–2:30pm and 6–11pm). Larger-than-life Australian chef David Laris's previous culinary stints in Hong Kong, Vietnam, Macau, and London (as executive chef of Mezzo) should make for some inspired "New World" cuisine. Seafood lovers should find the *foie gras,* oyster, and crustacean-stocked seafood bar to their liking.

New Heights (seventh floor; ✆ 021/6321-0909; daily 11:30am–3:30pm and 6–11:30pm) is the option for casual, more affordable bistro-type fare, with rooftop views of the Bund and Pǔdōng rivaling that of M on the Bund next door. Dinner for two should be in the ¥400 ($50) range. In the back of New Heights is a music lounge, **Third Degree** (daily 7pm–2am), which serves up live music with its cocktails.

Three on the Bund is located at Zhōngshān Dōng Yī Lù 3 (entrance on side street at Guǎngdōng Lù 23; ✆ 021/6323-3355; www.threeonthe bund.com). Take the metro to Hénán Zhōng Lù.

around ¥380/$45). That this typically festive and brightly lit restaurant is often full is a testament to Shànghǎi's new wealth; your average diner on any given night will likely be a government official, China's next billionaire, or a Japanese and Southeast Asian crab aficionado with kilos of disposable income. Crab dominates the menu, of course, from dumplings and soup to the whole hairy monster, which is typically steamed and eaten with a dipping sauce of ginger, soy sauce, and black vinegar. True crab aficionados then put the whole crab back together after eating, as if it had never been dismantled, piece by succulent piece. Wash it all down with the restaurant's famous Shàoxīng wine.

Fúzhōu Lù 603 (west of Zhèjiāng Zhōng Lù); see map p. 118. ℂ 021/6322-3673. Reservations required. Meal for 2 ¥400 – ¥800 ($50–$100). AE, DC, MC, V. Daily 11am–1pm and 5–8:30pm. Metro: Hénán Zhōng Lù.

EXPENSIVE

Shànghǎi Uncle (Hǎishàng Āshū) ★★★ SHÀNGHǍI   If you only get to try one Shanghainese meal, let it be here. Opened by "Uncle" Lǐ Zhōnghéng, gourmet, restaurant-owner (11 outlets) from Hong Kong, and son of a *New York Times* food critic, this rave worthy restaurant touts old Shànghǎi favorites given a modern makeover. Menu favorites include pine seed pork rip, so tender it falls right off the bone before it melts in your mouth; Shànghǎi traditional smoked fish; Uncle's crispy pork of flame, cooked five ways while preserving its crispy skin and tender flesh; and the fusion-influenced cheese baked lobster with homemade noodles. The inspired dry scallop and dry shrimps on Peking pancakes with XO sauce take even the most jaded Chinese diners by wonderful surprise. Shànghǎi Uncle has been so successful that it has sprouted three outlets in as many years, with this branch in the cavernous basement of the Bund Center being the newest and the largest. The decor is all modern Shànghǎi with brash red walls, fake palm trees, and an elevated central platform enclosed by a curtain of golden beads. Mezzanine booths offer the best viewing spots. Make your reservation now.

Yán'ān Dōng Lù 222, Wàitān Zhōngxīn (Bund Center), Basement (between Hénán Zhōng Lù and Jiāngxī Zhōng lù); see map p. 118. ℂ 021/6339-1977. Xúhuì branch: Tiānyáoqiáo Lù 211, 2nd floor (north of Nándān Dōng Lù), ℂ 021/6464-6430. Reservations highly recommended. Meal for 2 ¥160 – ¥250 ($20–$31). AE, DC, MC, V. Daily 11am–11pm. Metro: Hénán Zhōng Lù.

MODERATE

Gōngdélín *Overrated* VEGETARIAN   Shànghǎi's most well-known vegetarian restaurant has over a half century of experience and has grown a bit stodgy, not to mention greasy in its old age. Its renown still counts for something, though, as crowds continue to pack in here for the *sùjī* (vegetarian chicken), *sùyā* (vegetarian duck), and other mock imitations of fowl, pork, seafood, and various traditional Chinese dishes, all cleverly made from tofu and soy products. There's a takeout counter near the main entrance if you chance by during the day while shopping.

Nánjīng Xī Lù 445 (south side of Nánjīng Xī Lù, between Rénmín Gōngyuán and Chéngdū Běi Lù); see map p. 118. ℂ 021/6327-0218. Reservations recommended on evenings and weekends. Meal for 2 ¥75 – ¥200 ($9–$24). AE, DC, MC, V. Daily 6:30–9:30am, 11am–2pm, and 5–8pm. Metro: Shímén Yī Lù.

INEXPENSIVE

Yúnnán Měishí Yuán (Yúnnán Gourmet) YÚNNÁN   Strictly prole dining by way of Southwest China, this small eatery in the Raffles City shopping complex offers typical Yúnnán staples like *guòqiáo mǐxiàn* (crossing-the-bridge noodles—various meats, vegetables, and noodles cooked in a piping-hot, oil-layered broth), *qìguō jī* (chicken steamed with Chinese herbs), and even *dà jiùjià* (rice-flour pastry stir-fried with meat and vegetables), seldom seen outside Yúnnán Province. The food is not the most authentic, but it seems to satisfy the Shanghainese curiosity about minority cuisine.

Xīzàng Zhōng Lù 268, B1–19/20 (basement of Raffles City at intersection with Fúzhōu Lù); see map p. 118. ℂ 021/6340-3076. Meal for 2 ¥40 – ¥75 ($4.80–$9). No credit cards. Daily 10am–10pm. Metro: Rénmín Gōngyuán or Rénmín Guǎngchǎng.

3 Lúwān District (French Concession)

VERY EXPENSIVE

Lan Kwai Fong at Park 97 ★★ INTERNATIONAL Located in Fùxīng Gōngyuán, the oh-so-chic Park 97, one of Shànghǎi's trendiest restaurant complexes since 1997 now comprises four outlets, direct from Hong Kong. The decor throughout is a blend of Art Deco elegance in the restaurants with large windows affording views of the surrounding park, and chintzy bright-red velour in the bar and lounges. This is a great place to relax during the day and an optimal place to see and be seen: You'll get attention not only from the waitstaff but also from other patrons discreetly checking each other out, and from curious Shanghainese ambling through the park. Outside tables during warm weather provide the best viewing spots.

    Baci Italian Cuisine is justifiably known for its fresh pasta dishes and very thin-crusted pizzas, but its most popular offering is its weekend brunch, with sets ranging from ¥97 to ¥180 ($12–$23), including cocktail, pastries, and limitless tea/coffee. A children's menu is also available for brunch. **Tokio Joe** has sushi creations and delicious rolls, with three-course set meals priced from ¥60 to ¥110 ($7.20–$13). **California Club** is a very hip and loud disco (aesthetically and acoustically) that opens onto Baci; while **Upstairs at 97** is a lounge bar with a slightly mellower live band (usually jazz or Latin) but no less lively a crowd.

Gāolán Lù 2 (inside west gate of Fùxīng Gōngyuán); see map p. 122. ✆ 021/5383-2328 (Baci/Tokio Joe/California Club). Reservations recommended on weekends. Main courses ¥50 – ¥250 ($6–$30). AE, DC, MC, V. Baci open daily 11:30am–11pm. Tokio Joe open Mon–Fri 11:30am–2:30pm and 6–11pm; Sat–Sun 11:30am–6pm (lunch) and 6–11pm. California Club and Upstairs at 97 open daily 9pm–2am ('til 4am Fri–Sat). Metro: Huángpí Nán Lù.

Xīn Tiāndì Restaurant Mall ★★★ INTERNATIONAL A Starbucks stands at its entrance, the First National Congress of the Communist Party at its flanks, and in its midst, brilliant restorations of Shànghǎi's colonial Shíkù Mén ("stone gate") architecture. The place is **Xīn Tiāndì** (literally "New Heaven and Earth"), an upscale cultural mall where the moneyed East meets the moneyed West. Here you'll find the city's hottest dining spots, from actor Jackie Chan's own cafe (Star East) to what many consider the single best restaurant in the city (T8). Located downtown a block south of the Huángpí Nán Lù Metro station and bounded by Tàicāng Lù in the north, Zìzhōng Lù in the south, Huángpí Nán Lù to the east, and Mǎdāng Lù to the west, Xīn Tiāndì is a 2-block pedestrian mall (bisected by the east-west running Xìngyè Lù) with enough good eating to require weeks to experience it all. The best and the priciest are listed below. (See p. 122 for map.)

    T8 ★★★ (North Block, House 8; ✆ 021/6355-8999; lunch Wed–Mon 11:30am–2pm, dinner daily 6:30–11pm) is the restaurant whose service and chefs have quickly rivaled those at M on the Bund, only with less attitude. There's a new chef but little else has changed. Service and management are superb and unobtrusive, and clientele appears to be here more for the food than to be seen. The decor is super chic and the food is irresistible, especially the Sìchuān seared king prawns, the slow-cooked lamb, the Sìchuān pie, and the to-die-for chocolate addiction plate.

    Crystal Jade Restaurant ★★★ (see separate review on p. 99).

    Star East (Shànghǎi Dōngmèi) ★ (North Block, House 17, Unit 1; ✆ 021/6311-4991; daily 11:30am–2am), international film star Jackie Chan's slick five-story Cantonese restaurant and bar, where Western set meals are available as well.

La Maison (**Lèměisōng Fǎguó Cāntīng;** North Block, House 23, Unit 1; ℂ **021/3307-1010;** daily 11:30am–12:30am), a strictly French cafe, with French prices and its own bakery.

Va Bene (**Huá Wàn Yì**) ✿✿ (North Block, House 7; ℂ **021/6311-2211;** daily 11:30am–2:30pm and 5–11:30pm), an upscale Italian diner (from the owners of Hong Kong's Gaia) with warm Tuscan decor, patio dining, and a wide range of antipasti, pasta, and gourmet pizzas, all made from the freshest ingredients.

Paulaner Brauhaus (**Bǎoláinà**) ✿ (North Block, House 19–20; ℂ **021/ 6320-3935;** daily 11am–2am), the Shànghǎi standby praised for its excellent German food, with authentic brews to match.

Herbal Legend (**Bǎicǎo Chuánqí**) ✿ (South Block, House 1, Unit 1; ℂ **021/ 6386-6817;** daily 11am–1am), one of the healthiest "theme" restaurants you'll ever encounter, incorporating the use of Chinese medicinal herbs in its cooking, such as roasted lamb with *dāng gū*.

KABB (**Kǎibó Xīcāntīng**) ✿ (North Block, House 5, Unit 1; ℂ **021/ 3307-0798;** Mon–Fri 9:30am–midnight, Sat–Sun 9:30am–2am), a spiffy American bar and comfort food cafe.

Luna ✿ (North Block, House 15, Unit 1; ℂ **021/6336-1717;** daily 11:30am–1:30am), a Continental cafe with heavenly surroundings.

Really Good Seafood (**Zhēndèhǎo Hǎixiān Cāntīng**) ✿ (South Block, House 1; ℂ **021/6387-5757;** daily 11am–2pm and 5–10pm), a modern elegant Chinese restaurant delivering what its name promises, but at high prices. Lunch sets (under ¥80/$10 per person) are considerably more affordable.

Yè Shànghǎi ✿✿ (South Block, House 6; ℂ **021/6311-2323;** daily 11:30am–2:30pm and 5:30–11pm), an elegant touch of old Shànghǎi, which Hong Kong visitors claim is better than the original back home.

Zen (**Xiānggǎng Cǎidié Xuān**) ✿ (South Block, House 2; ℂ **021/ 6385-6395;** daily 11:30am–11:30pm), a modern Cantonese restaurant by way of Hong Kong, with excellent dim sum for lunch.

EXPENSIVE

Hazara (**Hāzhālā**) ✿ INDIAN   Located on the grounds of the Ruìjīn Hotel, Hazara, one of two restaurants under the aegis of the bar Face (the other is the Thai restaurant Lan Na Thai), has recently moved from its former tent-enclosed though highly ambient quarters to a considerably tighter space behind the Face mansion. In its current incarnation, concrete floors and steel I-beam ceilings mix uneasily with antique tables and Indian statues. If you can ignore the rather claustrophobic effect, the service is still top-notch, and the food is quite fine and tasty. Of course it's also pricier than it should be. The house specialty, *raan e hazara* (baby lamb leg marinated in spices and grilled in a tandoori oven), is worth splurging for, as is the high calorie *murgh malai* butter chicken, but appetizers are fairly pedestrian and vegetable dishes merely average.

Ruìjīn Èr Lù 118 (Building 4, Ruìjīn Bīnguǎn, between Yǒngjiā Lù and Fùxīng Zhōng Lù); see map p. 122. ℂ 021/6466-4328. Reservations required. Meal for 2 ¥300–¥500 ($38–$62). AE, DC, MC, V. Sun–Thurs 5:30–10:30pm; Fri–Sat 5:30–11pm. Metro: Shǎnxī Nán Lù.

Lan Na Thai (**Lán Nà Tài**) ✿✿ THAI   This popular Thai restaurant is located on the second floor of a beautiful colonial mansion on the north end of the Ruìjīn Hotel estate. Look for signs to Faces, which is the elegant lounge on the main floor. Upstairs, carved Thai wall panels hang on blue walls and the tables overlook the estate and courtyard below. The clientele is mostly foreign, but the chef is most assuredly from Thailand, as are many of the genuine fresh ingredients. The prawn cake, satays, and papaya salad are superb, as are the soft-shell crabs, hot spicy seafood stir-fry (Phad Talay Nim Prik Paow), and green curry. Service is discreet and gracious, making this an ideal spot for a relaxing lunch or fine candlelit dinner.

Ruìjīn Èr Lù 118 (Building 4, Ruìjīn Guest House; south of Fùxīng Zhōng Lù); see map p. 122. © 021/6466-4328. Reservations recommended on weekends. Meal for 2 ¥200 – ¥320 ($25–$40). AE, DC, MC, V. Daily 11:30am–2:30pm and 5:30–11pm. Metro: Shǎnxī Nán Lù.

La Seine (Sàinà Hé Fǎguó Cāntīng) ★★ FRENCH   With French cuisine being hit-or-miss in this town, that this restaurant in the Somerset Grand service apartments bagged the prize for best French dining from the English-language monthly *that's Shanghai* in 2003 qualifies it as a hit. The diverse international crowd certainly seems to appreciate everything from the artfully presented dishes to the professional Hong Kong management. Decor is a funky sea of purple, from the walls, adorned with French posters, to the thick drapes and plush high-backed chairs. All the usual French favorites are well represented, with the *foie gras du chef* and *escargots* appetizers, beef tenderloin with goose liver, and sinful desserts such as the Earl Grey crème brûlée and the hot coffee chocolate cake with raspberry sauce just a few of the dishes making an impression. Weekday buffet lunches (¥68 – ¥108/$8.50–$13) and weekend buffet brunches (¥78/$9.50) are an incredible bargain.

Jǐ'nán Lù 8 (west block of Somerset Grand, south of Huáihǎi Gōngyuán, 2 blocks east of Huángpí Nán Lù); see map p. 122. © 021/6384-3722. Reservations recommended. Main courses ¥75 – ¥150 ($9–$19). AE, DC, MC, V. Daily 11:30am–2:30pm and 6pm–midnight. Metro: Huángpí Nán Lù.

MODERATE

1931 Bar and Restaurant SHÀNGHǍI   Formerly attractive because of its romantic colonial Shànghǎi setting, this small restaurant has recently undergone a renovation in favor of a more traditional Western look (flower wallpaper, thick drapes, upholstered chairs). Happily, traces of old Shànghǎi remain—wall posters of the 1930s, tiny intimate tables, and waitresses clothed in traditional *qípáo* dresses (high collar, side slits)—making this a still-pleasant spot to drop in for a Shànghǎi lunch, a light dinner, or late-night drinks. Popular menu items include lamb or duck scallion pancakes, Shànghǎi fried noodles, and Yù Yuán Garden fried dumplings, though the dishes are mostly just average. For tipplers, there's a full bar with a range of reasonably priced liquors, as well as coffees, teas, and fresh juices.

Màomíng Nán Lù 112 (south of Huáihǎi Zhōng Lù); see map p. 122. © 021/6472-5264. Meal for 2 ¥100 – ¥220 ($13–$27). AE, DC, MC, V. Daily 11:30am–1am. Metro: Shǎnxī Nán Lù.

Crystal Jade Restaurant (Fěicuì Jiǔjiā) ★★★ *Value* CANTONESE/DIM SUM/SHÁNGHǍI   This consistently superb restaurant chain out of Singapore (where they have more than two dozen outlets) is serving up arguably the best *xiǎolóng bāo* (steamed dumplings with broth) and *lāmiàn* (hand-pulled noodles) south of the Yángzǐ. Hong Kong and Singapore expats in the know flock to this somewhat loud restaurant on the second floor of the southern annex of Xīn Tiāndì, where you can watch the chefs skillfully hand-pull the noodles you'll soon be eating. Dim sum dominates lunchtime, but must-tries at any time of day or night include the Shànghǎi steamed pork dumplings (the aforementioned *xiǎolóng bāo*), the *lā miàn* in Sìchuān style (exquisitely fine noodles with just the right consistency in a spicy peanut broth), and the deep-fried stuffed scallop with pepper and salt. Service is efficient and attentive. Reserve in advance or risk a long wait.

Xìnyè Lù 123 Lòng, Xīn Tiāndì, Nánlǐ 6–7, 2nd floor–12A & B (1 block south of Tàicāng Lù and east of Mǎdāng Lù); see map p. 122. © 021/6385-8752. Reservations required. Meal for 2 ¥80 – ¥200 ($10–$25). AE, DC, MC, V. Mon–Sat 11:30am–3:30pm and 5–10:30pm; Sun 10:30am–3:30pm and 5–10:30pm. Metro: Huángpí Nán Lù.

Dī Shuǐ Dòng ★★ *Finds* HÚNÁN   Rivaling Sìchuān cuisine in spiciness (though relying more on straight chilies and less on the mind-numbing, tongue-lashing peppercorn), the lesser-known cooking of Húnán Province has been steadily amassing a legion of local devotees. Leading the Húnán invasion has been the wonderful Dī Shuǐ Dòng, reached by a flight of rickety wooden stairs inside a small French concession storefront. Upstairs is a rough-hewn simulation of a Húnán village, with tiled roofs, fake foliage, batik-clad waitstaff, and popular Chinese love songs bleating in the background. Highly recommended are the *làzi jǐdīng* (spicy chicken nuggets), *suān dòujiǎo ròuní* (diced sour beans with minced pork), *duòjiāo yútóu* (fish head steamed with red chili), and *xiāngwèi hóngshǔ bō* (fragrant sweet potato in monk's pot). Or order just about anything in sight and plenty of cold beer to douse the fiery flames in your mouth. Service is no-nonsense, even occasionally impatient, but the food is superb and shouldn't be missed.

Màomíng Nán Lù 56 (north of Chánglè Lù); see map p. 122. ✆ 021/6253-2689. Meal for 2 ¥80 – ¥140 ($10–$18). No credit cards. Daily 11am–12:30am. Metro: Shǎnxī Nán Lù.

Trattoria Isabelle (Yīshābèi'ěr) ★ *Finds* ITALIAN   Miss this little trattoria hidden in a modest three-story house off the pedestrian street Yándāng Lù and you'll miss out on some of Shànghǎi's tastiest Italian home cooking. This is a thoroughly charming and unpretentious restaurant all the way from its simple decor—wooden floors, pink tablecloths, and fresh flowers—to its discreet and friendly service, to its uncomplicated and comforting food. Steak and fish are available, but it's the pastas—relying on simple sauces such as tomato, pesto, seafood, and chicken and mushroom—that keep the expats-in-the-know coming back. It's hard to find a better deal in town than the pasta lunch set (¥28 – ¥40/$3.50–$5, including salad and coffee), or the ¥30 ($3.75) and under cocktails. *Benissimo.*

Xīn Ān Lù 139 (east of Yándāng Lù, between Náncāng Lù and Huáihǎi Zhōng Lù); see map p. 122. ✆ 021/5386-0827. Reservations recommended in evenings. Main courses ¥30 – ¥90 ($3.75–$12). No credit cards. Daily 11:30am–2pm and 5:30–11pm. Metro: Shǎnxī Nán Lù.

Zǎo Zǐ Shù ★ *Finds* VEGETARIAN   This restaurant's name literally means "jujube tree," but the three characters that greet visitors upon arrival also cleverly play on the pun *zǎo chī sù,* advocating the early adoption of a vegetarian diet. Pleasant and contemporary, the restaurant takes its mission seriously: Fruit is served as an appetizer; organic tea is the norm; alcohol, dairy, and MSG are shunned; and smoking is definitively prohibited. The bean curd skin roll is a delicious appetizer and you can't go wrong with most of the pure vegetable dishes, though the fake meat dishes don't hold up as well. Avoid the vegetarian steak with pepper sauce. Spinach dumplings and soup noodles with vegetables are also hearty alternatives for those less inclined to edible fungi. Friendly service and tasty fare that's less oily than that at other vegetarian outlets means this restaurant is often full. To distract the waiting masses, there's an adjoining store selling vegetarian foodstuffs.

Sōngshān Lù 77, 1st Floor (inside the Shànghǎi Huánggōng complex, south of Huáihǎi Lù, 1 block east of Huángpí Nán Lù); see map p. 122. ✆ 021/6384-8000. Reservations recommended. Meal for 2 ¥60 – ¥100 ($7.50–$13). AE, DC, MC, V. Daily 10:30am–9pm. Metro: Huángpí Nán Lù.

INEXPENSIVE

Xīn Wàng HONG KONG   Informal, inexpensive, yet tasty dining at its best, this small chain dishes up a hodge-podge of Chinese comfort foods guaranteed to please all comers. Rice, noodles, and congee form the base of most dishes, after which it's strictly variation on a theme. *Yángzhōu chǎofàn* (fried rice),

Coffee, Tea & Something Else

The number of Western-style coffee bars that have sprouted in Shànghǎi in the last few years can almost make you forget that the Chinese have traditionally been tea drinkers. You can credit (or blame) Starbucks (which at last count had 36 outlets in Shànghǎi) for the java jolt, but if you are in need of a caffeine fix, consider branching out and spreading the wealth a little. The following is a list of unusual local teahouses and cafes that offer much more than your average cup of overpriced joe:

Bonomi Café (Zhōngshān Dōng Yī Lù 12, room 226; ✆ **021/6329-7506**; Mon–Fri 8:30am–6pm, Sat 10am–4pm). While strolling the Bund, drop in for a cup of coffee at this second-floor Italian-style cafe located in one of Shànghǎi's great colonial buildings.

Old China Hand Reading Room (Shàoxīng Lù 27, by Shǎnxī Nán Lù, Xúhuì; ✆ **021/6473-2526**; daily 10am–midnight). The most charming coffee house in town, it has Qīng Dynasty furniture, old manual typewriters, and beautiful photographs taken by owner and photographer Deke Erh. Sip your tea, coffee, or fruit juice while browsing through hundreds of old and new books and magazines.

Old Film Café (Duōlún Lù 123, near Sìchuān Běi Lù, Hóngkǒu; ✆ **021/5696-4763**; daily 10am–1am). A bit out of the way up by the Duōlún Lù Commercial Street (p. 158), but here is a rare opportunity for film lovers to see some Chinese and Russian films dating back to the 1920s. Order a cuppa, select a flick, and settle in for some culture with your caffeine.

Wagas (Huáihǎi Zhōng Lù 300, Hong Kong New World, B107, Lúwān; ✆ **021/6335-3739**; daily 9:30am–9pm). Who needs Starbucks when you can have *illy* coffee? Wagas serves it straight up, with lounge chairs, a mellow soundtrack, gourmet panini, and a lot of healthy menu items like smoothies. There's another branch at Nánjīng Xī Lù 1168, CITIC Square, LG12A (✆ **021/5292-5228**).

---

xiānxiā yúntūn miàn (shrimp wonton noodles in soup), *mìzhī chāshāo fàn* (barbecue pork rice)—they're all here along with casseroles, simple sandwiches, fruit juices, and milk teas. The scene is typically chaotic, the waitstaff is usually harried, but the food is delivered quickly. There is another popular branch at Hànkǒu Lù 309 (✆ **021/6360-5008**).

Chánglè Lù 175 (between Màomíng Nán Lù and Ruìjīn Yī Lù); see map p. 122. ✆ **021/6415-5056**. Meal for 2 ¥40 – ¥60 ($5–$7.50). No credit cards. Daily 7am–5am. Metro: Shǎnxī Nán Lù.

4 Xúhuì District (Southwest Shànghǎi)

VERY EXPENSIVE

La Villa Rouge (Xiǎo Hóng Lóu) ★★★ CONTINENTAL/FUSION
Located on the western edge of Xújiāhuì Park in a 1921 red brick mansion that was once the original EMI Recording Studios, this trendy new (2002) restaurant evokes a wonderfully dreamy bygone era with its dark wood paneling, grand

staircases, antique wallpaper, large glass windows, and traditional recording instruments. 1930s Chinese pop classics play in the background as fashionably dressed diners dig discreetly into dishes more fusion than traditional French, all prepared by a team of Japanese chefs. Service is very attentive and individualized. Degustation menus (¥480 – ¥580/$60–$73 per person) are the way to go if you're blessed with an expense account or rich relatives; typical a la carte items such as beluga caviar, foie gras, lobster, and beef tenderloin can add up as well. For those watching their wallets and waistlines, ¥198 ($25) will get you in the door for a set lunch. Coffees and beers (¥40 – ¥50/$5–$6) are not the most expensive in town, making an after-dinner drink in the bar or on the patio during warmer months a classy way to spend an evening.

Héngshān Lù 811 (in Xújiāhuì Gōngyuán); see map p. 122. ② 021/6431-9811. Reservations required. Main courses ¥190 – ¥420 ($24–$52). AE, DC, MC, V. Daily 11:30am–10pm (bar is open until 1am/2am Fri–Sat). Metro: Héngshān Lù or Xújiāhuì.

EXPENSIVE

Dà Jiāng Hù (O-edo) 🎍 JAPANESE   Japanese fine dining this is not, but who wants morsel-size food too beautiful to eat when you can gorge like a sumo wrestler on unlimited quantities of sushi and tempura? Though there are several prix-fixe all-you-can-eat Japanese restaurants in town, Dà Jiāng Hù is one of the longest standing and most reliable. For ¥200 ($25) per person, you can have unlimited amounts of raw fish, broiled meats, grilled vegetables, and noodles in a pleasant, relaxed setting. There's also free-flowing sake and beer, so come early and stay awhile.

Dōnghú Lù 30 (north of Huáihǎi Zhōng Lù); see map p. 122. ② 021/5403-5877. Reservations recommended. Meal for 2 ¥400 ($50). AE, DC, MC, V. Daily 5–10:30pm. Metro: Chángshú Lù.

Le Garçon Chinois (Lè Jiā Ěr Sōng) 🎍🎍 SPANISH   One of the victims of the SARS-driven downturn, this restaurant with the funny French name resurfaced in early 2004 as a Spanish restaurant, and a lovely one at that. Currently occupying only the first floor of an old mansion in an alley off Héngshān Lù, Le Garçon Chinois oozes elegance in its blend of dark wood wall paneling, white tablecloths, and low candlelight. Diners speak in hushed whispers, perhaps too engrossed in the assorted tapas, the hot roasted gazpacho, the paella for two, or the fine lacquered pork ribs. The awe spills over to the chocolate soup dessert, guaranteed to be like nothing you've ever tasted or drunk. Let's hope this boy stays around for a while.

Héngshān Lù, Lane 9, no. 3 (between Dōngpíng Lù and Wūlǔmùqí Lù); see map p. 122. Reservations recommended. ② 021/6445-7970. Main courses ¥75 – ¥150 ($9–$19). AE, DC, MC, V. Daily 6–10:30pm. Metro: Héngshān Lù or Chángshú Lù.

Paulaner Brauhaus (Bǎoláinà) 🎍 GERMAN   Highly popular with local businessmen and their families, Shànghǎi's biggest beer house is a massive 1930s three-story structure isolated from the road by a large green courtyard that serves as a summer beer garden. The in-house German-style brewery makes its own Münchner ale and lager, which goes down well with heaps of sauerkraut, sausages, cabbage, and bratwurst. A second branch has opened in trendy Xīn Tiāndì downtown.

Fēnyáng Lù 150 (2 blocks east of Héngshān Lù, near the Dōngpíng Lù intersection); see map p. 122. ② 021/6474-5700. Main courses ¥80 – ¥160 ($9.60–$19). AE, DC, MC, V. Mon–Fri 5:30pm–2am; Sat–Sun 11am–4pm and 5:30pm–2am. Metro: Chángshú Lù.

Simply Thai (Tiāntài Cāntīng) ★★ THAI   This restaurant off trendy Héngshān Lù is the top choice with many Shànghăi expatriates (Thais included) for unpretentious, authentic, and reasonably priced Thai food. The setting is a cozy two-story cottage with olive green walls adorned with simple Thai friezes, and the food is comfortingly familiar with a few interesting twists. Especially pleasing are the refreshing pomelo (grapefruit) salad with pineapple appetizer, *tom yam* shrimp soup, panaeng pork curry, and seafood with glass noodle salad. The busy waitstaff puts on a friendly face. Patio dining in the warmer months provides a lovely respite from the city bustle. There is another branch at Xīn Tiāndì (✆ **021/6326-2088**).

Dōngpíng Lù 5, Unit C (between Héngshān Lù and Yuèyáng Lù); see map p. 122. ✆ **021/6445-9551**. Reservations recommended. Meal for 2 ¥150 – ¥300 ($18–$36). AE, DC, MC, V. Daily 10am–1am. Metro: Héngshān Lù or Chángshú Lù.

MODERATE

Indian Kitchen (Yìndù Xiăochú) ★★ INDIAN   This small, cozy restaurant deep in the heart of the French Concession is an all-around favorite with locals and expatriates for authentic and very reasonably priced Indian food. A glass-enclosed kitchen allows you see Indian chefs whipping up nan and *dosas,* and skewering the tandoori chicken you'll soon be eating. The extensive picture menu takes into account local tastes (crab masala, anyone?), but for the most part covers all the Indian classics, and well. Besides the signature chicken tandoori, the mutton curry and the flaky spring onion *parotas* are especially fine. Staff seems a little hesitant at times, but the line that forms nightly outside the door should be plenty reassuring.

Yŏngjiā Lù 572 (between Yuèyáng Lù and Wūlŭmùqí Nán Lù); see map p. 122. ✆ **021/6473-1517**. Reservations recommended. Meal for 2 ¥130 – ¥200 ($16–$25). AE, DC, MC, V. Daily 11am–2:30pm and 5–11pm. Metro: Héngshān Lù.

Lái Fú Lóu ★ HOT POT   Unlike most hot pot restaurants, which are packed, chaotic, and decor-free, Lái Fú Lóu offers some of the most elegant hot pot dining in town. Decor is sleek with soft gray chairs and dark brown wooden tables spaced far apart, affording diners some welcome privacy. Your biggest decision will be to pick your soup base: There's a wide variety here to choose from, including a special chicken soup stock, fish, or pig bone soup. Many folks opt for the *yīnyáng* version, which contains both a potent spicy stock and a more benign pork-based broth. Besides all the usual meat and vegetable ingredients, the restaurant also specializes in hand-made *yúwán* (fish balls) and *dànjiăo* (egg-wrapped dumplings).

Huáihăi Zhōng Lù 1416, 2nd Floor (at intersection of Fùxīng Xī Lù); see map p. 122. ✆ **021/6473-6380**. Reservations recommended. Meal for 2 ¥80 – ¥120 ($10–$15). AE, DC, MC, V. Daily 11am–4am. Metro: Chángshú Lù.

O'Malley's (Ōu Mă Lì Cāntīng) ★ (Kids) IRISH   Best known as one of Shànghăi's top bars and music spots, O'Malley's also sports a menu of Irish, English, and American favorites that range from bangers and mash to hearty helpings of mashed potatoes and flavorful steaks and burgers. Service is friendly and efficient. The old two-story mansion has been decorated like a down-and-out Irish pub, with plenty of cozy booths and tables on its main floor and balcony. In summertime, the large front lawn offers courtyard dining and a children's playground, a handy feature during popular weekend brunches. The beers, of course, are quite good, as is the live Irish dance music that runs from 8:30pm to midnight Tuesday through Sunday.

Táojiāng Lù 42 (1 block west of Héngshān Lù); see map p. 122. ✆ **021/6437-0667** or 021/6474-4533. Meals ¥80 – ¥150 ($9.60–$18). AE, MC, V. Daily 11am–1:30am. Metro: Héngshān Lù or Chángshú Lù.

Shànghǎi's Best for Brunch

Calling all gluttons! When it comes to chowing down, Shànghǎi's restaurants know how to put on a buffet. Weekend brunches (mostly held in the big hotels Sun 11am–2:30pm) are not necessarily cheap (and a 15% gratuity is added to your tab), but they are sumptuous events and extremely popular among expatriates and Shànghǎi residents alike. Here's a sampling of the best hotel brunches:

Café Studio in the Four Seasons (Wēihǎi Lù 500; ☎ 021/6256-8888) sets the Shànghǎi standard high with a full international spread of Boston lobsters, Chinese dim sum, a sushi and sashimi counter, carved meats, sumptuous desserts, and more, with as much Moët & Chandon as you want for ¥318 ($40). The **Marriott Café** at the JW Marriott (Nánjīng Xī Lù 399; ☎ 021/5359-4969, ext. 6422) outdoes the competition with its 360 degree bubbly brunch: a feast of sushi, oysters, lobsters, and free-flowing champagne (¥298/$37; ¥238/$29 without) against a backdrop of stunning city views and live jazz. **The Stage** in the Westin Hotel (Hénán Zhōng Lù 88; ☎ 021/6335-1888) has garnered raves for its kids' corner; parents can now feast the afternoon away (¥298/$37 with free-flowing champagne; ¥195/$24 without; ¥95/$12 for children) while their children play under supervision. All the way out in Pǔdōng, **Second Deck** *Kids* at the Novotel Atlantis (Pǔdōng Dà Dào 728; ☎ 021/5036-6666) also attracts families with a special kids' buffet complete with magic, acrobatics, games, and face-painting at the Dolfi Kids Corner (¥258/$32 for brunch with free-flowing champagne).

Outside the hotels, **M on the Bund** (p. 94) offers the best views to go with your Bloody Mary's and eggs Benedict, while Baci at **Park 97** (p. 97) has a kids' brunch menu and the whole park outside for the little tykes to roam.

Shànghǎi Lǎo Zhàn (Ye Olde Station Restaurant) ⭐ SHÀNGHǍI

Located in a 1921 French monastery, this 4-year-old restaurant easily boasts one of the most atmospheric and nostalgic colonial settings in town. A mosaic-tiled corridor, lined with traditional lamps, antique gramophones, old photos, and even a painting of Jesus Christ, leads to a main dining hall where you can find the real novelty of this restaurant: two traditional railway carriages (an 1899 German wagon once serving the Qīng empress dowager Cíxǐ Tàihòu, and a 1919 Russian carriage used by Sòng Qīnglíng or Mme. Sun Yat-sen) running off the side of the building and providing additional seating. The food holds its own well enough, with traditional Shànghǎi dishes such as sautéed fresh shrimps, fried hairy crab (seasonal), special vegetarian duck, powdered crabmeat with tofu, and mushroom and vegetable buns making an impression. Don't expect the royal treatment in this Orient Express, as service is mostly perfunctory.

Cáoxī Běi Lù 201 (opposite the Xújiāhuì Cathedral); see map p. 122. ☎ 021/6427-2233. Reservations recommended. Meal for 2 ¥120 – ¥320 ($15–$40). No credit cards. Daily 11am–2:30pm and 5:30–10:30pm. Metro: Xújiāhuì.

Shànghǎi Xīnjiāng Fēngwèi Fàndiàn *Finds* UIGHUR   Got lamb? North-

west Chinese cuisine, which has always been more popular in northern cities like

Běijīng, has arrived in Shànghǎi with a vengeance judging by the number of Uighur restaurants that have opened in the last few years. One of the busiest, this spot, located in the southwest part of town and decorated with fake foliage and a miniature model of Xīnjiāng Province's Tiān Shān (Heavenly Lake), treats patrons to a fun, raucous, and hearty dining experience complete with whooping and dancing waiters. The Uighurs are Muslim, so lamb dominates the Chinese-only menu. Definitely try the juicy *kǎo quányáng* (roast lamb at ¥38/$4.75 per 500g/1.1 lb.), though if you plan to dine after 7pm, call ahead and reserve a portion, as this popular dish often runs out early. Other favorites include *kǎo yángròu* (barbecue lamb skewers), *báopí yángròu juǎn* (minced lamb wrapped in pancakes), and *lǎohǔ cài,* a refreshing Xīnjiāng salad of cucumbers, tomatoes, and red onions. Noodles *(miàntiáo)* or baked bread *(bǐng)* make good accompaniments, as does Xīnjiāng black beer *(Xīnjiāng píjiǔ).*

Yíshān Lù 280 (south of Nándān Lù); see map p. 122. ② 021/6468-9198. Reservations highly recommended. Meal for 2 ¥120 – ¥240 ($15–$30). No credit cards. Daily 3pm–2am (nightly dancing at 7:30pm). Metro: Xújiāhuì (20 min. away).

Xien Yue Hien (Shēn Yuè Xuān) CANTONESE/DIM SUM   Nestled in the sprawling Dīngxiāng Huāyuán, a residence and garden built by the Qīng Dynasty military commander Lǐ Hóngzhāng for his eponymous concubine Dīng Xiāng, this two-story restaurant-in-a-mansion is often cited as one of the city's best bets for a dim sum brunch primarily because of its lovely garden setting. It certainly isn't because of the inattentive and apathetic service (which makes the 10% service charge all the more egregious). The usual dim sum suspects are all here, with notables being the steamed shrimp dumplings, the barbecue pork cake, the parsley ravioli, and the baked black sesame tart. For dinner, there's plenty of fresh seafood, including steamed bean curd with shrimps and silverfish, and fat green crab with mashed garlic and ginger sauce. When you make your reservation, ask for a table by the window.

Huáshān Lù 849 (inside Dīngxiāng Huāyuán between Wǔkāng Lù and Fùxīng Xī Lù); see map p. 122 ② 021/6251-1166. Reservations highly recommended. Meal for 2 ¥100 – ¥250 ($13–$31); subject to 10% service charge. AE, DC, MC, V. Mon–Fri 11am–midnight; Sat–Sun 7am–midnight. No Metro.

INEXPENSIVE

The Grape (Pútao Yuán Jiǔjiā) *Value* SHÀNGHǍI   Located in part of a stunning domed former Russian Orthodox church (though little of it is obvious in today's restaurant), the Grape was one of the first Shànghǎi eateries to attract foreign residents. Today, this friendly, down-to-earth (except for the clusters of plastic grapes that hang overhead) cafe keeps a core group of expats and locals happy with its reasonably priced homemade Shànghǎi cuisine and friendly service. The phoenix tail shrimps with garlic, steamed clams with eggs, spicy chicken, and braised fresh bamboo shoots are all worth trying.

Xīnlè Lù 55 (2 blocks west of Shǎnxī Nán Lù, between Huáihǎi and Yán'ān Lù); see map p. 122. ② 021/6472-0486. Meal for 2 ¥60 – ¥120 ($7.20–$14). No credit cards. Mon–Fri 11am–2am; Sat–Sun 8am–2am. Metro: Shǎnxī Nán Lù.

5 Jìng Ān District (Northwest Shànghǎi)

VERY EXPENSIVE

Shintori Null II (Xīndūlǐ Wúèr Diàn) ★★ JAPANESE   This nouvelle Japanese restaurant in the western part of the French concession is the epitome of cool if you like dining in a cold and dystopian industrial bunker. A bamboo-lined concrete walkway and silent automatic sliding doors lead to the main dining pit, which features a long communal table in the center—a recent trend in Shànghǎi's hippest restaurants—and an all-chrome open kitchen in the back; the second floor has some of the best perches for people-watching as well as private dining areas sectioned off by blinds. As expected, the crowd is well heeled, black-clad, and a bit precious. Sushi and sashimi are fresh and popular, but a fun way to go may be to make a meal from a selection of appetizers such as cuttlefish in butter sauce, grilled codfish with *monomiso,* foie gras on radish, and vermicelli noodles served in an ice bowl. Service is efficient and friendly, which lends some much-needed warmth to the place.

Jùlù Lù 803 (west of Fùmín Lù); see map p. 126. ℂ 021/5404-5252. Reservations required. Meals for 2 ¥250 – ¥600 ($31–$75). AE, DC, MC, V. Mon–Fri 5:30–10:30pm; Sat–Sun 11:30am–2pm and 5:30–10:30pm. Metro: Chángshú Lù.

Sìchuān Court ★★ SÌCHUĀN   This restaurant on the 39th floor of the Hilton Hotel has been serving quality Sìchuān cuisine long before it became fashionable on China's Eastern seaboard and is today one of the most reliable, if more expensive, options in town. The environment is strictly formal, with pristine white tablecloths, carved wood panels, expansive views, and an upscale, hushed crowd, while the food is first-rate, dressed up in spices flown in daily from Sìchuān. Signature dishes include the Sìchuān treasure box featuring an assortment of cold appetizers, sautéed prawns and pine seeds with hot garlic chili sauce, braised sliced cod with minced pork in chili sauce, and sautéed green beans. The *dāndān miàn* (noodles in spicy peanut sauce) here is flavorful without being overwhelming. The well-trained staff ably balances attention and privacy.

Huáshān Lù 250, 39th Floor (top floor of the Hilton Hotel); see map p. 126. ℂ 021/6248-0000, ext. 1850. Reservations required. Meal for 2 ¥250 – ¥350 ($30–$44). AE, DC, MC, V. Daily 6–10:30pm. Metro: Jìng Ān Sì.

EXPENSIVE

Bali Laguna (Bālí Dǎo) ★ INDONESIAN   Bali Laguna is widely acclaimed for its exquisite setting, perched over a lily pond in the heart of Jìng Ān Park. With an exotic Southeast Asian decor, views of the surrounding garden, and discreet sarong-clad waitstaff, there are few more genteel or romantic places to dine in Shànghǎi. The food is fairly authentic, rated above average though falling short of a rave. Tasty choices include *otak-otak* (grilled fish cake), king prawns with vermicelli and lemon grass, and stir-fried mushrooms with herbs and vegetables. Dining is on the second floor; reserve ahead for a window table. The bar on the first floor is open nightly until 2am.

Huáshān Lù 189 (inside southwest entrance to Jing Ān Park); see map p. 126. ℂ 021/6248-6970. Reservations recommended. Meal for 2 ¥150 – ¥250 ($19–$31). AE, DC, MC, V. Daily 11am–2:30pm and 6–10pm. Metro: Jìng Ān Sì.

Cochinchina (Ōuyuè Niándài) ★ VIETNAMESE   Located in a lovely old colonial mansion, Shànghǎi's longest-standing Vietnamese restaurant presents reasonably authentic Indochinese fare with a Shànghǎi twist. With ample windows and courtyard dining, the upscale decor evokes the early French colonial days of Southeast Asia as it was over a century ago. Service can best be described as genteel, the food above average, though short of completely authentic. The green papaya salad and fresh spring rolls make good starters and the soft shell crab a tasty main.

Jùlù Lù 889, Block 11 (east of Chángshú Lù, 1 block south of Yán'ān Lù); see map p. 126. ℂ 021/6445-6797. Meal for 2 ¥300 – ¥400 ($38–$50). AE, DC, MC, V. Daily 11am–10:30pm. Metro: Chángshú Lù.

Itoya (Yī Téng Jiā) ★ *Value* JAPANESE   This branch of a small chain in Shànghăi is intimate and stylish, and offers some of the most reliable and straight-forward Japanese food in town. A simple Japanese decor prevails (including private tatami mat rooms and a small sushi bar), and the service is friendly and helpful. The menu bulges with all the Japanese staples you'd expect, like noodles, tempura, and more. Sushi and sashimi selections are fresh, abundant, and popular, with more exotic and expensive choices like sea bream and lobster sashimi also available. Lunch specials (¥50 – ¥120/$6.25–$15) served with entrée, rice, soup, vegetables, and tea/coffee are a bargain, and dinner sets (¥100 – ¥225/$13–$28) are also popular. The majority of the Japanese clientele certainly seems to approve.

Nánjīng Xī Lù 1515, 1st Floor (inside Kerry Center/Jiālì Zhōngxīn, at Tóngrén Lù); see map p. 126. ⒸⒸ 021/5298-5777. Reservations recommended. Meal for 2 ¥200 – ¥500 ($25–$60). AE, DC, MC, V. Daily 11am–11:30pm. Metro: Jìng Ān Sì.

Kaveen's Kitchen (Zhèngzōng Yìndù Cài) ★ INDIAN   This small, cozy restaurant atop the Old Manhattan Bar serves some of the more reliably authentic North Indian grub in town. The place is wonderfully atmospheric, with Indian furnishings, tapestries hanging on the maroon walls, and lilting background music (crucial for countering the din from below). Owner Vic (who named the restaurant after his son) attends every table to make sure your order is just right. Worth trying are the tandoori chicken, the perfectly balanced mutton curry, and the subtly flavored eggplant with potatoes *(aloo bhengan)*. Wash it all down with some lassis (a yogurt drink), beer, or honest-to-goodness *chai* tea. The only gripe is that portions run small. Happily for pub-crawlers, the place is open until 4am. The ¥38 ($4.80) business lunch, which includes two main dishes, nan, rice, and a drink, is one of the better deals around.

Huáshān Lù 231, 2nd Floor (opposite Hilton Hotel, inside Old Manhattan Bar); see map p. 126. Ⓒ 021/ 6248-2777. Reservations recommended. Meal for 2 ¥150 – ¥240 ($19–$30). No credit cards. Daily 11:30am–2:30pm and 5:30pm–4am. Metro: Jìng Ān Sì.

Méilóngzhèn ★ SHÀNGHĂI   Established in 1938, Méilóngzhèn is a Shànghăi institution that still draws the crowds after all these years. Its cuisine has evolved over time from strictly regional fare to one incorporating the spices, vinegars, and chilies of Sìchuān cooking. Seafood is featured prominently, and popular favorites include deep-fried eel, lobster in pepper sauce, Mandarin fish with noodles in chili sauce, Sìchuān duck, and Méilóngzhèn special chicken, served in small ceramic pots. The atmosphere is a bit stodgy with old-fashioned Qīng Dynasty furniture and carved wooden paneling. Staff alternates between attentive and harried. There is another branch in the Westgate mall at Nánjīng Xī Lù 1038 (Ⓒ **021/6255-6688**).

Nánjīng Xī Lù 1081, Building 22 (east of Shànghăi Centre at Jiāngníng Lù); see map p. 126. Ⓒ 021/ 6253-5353. Reservations recommended. Meal for 2 ¥120 – ¥240 ($14–$29). AE, DC, MC, V. Daily 11am–2pm and 5–10pm. Metro: Shímén Yī Lù.

Mesa (Méisà) ★★ CONTINENTAL   The brainchild and handiwork of the original chef of T8 and one of the owners of the bar Face, Mesa (opened Nov 2003) is intended to be, in the words of the owners, "a place *we* would like to go eat," which roughly translates to a comfortable, unpretentious restaurant serving the comfort foods of home. Don't expect a casual diner, though, as this modern minimalist restaurant with stark walls, floor-to-ceiling windows, an open kitchen, and a communal serving table (hence "mesa," which means table in Spanish) still quietly screams fine dining. The menu which makes good use of fresh local ingredients changes frequently, but established favorites include the soy and ginger salmon with green tea soba, the T-bone steak, and the beef pie. Wines, chosen from an impressive list, are served in specially imported glasses. And save room for dessert, which is all home made and ranges from a sinful Rocky Road "pie" to an only slightly less sinful flourless chocolate cake. Alfresco dining on the second-floor patio is planned for the warmer months.

Jùlù Lù 748 (east of Fùmín Lù); see map p. 126. © 021/6289-9108. Reservations required. Main courses ¥90 – ¥200 ($11–$25). AE, DC, MC, V. Mon–Fri 6–11pm; Sat–Sun 9:30am–5pm and 6–11pm. Metro: Chángshú Lù.

MODERATE

Bǎoluó *Finds* *Value* SHÀNGHǍI   One of the few constants in this ever-changing town is the long line that invariably forms outside Bǎoluó every evening. A seemingly tiny diner occupying a mere unit in a row of tightly packed Chinese houses until you step inside, the restaurant actually stretches four houses deep, every square inch buzzing with barely controlled chaos. The story goes that Bǎoluó's owner—a bicycle repairman who lived in this very lane—started the restaurant in his own home but gradually bought up his neighbors' houses as business boomed. The extensive Chinese-only menu features many local favorites given a slight twist, including *huíguō ròu jiābǐng* (twice-cooked lamb wrapped in pancakes), *sōngshǔ lúyú* (sweet-and-sour fried fish), *xièfěn huì zhēnjūn* (braised mushroom with crabmeat), and the more unusual *qīngzhēn dòuní* (creamy mashed beans).

Fùmín Lù 271 (north of Chánglè Lù, 1 block east of Chángshú Lù); see map p. 126. © 021/6279-2827. Reservations highly recommended. Meal for 2 ¥80–¥140 ($10–$18). No credit cards. Daily 11am–6am. Metro: Chángshú Lù.

Bì Fēng Táng CANTONESE/DIM SUM   The alfresco branch of this local eatery, known for its dim sum, opened here in the summer of 1999. While it has festive indoor dining (with a fishing village look), it is hugely popular on nice days because of its sidewalk setting: Tables under big umbrellas are partitioned off with bamboo fencing, red lanterns are hung out, and the twinkling lights are fired up every night. The dim sum and other Shànghǎi and Chinese dishes (of average quality) are served until dawn. There's another popular branch at Chánglè Lù 175 (near Jǐn Jiāng Fàndiàn).

Nánjīng Xī Lù 1333 (1 block west of Shànghǎi Centre); see map p. 126. © 021/6279-0738. Meal for 2 ¥80–¥200 ($10–$25). AE, DC, MC, V. Mon–Fri 10am–5am; Sat–Sun 8am–5am. Metro: Jìng Ān Sì.

Value Chinese on the Cheap

Fast, tasty, and cheap Chinese food can always be found in the point-and-choose **food courts** that blanket the basements (usually) of the large shopping malls and department stores. A multitude of stalls proffer everything from basic stir-fries to Hong Kong–style dim sum, Southern-style casseroles to Northern-style noodles and dumplings. Simply point and choose from the dishes or models on display. Prices are very reasonable, allowing you to try a variety of dishes. You will have to purchase coupons or a card to pay for your food at each stall. The **Megabite** (Dàshídài) food courts in Hong Kong Plaza (Huáihǎi Zhōng Lù 282, Lúwān) and Raffles City Mall (Xīzàng Zhōng Lù 268, Huángpǔ) are excellent places to sample the goods.

Cū Cài Guăn ★★ CANTONESE   This lively and popular Cantonese eatery is owner Hong Kong film producer and gourmet Cài Lán's attempt to get back to the food he grew up eating during the lean years of World War II. Not that you'll be in for a dull evening. The highly exotic menu (in Chinese only) proves that there's no part of a pig that can't be eaten. Trotters, brains, knuckles, and kidneys are all fair and rather delicious game. Even today's more health conscious but nostalgic Chinese will break down and sneak an order of *zhūyóu lăofàn*, a simple but wonderfully fragrant dish of rice flavored with lard and soy sauce, a staple for many Chinese during leaner times. More benign but equally tasty dishes include *rìbĕn jièmò chăo niúliŭlì* (wasabi stir-fried beef), *XO jiàng chăo sìjìdòu* (stir-fried string beans in XO sauce), *shèngguā chăo zhūjìngròu* (crispy-skinned pork dipped in a spicy sauce), *shuĭjīng xiārén* (stir-fried shrimp), and *cōngyóu bĭng* (scallion pancakes). Or order from the tanks of live seafood on the first floor. Colorful murals and photographs of Hong Kong pop stars and actors surround diners on both floors. If you're alert, you may even spot one of them in person.

Xīnzhá Lù 1697 (north of Bĕijīng Xī Lù, at intersection with Chángdé Lù); see map p. 126. ☏ 021/6255-3633. Reservations recommended. Meal for 2 ¥100–¥180 ($13–$23). No credit cards. Daily 11am–11pm. Metro: Jìng Ān Sì.

Malone's (Mălóng Mĕishì Jiŭlóu) AMERICAN   Originally part of a chain from Canada (opened in 1994), Malone's is a sports bar and restaurant in the American image, complete with wooden floors, dartboards, a pool table, a small stage, and a dance floor. The TV monitors over the long bar are tuned to international sports programs, and a decent dance band plays until closing on weekends. The 100-entry menu is a comprehensive if overpriced version of American sports bar fare, with potato skins, Buffalo wings, fries, sandwiches, grilled steaks, and gigantic hamburgers. Unfortunately, service has been haphazard of late, so don't count on the young, woefully inexperienced waitstaff always getting your order right.

Tóngrén Lù 255 (2 blocks northwest of Shànghăi Centre); see map p. 126. ☏ 021/6247-2400. www.malones.com.cn. Main courses ¥80–¥180 ($10–$23). AE, DC, MC, V. Daily 9:30am–2am; Sat–Sun brunch 11am–4pm. Metro: Jìng Ān Sì.

INEXPENSIVE

Element Fresh (Yuán Sù) ★ AMERICAN   Even for a city as international and modern as Shànghăi, finding a reasonably priced, delicious fresh salad on a consistent basis is not as easy as you might imagine. Thankfully, this hip eatery in the Shànghăi Center, established by two Americans sensing a niche for healthy dining, serves up a range of soups, salads, and sandwiches that are fresh, light, healthy, and an instant cure for any homesickness. In general, the salads fare better than the sandwiches, and the pumpkin soup is worth trying. Also on the menu is a slew of smoothies, fresh fruit and vegetable juices, pastas, and a handful of Asian set meals, as well as some very popular breakfast sets. The place is jam-packed at lunchtime; patio dining during the warmer months brings out the crowds as well.

Nánjīng Xī Lù 1376, no. 112 (ground floor, Shànghăi Centre); see map p. 126. ☏ 021/6279-8682. Reservations recommended. Main courses ¥35–¥85 ($4.50–$11). AE, DC, MC, V. Daily 7am–11pm. Metro: Jìng Ān Sì.

Wáng Jiā Shā DUMPLINGS/SHÀNGHĂI   This is as down home and plain an eatery as you'll find in the middle of Nánjīng Lù, but it's also one of the city's most popular and trusty standbys for inexpensive dining. There is no English menu but all of Shànghǎi's signature snacks are here: *xièfěn xiǎolóng* (crabmeat and pork dumplings), *xièfěn shēngjiān* (crabmeat and pork buns steamed in oil), *xiāròu xiǎohúntun* (soup wontons with shrimp filling), and *liǎngmiàn huáng* (noodles pan-fried on both sides). This is also a good place to sample Shànghǎi's famous desserts such as *bābǎofàn* (eight-treasure sticky rice) and *dòushā sūbǐng* (crispy pastry with mashed bean filling). To partake of the chaos, pay for your selections first (look for a harried waitress at the counter in the middle of the room), queue to order, then find an empty spot at the plastic tables and benches. All that remains is to slurp, loudly and with gusto.

Nánjīng Xī Lù 805 (just west of Shímén Èr Lù); see map p. 126. ✆ 021/6258-6373. Meal for 2 ¥20–¥40 ($2.50–$5). No credit cards. Daily 7am–9pm. Metro: Shímén Yī Lù.

6 Chángníng District/Hóngqiáo Development Zone (West Shànghǎi)

VERY EXPENSIVE

The Door (Qián Mén) ★★ CONTINENTAL   Housed on the third floor of an old Tudor mansion, this luxurious dinner spot in west Shànghǎi, popular with the well-heeled Hóngqiáo set, has to be seen to be believed. The cavernous, incense-scented loft is littered with antique Chinese and Asian furniture, from large Buddha statues and silk wallpapers to Míng Dynasty tables and chairs, all the result of the designer's travels through Asia. For better or worse, this aesthetic embarrassment of riches (your eye keeps wanting to move off your food to the eye candy on the walls) can't help but trump the food, which is in itself not bad. The menu, updated every 2 weeks, is international with some fusion influence. Appetizers, such as the foie gras and bisque, fare especially well, while the steak, sea bass, and stuffed squab mains are worth trying.

Hóngqiáo Lù 1468, 3rd floor (off Yán'ān Xī Lù, east of Gǔběi Lù); see map p. 134. ✆ 021/6295-3737. Reservations recommended. Main courses ¥150–¥280 ($19–$35). AE, DC, MC, V. Daily 6pm–2am. No Metro.

EXPENSIVE

Dynasty (Mǎn Fú Lóu) ★★ CANTONESE/DIM SUM   Long regarded as one of Shànghǎi's top Cantonese restaurants, Dynasty defends its turf with an elegant setting and extensive menu. The dishes are prepared by the same chefs (many from Hong Kong) who routinely cater dinners for visiting heads of state at special banquets and luncheons. The large tables with white tablecloths and the open dining space are thoroughly Cantonese, like the menu, where you can't go wrong with the fresh seafood dishes (prawns and lobster are good bets) or the dim sum lunch.

Yán'ān Xī Lù 2099 (3rd floor, Renaissance Yangtze Shànghǎi Hotel); see map p. 134. ✆ 021/6275-0000, ext. 2230. Reservations required. Meal for 2 ¥200–¥400 ($25–$50). AE, DC, MC, V. Daily 11am–2:30pm and 6–10:30pm. No Metro.

MODERATE

1221 ★★ SHÀNGHǍI   Located at the end of an alley between the center of town and the Hóngqiáo district, the classy "One-Two-Two-One (Yī Èr Èr Yī)" has been quietly serving consistently fine food at reasonable prices for the last 6 years. Offering Shànghǎi cuisine (with a touch of East/West fusion cooking) that's neither too greasy nor too sweet, this chic, tastefully decorated restaurant has a large and endearingly loyal following in the expatriate and business community. Most things on the menu will delight, but some standouts include drunken chicken, Shànghǎi smoked fish, lionhead meatballs, and braised pork with preserved vegetables. Also worth trying are the stir-fried shredded beef with *yóutiáo* (a fried salty donut), and the crispy duck. Wash it all down with eight-treasure tea *(bābǎochá)*, steeped with streams of hot water skillfully poured from long-sprouted teapots. The efficient, no-nonsense service could be friendlier but that seems a small quibble in an otherwise excellent dining experience.

Yán'ān Xī Lù 1221 (between Pānyú Lù and Dīngxī Lù); see map p. 134. ☎ 021/6213-6585. Reservations recommended. Meal for 2 ¥120 – ¥250 ($15–$30). AE, DC, MC, V. Daily 11am–2pm and 5:30–11pm. No Metro.

Bā Guó Bù Yī 🔆🔆 SÌCHUĀN   This deservedly popular eatery in the Gǔběi Xīnqū area serves some of the heartiest and most authentic Sìchuān fare in town. Crowds throng nightly to this two-story glass-front complex not for its fake foliage and batik theme, but for its kitchen, which pulls no punches where the Sìchuān peppercorn is concerned. The menu is in Chinese only but has plenty of chili alerts to warn the neophyte. Start your evening with the *fùqī fèipiàn* appetizer (cold beef and tongue doused in chili oil and peanuts), then graduate to *làzi jīdìng* (chicken nuggets in a sea of red chili peppers), *huíguō ròu* (twice-cooked pork with chili and scallions), and the delicious *shuǐzhǔ yú* (fish slices and vegetables in a flaming spicy broth), closing with *dāndān miàn* (noodles in spicy peanut sauce). In between, be kind to yourself with lots of cold water and beer breaks; you'll need them to put out the three-alarm fire in your mouth. A second branch is at Dīngxī Lù 1018 (☎ 021/5239-7779).

Hóngqiáo Lù 1676 (east of Shuǐchéng Lù); see map p. 134. ☎ 021/6270-6668. Reservations required. Meal for 2 ¥80 – ¥160 ($10–$20). No credit cards. Daily 11:30am–2pm and 5–9pm. No Metro.

Frankie's Place (Fǎlánqí Cāntīng) 🔆 SINGAPOREAN   Despite several relocations and the occasional dip in the quality of food, Frankie's has been serving mostly mouthwatering Singaporean and Malaysian fare for over a decade. Weekends bring out Singaporean expatriates hungry for their fix of curries and chili *blachan* (chili mixed with shrimp paste). While the decor may be dull (fake vines and cane chairs are minor nods to the tropics), the spicy food certainly is not. The *laksa* (rice noodles in a spicy coconut soup), *beef rendang* (dry curry beef), fish curry, *char kuay teow* (spicy stir-fried flat rice noodles), and *nasi lemak* (coconut rice with fried fish, egg, and peanuts) all hit the spot with their reasonably authentic flavors and ingredients. The only complaint is that portions run small. Weekday set lunches at ¥20 ($2.50; an entree plus coffee/tea) are a steal. The restaurant's current location in the western part of town is a bit inconvenient for tourists, and owner Frankie has indicated that he may be at a new address by the time you read this, though the phone number should remain the same.

Gǔběi Lù 1477 (east side of Gǔběi Lù just north of Gǔyáng Lù); see map p. 134. ☎ 021/6209-1955. Reservations recommended on weekends. Meal for 2 ¥60 – ¥140 ($7.50–$18). AE, DC, MC, V. Daily 6am–midnight. No Metro.

INEXPENSIVE

Lǎo Tán 🔆 *Finds* GUÌZHŌU   Some pleasantly authentic Miáo minority cuisine from Southeastern China's Guìzhōu Province can now be found in Shànghǎi in this boisterous and always crowded second-floor restaurant tucked away just east of the Crowne Plaza hotel. Food obviously takes priority over the unassuming decor (blank white walls), though there are nice ethnic touches like pillars studded with bits of broken china, mosaic-topped tables anchored by stones, and batik-clad waitstaff. Sour and spicy flavors dominate but do not overwhelm. Try the tangy *suān jiāngdòu làròu* (sour diced long beans with chilies and smoked bacon), the tender *huǒyàn niúròu* (beef with red and green peppers on a bed of leeks cooked over a slow flame), the fiery *gānguōjī guōzi* (spicy chicken with peppers), and the hearty *gānbiān tǔdòu* (fried potato pancake)—a perfect accompaniment to just about any dish. Service is brusque only because it's astonishingly fast.

Xìngfú Lù 42, 2nd Floor (north of Fǎhuázhèn Lù, 1 block east of Fānyú Lù); see map p. 134. ℂ 021/6283-7843. Reservations highly recommended. Meal for 2 ¥60 – ¥100 ($7.50–$13). No credit cards. Daily 11am–2pm and 5–11pm. No Metro.

7 Pǔdōng New Area

VERY EXPENSIVE

Canton (Yuè Zhēn Xuān) ★★★ CANTONESE/DIM SUM   With a 360-degree view from this grand height (55 floors up), elegant decor, impeccable service, and master chefs from Hong Kong, the Grand Hyatt's Canton is the most luxurious restaurant for haute Cantonese cuisine in Shànghǎi. The cozy balcony seating is partitioned by gold leaf glass screens etched with Chinese calligraphy, and there are ceremonial gates at the entrance fashioned from hand-chiseled limestone. Table service is stylish as well. The shark's fin and bird's nest soups are superb; most of the seafood dishes are wonderfully light; and the dim sum dumplings are filled with delicate mixtures of shark's fin, mushrooms, and greens. Reserve a few days in advance to get a window seat.

Shìjì Dà Dào 88 (55th floor, Jīn Mào Tower, Grand Hyatt Hotel); see map p. 130. ℂ 021/5049-1234, ext. 8898. Reservations required. Meal for 2 ¥200 – ¥400 ($25–$50). AE, DC, MC, V. Daily 11:30am–2:30pm and 5:30–10pm. Metro: Lùjiāzuǐ.

Danieli's (Dānní'àilì) ★★★ ITALIAN   Italian fine dining at its best, which in this case includes an extensive wine list and the city at your feet, this restaurant atop the St. Regis Hotel is well worth a special trip out to Pǔdōng. Tasteful and elegant, the restaurant is laid out with an open kitchen and a handful of window tables, which you should request when you make your reservation. Service is highly attentive, and the waitstaff unerringly seems to know when to replenish the *ciabatta* bread that has gone cold. The menu, which changes every few months, features all manner of excellent *pesci* and *carni,* but it's the pastas that fans love (giving this restaurant "the best pasta" award in a local expatriate dining magazine competition). In particular, the porcini mushroom, lobster, and arugula risotto is buttery and flavorful, and the homemade pumpkin and amaretto-filled ravioli is sinfully rich. Save room for the warm pear tart topped with mascarpone and parmigiana ice cream with walnut sauce, all washed down with some delightfully bracing *illy* coffee.

Dōngfāng Lù 877 (29th floor, St. Regis Hotel); see map p. 130. ℂ 021/5050-4567. Reservations required. Main courses ¥90 – ¥250 ($11–$31). AE, DC, MC, V. Daily 11:30am–2:30pm and 5:30–10pm. Metro: Lùjiāzuǐ.

EXPENSIVE

Shànghǎi Uncle (Hǎishàng Āshū) ★★★ SHÀNGHǍI   Enough good cannot be said about this highly accomplished restaurant serving up the best nouvelle Shànghǎi cuisine in town. This branch, located on the eighth and ninth floors of one of Pǔdōng's more popular shopping complexes, sees its traffic influenced more by the mall crowd (the mall closes at 10pm), but the food here is of a similarly high quality as its Pǔxī counterparts (p. 96). Its succulent and tender pork dishes, and the cold and lightly salted ox tongue appetizer, can turn even the most diehard vegetarians into carnivores.

Zhāngyáng Lù 500, Pǔdōng Shídài Guǎngchǎng/Pǔdōng Times Square, 8th–9th floors (between Pǔdōng Nán Lù and Láo Shān Xī Lù); see map p. 130. ℂ 021/5836-7977. Reservations highly recommended. Meal for 2 ¥160 – ¥250 ($20–$31). AE, DC, MC, V. Daily 11am–11pm. Metro: Dōngcāng Lù or Dōngfāng Lù.

MODERATE

Hánpǔ Yuán (Hanpo Garden) ⚝ KOREAN   This Korean restaurant in the shadow of the Jīn Mào Tower is bright and airy, if otherwise unremarkably decorated. No matter, as it's the food that takes center stage. There are a variety of Korean standards, but opt for the barbecue, which is hand-grilled for you by friendly waitstaff decked out in Korean attire. The short ribs, marinated in more than 20 ingredients are especially delicious, as is the *bulgolgi*. There is, of course, the full complement of kimchi, various cold vegetable dishes, rice, and soup. You can also mix it up with some seafood pancake or the delicious spicy fish in a stone casserole.

Huāyuán Shíqiáo Lù 162 (across from the no. 6 exit of the Jīn Mào Tower); see map p. 130. ✆ 021/5888-9988. Reservations recommended. Meal for 2 ¥120 – ¥180 ($15–$25). AE, DC, MC, V. Daily 11am–10pm. Metro: Lùjiāzuǐ.

Sū Zhè Huì (Jade Garden) ⚝ SHÀNGHǍI   This branch of one of the more highly regarded and popular Shànghǎi chain restaurants offers diners its signature local dishes as well as Hong Kong–style dim sum in a classy and refined setting. Unadorned glass panels, marble floors, cream-colored chairs, and muted lighting all take a back seat to the food here. Not everything on the menu excites, so pick well: tea-smoked duck, wine-preserved green crab, and *mìzhī huǒfāng* (pork and taro in candied sauce) are all house specialties that live up to their renown; the noodles with scallions and small shrimp are some of the most delicious in town; and *qícài dōngsǔn* (fresh winter shoots with local greens) is something you're unlikely to get back home. Service is highly efficient.

Dōngfāng Lù 877 (just north of the St. Regis hotel); see map p. 130. ✆ 021/5058-6088. Meal for 2 ¥77 – ¥120 ($9.60–$14). AE, DC, MC, V. Daily 11am–11pm. Metro: Dōngfāng Lù.

INEXPENSIVE

Cháng Ān Dumplings (Cháng Ān Jiǎozi Lóu) *Value* DUMPLINGS   Having moved from its Yúnnán Lù address in Pǔxī to Pǔdōng in 2002, this once-famous local institution has seen a drop-off in customers. Now it's a no-frills *jiǎozi* joint popular with neighborhood locals. The usual Běijīng staples are here, including simple *shuǐjiǎo* (boiled dumpling) and the usual pork and leek dumplings (*jiǔcài ròu jiǎo*). Go for the *pínglóng* mixed sampler, which is a steamer of meat, vegetable, and seafood dumplings.

Pǔdōng Dà Dào 1588 (at intersection with Mínshēng Lù); see map p. 130. ✆ 021/5885-8416. Meal for 2 ¥20 – ¥40 ($2.50–$5). No credit cards. Daily 6:30am–9pm. No Metro.

8 Nánshì District (Old Town)

EXPENSIVE

Lǔ Bō Láng ⚝ *Overrated* SHÀNGHǍI   Housed in a three-story traditional Chinese pavilion just south of Yù Yuán and Jiǔ Qū Qiáo (Bridge of Nine Turnings), this restaurant has become a *de rigueur* stop on the average tourist itinerary strictly on the basis of its celebrity guest list. As the portraits on the second- and third-floor walls attest, some of its most famous visitors have included Queen Elizabeth II, Fidel Castro, and President Bill Clinton, none of whom will likely tell you the food is good enough though hardly the best in town. Specialties such as the seasonal *Yángchéng Hú* crab, shark's fin, and President Clinton's favorite *sānsī méimao sū* (eyebrow-shaped pasty stuffed with pork, bamboo, and mushrooms) sell well, though prices are generally inflated. The automatic 10% service charge is a guarantee that you won't get much in the way of service.

Yùyuán Lù 115 (south shore of teahouse lake); see map p. 138. ✆ 021/6328-0602. Reservations recommended. Meal for 2 ¥120 – ¥250 ($14–$30). AE, DC, MC, V. Daily 7am–12:30am. Metro: Hénán Zhōng Lù.

Shànghǎi's Favorite Dumpling

Xiǎolóng bāo, literally "little steamer buns," are popular in many parts of China, but nowhere more so than in the Shànghǎi region. The characteristic that distinguishes this little dumpling from all others is the hot broth inside that will trickle into your mouth, or squirt onto your neighbor's lap, depending on how you handle it. *Xiǎolóng bāo* is made by wrapping ground pork and a gelatinous soup in as thin a dough wrapper as possible. Sometimes, powdered crabmeat is added *(xièfěn xiǎolóng).* After steaming, the gelatin has melted and the pork is bathed in a delicious hot oil, all *inside* the wrapper. *Tip:* Never bite directly into a *xiǎolóng bāo* right out of the steamer, as the scalding broth can cause some serious tongue damage! Expert *xiǎolóng bāo* eaters usually hold the top of the dumpling with their chopsticks, with a spoon underneath. Nibble at the skin on top and let the broth trickle onto the spoon, or wait a few seconds for the broth to cool, then slurp the whole thing into your mouth. If desired, you can add some vinegar and ginger.

MODERATE

Shànghǎi Lǎo Fàndiàn (Shànghǎi Classic Restaurant) ☆ SHÀNGHǍI
While neighboring Lǚ Bō Láng has been getting all the attention, this classic restaurant has been quietly serving original (and better) Shànghǎi dishes since 1875. Reportedly built on the site of a restaurant personally approved by the Qiánlóng emperor (reign 1736–95), this restaurant was renovated in the last few years and is now located on the second-floor atrium of a three-star hotel. Old posters and antique rickshaws lend a traditional touch, but the highlight here is the food which even appeals to young Shanghainese who might usually be counted on to shun such stodgy establishments. Perennial favorites include the eight treasure duck (stuffed with glutinous rice cooked with eight ingredients including mushrooms, chicken, and various beans), deep-fried shrimps, and *kòu sān sī* (julienne strips of tofu skin, ham, and bamboo).

Fúyòu Lù 242 (northwest of Yù Yuán, at intersection of Jiùjiàochǎng Lù); see map p. 138. ℂ 021/6355-2275. Reservations highly recommended. Meal for 2 ¥160 – ¥240 ($20–$30). AE, DC, MC, V. Daily 11am–2pm and 5–9pm. Metro: Hénán Zhōng Lù (1 mile away).

INEXPENSIVE

Chūnfēng Sōngyuè Lóu VEGETARIAN   Located in the Yù Yuán commercial complex but slightly away from its jam-packed center, this restaurant dating to 1910 serves traditional vegetarian food (lots of imitation meat and stewed foods made of tofu and soy products), noodles, and dumplings at reasonable prices. More "formal" dining on the second floor (open at 11am) offers signature dishes (some of which have wall photo displays) such as *càixīn xièhuángyóu* ("crab" actually made of carrot, mushroom, and bamboo among other ingredients), *chénpí sùyā* (orange peel "duck"), and *xiānggū càibāo* (vegetable steamed buns). For cheaper and more casual dining on the first floor, try the vegetarian spring rolls *(chūnjuǎn,* ¥4/50¢) and the award-winning *xiānggū miànjīn miàn* (noodle soup with gluten and mushrooms, ¥6/75¢), though you may want to ask for *shǎo yóu* ("less oil").

Bǎilíng Lù 23 (corner of Jiùjiàochǎng Lù); see map p. 138. © 021/6355-3630. Meal for 2 ¥80 – ¥140 ($10–$18). No credit cards. Daily 6:30am–8pm. No Metro.

Nánxiáng Mántou Diàn DUMPLINGS   Tired of wandering around Old Town? This two-story dumpling restaurant just west of the Bridge of Nine Turnings (Jiǔ Qū Qiáo) would be the ideal place to take a load off and refortify with some of Shànghǎi's most famous snacks if it weren't always jammed to the rafters with scores of liked-minded tourists. What they all come for is the award-winning *Nánxiáng xiǎolóng* (¥8/$1 for a steamer of 16 dumplings), steamed pork dumplings with delicious broth that squirts all over the moment you bite into the wrapper. Impossibly long lines form for the takeout counter on the first floor where glass windows allow you to watch the cooks at work. Three dining rooms on the second floor offer a greater choice of snacks, including spring rolls with crab stuffing and salty cashew nut crisps. There's a picture menu to help in ordering; otherwise, just point or wait for help, which may be a while coming.

Yùyuán Lù 85 (west shore of teahouse lake); see map p. 138. © 021/6355-4206. Meal for 2 ¥16 – ¥80 ($2–$10). No credit cards. Daily 7am–8pm. Metro: Hénán Zhōng Lù (1 mile away).

6

What to See & Do in Shànghǎi

Shànghǎi has precious few sights on the scale of the Forbidden City or the Great Wall, but the treasures it does have—its colonial neighborhoods, historic homes, museums, parks, and shopping avenues, not to mention Asia's most famous street—speak to a unique legacy all its own. This chapter describes Shànghǎi's treasures, with a special focus on the city's four top attractions: the **Bund, Yù Yuán** (and **Old Town**), the **Shànghǎi Museum,** and the **Huángpǔ River Cruise.**

The average tourist usually blows through town in about 2 days, but 3 days is a minimum to do any real sightseeing, as attractions are scattered all over the city. Even then, Shànghǎi is about more than just its buildings. The city that's one of the most exciting in the world demands time to soak in its energy, to appreciate its complexity, and to sample its many offerings, which may not be apparent on the surface. Bear in mind that sights outside Shànghǎi, such as Sūzhōu, Hángzhōu, or the water villages of Nánxún, and Tónglǐ (all covered in chapter 10) require day trips.

HOW TO SEE SHÀNGHǍI

The best way to see Shànghǎi is on your own, armed with a good map, this book, and using a combination of taxis, subways, and your own two feet. Transportation facilities and many of the sights described here are very user-friendly, even for the non-Chinese-speaking, first-time visitor.

Of course, if you are severely pressed for time and only have a day, an **organized tour** in the company of an English-speaking guide can be a hassle-free if superficial way to cover the major sights. Your hotel travel desk or a travel agency (see "Organized Tours" later in this chapter) can arrange this.

The last and least advised option is to hire a car for the day through your hotel, an expensive option that will easily cost you upwards of ¥800 ($100) a day for a car and driver. It's cheaper if you hire a taxi for the day yourself on the streets.

SUGGESTED ITINERARIES

Several of the top attractions are within walking distance of each other (**Nánjīng Lù,** the **Bund, Old Town, Yù Yuán**), but others are a considerable distance apart, making taxis almost mandatory to take in everything during a short visit.

If You Have 1 Day

Start your only day in Shànghǎi with a visit to the **Nánjīng Lù Pedestrian Mall** (at Xīzàng Lù). If you don't feel like walking all the way down to the Bund, there's a tram that can take you as far as Hénán Lù, from where it's a short walk to the **Bund.** From there, head down to **Old Town** and **Yù Yuán,** finishing up with a tour of the fabulous **Shànghǎi Museum** in the late afternoon. In the evening there should be just enough time for dinner at your hotel and an **acrobatics** show or a fine dinner at **M on the Bund** or a restaurant in **Xīn Tiāndì.** If you prefer everything arranged for you, book a group tour of the city through your hotel tour desk. This will give you a chance to see some of the top attractions (**Yù Yuán,** the **Bund,** the **Oriental Pearl TV Tower** or the **Jīn Mào Tower,** the **Jade Buddha Temple,** and perhaps **People's Square**), with a full Shànghǎi lunch included. Either way, you won't have trouble sleeping.

If You Have 2 Days

Two days should give you time to take in the very top attractions (such as the Bund, Yù Yuán, and the Shànghǎi Museum), with a little time left over for shopping and browsing the historic neighborhoods. You can also visit the **Jade Buddha Temple** if you haven't already, and either the **Oriental Pearl TV Tower** (and the **Shànghǎi Historical Museum**) or the **Jīn Mào Tower** in Pǔdōng, where you'll be treated to some stunning city views. On the second afternoon, take a cruise on the **Huángpǔ River** or spend it strolling the **French Concession** with stops at some of its attractions (the residences of **Soong Ching-ling** and **Sun Yat-sen, Fùxīng Park,** site of the **First Communist Congress** at **Xīn Tiāndì,** and the **Shànghǎi Museum of Arts and Crafts**). An evening's dining and stroll through **Xīn Tiāndì** gives a taste of past, present, and future Shànghǎi.

If You Have 3 Days

Three days is the minimum to do much Shànghǎi sightseeing. It requires 2 days just to take in the top sites listed in the 1-day and 2-day itineraries. On the third day,

you should have time to wander farther afield with stops at a **Children's Palace** and one of the religious sites such as the **Ohel Moshe Synagogue,** the **Xújiāhuì Cathedral** (and the **Bibliotheca Zi-ka-wei** if it's a Sat), or the **Lónghuá Temple and Pagoda.** If none of these sites grabs you, consider a day trip, guided or on your own, to **Tónglǐ, Nánxún,** or **Sūzhōu.**

If You Have 4 Days or More

This will give you time to take a look at Shànghǎi's top attractions, although a week would be better. Much of what gives Shànghǎi its special quality is the mix of the traditional Chinese with the colonial European with the very modern; all this is reflected in its fascinating blend of period and modern architecture, something best appreciated at your leisure in the streets. Shànghǎi's shopping streets, riverfront, Old Town, French Concession, and even the Pǔdōng New Area are rewarding areas for a stroll (see chapter 7, "Shànghǎi Strolls," for detailed itineraries of walking tours). At People's Square, in addition to a mandatory visit to the Shànghǎi Museum, there are also opportunities for a tour of the adjacent **Grand Theater** and the fascinating **Shànghǎi Urban Planning Exhibition Center.** Old Town has several temples, a myriad of small alleys, and part of the old city wall worth exploring. There's also **Lǔ Xùn Park, Duōlún Lù Cultural Street,** and the **Shànghǎi Botanical Gardens.** You can also head out on an overnight trip to **Hángzhōu** or **Sūzhōu.**

1 The Bund (Wài Tān)

The Bund (which means the Embankment) refers to Shànghǎi's famous waterfront running along the west shore of the Huángpǔ River, forming the eastern boundary of old downtown Shànghǎi. Once a muddy towpath for boats along the river, the Bund was where the foreign powers that entered Shànghǎi after the

Huángpǔ (Downtown) & Hóngkǒu (Northeast Shànghǎi)

¥ Ban
✉ Post Office
PSB Public-Security Visas

Hongkou Football Stadium ■

HONGKOU
ZUQIU CHANG

LUXUN
PARK

①

②

③

DONG BAOXING
LU

SICHUAN
BEI LU
PARK

BAOSHAN LU

⑤

✉

Suzhou River

XINZHA LU

HENAN ZHONG LU

HUANGPU

⑯

⑧

RENMIN
GONGYUAN

Shanghai Municipal
Government Building

Nanjing Xi Lu

PEOPLE'S
PARK

⑳

⑱

⑲

⑰

⑮

㉖

㉔

㉓

㉒

㉑

㉝ ㉞

㉟

㉛

㉜

Yifu Theatre

⑫ ⑭

⑬

⑪

㉗ ㉘

㉙

㉚

RENMIN
GUANGCHANG

PEOPLE'S
SQUARE

㊱

Wusheng Lu

Renmin Da Dao

㊳

㊲

㊴

Shanghai
Concert Hall

Yan'an Dong Lu

HEPING PARK

Siping Lu

Lu

UNDER CONSTRUCTION

HONGKOU

Zhoujiazui Lu

Gaoyang Lu

Gongping Lu

Zhoushan Lu

Baoaing Lu

Kunming Lu

Changyang Lu

④

Huoshan Lu

Huimin Lu

Yangshupu Lu

Dong Changzhi Lu

Dong Daming Lu

International Passenger Terminal ■

Huangpu Lu 7

Huangpu River

BUND SIGHTSEEING TUNNEL

YAN'AN DONG LU TUNNEL

Oriental Pearl ■ TV Tower

LUJIAZUI Ⓜ

PUDONG
(SEE "PUDONG (EAST OF RIVER)" MAP)

Huangpu Cruise ■ Dock

Jinmao Tower ■

ravel
gency

Zhongshan Dong Er Lu

BUND PROMENADE

DONGCHANG LU Ⓜ

黄浦
Huángpǔ

虹口
Hóngkǒu

Key for Huángpǔ & Hóngkǒu

ACCOMMODATIONS ■

Broadway Mansions Hotel 6
(Shànghǎi Dàshà)
上海大厦

Howard Johnson Plaza Hotel 19
(Gǔ Xiàng Dàjiǔdiàn)
古象大酒店

JW Marriott (Wànháo Jiǔdiàn) 28
万豪酒店

Pacific Hotel (Jīnmén Dàjiǔdiàn) 24
金门大酒店

Park Hotel (Guójì Fàndiàn) 25
国际饭店

Peace Hotel (Hépíng Fàndiàn) 7
和平饭店

Pǔjiāng Fàndiàn (Pǔjiāng Hotel) 8
浦江饭店

Ramada Plaza Shànghǎi 21
(Nán Xīnyǎ Huáměidá Dàjiǔdiàn)
南新雅华美达大酒店

Sofitel Hyland Hotel (Hǎilún Bīnguǎn) 16
海伦宾馆

The Westin Shànghǎi 12
(Shànghǎi Wēisītīng Dàfàndiàn)
上海威斯汀大饭店

Yángzǐ Fàndiàn (Yangtze Hotel) 34
扬子饭店

YMCA Hotel (Qīngnián Huì Bīnguǎn) 39
青年会宾馆

DINING ◆

Gōngdélín 27
功德林

Huáng Hé Lù Měishí Jiē 26
(Huáng Hé Lù Food Street)
黄河路美食街

M on the Bund 9
(Mǐshì Xīcāntīng)
米氏西餐厅

Shànghǎi Uncle 14
(Hǎishàng Āshū)
海上阿叔

Three on the Bund 1
(Wài Tān Sān Hào)
外滩三号

Wáng Bǎo Hé 20
王宝和

Yúnnán Lù Měishí Jiē 38
(Yúnnán Lù Food Street)
云南路美食街

Yúnnán Měishí Yuán 35
(Yúnnán Gourmet)
云南美食园

Zhápǔ Lù Měishí Jiē 5
(Zhápǔ Lù Food Street)
闸浦路美食街

Travel Tip: He who finds the best hotel deal has more to spend on facials involving knobbly vegetables.

Hello, the Roaming Gnome here. I've been nabbed from the garden and taken round the world. The people who took me are so terribly clever. They find the best offerings on Travelocity. For very little cha-ching. And that means I get to be pampered and exfoliated till I'm pink as a bunny's doodah.

travelocity®

1-888-TRAVELOCITY / travelocity.com / America Online Keyword: Travel

黄浦 **Huángpǔ**   虹口 **Hóngkǒu**

Lúwān (French Concession) & Xúhuì (Southwest Shànghǎi)

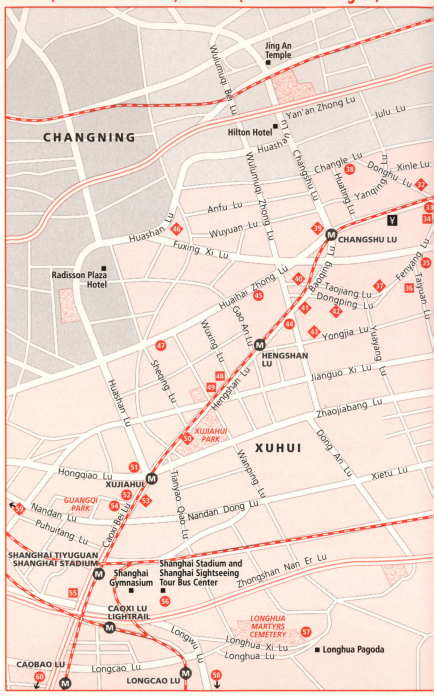

Jing An Temple

CHANGNING

Wulumuqi Bei Lu

Yan'an Zhong Lu

Julu Lu

Hilton Hotel

Huashan Lu

Changshu Lu

Changle Lu

Donghu Lu

Xinle Lu

38

32

Huating Lu

Yanqing Lu

Anfu Lu

Wulumuqi Zhong Lu

33

34

¥

Huashan Lu

46

Wuyuan Lu

39

M CHANGSHU LU

Fuxing Xi Lu

Baoqing Lu

35

Radisson Plaza Hotel

Huaihai Zhong Lu

40

Taojiang Lu

Fenyang Lu

37

Taiyuan Lu

36

45

Gao An Lu

Dongping Lu

42

Wuxing Lu

41

44

43

Yongjia Lu

Yuayang Lu

47

Sheqing Lu

Huashan Lu

48

Hengshan Lu

M HENGSHAN LU

Jianguo Xi Lu

49

Zhaojiabang Lu

50

XUJIAHUI PARK

XUHUI

Dong An Lu

Hongqiao Lu

51

M

Wanping Lu

Xietu Lu

XUJIAHUI

Tianyao Qiao Lu

52

Caoxi Bei Lu

53

59

Nandan Lu

GUANGQI PARK

54

Nandan Dong Lu

Puhuitang Lu

SHANGHAI TIYUGUAN
SHANGHAI STADIUM

M

Shanghai Gymnasium

Shanghai Stadium and Shanghai Sightseeing Tour Bus Center

Zhongshan Nan Er Lu

55

CAOXI LU LIGHTRAIL

56

M

LONGHUA MARTYRS CEMETERY

57

CAOBAO LU

Longcao Lu

Longwu Lu

Longhua Xi Lu

Longhua Lu

Longhua Pagoda

60

M

LONGCAO LU

58

122

Key for Lúwān & Xúhuì

ACCOMMODATIONS ■

City Hotel (Chéngshì Jiǔdiàn) 29
城市酒店

Héngshān Bīnguǎn 49
(Héngshān Hotel)
衡山宾馆

Huá Tíng Hotel & Towers 55
(Huá Tíng Bīnguǎn)
华亭宾馆

Jǐn Jiāng Tower 21
(Xīn Jǐn Jiāng Dàjiǔdiàn)
新锦江大酒店

Jǐn Jiāng Hotel 23
(Jǐn Jiāng Fàndiàn)
锦江饭店

Okura Garden Hotel Shànghǎi 26
(Huāyuán Fàndiàn)
花园饭店

Regal International East Asia Hotel 48
(Fùháo Huánqiú Dōngyà Jiǔdiàn)
富豪环球东亚酒店

Ruìjīn Bīnguǎn 18
(Ruìjīn Hotel)
瑞金宾馆

Shànghǎi Conservatory of Music
  Guest House 34
(Shànghǎi Yīnyuè Xuéyuàn)
上海音乐学院

Tàiyuán Biéshù (Tàiyuán Villa) 36
太原别墅

ATTRACTIONS ●

Fùxīng Gōngyuán (Fùxīng Park) 10
复兴公园

Guójì Lǐbài Táng 44
(Héngshān Community Church)
国际礼拜堂

Jǐn Jiāng Amusement Park 60
(Jǐn Jiāng Lèyuán)
锦江乐园

Lónghuá Sì (Lónghuá Temple) 57
龙华寺

Ocean World (Hǎiyáng Shìjiè) 56
海洋世界

Shànghǎi Library 45
(Shànghǎi Túshūguǎn)
上海图书馆

Shànghǎi Library Bibliotheca Zi-Ka-Wei 52
(Shànghǎi Túshūguǎn
  Xújiāhuì Cángshū Lóu)
上海图书馆徐家汇藏书楼

Shànghǎi Museum of Arts and Crafts 35
(Shànghǎi Gōngyì
Měishù Bówùguǎn)
上海工艺美术博物馆

Shànghǎi Music Conservatory
  Oriental Musical Instrument Museum 33
(Shànghǎi Yīnyuè Xuéyuàn Dōngfāng
  Yuèqì Bówùguǎn)
上海音乐学院东方乐器博物馆

Shànghǎi Public Security Museum 16
(Shànghǎi Gōng'ān Bówùguǎn)
上海公安博物馆

Shànghǎi Zhíwùyuán 58
(Shànghǎi Botanical Gardens)
上海植物园

Site of the First National Congress of the
  Communist Party 6
(Zhōnggòng Yīdà Huìzhǐ)
中共一大会址

Sòng Qìnglíng Gùjū 47
(Soong Ching-ling's Former Residence)
宋庆龄故居

Sūn Zhōngshān Gùjū Jìniànguǎn 13
(Sun Yat-sen's Former Residence)
孙中山故居纪念馆

Xīn Tiāndì (New Heaven and Earth) 5
新天地

Xújiāhuì Tiānzhǔtáng 54
(St. Ignatius Cathedral)
徐家汇天主堂

Zhōu Gōng Guǎn 12
(Zhōu Ēnlái's Former Residence)
周公馆

卢湾　徐汇
Lúwān　**Xúhuì**

124

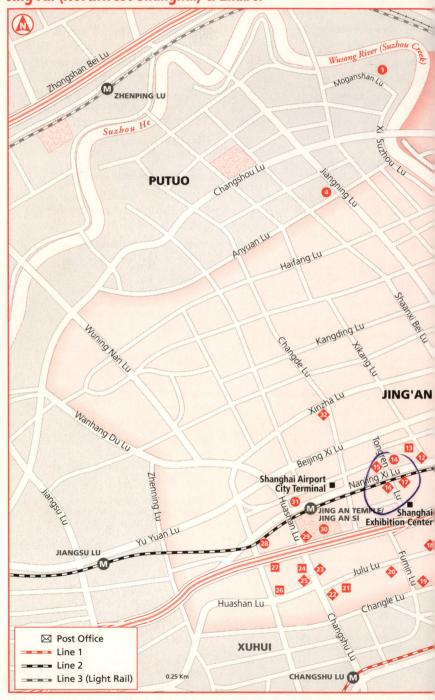

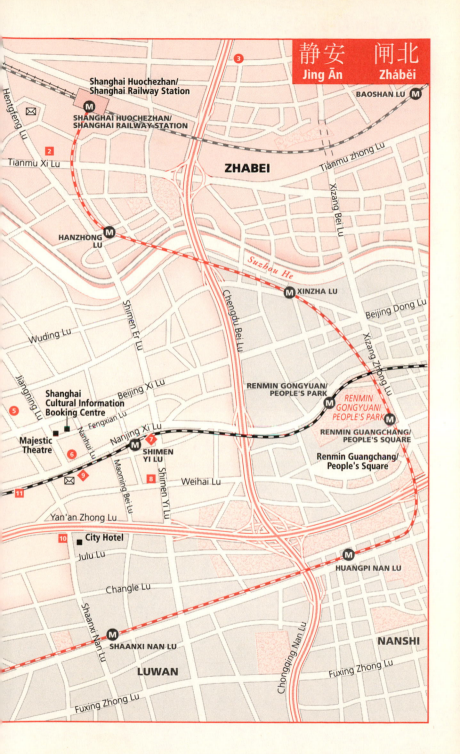

静安　闸北
Jìng Ān　**Zhábĕi**

BAOSHAN LU Ⓜ

Shanghai Huochezhan/
Shanghai Railway Station

Ⓜ
**SHANGHAI HUOCHEZHAN/
SHANGHAI RAILWAY STATION**

ZHABEI

Hengfeng Lu

⊠

❷

Tianmu Xi Lu

Tianmu zhong Lu

Xizang Bei Lu

❸

**HANZHONG
LU** Ⓜ

Suzhou He

Ⓜ **XINZHA LU**

Beijing Dong Lu

Chengdu Bei Lu

Shimen Er Lu

Wuding Lu

Xizang Zhong Lu

**RENMIN GONGYUAN/
PEOPLE'S PARK**

Jiangning Lu

❺

Beijing Xi Lu

Ⓜ *RENMIN
GONGYUAN/
PEOPLE'S PARK*

**Shanghai
Cultural Information
Booking Centre**

Fengxian Lu

Nanhui Lu

Nanjing Xi Lu

**RENMIN GUANGCHANG/
PEOPLE'S SQUARE** Ⓜ

**Majestic
Theatre**

❻

Ⓜ ❼
**SHIMEN
YI LU**

**Renmin Guangchang/
People's Square**

Maoming Bei Lu

⊠ ❾

❽

Shimen Yi Lu

Weihai Lu

❶❶

Yan'an Zhong Lu

❶⓪ ■ **City Hotel**

Julu Lu

Ⓜ **HUANGPI NAN LU**

Changle Lu

Shaanxi Nan Lu

Chongqing Nan Lu

NANSHI

Ⓜ **SHAANXI NAN LU**

Fuxing Zhong Lu

LUWAN

Fuxing Zhong Lu

127

Key for Jìng Ān & Zhábĕi

ACCOMMODATIONS ■

Four Seasons Hotel Shànghǎi **8**
(Shànghǎi Sìjì Jiǔdiàn)
上海四季酒店

Héngshān Moller Villa **10**
(Héngshān Mǎlè Biéshù Fàndiàn)
衡山马勒别墅饭店

Hilton Hotel **24**
(Jìng Ān Xīěrdùn Dàjiǔdiàn)
静安希尔顿大酒店

Holiday Inn Downtown Shànghǎi **2**
(Shànghǎi Guǎngchǎng Chángchéng Jiàrì Jiǔdiàn)
上海广场长城假日酒店

Hotel Equatorial (Guójì Guìdū Dàjiǔdiàn) **27**
国际贵都大酒店

Jù Yīng Bīnguǎn **21**
巨鹰宾馆

Portman Ritz-Carlton Hotel **13**
(Shànghǎi Bōtèmàn Lìjiā Dàjiǔdiàn)
上海波特曼丽嘉酒店

Shànghǎi Hotel **26**
(Shànghǎi Bīnguǎn)
上海宾馆

Shànghǎi JC Mandarin **11**
(Shànghǎi Jǐncāng Wénhuá Dàjiǔdiàn)
上海锦沧文华大酒店

ATTRACTIONS ●

Children's Municipal Palace **28**
(Shì Shàonián Gōng)
市少年宫

Jìng Ān Gōngyuán **30**
(Jìng Ān Park)
静安公园

Jìng Ān Sì **31**
(Jìng Ān Temple)
静安寺

Ohel Rachel Synagogue **5**
(Lāxīěr Yóutài Jiàotáng)
拉西尔犹太教堂

Shànghǎi Circus World **3**
(Shànghǎi Mǎxì Chéng)
上海马戏城

Yù Fó Sì **4**
(Jade Buddha Temple)
玉佛寺

SHOPPING ●

50 Mògān Shān Lù **1**
莫干山路 50 号

Shànghǎi Centre **14**
(Shànghǎi Shāngchéng)
上海商城

Westgate Mall **6**
(Méilóngzhèn Guǎngchǎng)
梅龙镇广场

静安　闸北
Jìng Ān　**Zhábĕi**

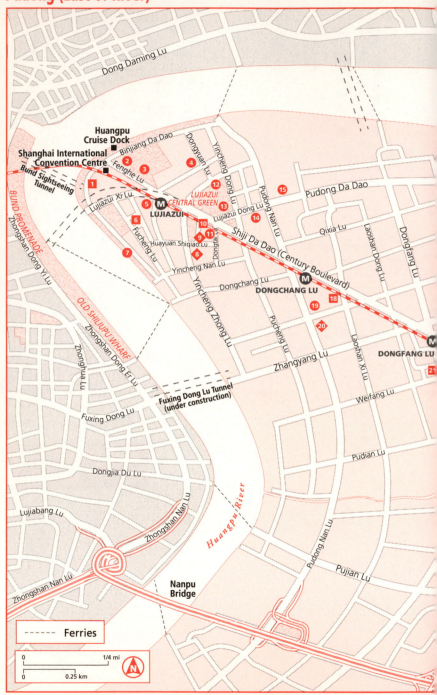

Dong Daming Lu

Huangpu Cruise Dock

Shanghai International Convention Centre

Bund Sightseeing Tunnel

Binjiang Da Dao

Fenghe Lu

Dongyuan Lu

Yincheng Dong Lu

LUJIAZUI CENTRAL GREEN

Pudong Da Dao

Pudong Nan Lu

Qixia Lu

Laoshan Dong Lu

Dongfang Lu

Lujiazui Xi Lu

LUJIAZUI

Lujiazui Dong Lu

Shiji Da Dao (Century Boulevard)

Fucheng Lu

Huayuan Shiqiao Lu

Dongchang Lu

DONGCHANG LU

Pucheng Lu

Yincheng Nan Lu

Yincheng Zhong Lu

Dongta Lu

Laoshan Xi Lu

DONGFANG LU

BUND PROMENADE

Zhongshan Dong Yi Lu

OLD SHILIUPU WHARF

Zhongshan Dong Er Lu

Zhonghua Lu

Fuxing Dong Lu

Fuxing Dong Lu Tunnel (under construction)

Zhangyang Lu

Weifang Lu

Dongjia Du Lu

Pudian Lu

Lujiabang Lu

Zhongshan Nan Lu

Huangpu River

Pudong Nan Lu

Pujian Lu

Zhongshan Nan Lu

Nanpu Bridge

- - - - Ferries

0   1/4 mi
0   0.25 km

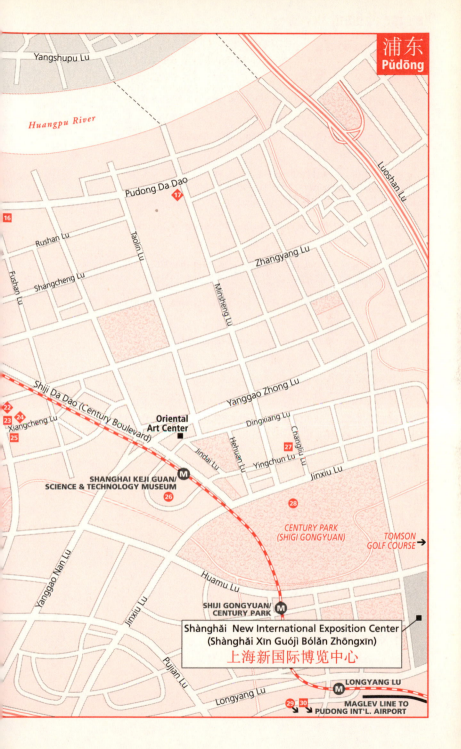

Yangshupu Lu

Huangpu River

Luoshan Lu

Pudong Da Dao **17**

16

Rushan Lu

Taolin Lu

Zhangyang Lu

Minsheng Lu

Fushan Lu

Shangcheng Lu

Shiji Da Dao (Century Boulevard)

Yanggao Zhong Lu

22
23 **24**
Xiangcheng Lu
25

Oriental Art Center

Dingxiang Lu

Changliu Lu

27

Jindai Lu

Hehuan Lu

Yingchun Lu

Jinxiu Lu

SHANGHAI KEJI GUAN/ SCIENCE & TECHNOLOGY MUSEUM

Ⓜ

26

28

CENTURY PARK (SHIGI GONGYUAN)

TOMSON GOLF COURSE →

Yanggao Nan Lu

Huamu Lu

Jinxiu Lu

SHIJI GONGYUAN/ CENTURY PARK Ⓜ

Shànghǎi New International Exposition Center
(Shànghǎi Xīn Guójì Bólǎn Zhōngxīn)
上海新国际博览中心

Pujian Lu

LONGYANG LU
Ⓜ

Longyang Lu

29 **30**
↓   ↓

MAGLEV LINE TO PUDONG INT'L. AIRPORT

Key for Pŭdōng

ACCOMMODATIONS ■

Courtyard by Marriott Hotel Pŭdōng (Shànghǎi Qílǔ Wànyí Dàjiǔdiàn) **21**
上海齐鲁万怡大酒店

Grand Hyatt Shànghǎi (Shànghǎi Jīn Mào Jūnyuè Dàjiǔdiàn) **10**
上海金茂君悦大酒店

Holiday Inn Pŭdōng (Shànghǎi Pŭdōng Jiàrì Jiǔdiàn) **25**
上海浦东假日酒店

Hotel Inter-Continental Pŭdōng Shànghǎi **18**
Shànghǎi Xīnyà Tāngchén Zhōujì Dàjiǔdiàn)
上海新亚汤臣洲际大酒店

Oriental Riverside Hotel Shànghǎi (Dōngfāng Bīnjiāng Dàjiǔdiàn **1**
东方滨江大酒店

Pŭdōng Shangri-La Hotel (Pŭdōng Xiānggélǐlā Fàndiàn) **6**
浦东香格里拉大酒店

Renaissance Shànghǎi Pŭdōng Hotel (Shànghǎi Chúndà Wànlì Jiǔdiàn) **27**
上海淳大万丽酒店

St. Regis Shànghǎi (Shànghǎi Ruìjí Hóngtǎ Dàjiǔdiàn) **23**
上海瑞吉红塔大酒店

Novotel Atlantis Shànghǎi (Hǎishén Nuòfùtè Dàjiǔdiàn) **16**
海神诺富特大酒店

Ramada Pŭdōng Airport (Shànghǎi Jīchǎng Huáměidá Dàjiǔdiàn) **30**
上海机场华美达大酒店

DINING ◆

Canton (Yuè Zhēn Xuān) **9**
粤珍轩

Danieli's (Dānní'àilì) **24**
丹尼艾丽

Shànghǎi Uncle (Hǎishàng Āshū) **20**
海上阿叔

Hánpǔ Yuán (Hanpo Garden) **8**
韩浦园

Sū Zhè Huì (Jade Garden) **22**
苏浙汇

Cháng Ān Dumpling (Cháng Ān Jiǎozi Lóu) **17**
长安饺子楼

浦东
Pǔdōng

Chángníng/Hóngqiáo Development Zone (West Shànghǎi)

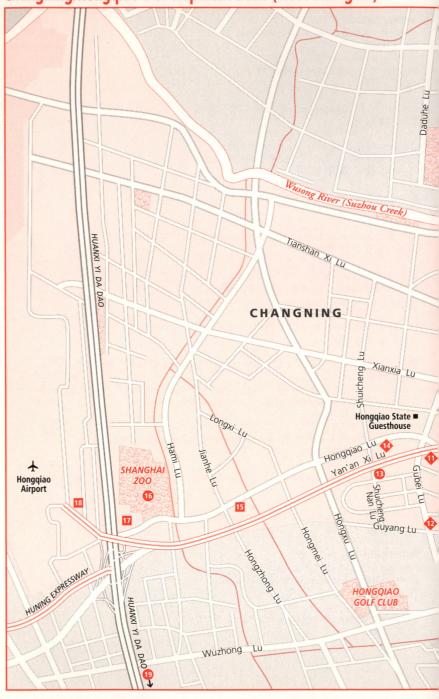

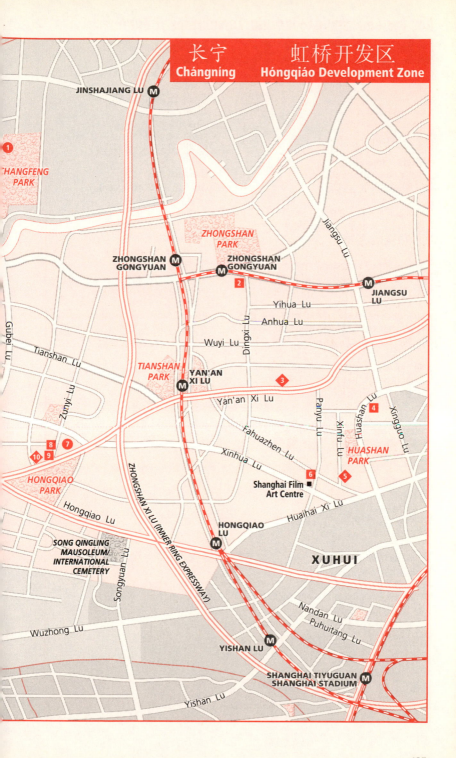

长宁
Chángníng

虹桥开发区
Hóngqiáo Development Zone

JINSHAJIANG LU Ⓜ

❶
HANGFENG
PARK

ZHONGSHAN
PARK

ZHONGSHAN
GONGYUAN Ⓜ

ZHONGSHAN
GONGYUAN Ⓜ

Jiangsu Lu

JIANGSU
LU Ⓜ

②

Yihua Lu

Anhua Lu

Dingxi Lu

Wuyi Lu

Gubei Lu

Tianshan Lu

TIANSHAN
PARK

YAN'AN
XI LU Ⓜ

③

Yan'an Xi Lu

Zunyi Lu

④

Panyu Lu

Xinfu Lu

Huashan Lu

Xingguo Lu

HUASHAN
PARK

Fahuazhen Lu

❽ ❼

❿ ❾

HONGQIAO
PARK

Xinhua Lu

⑥

⑤

Shanghai Film
Art Centre ■

Huaihai Xi Lu

Hongqiao Lu

SONG QINGLING
MAUSOLEUM/
INTERNATIONAL
CEMETERY

Songyuan Lu

ZHONGSHAN XI LU (INNER RING EXPRESSWAY)

HONGQIAO
LU Ⓜ

XUHUI

Wuzhong Lu

Nandan Lu

Puhuitang Lu

YISHAN LU Ⓜ

SHANGHAI TIYUGUAN
SHANGHAI STADIUM Ⓜ

Yishan Lu

Key for Chángníng/Hóngqiáo Development Zone

ACCOMMODATIONS ■

Crowne Plaza Shànghǎi **6**
(Shànghǎi Yínxīng Huángguān Jiǔdiàn)
上海银星皇冠假日酒店

Cypress Hotel **18**
(Lóngbǎi Fàndiàn)
龙柏饭店

Mayfair Hotel **2**
(Bālí Chūntiān Dàjiǔdiàn)
巴黎春天大酒店

Radisson Plaza Xīng Guó Hotel **4**
(Shànghǎi Xīng Guó Bīnguǎn)
上海兴国宾馆

Renaissance Yangtze Shànghǎi Hotel **9**
(Shànghǎi Yángzǐ Jiāng Dàjiǔdiàn)
上海扬子江万丽大酒店

Shànghǎi International Airport Hotel **19**
(Shànghǎi Guójì Jīchǎng Bīnguǎn)
上海国际机场宾馆

Shànghǎi Marriott Hotel Hóng Qiáo **15**
(Shànghǎi Wànháo Hóng Qiáo Dàjiǔdiàn)
上海万豪虹桥大酒店

Sheraton Grand Tài Píng Yáng **8**
(Xǐ Lái Dēng Háo Dá Tài Píng Yáng Dà Fàndiàn)
喜来登豪达太平洋大饭店

DINING ◆

1221 **3**

Bā Guó Bù Yī **14**
巴国布衣

Dynasty (Mǎn Fú Lóu) **10**
满福楼

Frankie's Place (Fǎlánqí Cāntīng) **12**
法兰奇餐厅

Lǎo Tán **5**
老坛

The Door (Qián Mén) **11**
乾门

ATTRACTIONS ●

Aquaria 21 **1**
(Shànghǎi Chángfēng Hǎiyáng
Shìjiè)
上海长风海洋世界

Dino Beach **19**
(Rèdài Fēngbào Shuǐshàng Lèyuán)
热带风暴水上乐园

Shànghǎi Zoo **16**
(Shànghǎi Dòngwùyuán)
上海动物园

SHOPPING ●

Carrefour (Jiālèfú) **13**
家乐福

Hóng Qiáo Friendship **7**
Shopping Centre
(Hóng Qiáo Yǒuyì Shāngchéng)
虹桥友谊商城

长宁
Chángníng

虹桥开发区
Hóngqiáo Development Zone

Key for Nánshì (Old Town) & Southeast Shànghǎi

南市
Nánshì

DINING ◆

Chūnfēng Sōngyuè Lóu 7
春风松月楼

Lǜ Bō Láng 6
绿波廊

Nánxiáng Mántou Diàn 5
南翔馒头店

Shànghǎi Lǎo Fàndiàn 1
(Shànghǎi Classic Restaurant)
上海老饭店

SHOPPING ●

Dàjìng Lù Market 11
(Dàjìng Lù Shìchǎng)
大境路市场

Dǒngjiādù Fabric Market 17
(Dǒngjiādù Lù Zhīpǐn Shìchǎng)
董家渡路织品市场

Fúyòu Market/Cáng Bǎo Lóu 10
福佑市场／藏宝楼

ATTRACTIONS ●

Báiyún Guàn 12
白云观

Chénghuáng Miào 8
(Temple of the Town God)
城隍庙

Chénxiāng Gé 2
沉香阁

Dǒngjiādù Tiānzhǔtáng 16
(Dǒngjiādù Catholic Church)
董家渡天主堂

Húxīn Tíng Teahouse 4
(Húxīn Tíng Cháshè)
湖心亭茶社

Museum of Folk Art 18
(Mínjiān Shōucángpǐn Chénlièguǎn)
民间收藏品陈列馆

Shànghǎi Old City Wall and Dàjìng
  Gé Pavilion 13
(Shànghǎi Gǔ Chéngqiáng Dàjìng Gé)
上海古城墙大镜阁

Shànghǎi Lǎo Jiē 9
(Shànghǎi Old Street)
上海老街

Wén Miào (Confucius Temple) 15
文庙

Xiǎo Táoyuán Qīngzhēn Sì 14
(Small Peach Garden Mosque)
小桃园清真寺

Yù Yuán (Yù Garden) 3
豫园

Nánshì & Southeast Shànghǎi

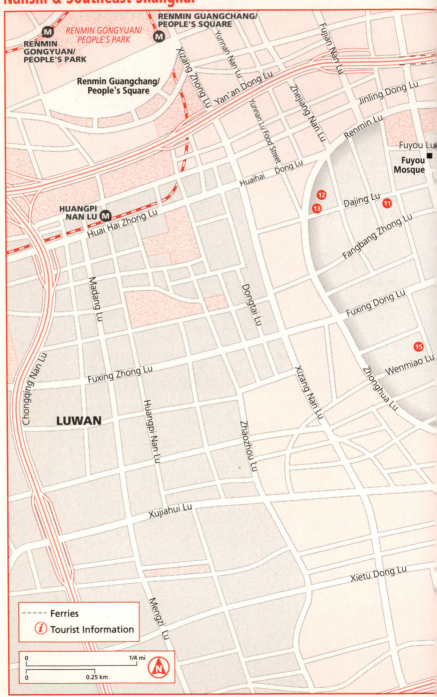

RENMIN GUANGCHANG/
PEOPLE'S SQUARE

*RENMIN GONGYUAN/
PEOPLE'S PARK*

RENMIN
GONGYUAN/
PEOPLE'S PARK

Fujian Nan Lu

Yunnan Nan Lu

Xizang Zhong Lu

Yan'an Dong Lu

Renmin Guangchang/
People's Square

Zhejiang Nan Lu

Jinling Dong Lu

Renmin Lu

Yunnan Lu Food Street

Fuyou Lu

**Fuyou
Mosque**

Huaihai   Dong Lu

HUANGPI
NAN LU

Dajing Lu

⑫
⑬
⑪

Huai Hai Zhong Lu

Fangbang Zhong Lu

Madang Lu

Dongtai Lu

Fuxing Dong Lu

⑮
Wenmiao Lu

Chongqing Nan Lu

Fuxing Zhong Lu

Xizang Nan Lu

Zhonghua Lu

LUWAN

Huangpi Nan Lu

Zhaozhou Lu

Xujiahui Lu

Xietu Dong Lu

Mengzi Lu

- - - - Ferries

ⓘ Tourist Information

0   1/4 mi

0   0.25 km

N

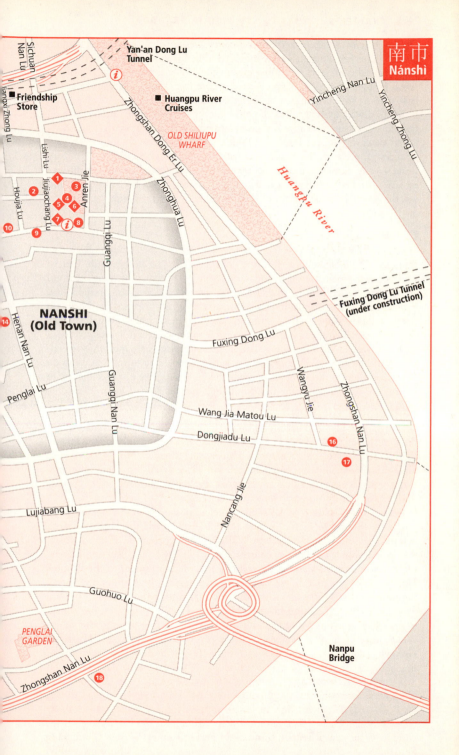

南市
Nánshi

Yan'an Dong Lu
Tunnel

i

■ Friendship
Store

■ Huangpu River
Cruises

*OLD SHILIUPU
WHARF*

Sichuan
Nan Lu

Jiangxi Zhong Lu

Lishi Lu

Houjia Lu

Jiujiaochang Lu

Anren Jie

Zhongshan Dong Er Lu

Zhonghua Lu

Guanqi Lu

Huangpu River

Yincheng Nan Lu

Yincheng Zhong Lu

◆ 1
◆ 2
◆ 3
◆ 4
◆ 5
◆ 6
◆ 7
◆ 8
i
◆ 9
10

Fuxing Dong Lu Tunnel
(under construction)

**NANSHI
(Old Town)**

14

Henan Nan Lu

Penglai Lu

Guanqi Nan Lu

Fuxing Dong Lu

Wang Jia Matou Lu

Dongjiadu Lu

Wangyu Jie

Zhongshan Nan Lu

16
17

Lujiabang Lu

Nancang Jie

Guohuo Lu

*PENGLAI
GARDEN*

Zhongshan Nan Lu

18

**Nanpu
Bridge**

Opium War of 1842 erected their distinct Western-style banks and trading houses. From here Shànghǎi grew into a cosmopolitan and thriving commercial and financial center, Asia's leading city in the 1920s and 1930s. Many of the awesome colonial structures you see today date from that prosperous time and have become an indelible part of Shànghǎi's cityscape.

Today, a wide avenue fronts the old buildings while a raised promenade on the east side of the road affords visitors pleasant strolls along the river and marvelous views of both the Bund and Pǔdōng across the river. Pǔdōng's new skyscrapers and modern towers—constituting Shànghǎi's "21st Century Bund"—may dominate today's skyline, but the city's core identity and history are strictly rooted in this unique strip on the western shore. For years, the Bund was the first sight of Shànghǎi for those arriving by boat; it should be your first stop as well.

ESSENTIALS

Stretching for 1.6km (1 mile) along the western edge of the Huángpǔ River, the Bund runs from Sūzhōu Creek in the north to Jīnlíng Lù in the south. On the west side of the main avenue (Zhōngshān Dōng Yī Lù) that runs along the Bund are the colonial edifices of yore, while the eastern side is taken by the **Bund Promenade,** a raised embankment that acts as a dike against the Huángpǔ River, because downtown itself, situated on a soggy delta, is slowly sinking below the river level. The Bund is pleasant to stroll at any hour but is often crowded with tourists and vendors selling snacks and souvenirs. Early mornings see taichi practitioners and ballroom dancers out in force. Early to mid-morning on weekdays is best for avoiding the crowds and for photography. If possible, try to return here at night when the Bund buildings are all aglow.

EXPLORING THE BUND

The highlights of the Bund are undoubtedly the colonial-era buildings lining the west side of Zhōngshān Dōng Yī Lù, standouts of which include the **former British Consulate,** the **Customs House,** the **former Hong Kong and Shànghǎi Bank,** and the **Peace Hotel.** For more details on these buildings, many of which have been skillfully restored, and a more complete walking guide to this gallery of European architecture, see chapter 7, "Shànghǎi Strolls."

Besides its landmark colonial architecture, however, the Bund has a few other small attractions. On its north end, Sūzhōu Creek enters the Huángpǔ River beneath the 18m-wide (60-ft.) iron **Wàibáidù Bridge,** built in 1906 to replace the original wooden toll bridge constructed in 1856 by an English businessman. On the river shore now stands a granite obelisk, the **Monument to the People's Heroes,** dedicated to Chinese patriots (as defined by the Communist Party), beginning in the 1840s. It was erected in 1993 and contains a small historical gallery at its base, the **Bund History Museum** (daily 9am–4:15pm; free admission), which contains a few artifacts and some interesting photographs of the Bund. Just south of the monument, at street level, is the park **Huángpǔ Gōngyuán** (daily 6am–6pm in winter, until 10pm in summer; free admission), originally the British Public Gardens built in 1868. In the early days, only Chinese servants accompanying their foreign masters were allowed to enter the park. Dogs were also prohibited, leading in later years to the apocryphal NO CHINESE OR DOGS ALLOWED sign being attributed to the park. The park was eventually opened to Chinese in 1926. South of here, across from the Peace Hotel, is the entrance to the new pedestrian **Bund Sight-Seeing Tunnel (Wàitān Guānguāng Suìdào;** Mon–Thurs 8am–10pm, Fri–Sun 8am–10:30pm; admission ¥40/$5

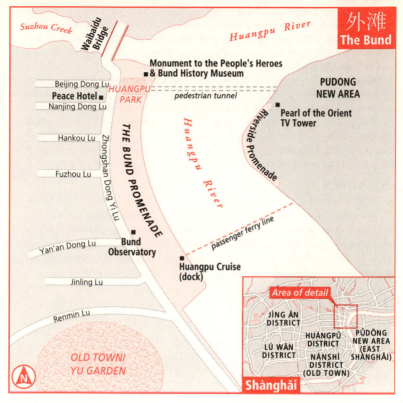

*Monument to the People's Heroes
■ & Bund History Museum*

Suzhou Creek

Waibaidu Bridge

Huangpu River

**PUDONG
NEW AREA**

Beijing Dong Lu
Peace Hotel ■
Nanjing Dong Lu

HUANGPU
PARK

pedestrian tunnel

■ **Pearl of the Orient
TV Tower**

Hankou Lu

Huangpu River

Fuzhou Lu

THE BUND PROMENADE

Zhongshan Dong Yi Lu

Riverside Promenade

Yan'an Dong Lu

■ **Bund
Observatory**

passenger ferry line

Jinling Lu

■ **Huangpu Cruise
(dock)**

Renmin Lu

Area of detail

JÌNG ĀN
DISTRICT

HUÁNGPŬ
DISTRICT

PŬDŌNG
NEW AREA
(EAST
SHÀNGHĂI)

LÙ WĀN
DISTRICT

NÁNSHÌ
DISTRICT
(OLD TOWN)

OLD TOWN/
YU GARDEN

Shànghăi

round-trip, ¥30/$4 one-way) located under the Huángpǔ. Complete with tram cars and light show, the tunnel connects downtown Shànghǎi to the Pǔdōng New Area and the Oriental Pearl TV Tower. Also here is a **statue of Chén Yì,** Shànghǎi's first mayor after 1949 and a dead ringer for Máo Zédōng, at least in bronze.

Farther south down the Bund Promenade are scores of vendors, a few restaurants, and excellent overlooks facing the river. Near the southern end of the promenade are the docks for the Huángpǔ River cruises (p. 147). You'll also notice the picturesque **Signal Tower,** a slender round brick tower that served as a control tower for river traffic during colonial days. First built in 1884, the tower was rebuilt in 1907, and also relayed weather reports. In 1993 during the widening of Zhōngshān Lù, it was moved 20m (65 ft.) to its current site. Today, a handful of photographs inside show the early days of the Bund, but you can no longer climb to the lookout.

Impressions

Seen from the river, towering above their couchant guardian warships, the semi-skyscrapers of the Bund present, impressively, the facade of a great city.

—Christopher Isherwood, 1937

Yù Yuán (Yù Garden)

Yù Yuán is a pleasant enough, well-contained classical Chinese garden, if not quite the loveliest of its kind, as local boosters would have you believe. Bearing the burden of being the most complete classical garden in urban Shànghǎi and therefore a must-see for every tourist, this overexposed garden overflows daily with hordes of visitors, and is no longer the pastoral haven it once was. Built between 1559 and 1577 by local official Pān Yǔnduān as the private estate for his father, Yù Yuán (meaning Garden of Peace and Comfort) is a maze of Míng Dynasty pavilions, elaborate rockeries, arched bridges, and goldfish ponds, all encircled by an undulating dragon wall. Occupying just 2 hectares (5 acres), it nevertheless appears quite expansive, with room for 30 pavilions.

ESSENTIALS

Yù Yuán is located at the heart of Old Town (Nánshì), a few blocks southwest of the Bund in downtown Shànghǎi (nearest Metro: Hénán Zhōng Lù, which is still a mile away). The main entrance and ticket window (© 021/6355-5032) are on the north shore of the Húxīn Tíng pond. It is open daily from 8:30am to 5pm (last ticket 4:45pm), and admission is ¥30 ($3.75). The least crowded time to visit is early morning. Allow 2 hours for a leisurely tour of this site.

EXPLORING YÙ GARDEN

The layout of Yù Yuán, which contains several gardens-within-gardens, can make strolling here a bit confusing, but if you stick to a general clockwise path from the main entrance, you should get around most of the estate and arrive eventually at the Inner Garden (Nèi Yuán) and final exit. The major sites from the northern entrance clockwise to the east and south are as follows:

SĀNSUÌ TÁNG (THREE EARS OF CORN HALL)   This is the first and largest of the garden's grand pavilions, although it was built in 1760 after Yù Yuán had been sold to a group of merchants. The highlight here is the fine window and wood beam carvings of rice, millet, wheat, fruit, and other emblems of a plentiful harvest. The building was used as a meeting place for local officials and for proclaiming Imperial announcements.

YÁNGSHĀN TÁNG (HALL FOR VIEWING THE GRAND ROCKERY)   Immediately north of the Three Ears of Corn Hall, this graceful two-story tower with upturned eaves serves as the entrance to the marvelous rock garden behind. Its upper story, known as Juǎnyǔ Lóu (Chamber for Gathering Rain), provides a fine view of the Grand Rockery.

DÀ JIǍ SHĀN (THE GRAND ROCKERY)   A pond separates the viewing hall from the Grand Rockery, which consists of 2,000 tons of rare yellow stones fused together with rice glue and designed by a famous garden artist of the Míng, Zhāng Nányáng. The twisted mountainlike sculpture, intended to evoke peaks, ravines, caves, and ridges, stands 14m (46 ft.) high and was the highest point in the city during the garden's construction. East of the pond is **Jiàn Rù Jiǎ Jǐng (The Corridor for Approaching the Best Scenery);** notice the beautiful vase-shaped doorframes. Off the corridor to the east you'll find the small **Yúlè Xiè (Pavilion for Viewing Frolicking Fish)** with schools of happy carp and goldfish swimming in a stream that appears much longer than it actually is (less than 50m/164 ft.). Northeast of the rockery is the **Cuì Xiù Táng (Hall of Gathering Grace);** to the east is **Wànhuā Lóu (Pavilion of Ten Thousand Flowers),** where a 4-century-old gingko tree stakes out the front courtyard.

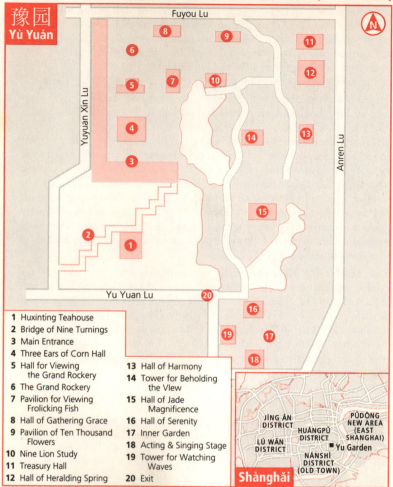

豫园
Yù Yuán

1 Huxinting Teahouse
2 Bridge of Nine Turnings
3 Main Entrance
4 Three Ears of Corn Hall
5 Hall for Viewing
   the Grand Rockery
6 The Grand Rockery
7 Pavilion for Viewing
   Frolicking Fish
8 Hall of Gathering Grace
9 Pavilion of Ten Thousand
   Flowers
10 Nine Lion Study
11 Treasury Hall
12 Hall of Heralding Spring

13 Hall of Harmony
14 Tower for Beholding
   the View
15 Hall of Jade
   Magnificence
16 Hall of Serenity
17 Inner Garden
18 Acting & Singing Stage
19 Tower for Watching
   Waves
20 Exit

Shànghǎi

JÌNG ĀN
DISTRICT

HUÁNGPǓ
DISTRICT

PǓDŌNG
NEW AREA
(EAST
SHANGHAI)

LÚ WĀN
DISTRICT

NÁNSHÌ
DISTRICT
(OLD TOWN)

■ Yu Garden

DIǍN CHŪN TÁNG (HALL OF HERALDING SPRING) If you continue east from the Grand Rockery and the Pavilion of Ten Thousand Flowers, you will come to two halls in the northeast section of Yù Yuán: the northern Cángbǎo Lóu (Treasury Hall), and the most famous historical building in the garden, Diǎn Chūn Táng (Hall of Heralding Spring). It was here in 1853 that the secret Small Sword Society (Xiǎodāo Huì) plotted to join the peasant-led Tàipíng Rebellion based in Nánjīng that aimed to overthrow the Qīng Dynasty. The uprising was a bloody one in Shànghǎi, forcing countless Chinese to flee into the British Concession. Rebels ruled the Chinese city for a year before being put down by a combination of Chinese and Western soldiers. Today there is a small collection of uprising artifacts in this hall, including weapons and coins minted by the rebels.

HÉXÙ TÁNG (HALL OF HARMONY) South of the rebels' old headquarters, past the **Kuài Lóu (Tower of Joy)** perched atop a pile of rocks, is the glass-enclosed Hall of Harmony, worth stepping inside to examine its display of old Qīng Dynasty furniture, fashioned by hand from banyan tree roots.

Just to the west of this hall is a wonderful **dragon wall** with a lifelike clay carving of a dragon's head perched at the end and gray tiles along the top evoking the dragon's body. Such walls are used throughout to divide the garden into different sections. A detour west of this wall leads to a bamboo grove and eventually to the airy **Jiǔshī Xuān (Nine Lion Study).**

YÙ HUÁ TÁNG (HALL OF JADE MAGNIFICENCE)   This hall opens into a southern courtyard with the most celebrated stone sculpture in the garden, **Yù Líng Lóng (Exquisite Jade Rock).** This honeycomb slab was reportedly originally procured by the Huìzōng emperor of the Northern Sòng (reigned 1100–26) from the waters of Tài Hú (Lake Tài) where many of the bizarre rocks and rockeries found in classical Chinese gardens were submerged to be naturally carved by the currents. Such rocks represent mountain peaks in classical Chinese garden design, and this rock satisfies the three elements of appearance (that it be rough, craggy, and pitted). Water poured into the top of this boulder will spurt out through its numerous holes; incense lighted at its base will swirl outward from its openings. Destined for the emperor, the rock was reportedly shipwrecked in the Huángpǔ River, and later retrieved by Pān Yǔnduān and placed here across from his study.

NÈI YUÁN (INNER GARDEN)   South of Exquisite Jade Rock is the entrance to the Inner Garden, which was constructed in 1709 and made a part of Yù Yuán only in 1956. This is often the quietest section of the garden, particularly in the morning. Its Hall of Serenity (Jìngguān Táng) at the north entrance and Tower for Watching Waves (Guāntāo Lóu) are magnificent, as is the ornately carved Acting and Singing Stage (Gǔ Xìtái) to the south. Local artists and calligraphers sometimes use these and other pavilions to display (and sell) their works. The exit from Yù Yuán is located next to the Inner Garden entrance (west); it puts you on Yùyuán Lù, which leads back to the Old Town pond and the Húxīngtíng Teahouse.

3 Shànghǎi Museum (Shànghǎi Bówùguǎn)

Frequently cited as the best museum in China, the Shànghǎi Museum has 11 state-of-the-art galleries and three special exhibition halls arranged on four floors, all encircling a spacious cylindrical atrium. The exhibits are tastefully displayed and well lit, and explanatory signs are in English as well as Chinese. For size, the museum's 120,000 historic artifacts cannot match the world-renowned Chinese collections in Běijīng, Taipei, and Xī'ān, but are more than enough to fill the galleries on any given day with outstanding treasures. Many foreign visitors to the museum often rank it as Shànghǎi's very best site.

ESSENTIALS

Located downtown on the south side of People's Square (Rénmín Guǎngchǎng) at Rénmín Dà Dào 201 (© 021/6372-3500), the museum has its main entrance on the north side of the building, facing the three monumental structures that now occupy the north half of the square (Grand Theatre to the west, City Hall in the middle, Shànghǎi Urban Planning Exhibition Center to the east). Metro Lines 1 and 2 both have their main stations on the northeast corner of People's Square. The Shànghǎi Museum is open Sunday through Friday from 9am to 5pm (no tickets sold after 4pm) and on Saturday from 9am to 8pm (no tickets sold after 7pm). Admission is ¥20 ($2.50). If you plan on seeing other attractions in People's Square, consider buying a combination ticket (see box below). Audio phones providing narratives of the major exhibits in English,

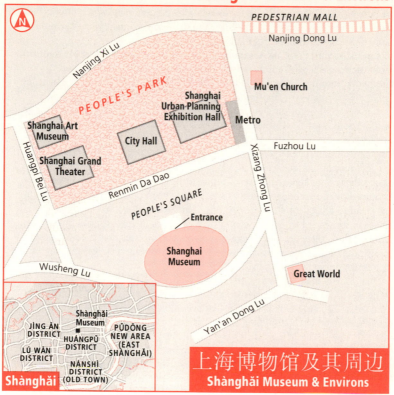

French, Japanese Spanish, German, and Italian are available for rent (¥40/$5 plus a deposit of ¥400/$50 or your passport) at the counter to your left as you enter the lobby.

EXPLORING THE SHÀNGHǍI MUSEUM (SHÀNGHǍI BÓWÙGUǍN)

Unlike many museums in China, the Shànghǎi Museum is arranged by theme rather than by dynasty. Though visitors all have their individual favorites, the Bronze Gallery and the Stone Sculpture Gallery on the first floor and the Painting Gallery on the third floor are generally considered the most impressive. Elevators, escalators, and stairways serve each floor. There is a large gift shop on the ground floor that sells museum reproductions, books, postcards, and gifts; and there are smaller shops on the other floors.

Begin your tour on the first floor at the **Ancient Chinese Bronze Gallery,** which boasts a marvelous collection of over 400 bronzes from the 18th to the 3rd centuries B.C. typically reserved for use only by nobles and royalty. Standouts include two wine vessels with animal mask designs, one in the shape of an ox (*zūn*) and the other a traditional pot (*hé*) used by the king of Wú, both dating from the Late Spring and Autumn Period (770–476 B.C.). There's also a typical food vessel on three legs (*dǐng*) from the Western Zhōu Dynasty (1100–771 B.C.), the shape of which is said to be the inspiration for the museum building, which certainly resembles an ancient *dǐng* from afar. The **Ancient Chinese Sculpture Gallery** has sculptures spanning the Warring States period to the Míng Dynasty

(475 B.C.–A.D. 1644), including a kneeling clay figure playing a bamboo flute from the Eastern Hàn (A.D. 25–200) and a Buddhist image of Sakyamuni in stone from the Northern Qí (A.D. 550–577).

On the second floor, the **Ceramics Gallery** contains many tricolor figurines from the magnificent Táng Dynasty (A.D. 618–907) and delicately painted and fired pots from the Míng Dynasty (A.D. 1368–1644) kilns at Jǐngdé Zhèn; the gallery is definitely worth a tour if you love your china.

On the third floor, the **Painting Gallery** contains many ancient original art works on silk scrolls, including landscapes from the Míng Dynasty and Buddhist scrolls from the Táng and Sòng (A.D. 960–1279) dynasties. Typical is the ink brush scroll by Emperor Zhào Jí (A.D. 1083–1135) of the Sòng Dynasty titled for its subjects, *Willow, Crows, Reed, and Wild Geese.* The **Calligraphy Gallery** shows the various styles of artistic "handwriting" developed in China over many centuries, with specimens as old as the Táng Dynasty. Altogether, the museum owns some 15,000 of these fine scrolls. The **Seal Gallery** has intricate carved chops in stone used by emperors and their courts to notarize official documents. On this floor there are also displays showing the basic elements of calligraphy, explaining the relationship between Chinese painting and calligraphy, and demonstrating how the artists' tools were used.

The fourth floor has a splendid **Jade Gallery,** with intricately carved jade wine vessels, jewelry, and ornaments, some from as early as the Liángzhū Culture (31st–22nd c. B.C.). The **Coin Gallery** displays coins that predate the First Emperor's reign (221–207 B.C.), as well as gold coins from Persia discovered on the Silk Road. The **Míng and Qīng Furniture Gallery** has elaborately carved screens inlaid with jade from the Qīng Dynasty (A.D. 1644–1911), a six-poster canopy bed, and a wonderful folding wooden armchair from the Míng Dynasty (A.D. 1368–1644). The **Minority Nationalities' Art Gallery** displays some lovely costumes, jewelry, dioramas, and ceremonial creations from the more remote, non-Hàn Chinese reaches of the Chinese empire, most of them dating from the early 20th century.

Tips People's Square Combo Tickets

If you are at People's Square and planning to tour more than one of its attractions (Shànghǎi Museum, Grand Theatre, Shànghǎi Urban Planning Exhibition Center, Shànghǎi Art Museum), it's best to buy a combination ticket (which includes entry to three locations). The good news is you can purchase these combo tickets at any of the four locations; the bad news is that each location offers slightly different options for touring. None offers a complete package, so if you want to tour all four, you'll have to pay full price at one of them (I suggest the Art Museum, which has the cheapest ticket at ¥20/$2.50). If you don't wish to visit all four, purchase your combo ticket at the place you *most* want to visit. In general, admission to the Shànghǎi Museum and Grand Theatre is ¥45 ($5.50); to the Museum, Theatre and Art Museum is ¥60 ($7.50); and to the Museum, Theatre and Urban Planning Exhibition Center is ¥70 ($9). Other combinations include: Grand Theatre and Urban Planning Exhibition Center for ¥60 ($7.50); and Museum, Art Museum, and Urban Planning Exhibition Center for ¥60 ($7.50).

4 Huángpǔ River Cruise

The Huángpǔ River (Huángpǔ Jiāng) is the city's shipping artery both to the East China Sea and to the mouth of the Yángzǐ River, which the Huángpǔ joins 29km (18 miles) north of downtown Shànghǎi. It has also become a demarcating line between two Shànghǎis, east and west, past and future. On its western shore, the colonial landmarks of the Bund serve as a reminder of Shànghǎi's 19th-century struggle to reclaim a waterfront from the bogs of this river (which originates in nearby Diānshān Hú or Lake Diānshān); on the eastern shore, the steel and glass skyscrapers of the Pǔdōng New Area point to a burgeoning financial empire of the future.

The Huángpǔ's wharves are the most fascinating in China. The port handles the cargo coming out of the interior from Nánjīng, Wǔhàn, and other Yángzǐ River ports, including Chóngqìng, 2,415km (1,500 miles) deep into Sìchuān Province. From Shànghǎi, which produces plenty of industrial and commercial products in its own right, as much as a third of China's trade with the rest of the world is conducted each year. A boat ride on the Huángpǔ is highly recommended: not only does it provide unrivalled postcard views of Shànghǎi past and future, but it'll also afford you a closer look at this dynamic waterway that makes Shànghǎi flow.

ESSENTIALS

There are several ways to tour the Huángpǔ River. If you have time, a 3½-hour (60km/37-mile) voyage along the Huángpǔ to the mouth of the Yángzǐ River and back allows for the most leisurely and complete appreciation of the river. There are also shorter river cruises (1–2 hr.) that ply the main waterfront area between the two suspension bridges, Yángpǔ Qiáo in the north and Nánpǔ Qiáo in the south, and an even shorter (30-min.) cruise from Pǔdōng (see "Quick Cruise from Pǔdōng" box on p. 148).

Several boat companies offer cruises, but the main one is the **Shànghǎi Huángpǔ River Cruise Company (Shànghǎi Pǔjiāng Yóulǎn)**, at Zhōngshān Dōng Èr Lù 219 (© **021/6374-4461**), located on the southern end of the Bund Promenade; there's another office further north at Zhōngshān Dōng Èr Lù 153. They have a daily full 3½-hour afternoon cruise (2–5:30pm) with the possibility of a full morning cruise during the summer. Prices for this cruise start at ¥70 ($9) and top out at ¥120 ($15), with the best ticket offering the most comfortable seats on the top deck, the best views, and drinks and snacks. This company also offers a nightly hour-long cruise from the Bund to the Yángpǔ Bridge (7 and 8:30pm) and another to the Lúpǔ Bridge in the south (7:30 and 9pm). Prices range from ¥35 to ¥70 ($4.30–$9). As well, there are hour-long cruises (¥25 – ¥35/$3–$4.50) on weekdays running every 2 to 3 hours between 9:30am and 10pm. Cruise schedules vary depending on the season, and on weekends additional cruises are sometimes added, so check ahead. Tickets can be purchased at the above offices or through your hotel desk.

CRUISING THE HUÁNGPŬ

Between the stately colonial edifices along the Bund, the glittering skyscrapers on the eastern shore of Pǔdōng, and the unceasing river traffic, there is plenty to keep your eyes from ever resting. Even on overcast days (the norm in Shànghǎi), the single greatest piece of eye candy as your boat pulls away is undoubtedly still the granite offices, banks, consulates, and hotels that comprise the Bund. Sadly for purists these days, however, the **Peace Hotel** with its stunning green pyramid roof and the **Customs House** with its big clock tower no longer have your undivided attention but

Quick Cruise from Pǔdōng

A brief (30-min.) but dramatic cruise along the Huángpǔ can be picked up on the Pǔdōng side of the river. The cruise won't get you far, only upriver to the old Shílìupǔ Wharf and back, 15 minutes each way, but the cityscapes on both sides will give you a sweeping perspective of Shànghǎi old and new.

Tickets for the Pǔdōng cruise can be purchased at the Oriental Pearl TV Tower ticket booth or at a kiosk near the dock (Dōngfāng Míngzhú Yóulǎn Mǎtóu; ℂ 021/5879-1888) on Fēnghé Lù. To reach the dock, walk along the northwest side of the TV Tower grounds on Fēnghé Lù, past the Insect Museum and the twin-globed Convention Center, straight on to the right-hand side of the sail-shaped pavilion on the river shore. Departures are 10, 11am, noon, 2, 3, and 4pm (more may be added during peak times); tickets are ¥30 to ¥40 ($4–$5). There are also night cruises (¥50/$6) departing nightly at 7 and 8pm from May to October.

have to compete with the towering 21st-century space-age skyscrapers that have sprouted in the background. Up close, though, the grandeur of the Bund is still undeniable.

As the ship heads north, downstream, it passes **Huángpǔ Park** across from the **Peace Hotel,** still considered by many to be the loveliest piece of architecture in Shànghǎi. Others prefer the architectural perfection of the **Jīn Mào Tower** on the opposite shore; it's certainly hard to take your eyes off the Jīn Mào as it tapers majestically upwards. Also on the Pǔdōng shore are the can't-miss Oriental Pearl Tower, the Shànghǎi International Convention Center with its twin glass globes, and a slew of hotels, offices, and malls of the Lùjiāzuǐ Financial Area.

Back on the western shore, north of Huángpǔ Park is **Sūzhōu Creek (Sūzhōu Hé),** formerly called the Wúsōng River. Originating in Tài Hú (Lake Tài), the 120km-long (72-mile) river was once much busier than the Huángpǔ, but silting in the lower reaches eventually diminished water traffic. The creek is spanned by **Wàibáidù Bridge,** which once linked the American concession in the north (today's Hóngkǒu District) and the British concession south of the creek. Eighteen meters (60 ft.) wide, with two 51m-long (171-ft.) spans, this bridge has seen all forms of traffic, from rickshaws to trams to motorcars. Elderly Shanghainese still recall the days of the Japanese occupation when they had to bow to Japanese sentries guarding the bridge and seek special permission to cross.

North of the Sūzhōu Creek hugging the west shore are the old "go-downs" or warehouses of the many foreign trading firms. This area, known as Hóngkǒu District, and the district to the east, Yángpǔ District, have been marked for rapid development after Pǔdōng, though new modern towers (all no more than 3 years old) have already started to stake out the skyline. Less than a mile farther on is the **International Passenger Terminal,** where cruise ships from Japan tie up. The Huángpǔ River jogs east at this point on its way to the Shànghǎi shipyards, where cranes and derricks load and unload the daily logjam of freighters from the world's other shipping giants (United States, Japan, Russia, Norway). Eventually, all of this waterfront will be developed into a series of marinas and a combination of industrial and recreational areas.

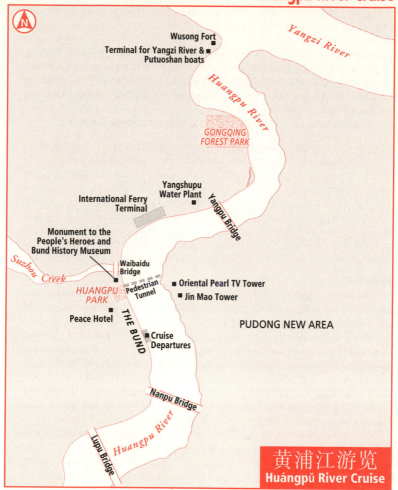

黄浦江游览
Huángpǔ River Cruise

Before the Huángpǔ slowly begins to curve northward again, you'll pass the English castle-style **Yángshùpǔ Water Plant** originally built by the British in 1882. The **Yángpǔ Cable Bridge,** like the **Nánpǔ Cable Bridge** to the south, is one of the largest such structures in the world. Boasting the longest span in the world, some 602m (1,975 ft.), the Yángpǔ Bridge is considered the world's first "slant-stretched" bridge. Its total length is about 7.6km (4¾ miles), and 50,000 vehicles pass over its six lanes daily.

What overwhelms river passengers even more than the long industrial shoreline is the traffic slinking up and down the waterway from the flotilla of river barges to the large rusting hulls of cargo ships. The Huángpǔ is, on the average, just 183m (600 ft.) wide, but more than 2,000 oceangoing ships compete with the 20,000 barges, fishing junks, and rowboats that ply the Huángpǔ every year. As the river curves north, you'll pass the small island, **Fùxīng Dǎo,** which is to be developed into an ecological and recreational theme park.

The Huángpǔ eventually empties into the mighty Yángzǐ River at **Wúsōng Kǒu,** where the water during high tide turns three distinct colors, marking the confluence of the Yángzǐ (yellow), the Huángpǔ (gray), and the South China Sea (green). Before this, there's an ancient **Wúsōng Fort,** from which the Chinese fought the British in 1842. The passenger terminal (**Wúsōng Passenger Terminal;** ✆ **021/5657-5500**) for Yángzǐ River cruises is also here. This marks the end of Shànghǎi's little river and the beginning of China's largest one. As your tour boat pivots slowly back into the narrowing passageway of the Huángpǔ, you can look forward to a return trip that should be more relaxed.

5 Temples, Churches, Mosques & Synagogues

Not known for its temples, Shànghǎi's most popular Buddhist shrine with visitors is the Jade Buddha Temple (Yùfó Sì). The Lónghuá Temple is also on the route of some tourists; its pagoda is the most interesting one in Shànghǎi. Shànghǎi also has several active Christian churches and an Islamic mosque where foreign visitors may worship or visit. But what really sets religious Shànghǎi apart, at least in China, is its Jewish legacy, most powerfully evoked by the reopening of the Ohel Moshe Synagogue as a museum and study center.

TEMPLES

Báiyún Guàn   This temple is one of only two Daoist temples in China to possess the precious Míng Dynasty Daoist Scripture *(dàozàng)*—the other is the much larger Báiyún Guàn in Běijīng. At press time, a brand-new apartment complex was forcing the temple to move from Xīlínhòu Lù (where it had been since 1863) to a spot near the old city wall (Dàjìng Gé). In its old incarnation, the two-story temple was housed in a lovely courtyard building with red walls, lattice windows and doors, and a beautiful ornamented roof (at press time, it was not known if the whole building would be moved, or just the temple). Incense-bearing supplicants pray before a dizzying array of gilded Daoist deities, each entrusted with a specific cause. If your timing is right, you may be able to catch a Daoist service, which is highly ritualized, often resembling pageants complete with music, chanting, and processing monks in colorful robes.

Dàjìng Lù, Nánshì (east of Rénmín Lù, next to Dàjìng Gé); see map p. 138. ✆ 021/6386-5800. Admission ¥2 (25¢). Daily 7:30am–4:30pm. Metro: Hénán Zhōng Lù (1 mile away).

Chénghuáng Miào (Temple of the Town God)   Every Chinese city once had its Temple of the Town God, the central shrine for Daoist worship. Shànghǎi's version dates from 1403 when local official Qín Yùbó, who had been posthumously designated as Shànghǎi's patron town god by the Míng Dynasty Hóngwǔ emperor (A.D. 1328–98), was finally honored with his own temple, though it didn't take on its present name until 1929. During the Cultural Revolution (1966–76), the temple, which had grown to become more of a marketplace, was destroyed. In the early 1990s, the temple and surrounding bazaar area, which encircled part of Yù Yuán, were extensively restored to become one large complex devoted to the god of commerce. The temple's main courtyard is usually jammed with worshippers praying before the statues of Huò Guāng (a local military hero) in the front hall, and the town god in the back. The smell of incense is overpowered only by the smell of money wafting from the nearby shops.

Fāngbāng Zhōng Lù 249, Nánshì (Old Town Bazaar, north side of Fāngbāng Zhōng Lù near Ānrén Lù); see map p. 138. ✆ 021/6386-5700. www.shchm.org. Admission ¥5 (60¢). Daily 8:30am–4pm. Metro: Hénán Zhōng Lù (1 mile away).

Chénxiāng Gé Pān Yǔnduān, the official who built Yù Yuán, had this Buddhist temple built to honor his mother in 1600. During the Cultural Revolution (1966–76) it was all but destroyed and abandoned. In 1989, restoration began, culminating in its reopening as a Buddhist nunnery and small Old Town tourist attraction in 1994. The centerpiece is an altar with a golden statue of the Buddha. The Buddha's vault is adorned with images of 384 disciples, created since 1990 by a single master craftsman. Guānyīn (the Goddess of Mercy) is highly venerated here as well.

Chénxiānggé Lù 29, Nánshì (1 block west off Jiùjiàochǎng Lù, the western boundary of the Old Town Bazaar); see map p. 138. ☎ 021/6328-7884. Admission ¥5 (60¢). Daily 7am–4pm. Metro: Hénán Zhōng Lù (1 mile away).

Jìng Ān Sì (Jìng Ān Temple) Always lively and crowded, this garishly decorated temple has the longest history of any shrine in Shànghǎi, about 17 centuries (though the shopping annex is more recent). Its chief antiquities are a Míng Dynasty copper bell (the Hóngwǔ Bell) that weighs in at 3,175 kilograms (3.5 tons) and stone Buddhas from the Northern and Southern States period (A.D. 420–589). Although its name means "Temple of Tranquillity," it is hardly the place for quiet meditation these days, nor was it in the past. Before 1949, this was Shànghǎi's richest Buddhist monastery, presided over by the Abbott of Bubbling Well Road (Nánjīng Xī Lù, as it was known in Colonial times because of a well that was located in front of the temple), an imposing figure who kept seven mistresses and a White Russian bodyguard. Today's Southern-style main halls are all recent renovations using Burmese teakwood (*yóumù*). Reconstructions (part of an expansion plan that seems hellbent on turning the temple into a marketplace) will continue into 2007. The temple is also the headquarters and repository for the Mí Sect, a Chinese-originated Buddhist discipline that was all but extinct until it was reintroduced from Japan in 1953.

Nánjīng Xī Lù 1686, Jìng Ān (corner of Huáshān Lù); see map p. 126. ☎ 021/6248-6366. Admission ¥5 (60¢); ¥30 ($3.75) 1st–15th day of Spring Festival (usually late Jan/Feb). Daily 7:30am–5pm. Metro: Jìng Ān Sì.

Lónghuá Sì (Lónghuá Temple) ★★ Shànghǎi's largest and most active temple is one of its most fascinating, featuring the city's premier pagoda, Lónghuá Tǎ. Local lore has it that the pagoda was originally built around 247 by Sūn Quán, the king of the Wú Kingdom during the Three Kingdoms period, but today's seven-story, eight-sided, wood and brick pagoda, like the temple, dates to the Sòng Dynasty (A.D. 960–1279). For a long time the tallest structure in Shànghǎi, today it's pretty (tiny bells hang from the eaves), just a little delicate, and can only be admired from a distance. The extensive temple grounds, on the north side of the newly created pedestrian street, are often crowded with incense-bearing supplicants. There are four main halls (only a century old), the most impressive being the third, Dàxióng Bǎo Diàn (Grand Hall) where a gilded statue of Sakyamuni sits under a beautifully carved dome, flanked on each side by 18 *arhats* (disciples). Behind, Guānyīn, the Goddess of Mercy, presides over a fascinating tableau representing the process of reincarnation: a boat in the bottom right corner indicates birth, while death awaits at the bottom left corner. The fourth hall, Sānshén Bǎo Diàn, features three incarnations of the Buddha. Behind the third and fourth halls is a basic but popular vegetarian restaurant (11am–2pm). Lónghuá is also famous for its midnight bell-ringing every New Year's Eve (Dec 31–Jan 1), which takes place in the three-storied Zhōng Lóu (Bell Tower) near the entrance. The tower's 3,000-kilogram (3.3-ton) bronze bell, cast in 1894, is struck 108 times to dispel all the worries said to be afflicting mankind. For a fee of ¥10 ($1.25), you, too, can strike the bell, but for three times only.

Lónghuá Lù 2853, Xúhuì; see map p. 122. ✆ 021/6456-6085. Admission ¥5 (60¢). Daily 7am–5pm. Metro: Shànghăi Tiyùguăn (a long, unpleasant walk; easier to reach by taxi).

Wén Miào (Confucius Temple)   Although there has been a Confucius temple in Shànghăi as early as 1267, today's temple was built at its current site in 1855, and was most recently restored in 1999 to celebrate the 2,550th birthday of China's Great Sage. In between, it has variously been a temple, school (where Confucian scholars came to study), public garden, and Children's Palace. Offering quiet refuge from the crowded streets of the old Chinese city, the temple, like all Chinese Confucian temples, features a *língxīn mén* (gate) leading to the main hall, Dàchéng Diàn. Inside are statues of Confucius flanked by his two disciples, Mèngzǐ (Mencius) and Yànhuī, and his two favorite musical instruments, a drum and set of bells. To the northeast, the Zūnjīng Gé, formerly the library, now houses a display of unusually shaped rocks. Southeast of Dàchéng Diàn, Mínglùn Táng was a former lecture hall, the Rúxué Shǔ (Confucian Study Hall) is now a small teapot museum, and back near the entrance, Kuíxīng Gé is a three-story 20m-high (66-ft.) pagoda dedicated to the god of liberal arts, and the only original structure left on these tranquil grounds. A lively book market is held here Sunday mornings.

Wénmiào Lù 215, Nánshì (north side of Wénmiào Lù, 1 block east of Zhōnghuá Lù); see map p. 138. ✆ 021/ 6407-3593. Admission ¥8 ($1). Daily 9am–4:30pm. No Metro.

Yù Fó Sì (Jade Buddha Temple) ★ *Overrated*   Though an active Buddhist monastery today (devoted to the Chán or Zen sect, which originated in China), the real emphasis at this temple, Shànghăi's most popular with visitors, is squarely on tourism. What the busloads come for are the temple's two gorgeous white jade Buddhas, each carved from an individual slab of Burmese jade and brought to Shànghăi in 1881 by the monk Huígēng, who was on his way back from Burma to his hometown on nearby Pǔtuó Shān (Pǔtuó Island). A temple was built in 1882 to house the statues, but was destroyed in a fire and rebuilt at the present site in 1918 with swirling eaves characteristic of the Song Dynasty architectural style. Northeast of the main Dàxióng Bǎo Diàn (Treasure Hall of the Great Hero), which contains golden images of the Buddhas of the past, present, and future, the Cángjīng Lóu houses the first of the two treasures: a lustrous, beatific, seated Buddha weighing 205 kilograms (455 lb.), measuring 1.9m (6 ft. 5 in.), and adorned with jewels and stones. The other Buddha is found northwest of the main hall in the Wòfó Sì, where a less impressive but still beautiful 1m-long (3 ft. 4 in.) sleeping Buddha reclines, his peaceful expression signaling his impending entry into nirvana. Opposite it is a much larger, coarser replica donated by the Singapore Buddhist Friendship Association in 1988.

Ānyuán Lù 170, Pǔtuó (northwest Shànghăi, west of Jiāngníng Lù, 6 long blocks north of Běijīng Xī Lù); see map p. 126. ✆ 021/6266-3668. Admission ¥15 ($1.80). Daily 8am–4:30pm. No Metro.

MOSQUES & CHURCHES

In addition to the places listed below, there are other cathedrals, churches, mosques, and places of worship in Shànghăi. For the locations and times of services, inquire at your hotel.

Dǒngjiādù Tiānzhǔtáng (Dǒngjiādù Catholic Church)   Located in the southern part of the old Chinese city, this was the first large cathedral in Shànghăi, built in 1853 in the early Spanish baroque style. It's a fine-looking building with arched roofs, thick pillars, and lotus-designed bas-reliefs inside.

Shé Shān Cathedral

For those who can't get enough of Shànghǎi's European-style churches, one of the best is located in Sōngjiāng County, a 40-minute trip from Shànghǎi. Situated on the western peak of Shé Shān (Shé Mountain), Shé Shān Cathedral (Shé Shān Táng) was originally built by the Jesuits in 1866 as the Holy Mother Cathedral, and rebuilt between 1925 and 1935 as the Basilica of Notre Dame. Laid out in the shape of a cross, this majestic brick structure has a 38m-tall (125-ft.) bell tower on top of which stands a replacement bronze Madonna and Child statue (the original was destroyed in the Cultural Revolution). Catholic pilgrims from neighboring areas flock here on Sundays and holy days, many of them making the trek up the hill via the south gate. Along the way are a number of shrines and grottoes. Alternatively, you can take a cable car (¥40/$5 round-trip, ¥30/$3.75 one-way). The church (✆ 021/5765-1521; daily 8am–4pm) holds Mass Monday to Saturday at 7am (6:30am in summer) and at 8am on Sunday (7:30am in summer). Behind the church is an astronomical **observatory** (✆ 021/5765-3423; daily 7:30am–5pm), founded in 1900 by the French Catholic Mission. The eastern half of Shé Shān consists mostly of a Forest Park and various recreational theme parks. To reach Shé Shān, take bus no. 1B (¥10/$1.25; 12 buses 7:45am–4:30pm) from the Shànghǎi Stadium Sightseeing Bus Center. Return buses run 7:20am to 4:30pm.

Chinese couplets are inscribed on both inside and outside walls, and four of the church bells are said to be original.

Dōngjiādù Lù 185, Nánshì (west of Zhōngshān Nán Lù); see map p. 138. ✆ 021/6378-7214. Services Mon–Sat 7am; Sun 6am, 8am. No Metro.

Guójì Lǐbài Táng (Héngshān Community Church)

Established in 1925 and also called the International Church, this is the best known of Shànghǎi's Protestant churches among foreign residents and visitors, and is the largest in use. The ivy-covered English-style building and grounds are beautiful, fully in keeping with this upscale colonial-style shopping district on the fringes of the French Concession. Special services for foreign passport holders are currently held here at 4pm on Sundays.

Héngshān Lù 53, Xújiāhuì (west of Wūlǔmùqí Nán Lù); see map p. 122. ✆ 021/6437-6576. Services Sun 7:30am, 10am (English translation available), 7pm. Metro: Héngshān Lù.

Mù'ēn Táng

Formerly known as the Moore Church, it was established by American missionaries in 1887 and expanded in 1931 to seat over 1,000 worshippers. It has built up a local membership that numbers in the thousands since reopening in 1979 after its closure during the Cultural Revolution (1966–76). Originally the Methodist church of Shànghǎi, this nondenominational church has a Chinese woman serving as its pastor. Two bishops were consecrated here in 1988, the first in China in 3 decades; the same year, American evangelist Billy Graham preached here.

Xīzàng Zhōng Lù 316, Huángpǔ Qū (east side of Rénmín Guǎngchǎng); see map p.118. ✆ 021/6322-5069. Services Sun 7:30am, 9am, 2pm, and 7pm. Metro: Rénmín Guǎngchǎng or Rénmín Gōngyuán.

Jewish Shànghăi

As China's most international city, Shànghăi experienced several waves of Jewish immigration, each leaving its mark. The first to arrive, in the late 1840s, were the Sephardic Jews. Businessmen who made their fortunes in opium and property, they built large estates, as many as seven synagogues, and were responsible for some of Shànghăi's finest architecture. The Sassoons, who emigrated from Baghdad in the mid–19th century, were the first Jewish family to make a fortune in Shànghăi, and both the Peace Hotel on the Bund and the villa estate next to the zoo (now the Cypress Hotel) were their creations. Silas Hardoon was a later Jewish real estate baron whose great estate was razed to make way for the Sino-Soviet Shànghăi Exhibition Center on Yán'ān Xī Lù (south of the Portman Hotel). Meanwhile, the Kadoories' legacy, the stunning "Marble House" on Yán'ān Xī Lù, is today the city's most popular and impressive Children's Palace.

The second wave of Jewish emigrants comprised Russian Jews fleeing the Bolsheviks at the beginning of the 20th century. They were followed in the 1930s by a third wave of European Jews who were fleeing Hitler, and who landed here only because Shànghăi was the only city in the world at that time willing to accept these "stateless refugees." Just before World War II, the numbers of Jews in Shànghăi topped 30,000. In February 1943, to appease the Germans who wanted the Japanese to implement the Final Solution in Shànghăi, the occupying force of the Japanese army forced the "stateless Jews" into a "Designated Area" in Hóngkŏu District (north of the Bund), marked by today's Zhōujiāzuĭ Lù in the north, Huìmín Lù in the south, Tōngbĕi Lù in the east, and Gōngpíng Lù in the west. Tens of thousands of Jews lived cheek by jowl in this "ghetto," where the local synagogue became the center of their material and spiritual life until the end of the war.

Xiăo Táoyuán Qīngzhēnsì (Small Peach Garden Mosque)   Shànghăi's largest and most active mosque dates from 1917 though the current reconstruction is from 1925. Its main prayer hall can hold several hundred worshippers (restricted to Muslim males only). There is a separate worship hall for women. The courtyard contains a minaret (for calls to prayer). Shànghăi's other mosque that welcomes foreign visitors is the Sōngjiāng Mosque (Sōngjiāng Qīngzhēnsì), located in the southwest suburb of Sōngjiāng (✆ **021/5782-3684**). Shànghăi's oldest mosque (1870) is at Fúyòu Lù 378.

Xiăo Táoyuán Jiē 52, Nánshì Qū (southwest of Chénghuáng Miào at Fùxīng Dōng Lù and Hénán Nán Lù); see map p. 138. ✆ 021/6377-5442. Daily sunrise–sunset. No Metro.

Xújiāhuì Tiānzhŭtáng (St. Ignatius Cathedral) ✸   Once known as St. Ignatius, this is Shànghăi's great cathedral, opened by the Jesuits who'd had a church here as early as 1608 (today's structure dates to 1910). The Jesuits were invited here by a local high-ranking Míng Dynasty official, landowner, and scientist, Xú Guāngqí (the district's name Xújiāhuì, means "Xú Family Village"), who was himself converted to Catholicism by the Jesuits' most famous missionary to China,

Travelers interested in the Jews in Shànghǎi can still visit that center, the **Ohel Moshe Synagogue (Móxī Huìtáng)**, Chángyáng Lù 62, Hóngkǒu (✆ **021/6512-0229** or 021/6541-6312). Built in 1927 by the Ashkenazi Jewish community of Shànghǎi, it no longer serves as a synagogue, but as a museum devoted to the Jews in Shànghǎi. The third floor has displays, period photographs, a list of Shànghǎi Jews, and a small bookstore. Visitors are welcome on weekdays from 9am to 4pm, but there's a comparatively steep entrance "donation" of ¥50 ($6.25). If you visit, there's a good chance you'll encounter a Mr. Wáng Fǎliáng of the synagogue, who can recount many stories of how the Chinese and Jewish refugees lived together under Japanese occupation.

The best way to visit this synagogue, Huǒshān Park (Huǒshān Gōngyuán), where there is a memorial to Jewish refugees, the Marble Hall, and the *nòngtáng* (lane) row houses of Hóngkǒu that formed Shànghǎi's "Little Vienna," is on the wonderful **"Tour of Jewish Shànghǎi"** ★ conducted by appointment with Dvir Bar-Gal (✆ **13002146702**; www.shanghai-jews.com).

The tour will also pass by the **Ohel Rachel Synagogue (Lāxīěr Yóutài Jiàotáng)** at Shǎnxī Běi Lù 500, behind the Portman Ritz-Carlton Hotel; now home to the Shànghǎi Education Commission. It was built in 1920 by Jacob Sassoon in memory of his wife Rachel, but except for the occasional VIP visitor (namely Hillary Clinton in 1998), the synagogue, now considered 1 of the world's 100 most endangered monuments, is usually closed to the public.

Travelers interested in learning more about the Jewish community in Shànghǎi, attending Shabbat dinners, or participating in religious services, should contact the **Shànghǎi Jewish Center**, Hóngqiáo Lù 1720, Shang-Mira Garden Villa no. 2 (✆ **021/6278-0225**; fax 021/6278-0223; www.chinajewish.org).

Matteo Ricci (1553–1610). Xú is buried in a public park named after him on Nándān Xī Lù, southwest of the cathedral. As a missionary center, the cathedral grounds once included a library, an orphanage, a college, a publishing house, and its own weather station. Today only the church, part of the school, and the recently reopened library (p. 167) remain. This largest of Shànghǎi's cathedrals, with space for over 2,500 inside, sports a gargoyled roof and twin red-brick spires which were destroyed in the Cultural Revolution (1966–76) and rebuilt in 1980. Its vast interior of altars, stone columns, Gothic ceilings, stained glass windows, and paintings of the Last Supper and Stations of the Cross, is yet another chapter in Shànghǎi's living history of European architecture, though there is currently a multi-year project underway to replace the traditional Western-style stained glass with glasswork imbued with Chinese motifs and characteristics (for example, using a phoenix, the traditional Chinese symbol for rebirth, to signify the Resurrection).

Pǔxī Lù 158, Xúhuì (west side of Cáoxī Běi Lù); see map p. 122. ✆ **021/6439-4298** or 021/6438-4632. Services Mon–Sat 6:15am, 7am, with an additional 6pm Mass on Sat; Sun 6am, 7:30am, 10am; open to visitors Sat–Sun 7:30–11am and 1–4pm. Metro: Xújiāhuì.

Other major Catholic churches include **Bóduōlù Táng (St. Peter's Church),** Chóngqìng Nán Lù 270, Lúwān (② **021/6467-0198**), originally built in 1933 but rebuilt in 1995, and which now holds services in English at 5pm Saturday, 10:30am Sunday, and 7pm on holy days; **Shèng Ruòsè Táng (St. Joseph's Church),** built in 1860 at Sìchuān Nán Lù 36, Huángpǔ (② **021/6328-0293** or 6336-5537); and **Jūnwáng Tiānzhǔ Táng (Christ the King Catholic Church),** also called the Good Shepherd Church, Jùlù Lù 361, Jìng Ān (② **021/6217-4608**).

Other active Protestant places of worship that open their doors to foreign worshippers include **Huái'ēn Táng (Shànghǎi Grace Church),** opened in 1910 at Shǎnxī Běi Lù 375, Jìng Ān (② **021/6253-9394**); **Jǐnglíng Táng (Youag John Allen Memorial Church),** built in 1923 at Kūnshān Lù 135, east from Sìchuān Běi Lù, Hóngkǒu (② **021/6324-3021** or 5539-1720), the place where Chiang Kai-shek wed Soong Mei-ling; and **Zhūshèng Táng (All Saints Church),** Fùxīng Zhōng Lù 425 at Dànshuǐ Lù (② **021/6385-0906**), a lively church in the French Concession that recently began holding services again.

6 Parks & Gardens

Shànghǎi's parks are splendid places for a stroll, combining scenic vistas with people-watching. They are particularly lively at dawn, when locals gather for their morning exercises ranging from *tàijí quán* (tai-chi) to ballroom dancing. Due to the scarcity of play space for children, nearly all parks have a children's section, however small or dilapidated.

In addition to those listed below, Shànghǎi has many smaller parks that offer some reprieve from the urban jungle. One of the newest is in the Xújiāhuì District, **Xújiāhuì Gōngyuán,** built in 1999 on the former grounds of the Great Chinese Rubber Works Factory and the EMI Recording Studio (today's glamorous La Villa Rouge restaurant), with entrances at Zhàojiābāng Lù in and the west at the intersection of Héngshāng Lù and Yúqìn Lù. The park has a man-made lake with a sky bridge running across the park, and offers a pleasant respite for Xújiāhuì shoppers. **Zhōngshān Gōngyuán,** Chángníng Lù 780, Chángníng District, built in 1914 as Jessfield Park, once contained the campus of St. John's University, Shànghǎi's first international college; today, it is known for its extensive rose and peony gardens, a large children's play area, and as the westernmost stop to date on the Metro Line 2.

Bīnjiāng Dà Dào (Riverside Promenade) ★   Pǔdōng's answer to the Bund, this strip of green along the east bank of the Huángpǔ River offers a fine view of the Bund at a distance. After dark, when the Bund's buildings are lit up and beacon lights sweep the river lanes, the view is one of the best in Shànghǎi. The Riverside Promenade also affords marvelous views of Pǔdōng's skyscrapers, and the Shànghǎi International Conference Center and its twin globes. Extending from Dōngchāng Lù and the river ferry terminal in the south to Táidōng Lù in the north, the 2.5km-long (1½-mile) promenade consists of manicured lawns, flower beds, and a broad walkway dotted with kiosks. Starbucks and Häagen-Dazs have staked out the best spots in the middle section around the Shangri-La hotel, so you can now have your view and your latte and ice cream too.

East shoreline, Huángpǔ River, Pǔdōng (entrances on either side of Lùjiāzuǐ Lù); see map p. 130. Free admission. Daily 6:30am–11pm (midnight in summer). Metro: Lùjiāzuǐ.

Fùxīng Gōngyuán (Fùxīng Park) ★ *Kids*   Formerly a private estate in the French Concession, Fùxīng Park was purchased by foreign residents and opened to the French public on July 14, 1909. It was popularly known as French Park, styled after your typical Parisian city park with wide, tree-lined walks and flower beds. Today, this is one of the city's most popular parks, home to a number of restaurants and nightclubs, as well as to pleasant fountains, a children's playground with a carousel and bumper cars, a rose garden to the east, 120 species of trees, and, near the north entrance, a statue of Karl Marx and Friedrich Engel before which Chinese couples often practice their ballroom dancing.

Gāolán Lù 2, Lúwān (west entrance Gāolán Lù, north entrance Yándāng Lù, southeast entrance Chóngqìng Nán Lù off Fùxīng Zhōng Lù); see map p. 122. ℂ 021/6372-6083. Admission ¥2 (25¢). Daily 6am–6pm. Metro: Huángpí Nán Lù.

Jìng Ān Gōngyuán (Jìng Ān Park)

This pleasant little park was completely remodeled in 1999 when the new Jìng Ān Metro station was created. Its north side consists of a sunken cement courtyard, flanked by a few shops, cafes, and the Metro entrance; the south side, dominated by a pond that is an artful re-creation of a classic Southern Chinese garden, is a pretty spot to stroll, people-watch, or enjoy an evening drink at the bar in the adjacent Indonesian restaurant (Bali Laguna). Mornings are a perfect time to watch (or join) tai chi classes, while Sunday morning (8:30–11am) brings out the polyglots (mostly Chinese who want to practice their English) to the multi-language corner *(wài yǔ jiǎo)* at the eastern end of the park.

Huáshān Lù 189, Jìng Ān (south of Jìng Ān Temple); see map p. 126. ℂ 021/6248-3238. Free admission. Daily dawn–very late. Metro: Jìng Ān Sì.

Lùjiāzuǐ Lùdì (Lùjiāzuǐ Central Green)

Located just north of the Jīn Mào Tower, this sprawling 10-hectare (330,000-sq.-ft.) park with an expansive lawn has a large lake in the shape of Pǔdōng; radiating from it are paths that outline a magnolia, the city flower of Shànghǎi. Clusters of willows, maples, and gingko trees provide plenty of shade. It's the kind of place that inspires impromptu picnics, kite flying, a lazy afternoon nap, and even hot-air ballooning in the warmer months. The park is so high-tech it even has a series of in-ground audio speakers that will occasionally pipe out New Age mood music.

Lùjiāzuǐ Lù 160, Pǔdōng (east of the Oriental Pearl TV Tower; north of the Jīn Mào Tower); see map p. 130. ℂ 021/5887-5487. Free admission. Open 24 hr. Metro: Lùjiāzuǐ.

Rénmín Gōngyuán/Rénmín Guǎngchǎng (People's Park/People's Square)

Shànghǎi's "Central Park" and central square are built on the site of colonial Shànghǎi's horse-racing track (dating to as early as 1863), once a favorite amusement for the British community and upper-class Chinese. Today the original 12 hectares (30 acres) of the racecourse have been parceled out into a quiet pleasant park in the north (complete with a small and occasionally scummy pond, rock garden, amusement rides, and clusters of old folks playing mahjong and chess) and Rénmín Guǎngchǎng (People's Square) to the south. Opened in 1951 and renovated in 1994, with an intermediary spell as a public reckoning ground during the early days of the Cultural Revolution (1966–76), the square is now Shànghǎi's cultural and traffic center, with an underground shopping arcade, the central subway station, the Shànghǎi Museum, the Grand Theatre, the 20-story Municipal Hall, and the Shànghǎi Urban Planning Exhibition Hall. Besides being a magnet for locals who come here to feed the pigeons, fly their kites, and gossip on the benches, the square, surrounded as it is by some of Shànghǎi's tallest and most modern buildings, is also a wonderful place to take in exactly how much Shànghǎi has grown up.

Nánjīng Xī Lù 231, Huángpǔ Qū (at Huángpí Lù); see map p. 118. ℂ 021/6372-0626. Park admission ¥2 (25¢). Daily 6am–6pm. Metro: Rénmín Gōngyuán.

Shànghǎi Zhíwùyuán (Shànghǎi Botanical Gardens) ★ *Kids*   Somewhat inconveniently located in the southwest part of town, the city's premier and largest garden offers a pleasant reprieve from the urban hustle, but is not worth a special trip unless you really like your plants. The extensive grounds, covering 81 hectares (200 acres), are divided into different sections featuring peonies, roses, bamboo, azaleas, maples, osmanthus, magnolias, and orchids (considered the best in China). There is also a garden of medicinal plants and a greenhouse dedicated to tropical plants, but the hallmark section is the Pénjǐng Yuán (Bonsai Garden), which requires a separate admission (¥7/90¢), with hundreds of bonsai displayed in a large complex of corridors, courtyards, pools, and rockeries. There are restaurants, exhibition halls, vendors' stalls and several children's playgrounds dotted throughout the park.

Lóngwú Lù 1111, Xúhuì; see map p. 122. ℂ 021/6451-3369. Admission ¥15 ($1.80) garden only; ¥40 ($5) includes Bonsai Garden and 3 other sections. Daily 6am–5pm summer, 7:30am–4:30pm winter. No Metro.

Shìjì Gōngyuán (Century Park) ★ *Kids*   Built to herald the new millennium, this sprawling 140-hectare (347-acre) park lies at the southern terminus of Century Boulevard (Shìjì Dà Dào), which runs from the Oriental Pearl TV Tower. Designed by a British firm, the park is divided into seven scenic areas including a minigolf course, a beach area complete with man-made cobblestone beach, a bird-protection area, and an international garden area. The center of the park contains a lake where fishing poles and paddleboats can be rented. There's plenty here to distract the kids, but it's an even better place to watch local families enjoying themselves.

Jínxiù Lù 1001, Pǔdōng (south entrance at Huāmù Lù, next to Metro station); see map p. 130. ℂ 021/ 3876-0588. Admission ¥10 ($1.20). Daily 7am–6pm (to 5pm Nov 16–Mar 15). Metro: Shìjì Gōngyuán.

7 Museums & Mansions

In its quest to become the cosmopolitan and culturally savvy city worthy of hosting the World Expo in 2010, Shànghǎi has set a mildly ambitious goal of having 100 museums up and running by that time. To meet this quota, everything from navy ships to Chinese medicines has been encased in glass and given its own building. Many of Shànghǎi's museums and historic residences are housed in the European mansions and estates of colonial Shànghǎi where the setting is often the chief attraction. While lighting and display are seldom state-of-the-art and English signage can be spotty or nonexistent, simply touring these fine storehouses is fascinating enough. To spare the time-limited visitor, what follows is a list of the more worthwhile sights. No doubt by the time you read this there will be that many more new museums to choose from.

Duōlún Lù Culture Street (Duōlún Lù Wénhuà Jiē) ★ *Finds*   A 20-minute walk south from Lǔ Xùn Gōngyuán (Lǔ Xùn Park and Memorial Hall) is Duōlún Lù, Shànghǎi's culture street, a 1998 attraction angling off Sìchuān Běi Lù in the historic Hóngkǒu District. This district north of the Bund was the original American Concession but merged with the British Concession to form the International Settlement in colonial Shànghǎi. By the time the writer Lǔ Xùn (p. 159) moved into the neighborhood in the 1930s, the area had become a Japanese enclave. Other famous progressive artists and writers (Máo Dùn, Guō Mòruò, Dīng Líng), many of who were part of the League of Leftist Writers, lived here as well during that time, making this area around Duōlún Lù (formerly Darroch Rd.) known as a cultural and literary center. The stately brick homes and shops on this ½-mile (.8km) stretch of the street have been preserved and refurbished, and cars are now banned, making it a fine pedestrian mall of bookshops, teahouses, antiques shops, and historic homes. As you enter from Sìchuān Běi Lù, the new Duōlún Art Gallery (no. 27; ℭ **021/6587-6902;** daily 9am–5pm; admission ¥20/$2.50) on your left showcases the works of international modern artists. A few doors down at no, 59, the Chinese-styled Hóng Dé Táng (Great Virtue Christian Church) built in 1928 now houses art and embroidery stores. The street curves to the right, passing the stately bell tower Xī Shí Zhōng Lóu (no. 119); the wonderful Old Film Café (no. 123) where you can sip coffee while watching old Chinese movies from the 1920s and 1930s; and antiques and curio shops selling everything from art to Máo memorabilia. At Lane 201, no.2 is the League of Leftist Writers Museum (daily 9:30am–4:30pm; admission ¥5/60¢). A coin museum, Jīnquán Qiánbì Bówùguǎn (daily 9am–5pm; admission ¥10/$1.20), down a right side street of the same name, is housed in a lovely French-style mansion that was a Japanese solider garrison in the late 1930s. The last architectural treasure on the curving lane is the Kǒng Residence, a splendid 1924 creation sadly not open for public viewing. The street is not really worth a special trip out here, but if you're interested in Shànghǎi's colonial architecture, or if your travels take you to Hóngkǒu, then Duōlún Lù is a must.

Duōlún Lù at Shǎnxī Běi Lù, Hóngkǒu (3 blocks north of Dōng Bǎoxìng Lù Light Rail Station); see map p. 118. Free admission. Daily sunrise–late. No Metro. Light Rail: Dōng Bǎoxìng Lù.

Lǔ Xùn Park and Memorial Hall/Former Residence of Lǔ Xùn (Lǔ Xùn Gōngyuán/Lǔ Xùn Gùjū)

What was originally Hóngkǒu Park (1905), once a foreigners' park opened to the Chinese only in 1928, has been renamed for China's best-known 20th-century writer, Lǔ Xùn (1881–1936), who lived in this neighborhood from 1927 until his death. Known as the "father of modern Chinese literature" because of his role in developing the modern style of Chinese prose as well as in helping simplify the Chinese script, Lǔ Xùn was a prolific writer who translated science-fiction novels into Chinese just as easily as he penned scathing critiques of Confucianism and the alternately submissive and arrogant Chinese character. Extolled as a political revolutionary (Máo Zédōng penned an inscription on Lǔ Xùn's tomb which lies at the north end of the park), Lǔ Xùn was himself deliberately never a member of the Communist party. One can only imagine what his scathing pen would have had to say about China's current headlong rush into capitalism. At the eastern end of the park is a memorial hall devoted to his life, the Lǔ Xùn Jìniànguǎn. The main exhibit room on the second floor displays his many books and old photographs, as well as his hat, goatskin gown, and death mask. Signs are in English. There's also a bookstore here selling English-language copies of some of his most famous works, such as *The Story of Ah Q.* A 10-minute walk east of the park, **Lǔ Xùn's Former Residence** is a three-story brick house where he lived from 1933 to his death, and largely decorated as it was then. Exhibits here include an original writing brush as well as a clock marking his exact time of death on October 19, 1936: 5:25am.

Jiāngwān Dōng Lù 146, Hóngkǒu; see map p. 118. ℭ **021/5696-2894.** Park admission ¥2 (25¢); includes Lǔ Xùn's tomb. Daily 6am–6pm. Lǔ Xùn Memorial Hall (inside park on east side; ℭ **021/5666-9711**); admission ¥8/$1; daily 9am–4pm. **The Former Residence of Lǔ Xùn,** Shānyīn Lù 9 Lane 132, Hóngkǒu (from park, take a left out the main entrance, follow Tián'ài Lù south until it curves left onto Shānyīn Lù); admission ¥4 (50¢); daily 9am–4pm. No Metro. Light Rail: Hóngkǒu Zúqiú Chǎng.

Moller Mansion (Héngshān Mălè Biéshù)

Garish, hideous, and mesmerizing at the same time, it's hard to take your eyes off this gigantic gingerbread mansion at Yán'ān Zhōng Lù in the northwest corner of the French Concession. An eclectic mix of architectural styles from faux Gothic to Tudor, this mansion of brown-tiled steeples, gables, and spires was built by a Swedish shipping magnate Eric Moller in 1936, so the apocryphal story goes, for his daughter who envisioned the house in a dream, a version since debunked by the daughter herself. Whatever the genesis, the flamboyant house, with its marble pillars, chandeliers, dark wood paneling, and beautiful stained glass windows epitomized the excesses of colonial Shànghăi. Previously closed to the public in its incarnation as the headquarters of the Shànghăi Communist Youth League, the mansion has been restored and is now an overpriced boutique hotel. Unfortunately, the restoration included the addition of several ugly imitation buildings in the back. Whatever was said about the original mansion, it was at least that: original.

Shănxī Nán Lù 30, Jìng Ān (intersection with Yán'ān Zhōng Lù); see map p. 126. *C* 021/6247-8881. Open 24 hr. Metro: Shănxī Nán Lù.

Museum of Folk Art (Mínjiān Shōucángpǐn Chénlièguăn)

Another step closer to reaching Shànghăi's planned 100 museums, this one showcases collections of just about any folk arts and crafts you can think of, which can be quite interesting if you like your Chinese tchotchkes. Rotating exhibits have included tiny shoes for bound feet, and 1930s cigarette labels. If this doesn't grab you, come see the significantly more interesting building housing the exhibits. This was the original Sānshān Guild Hall (Sānshān Huìguăn), the only one remaining of several guildhalls that used to dot the neighborhood. Funded by merchants from Fújiàn Province, it was built in 1909, in a traditional style with upturned eaves, carved beams, and colorfully painted rafters. The stage, in particular, stands out for its elaborate carvings.

Zhōngshān Nán Yī Lù 1551, Nánshì (at Nán Chēzhàn Lù, 2 blocks east of Xīzàng Nán Lù); see map p. 138. *C* 021/6313-5582. Admission ¥4 (50¢). Daily 9am–4pm. No Metro.

Shànghăi Art Museum (Shànghăi Měishùguăn) ★

Relocated in 2000 to the historic clock tower building on the northwest end of People's Square, the museum is more to be seen for its 1930s monumental interior architecture than for its art. The artworks in the 12 exhibit halls are certainly worthy of note, ranging from modern traditional oils to recent pop canvases, but they are overwhelmed by the fastidiously restored wood and marble interiors of this 1933 five-story neoclassical landmark. People's Square, today's Rénmín Guăngchăng, was a racecourse in colonial times, and today's clock tower, erected in 1933, marks the location of the original grandstand of 1863. After 1949, the building was used as the Shànghăi Museum and the Shànghăi Library. Today, in addition to the artwork, there is a classy American restaurant, Kathleen's 5, on the fifth floor. *Note:* If you're going to visit more than one attraction in People's Square, consider buying a combination ticket (see box in the Shànghăi Museum section, p. 146).

Nánjīng Xī Lù 325, Huángpǔ (northwest edge of People's Park at Huángpí Lù); see map p. 118. *C* 021/6327-2829. www.sh-artmuseum.org.cn. Admission ¥20 ($2.50). Daily 9am–5pm (last tickets sold 4pm). Metro: Rénmín Gōngyuán.

Shànghăi Bank Museum (Shànghăi Shì Yínháng Bówùguăn)

Another notch in the Shànghăi museum belt, this one would seem to be a natural for this finance-oriented city. Unfortunately, at press time (when it was also undergoing extensive renovations), the museum is only open to tour groups with prior arrangements, which seems odd given how much the museum is being advertised around town. Chronicling the history of Chinese banking from the Míng Dynasty (1368–1644) to the present are over 2,000 relics including photographs of old-fashioned private banks, an account recording machine from the 1920s, and even a "6-billion-yuan" paper note (which could only buy 70 grains of rice during the period just before the 1949 revolution). If this interests you, call the museum to see if you can't somehow sweet-talk your way in. Enough public requests may make them change their entrance policy.

Pǔdōng Dà Dào 9, 7th floor, Pǔdōng (inside the Industrial and Commercial Bank building, at intersection with Pǔdōng Nán Lù); see map p. 130. ☎ 021/5878-8743. Admission ¥5 (60¢). Mon–Fri 9–11:30am and 1–4pm, by appointment only. Metro: Lùjiāzuǐ.

Shànghǎi Municipal History Museum (Shànghǎi Shì Lìshǐ Bówùguǎn) ★★

This excellent museum in the basement of the Oriental Pearl TV Tower in Pǔdōng tells the history of Shànghǎi with an emphasis on the colonial period between 1860 and 1949. Fascinating exhibits include dioramas of the Huángpǔ River, the Bund, Nánjīng Lù, and foreign concessions, evoking the colorful street life and lost trades of the 19th and early 20th centuries; dozens of models of Shànghǎi's classic avenues and famous buildings; and a vehicle collection with trolley cars (the city line opened in 1908), 1920s sedans, and a U.S. jeep (popular after World War II) among others. Other intriguing bits include a gorgeously ornate wedding palanquin, boulders marking the concessions' boundaries, and visiting chits used in brothels. The museum takes about an hour to tour. Tickets are purchased at the Oriental Pearl TV Tower gate. Audio headsets (¥30/$3.75) can enhance your visit but are not crucial, as displays are well annotated in English and Chinese.

Lùjiāzuǐ Lù 2, Oriental Pearl TV Tower basement, Pǔdōng; see map p. 130. ☎ 021/5879-3003. Admission ¥35 ($4.25). Daily 9am–9pm. Metro: Lùjiāzuǐ.

Shànghǎi Museum of Arts and Crafts (Shànghǎi Gōngyì Měishù Bówùguǎn) ★

This gorgeous three-story late French Renaissance mansion was built in 1905 for the French Concession chamber of industry director. The mansion's expansive lawns, sweeping marble staircases, stained glass windows, dark wooden paneling, and ceiling beams obviously appealed to many others as well, as it became the residence of Chén Yì, Shànghǎi's first mayor after 1949. For aficionados of Cultural Revolution (1966–76) history, it also served for a time as the residence of Lín Lìguǒ (Lín Biāo's son's mother-in-law) who tore down the glasshouse that used to be in the eastern section of the residence. After 1960, this became the Shànghǎi Arts and Crafts Research Center and its many rooms were converted into studios where visitors could watch artisans work at traditional handicrafts. Today, some of the artists' studios remain but it has been largely rearranged as a formal museum of the crafts produced in Shànghǎi over the past 100 years. On display are fine carvings in jade, wood, ivory, and bamboo, as well as gorgeously stitched costumes and tapestries, intricately painted vases and snuff bottles, and a variety of folk crafts from paper lanterns to dough figurines. A salesroom is attached, of course. Expect high prices but also high quality.

Fēnyáng Lù 79, Xúhuì (at intersection with Tàiyuán Lù); see map p. 122. ☎ 021/6431-1431. Admission ¥8 ($1). Daily 9am–4pm. Metro: Chángshú Lù.

Shànghǎi Music Conservatory Oriental Musical Instrument Museum (Shànghǎi Yīnyuè Xuéyuàn Dōngfāng Yuèqì Bówùguǎn) Finds

Located on the grounds of the Shànghǎi Music Conservatory, which was established in 1927, this new museum has a fascinating collection of musical instruments seldom seen in the West. There are four main exhibits covering (1) the instruments of ancient China, (2) modern Chinese musical instruments, (3) the instruments of China's ethnic minorities such as the Zhuàng, the Miáo, the Uighurs, and the Mongolians, and (4) folk instruments from around the world. The highlights are undoubtedly the ancient pieces, which range from an 8,000-year-old bone flute to the rare Táng Dynasty (618–907) five-stringed *pípa* and the Míng Dynasty (1368–1644) 25-string plucked zither. Unfortunately, the museum doesn't see many visitors, which sometimes leads to it being closed early. Also on the grounds is a wonderful colonial mansion, once the Brazilian consulate, which is now a guesthouse (p. 79) run by the conservatory.

Fēnyáng Lù 20, Xúhuì (east of Chángshú Lù, south of Huáihǎi Zhōng Lù); see map p. 122. ℭ 021/ 6437-0137, ext. 2132, or 021/6431-2157. Admission ¥10 ($1.25). Mon–Fri 9–11am and 1:30–5pm. Metro: Chángshú Lù.

Shànghǎi Natural History Museum (Shànghǎi Zìrán Bówùguǎn) ★ *Kids*

Unlike most of Shànghǎi's museums, which are glossy and modern, this museum, like its contents, has seemingly been frozen in time (specifically 1956 when the museum was first located here), which perversely makes it a rather delightful visit. There is the usual collection of animals, mummies, and fossils, including in the central atrium a complete specimen of a 140-million-year-old dinosaur skeleton from Sìchuān Province. The top floor houses a gallery of stuffed creatures, which have been known to scare some of the young ones (and a few adults, too). Much more interesting for adults is the building itself, a beautiful classical structure that used to be the Cotton Exchange in colonial days. The mosaic floors and stained glass windows in the lobby only hint at the grand building that once was.

Yán'ān Dōng Lù 260, Huángpǔ (at Hénán Nán Lù); see map p. 118. ℭ 021/6321-3548. Admission ¥5 (60¢). Daily 9am–3:30pm. Metro: Hénán Zhōng Lù.

Shànghǎi Public Security Museum (Shànghǎi Gōng'ān Bówùguǎn)

Big Brother's watching. This modern museum surveys the history of Shànghǎi's "homeland security," with a focus on its police department, originally established in 1854. There are few signs in English, but some very interesting artifacts. The second floor has miscellaneous relics, from uniforms and pistol cases to tiny spy cameras and stuffed homing pigeons, but the going gets good on the third floor with grizzly photos and actual weapons (saws, axes, sawed-off shotguns) from Shànghǎi's more famous cases. Look for a human skull impaled with a scissor blade, and the stuffed police dog (b. 1946, d. 1957). There are also items deemed threats to public security: gambling devices, opium pipes, pirated videos, drug paraphernalia, and even books on *Fǎlúngōng*. The fourth floor has displays on fire fighting and Shànghǎi's crime busters, while the fifth floor is, oddly, given to temporary art exhibits.

Ruìjīn Nán Lù 518, Lúwān (south of Xiétǔ Lù); see map p. 122. ℭ 021/6472-0256. Admission ¥8 ($1). Mon–Sat 9am–4pm. No Metro.

Shànghǎi Urban Planning Exhibition Centre (Shànghǎi Chéngshì Guīhuà Zhǎnshìguǎn) ★ *Finds*

Filmmakers and science-fiction writers have imagined it, but if you want to see what a city of the future is really going to look like, take yourself over to this museum on the eastern end of People's Square. Housed in a striking modern five-story building made of microlite glass, this is one of the world's largest showcases of urban development and is much more interesting than its dry name suggests. The highlight is on the third floor: an awesome vast scale model of urban Shànghǎi as it will look in 2020, a master plan full of endless skyscrapers punctuated occasionally by patches of green. The clear plastic models indicate structures yet to be built, and there are many of them. Beleaguered Shànghǎi residents wondering if their current cramped downtown houses will survive the bulldozer (chances are not good) need only look here for the answer. The fourth floor also offers displays on proposed forms of future transportation, including magnetic levitation (maglev), subway, and light-rail trains that are going to change even the face of the Bund. The rest of the building includes a U-shaped mezzanine with photographic exhibits of colonial and contemporary Shànghǎi, a temporary exhibit hall on the second floor, and a cafe and art gallery on the fifth. There are restaurants and retail outlets crafted in the style of 1930s Shànghǎi on the underground level that connects to the Metro. The museum is well worth an hour of your time. ***Note:*** If you're going to visit more than one attraction in People's Square, consider buying a combination ticket (see box in the Shànghǎi Museum section above, p. 146).

Rénmín Dà Dào 100, Huángpǔ (northeast of the Shànghǎi Museum; entrance on east side); see map p. 118. ✆ 021/6372-2077. Admission ¥25 ($3.10). Daily 9am–4pm (to 5pm Fri–Sun). Metro: Rénmín Guǎngchǎng.

Site of the First National Congress of the Communist Party (Zhōnggòng Yīdà Huìzhǐ)
This historic building of brick and marble—a quintessential example of the traditional Shànghǎi style of *shíkù mén* (stone-framed) houses built in the 1920s and 1930s—contains the room where on July 23, 1921, Máo Zédōng and 12 other Chinese revolutionaries founded the Chinese Communist Party. Also present were two Russian advisors. The delegates had to conclude their meeting on Nánhú Lake in Zhèjiāng Province when police broke up the party. The original teacups and ashtrays remain on the organizing table. As the anchor of the urban renewal project that spawned the open-air mall Xīn Tiāndì, this museum has been expanded to include several new galleries. There is the expected hagiographic treatment given the history of the Communist Party, but also more interesting displays of a Qīng Dynasty bronze cannon, swords and daggers used by rebels during the Tàipíng and Small Swords rebellions in 19th-century Shànghǎi, and a boundary stone used to demarcate the entrance to the British Concession, dated May 8, 1899.

Xīngyè Lù 76, Lúwān (south end of Xīn Tiāndì); see map p. 122. ✆ 021/5383-2171. Admission ¥3 (35¢). Daily 9am–4pm. Metro: Huángpí Nán Lù.

Sòng Qìnglíng Gùjū (Soong Ching-ling's Former Residence)
Soong Ching-ling (1893–1981) is revered throughout China as a loyalist to the communist cause. Born in Shànghǎi to a wealthy family, she married the founder of the Chinese Republic, Dr. Sun Yat-sen, in 1915. Unlike the rest of her family members (the most famous being her youngest sister Soong Mei-ling, who married Chiang Kai-shek) who all fled China after 1949, Soong Ching-ling stayed and was given many important political and cultural posts in the communist government. This 1920s villa, built by a Greek sea captain in the French Concession, served as her residence from 1948 to 1963. Little is changed at this two-story house with white walls and green shutters with many of the rooms much as Soong left them. Unfortunately, only the first floor living and dining areas are accessible; her upstairs office, bedroom, and the bedroom of her devoted maid, Lǐ Yàn'é, are closed to the public for conservation reasons. There are two black sedans in the garage, one presented to her by Stalin in 1952. A new annex just inside the gate displays relics from her life, including her Wesleyan College diploma, phonograph records, family photos, and letters from the likes of Indian

China's Sex Museum

When it opened in 1999 on the eighth floor of the Old Sincere Building on Nánjīng Lù, China's first and to date only official sex museum was welcomed by some as an indication of an increasingly progressive attitude in a puritanical empire where the sale of pornography is still ostensibly punishable by death. The creation of Professor Liú Dálín of Shànghǎi University, this pioneering **Museum of Ancient Chinese Sex Culture (Zhōgguó Gǔdài Xìng Wénhuà Bówùguǎn)** displayed most of his private collection of over 1,200 sex artifacts, many of them proof that China's putative Puritanism is really no more than a 60-year old yoke. Unfortunately, the new economics, which has led to some opening-up of Chinese society, has also resulted in the premature departure of the museum from Shànghǎi. The exorbitant rents in town have forced the private museum to move twice in the last 4 years, first from its busy Nánjīng Lù address to the isolated residential area Wǔdīng Lù in northwest Shànghǎi, and again in May 2004, to the town of Tónglǐ 80km (50 miles) away (the museum was running monthly deficits of ¥20,000 – ¥30,000/$2,420–$3,630 at Wǔdīng Lù). For at least the next decade the town negotiated a 10-year lease with Professor Liú; then, Shànghǎi's loss is Tónglǐ's gain (p. 242).

Prime Minister Jawaharlal Nehru and American correspondent Edgar Snow. Soong Ching-ling died in Běijīng in 1981 but is buried with her parents and her maid in the Wànguó Cemetery in western Shànghǎi.

Huáihǎi Zhōng Lù 1843, Xújiāhuì (east of Tiānpíng Lù); see map p. 122. © 021/6437-6268. Admission ¥8 ($1). Daily 9am–4:30pm. No Metro.

Sūn Zhōngshān Gùjū Jìniànguǎn (Sun Yat-sen's Former Residence) ⭐

Sun Yat-sen (1866–1925), beloved founder of the Chinese Republic (1911), lived here with his wife, Soong Ching-ling, from June 1918 to November 1924, when the address would have been 29 Rue de Moliere. Here Sun's wife later met with such literary stars as Lǔ Xùn and George Bernard Shaw (at the same dinner party) and political leaders including Vietnam's Ho Chi Minh (in 1933). Led by an English-speaking guide, visitors enter through the kitchen on the way to the dining room. Sun's study is upstairs, complete with ink stone, brushes, maps drawn by Sun, and a "library" of 2,700 volumes (look closer and you'll see they're merely photocopies of book spines). The bedroom and the drawing room contain more original furnishings, including an original "Zhōngshān" suit, similar to the later Máo suit. The backyard has a charming garden.

Xiāngshān Lù 7, Lúwān (west of Fùxīng Park at Sīnán Lù); see map p. 122. © 021/6437-2954 or 021/6385-0217. www.sh-sunyat-sen.com. Admission ¥8 ($1). Daily 9am–4:30pm. Metro: Shǎnxī Nán Lù.

Yínchuān Xiǎozhù (Lùjiāzuǐ Development Showroom)

A great oddity amidst all the modern skyscrapers of Pǔdōng, this traditional Chinese courtyard mansion, located at the southeast corner of the Lùjiāzuǐ Green, was the residence of a wealthy merchant named Chén Guìchūn. Originally built in 1917, this red and black brick house with ornately carved windows, doors, and balustrades was completely rebuilt in the late 1990s and today is a museum chronicling the rapid development of Pǔdōng. Displays, ranging from traditional looms and tools used by local farmers to photographs and models of the modern metropolis, are scant and annotated in Chinese only, but the house is lovely and worth a 15-minute round if you're in the area.

Lùjiāzuǐ Dōng Lù 15, Pǔdōng (a few blocks east of the Oriental Pearl TV Tower, southeast corner of Lùjiāzuǐ Green); see map p. 130. ✆ 021/5887-9964. Admission ¥5 (60¢). Daily 8:30am–8:30pm. Metro: Lùjiāzuǐ.

Zhōu Gōng Guǎn (Zhōu Ēnlái's Former Residence)

China's most revered leader during the Máo years, Premier Zhōu Ēnlái (1898–1976), used to stay at this ivy-covered house when he visited Shànghǎi in 1946. His old black Buick is still parked in the garage. The backyard has a small courtyard garden, where there is a statue of Zhōu. The house was used more as an office than residence, and it served before the revolution as the Communist Party's Shànghǎi office. Zhōu kept a spartan room on the first floor (his threadbare blankets are neatly folded on the bed); newspapers were produced on the second floor; and a dorm was maintained in the attic. Signs are in Chinese only.

Sīnán Lù 73, Lúwān (2 blocks south of Fùxīng Zhōng Lù); see map p. 122. ✆ 021/6473-0420. Admission ¥2 (25¢). Daily 9am–4pm. Metro: Shǎnxī Nán Lù.

8 Special Attractions

Many of Shànghǎi's top attractions aren't easily categorized. The city's many Children's Palaces, the historic Great World amusement center, and the world's tallest hotel are three examples of the many unusual sights you can view in Shànghǎi.

Children's Municipal Palace (Shì Shàonián Gōng) ★ Kids

Initiated by China's honorary president, Soong Ching-ling, Children's Palaces offer after-school programs for high-achieving children, with advanced instruction in music, art, science, sports, and computers. Of the two dozen children's palaces in the city, this is the largest, the nicest and the most visited. Besides meeting children and peeking in on their classes, you'll be able to admire the gorgeous colonial setting. Built between 1918 and 1931 by a Jewish family from Baghdad, the Kadoories, this sprawling mansion was known in colonial Shànghǎi as the Marble Hall for its grand hallways and gigantic marble ballroom with ornate fireplaces and glittering chandeliers, all reasonably well preserved despite years of children's activities. To tour this Children's Palace, it's best to call ahead for an appointment or make arrangements through CITS or your hotel concierge.

Yán'ān Xī Lù 64, Jìng Ān (near Huáshān Lù); see map p. 126. ✆ 021/6248-1850. Free admission. Mon–Fri 4:30–6pm; Sat–Sun 9am–4pm. Metro: Jìng Ān Sì.

Húxīngtíng Teahouse (Húxīn Tíng Cháshè) ★

Shànghǎi's quintessential teahouse has floated atop the lake at the heart of Old Town, in front of Yù Yuán, since 1784, built by area cotton-cloth merchants as a brokerage hall. Tea drinking was forbidden inside until the late 1800s, when it became what it is today. Believed to be the original model for Blue Willow tableware, the five-sided, two-story pavilion with red walls and uplifted black-tiled eaves has served everyone from visiting heads of state to local laborers. This is the place in Shànghǎi to idle over a cup of tea, seated in front of the open windows. Húxīngtíng (meaning "mid-lake pavilion") is reached via the traditional Bridge of Nine Turnings, so designed to deflect evil spirits who are said to travel only in straight lines.

Yùyuán Lù 257, Nánshì (at pond in the center of the Old Town Bazaar); see map p. 138. ✆ 021/6373-6950. Free admission. Daily 8:30am–10pm. Metro: Hénán Zhōng Lù.

Jīn Mào Tower (Jīn Mào Dàshà) ★★   This tallest building in China is, quite simply, sublime. Built in 1998 as a Sino-American joint venture, the Jīn Mào is currently the third tallest building in the world at 421m (1,379 ft.). Blending traditional Chinese and modern Western tower designs, the building, which boasts 88 floors (eight being an auspicious Chinese number), consists of 13 distinct tapering segments, with high-tech steel bands binding the glass like an exoskeleton. Offices occupy the first 50 floors, the Grand Hyatt hotel the 51st to the 88th floors, while a public observation deck on the 88th floor ("The Skywalk") offers views to rival those of the nearby Oriental Pearl TV Tower (its admission charge is also lower). High-speed elevators (9m/31ft. per second) whisk visitors from Level B1 to the top in less than 45 seconds. The view from there is almost too high, but exquisite on a clear day. You can also look down at the 152m-high (517-ft.) atrium of the Grand Hyatt. Enter the building through entrance 4.

Shìjì Dà Dào 2, Pǔdōng (3 blocks southeast of Oriental Pearl TV Tower); see map p. 130. ℂ 021/5047-5101. Admission ¥50 ($6); ¥30 ($3.80) seniors over 70. Daily 8:30am–9pm. Metro: Lùjiāzuǐ.

Oriental Pearl TV Tower (Dōngfāng Míngzhū Guǎngbō Diànshì Tǎ) ★
The earliest symbol of the new China, this hideous gray tower with three tapering levels of pink spheres (meant to resemble pearls) still holds a special place in many a local heart and is still one of the first stops in town for Chinese visitors. Built in 1994 at a height of 468m (1,550 ft.), it is hailed as the tallest TV tower in Asia and the third tallest in the world. Visit for the stunning panoramas of Shànghǎi (when the clouds and smog decide to cooperate) and the stellar Shànghǎi Municipal History Museum (reviewed earlier in this chapter) located in the basement. Various combination tickets are offered for tower and museum, but for most folks, the observation deck in the middle sphere (263m/870 ft. elevation), reached by high-speed elevators staffed by statistics-reciting attendants, is just the right height to take in Shànghǎi old and new, east and west. Those partial to vertiginous views can ascend to the "space capsule" in the top sphere (350m/1,092 ft. elevation).

Lùjiāzuǐ Lù 2, Pǔdōng; see map p. 130. ℂ 021/5879-1888. Admission ¥50 – ¥100 ($6–$12), depending on sections visited. Daily 8:30am–9:30pm. Metro: Lùjiāzuǐ (Exit 1).

Peace Hotel (Hépíng Fàndiàn) ★★★   This Art Deco palace is the ultimate symbol of romantic colonial Shànghǎi. Built in 1929 by Victor Sassoon, a British descendant of Baghdad Jews who'd made their fortune in opium and real estate, the building was originally part office/residential complex known as the Sassoon House, and part hotel, the Cathay Hotel, one of the world's finest international hotels in the 1930s. Sassoon himself had his bachelor's quarters on the top floor where he threw lavish parties for the city's top denizens. Stroll through the wings of the finely restored lobby, then take the elevator to the gorgeous eighth-floor ballroom. You can walk up to the roof and the garden bar for a superb view of the Bund, Nánjīng Lù, the hotel's famous green pyramid roof, and the Huángpǔ River. Unfortunately, this same view once enjoyed by the world's celebrities in the 1930s now comes with a cover charge of ¥50 ($6.25; one soft drink included).

Nánjīng Dōng Lù 20, Huángpǔ (on the Bund); see map p. 118. ℂ 021/6321-6888. Free admission. Daily 24 hr. Metro: Hénán Zhōng Lù.

Shànghǎi Grand Theatre (Shànghǎi Dà Jùyuàn) ★   A truly grand eight-story space-age complex of glass and more glass, Shànghǎi's Grand Theatre, boasting three theatres (the largest seating 1800), is the city's premier venue for international performances, dramas, and concerts. Guided tours enable you to view the main auditorium (second floor), the VIP Room (third floor), and the Ballet Studio (fifth floor). You can use the elevators or take the white marble stairs. Beautiful as the theatre is, of all the attractions around People's Square, this is the most overpriced. Better to invest in a combination ticket that covers entrance fees to one or more other attractions (see "People's Square Combo Tickets," p. 146).

Rénmín Dà Dào 300, Huángpǔ (across from the Shànghǎi Museum); see map p. 118. ✆ **021/6372-8702** or 021/6372-3833. Admission (for tours) ¥40 ($4.80). Tours daily 9–11am and 1–4pm. Metro: Rénmín Guǎngchǎng or Rénmín Gōngyuán.

Shànghǎi Library (Shànghǎi Túshūguǎn) Opened in 1996, this city library is a state-of-the-art facility with many modern reading rooms, including one devoted to foreign periodicals (fourth floor; Mon–Fri 8:30am–5pm). The collection includes almost two million rare scrolls, manuscripts, and books that can be viewed upon request, though you'll have to apply for a temporary library card. Downstairs, west of the main entrance, is a low-priced Internet cafe.

Huáihǎi Zhōng Lù 1557, Xúhuì (between Wūlǔmùqí Zhōng Lù and Húnán Lù, near American Consulate); see map p. 122 ✆ **021/6445-5555**. Free admission (but temporary library card at ¥10/$1.25 required to read publications). Daily 8:30am–8:30pm. Metro: Héngshān Lù.

Shànghǎi Library Bibliotheca Zi-Ka-Wei (Shànghǎi Túshūguǎn Xújiāhuì Cángshū Lóu) ⭐ *Finds* Bibliophiles, rejoice! In 1847, the Jesuits established as part of their mission in Xújiāhuì a library (Bibliotheca Zi-Ka-Wei), which has now been partially reopened to the public. The first of the two buildings that constitute the present library, a handsome four-story structure with balconies and dormer windows, was the seat of the Society of Jesus, built between 1867 and 1868 as the residence for Jesuit priests. On the second floor is a public reading room presided over by two boxwood friezes, one of St. Ignatius of Loyola on his deathbed, and the other of St. Francis. But the real treasure is in the adjacent two-story Bibliotheca built in 1897 with a first floor designed in a Chinese style with separate alcoves for the keeping of local records, and the second floor given over to the collection of Western books. Here, stacked neatly on wall-to-wall, floor-to-ceiling shelves are some 560,000 musty, fragile volumes in about 20 languages including Latin, English, French, German, Chinese, and Russian, and covering everything from literature and philosophy to politics, history, and religion. The oldest book, a Latin tome by John Duns Scotus, dates to 1515. There's a Chinese-Latin dictionary from 1723, and a French-Shanghainese-Latin dictionary as well. Remarkably, the library, which had become a part of the Shànghǎi City Library in 1956, did not lose a single volume during the Cultural Revolution (1966–76), as librarians defended the collection zealously from Red Guards. At press time, the Bibliotheca was only open for touring on Saturday afternoons, but the reading room is open to the public during regular business hours. Special-interest groups can call ahead to arrange a private tour.

Cáoxī Běi Lù 80, Xúhuì (just north of Xújiāhuì Cathedral); see map p. 122. ✆ **021/6487-4095**. Free 15-min. library tours are offered only on Sat 2–4pm. Reading room: Mon–Sat 9am–4pm. Metro: Xújiāhuì.

Shànghǎi Old City Wall and Dàjìng Gé Pavilion (Shànghǎi Gǔ Chéngqiáng Dàjìng Gé) In 1553 during the Míng Dynasty, Shànghǎi built a city wall to defend itself against Japanese pirates. Following the course of today's Rénmín Lù and Zhōnghuá Lù, the wall measured 8.1m (27 ft.) high, 4.8km (3 miles) around, and had 10 gates. All that remains today is 50m (160 ft.) of wall at this intersection of Dàjìng Lù and Rénmín Lù (the rest was pulled

---

Height Matters

While the West has dropped out of the race, China and its East Asian neighbors continue to compete to erect the world's tallest structures. Near what's currently the world's third-tallest skyscraper, the Jīn Mào Tower in Shànghăi (88 stories, 414m/1,381 ft.), ground has been broken for the Shànghăi World Financial Center. At 95 stories and 453m (1,509 ft.), this will be the world's tallest building if and when completed (2008). That's only if Hong Kong, Shànghăi's chief higher-is-better rival, doesn't get there first with its own tower at Union Square (108 stories, 473m/1,575 ft.), slated for completion in 2007.

---

down in 1912). The visible section of the remaining wall dates to the Qīng Dynasty, as is evident by brick markings bearing the names of Qīng emperors Xiánfēng (1851–61) and Tóngzhì (1862–74). The newly rebuilt Dàjìng Gé pavilion atop the wall was 1 of the 30 towers along the structure. There's a small exhibit here on life in the old Chinese city.

Dàjìnggé Lù 269, Nánshì (just east of intersection with Rénmín Lù); see map p. 138. ℂ 021/6385-2443. Admission ¥5 (60¢). Daily 9am–4pm. No Metro.

Shànghăi Stock Exchange (Shànghăi Zhèngquàn Jiāoyì Suŏ)   Opened in 1992, the Shànghăi Stock Exchange is China's largest. It recently moved to this new building, which is supposed to resemble an ancient Chinese coin with an open square in the middle, in the heart of Pŭdōng, Shànghăi's Wall Street. While visitors aren't permitted onto the trading floor, sometimes a tour of the exchange can be arranged through your hotel desk.

Pŭdōng Nán Lù 528, Shànghăi Securities Exchange Building, Pŭdōng; see map p. 130. ℂ 021/6880-8888. Mon–Fri 9–11:30am and 1–4pm. Metro: Dōngchāng Lù.

Xīn Tiāndì (New Heaven and Earth) ★★★   Shànghăi's trendiest lifestyle destination, this 2-block complex of high-end restaurants (some of Shànghăi's best), bars, shops, and entertainment facilities, mostly lodged in refurbished traditional Shanghainese *shíkù mén* (stone-frame) housing, is the first phase of the Tàipíng Qiáo Project, an urban renewal project covering 52 hectares (128 acres) that resulted in the relocation of 3,500 families. Busloads of domestic Chinese tourists traipse through in the evenings, Western visitors feel like they've never left home, and hip young Shanghainese flood here to enjoy the good life they feel they're due. Besides the many shopping and dining establishments (separately reviewed), there is a *shíkù mén* museum (at Xīnyeè Lù and Mădāng Lù) showcasing the interiors of a typical lane house.

Bounded by Tàicāng Lù, Huángpí Nán Lù, Zìzhōng Lù, and Mădāng Lù, Lúwān; see map p. 122. ℂ 021/3307-0337. Shíkùmén Museum admission ¥20 ($2.50). Museum daily 10am–10pm. Hours for restaurants and shops vary. Metro: Huángpí Nán Lù.

9 Especially for Kids

Compared to other Chinese cities, Shànghăi has a relatively large number of attractions for children. Listed elsewhere in this chapter, the Oriental Pearl TV Tower, the Jīn Mào Tower, and the Shànghăi Museum of Arts and Crafts may amuse the kids, but the following should appeal particularly to younger foreign travelers (and often to their parents, too) while in Shànghăi.

Aquaria 21 (Shànghǎi Chángfēng Hǎiyáng Shìjiè) ✦

This excellent underwater world aquarium features a "touch pool" so that kids can mingle with the sea life (crabs, starfish, urchins). The main tank is stocked with seahorses, tuna, turtles, rays, and patrolling sharks fed by keepers in diving suits. There's also an arena of penguins from Peru and Chile. In fact, you can journey through a series of aquatic habitats, from the Amazon River to Antarctica. Scuba gear is provided for those who want diving lessons.

Dà Dū Hé Lù 451, Chángníng (Gate 4, Chángfēng Gōngyuán, west of Inner Ring Rd.). ✆ **021/5281-8888**, ext. 6838. Admission ¥80 ($10) adults, ¥60 ($7.50) children 1–1.4m (39–55 in.), free for children under 1m (39 in.). Open daily 9am–5pm. No Metro. Light Rail: Jīnshājiāng Lù.

Dino Beach (Rèdài Fēngbào Shuǐshàng Lèyuán) ✦

The best water park in Shànghǎi boasts Asia's largest wave pool (.8 hectares/2 acres). As well, there are eight water slides, the longest measuring almost 150m (500 ft.), three swimming pools for kids, a mile-long river with rapids, and organized beach volleyball and water polo games. Factor in a slew of fast-food outlets, and you come up with the closest thing to an American-style water park in China.

Xīn Zhèn Lù 78, Mínghǎng (Qībǎo Zhèn, south of Shànghǎi-Hángzhōu Hwy.). ✆ **021/6478-3333**. www.dinobeach.com.cn. Admission ¥60 ($7.20) Mon and Wed–Fri, ¥80 ($9.60) Sat–Sun; children under 1.5m (59 in.) half-price; toddlers under .8m (32 in.) free; ¥30 ($3.60) Tues for all adults. Open summer only: daily 9am–9pm June 28–early Sept (except 2nd weekend of July to the 3rd weekend of Aug 9am–11pm). No Metro. Regular shuttle buses from Shànghǎi Stadium and Xīnzhuāng Metro stations (3km/2 miles from Dino Beach).

Great World (Dà Shìjiè)

Built in 1915 for the entertainment of the rich, this tower that looks like a multi-tiered wedding cake was an infamous gambling and vice den during the 1920s and 1930s but has since been converted into an entertainment center for the entire family. Among the kid-friendly attractions here are a Guinness Book of World Records gallery, a video game salon, a bumper car track, folk dancing shows, and acrobatic and martial arts performances. The live performances typically run all day from 9am to 6pm, while evening shows start at 7:30pm. Unfortunately, the building, looking rather the worse for wear, was closed at press time due to the road-widening project on Xīzàng Lù, and there's been no confirmation as to when it might reopen.

Xīzàng Nán Lù 1, Huángpǔ (at Yán'ān Dōng Lù). ✆ **021/6326-3760**, ext. 40, or 021/6374-6703. Admission ¥30 ($4). Daily 9am–9:30pm. Metro: Rénmín Guǎngchǎng.

Jǐn Jiāng Amusement Park (Jǐn Jiāng Lèyuán)

Shànghǎi's most complete modern amusement park, the Jǐn Jiāng has a loop-the-loop roller coaster, merry-go-rounds, and bumper cars, as well as a haunted house. There's also a special playground for preschoolers. The "Gorge Drifting Waterland" is a watersports area only open during summer and requiring a separate admission (¥30/$3.60; daily 10am–4:30pm).

Hóngméi Lù 201, Xúhuì (at Hùmíng Lù). ✆ **021/6436-4956**. Admission ¥60 ($7.50); includes 8 rides. Daily 8am–9pm summer, 8am–5pm winter. Metro: Jǐnjiāng Lèyuán.

Ocean World (Hǎiyáng Shìjiè)

This indoors water world is geared for preschoolers. Most pools are shallow enough for nonswimmers, and lifeguards are always on duty. There's a wading stream with Jacuzzi-jet seats, a wave beach, slides, fountains, and seesaws. For lunch, the Regal Shànghǎi East Asia's Hotel Top of the World Café is also in the stadium complex.

Tiānyáoqiáo Lù 666, Xúhuì (inside Shànghǎi Stadium). ✆ **021/6426-6068**. Admission ¥40 ($5) weekdays, ¥50 ($6) weekends. Mon–Fri 1–9pm; Sat–Sun 10am–9pm. Metro: Shànghǎi Tǐyùguǎn.

Shànghǎi Circus World (Shànghǎi Mǎxì Chéng) 🌟

This glittering modern arena for acrobatic and circus performances, opened in the northern suburbs in 1999, has a 1,638-seat circus theater with a revolving stage, computer-controlled lighting, and state-of-the-art acoustics. The complex also includes a gigantic animal house with rooms for elephants, tigers, lions, chimps, horses, and pandas. The celebrated Shànghǎi Acrobatic Troupe stages its 20-act performances here on a regular basis. This has been the venue for the annual Shànghǎi International Magic Festival and Competition, held in early November. Check with your hotel for the current performers, schedules, and tickets.

Gònghé Xīn Lù 2266, Zháběi (north of railway station, near Zháběi Gōngyuán). ℂ 021/5665-6622, ext. 2027. www.circus-world.com. Tickets ¥50–¥150 ($6–$18); "VIP" seats ¥280 ($34). Performances Wed, Fri, Sat 7:30pm. No Metro. Shànghǎi Center: Nánjīng Xī Lù 1376, 4th Floor, Jìng Ān. ℂ 021/5665-6622, ext. 2027. Tickets ¥50–¥100 ($6–$13). Daily 7:30pm.

Shànghǎi Natural Wild Insect Kingdom (Shànghǎi Dàzìrán Yěshēng Kūnchóng Guǎn)

The birds and the bees, the beetles and the butterflies, all your usual creepy crawlies are on display in this 2-year-old museum housing several galleries, including a tropical rainforest and a reptile cave. Some of the insect models can be pretty tacky to adult eyes, but kids like the interactive exhibits where they can feed critters and catch fish.

Fēnghé Lù 1, Pǔdōng (west of Oriental Pearl TV Tower, north of International Convention Center). ℂ 021/5840-6950. Admission ¥35 ($4.50) adults; ¥20 ($2.50) under 18. Mon–Fri 9am–5pm (to 9pm in summer). Metro: Lùjiāzuǐ.

Shànghǎi Ocean Aquarium (Shànghǎi Hǎiyáng Shuǐzú Guǎn) 🌟🌟

Shànghǎi's newest, biggest, and best aquarium, and Asia's largest, opened in 2002 in Pǔdōng, next to the Oriental Pearl TV Tower. Its state-of-the-art facilities boasts 28 exhibit areas for over 10,000 sea creatures from all continents: sharks, jellyfish, turtles, lionfish, sea otters, Yángzǐ sturgeon, and more. The centerpiece is the massive, sparkling $6.6-million glass-surround observation tunnel. Adventurous visitors can make special arrangements to dive in the shark tank, though it could well cost you an arm and a leg.

Yínchéng Běi Lù 158, Pǔdōng (east of Oriental Pearl TV Tower). ℂ 021/5877-9988. www.aquarium.sh.cn. Admission ¥110 ($13) adults, ¥65 ($7.80) seniors over 70, ¥70 ($8.40) children under 1.4m (55 in.), free for children under .8m (32 in.). Daily 9am–8:30pm. Metro: Lùjiāzuǐ.

Shànghǎi Science and Technology Museum (Shànghǎi Kējì Guǎn) 🌟🌟

This hands-on interactive science museum, opened in 2001, has received raves from expatriate families with children. There are five main interactive exhibits, which can be visited in any order. The "Earth Exploration" exhibit is a journey to the center of the Earth, complete with fossils. "Children's Technoland" has a walk-in heart and brain, as well as a simulated construction zone with soft foam bricks. The vast "Light of Wisdom" area has over a hundred interactive stations that bring scientific principles to life. "Cradle of Designers" gives you the chance to design your own cards or create your own video. "Spectrum of Life" is a simulated tropical rainforest with robotic beetles and a bat cave. There are also two brand-new IMAX 3D cinemas. Weekends are crowded here; best time to visit is on weekdays in the late afternoons, when the school excursions are over.

Shìjì Dà Dào 2000, Pǔdōng (north side Shìjì Gōngyuán). ℂ 021/6862-2000. Admission ¥60 ($7.20) adults, ¥45 ($5.60) high-school students, ¥20 ($2.50) children under 1.2m (4 ft.). Tues–Sun 9am–5:30pm (last ticket sold at 3:30pm). Metro: Shànghǎi Kējiguǎn.

Shànghǎi Wild Animal Park (Shànghǎi Yěshēng Dòngwùyuán)

Shànghǎi's only drive-through safari, home to some 5,000 animals (200 species), is located all the way out by the Pǔdōng International Airport. At least the South China tigers, lions, cheetahs, zebras, giraffes, camels, bears, elephants, hippos, and flamingos have more legroom here than in the Shànghǎi Zoo. Unfortunately, business has dropped off considerably since there were two human fatalities several years ago. Buses transport visitors through the grounds, and there's also a walk-through area with birds, monkeys, seals, and sea lions.

Nánfāng Gōnglù, Nánhuì (east Pǔdōng). © 021/5803-6000. Admission ¥80 ($10), half-price children under 1.2m (4 ft.). Daily 8am–5pm. No Metro.

Shànghǎi Zoo (Shànghǎi Dòngwùyuán)

One of China's best, this zoo still has a long way to go to equal the better preserves in the West. It was a private estate of the Sassoon family, then a city golf course, before its conversion to a zoo in 1954. There are plenty of open spaces for children to play, but the spaces for animals are quite confined and depressing. Expect the usual performing seals and elephants. The panda center, a 20-minute stroll northwest from the entrance, has small indoor and outdoor areas. There are about 6,000 specimens (600 species) here, as well as a children's zoo and recreation center with playground equipment and Ferris wheel.

Hóngqiáo Lù 2831, Chángníng (1 mile east of Hóngqiáo Airport). © 021/6268-7775. Admission ¥30 ($3.75), free for children under 1.2m (4 ft.). Daily Nov–Feb 7am–4:30pm, Mar and Oct 7am–5pm, Apr–Sept 6:30am–5pm. No Metro.

10 Organized Tours

Most Shànghǎi hotels have tour desks that can arrange a variety of day tours for guests. These tour desks are often extensions of **China International Travel Service (CITS),** with its head offices near the Shànghǎi Centre at Běijīng Xī Lù 1277, Guólù Dàshà (© **021/6289-4510** or 021/6289-8899, ext. 263; www.scits.com). The FIT (Family and Independent Travelers) department can be reached at fax 021/6289-7838. There's another branch at the Bund at Jīnlíng Dōng Lù 2 (© **021/6323-8770**) where you can purchase airline and train tickets. CITS operates many of the English-language group tours in Shànghǎi, even those booked in hotels. The only reason to go directly to the CITS office is to arrange a special tour, perhaps of sites not offered on the regular group tour list, or for a private tour with guide, driver, and car, but you will pay dearly for it.

If you have little time, **group tours** are convenient, efficiently organized, and considerably less expensive than private tours. These tours cost about ¥250 to ¥400 ($30–$48) per person. The **Jīn Jiāng Optional Tours Center,** which has its head office in the CITS building (Běijīng Xī Lù 1277, Room 611; © **021/ 6445-9525;** fax 021/6472-0184; www.jjtravel.com) and a branch office near the Jīn Jiāng and Okura Garden hotels at Chánglè Lù 191 (© **021/6445-9525** or 021/6466-2828, ext. 239/240) offer a typical group tour of Shànghǎi by bus, with English-speaking guide and lunch, for ¥250 ($31); sites include Yù Yuán, the Bund, Jade Buddha Temple, Xīn Tiāndì, People's Square, the Shànghǎi Museum, and a quick drive-by of Pǔdōng. Jīn Jiāng offers similar 1-day group tours to Sūzhōu (¥350/$42) and Hángzhōu (¥500/$60). Hotel desks have a wider range of group tour itineraries to select from, but at higher prices than those offered by the Jīn Jiāng Optional Tours Center.

Group tours aren't for everyone, as they are extremely rushed. At major sites, group tour participants are shown only a fraction of what's there. A good guide can outline the history and culture of a place, but there is usually no more than an hour to see a major site. Most of the commentary is delivered during the bus ride.

Of course, travel agencies can arrange in-depth private tours, customized to fit your itinerary or interest (such as education, art, food, or the martial arts). These tours include an English-speaking guide, driver, and private car for the day. The Jìn Jiāng Optional Tours Center offers a full-day private tour of the city, including door-to-door service, air-conditioned car, English-speaking guide, and lunch, at a cost of ¥950 ($114) for one person, ¥550 ($66) each for two people, or ¥480 ($58) each for three or four people. Travel agencies and hotel tour desks can also act as ticketing agents for nighttime entertainment, too (such as acrobatics, opera, circus, Peace Hotel Jazz Bar, Huángpǔ River cruises).

In addition to CITS and Jìn Jiāng, another proven private travel agency providing group day tours, private tours, tickets, and hotel bookings to international clients is the **Shànghǎi Spring International Travel Service,** Dīngxī Lù 1558 (ⓒ **021/6251-5777;** fax 021/6252-3734; www.china-sss.com), which also maintains a 24-hour Tourist Information Line (ⓒ **021/6252-0000**).

The **Shànghǎi Sightseeing Bus Center,** located under the no. 5 staircase at Gate 12 of the Shànghǎi Stadium (Tiānyáoqiáo Lù 666; ⓒ **021/6426-5555**), runs 10 in-town sightseeing bus lines (see "Getting Around" in chapter 3, p. 53), and multiple tours, both guided and unguided, to destinations like Tónglǐ, Nánxún, Sūzhōu, and Hángzhōu, but tour guides speak Chinese only. (See chapter 10 for information on how to tour the above listed towns.)

11 Staying Active

Most visitors to Shànghǎi do not come intending to pursue outdoor recreation or sports, but there is a wide range of such activities. Hotels routinely offer exercise machines, weights, aerobic and workout areas, swimming pools, locker rooms, and, less often, tennis and squash courts, all at little or no charge to their guests. It is possible to use some hotels' fitness facilities even if you are not a guest (although the fees can be steep). Joggers in Shànghǎi will find the early morning streets and public parks conducive to running. Shànghǎi has its own annual international marathon, the Toray Cup (run in mid-Nov).

Golf and bowling are two of the most popular recreational sports in Shànghǎi, pursued by well-to-do locals, foreign residents, and overseas visitors, but kite-flying, traditional *tàijí quán,* and even go-cart racing can also be enjoyed if time and energy allow.

Spectator sports include Formula One racing, professional basketball, interleague soccer, and international badminton.

ACTIVITIES FROM A TO Z

BOWLING (BǍOLÍNG QIÚ) Bowling experienced a boom in China during the 1990s, when over 15,000 alleys were built, many of them in Shànghǎi. There are good alleys in the Cypress, Equatorial, Huá Tíng, Jìn Jiāng, and especially the Regal International East Asia hotels. The Buckingham Bowling Alley at Dìngxī Lù 825 (ⓒ **021/6281-9988**) is popular with foreign residents. Rates run from ¥10 to ¥30 ($1.20–$3.60) per line at Shànghǎi bowling halls, depending on the quality of the facility and the time of day (the later, the more expensive); shoe rentals toe the line at ¥3 to ¥10 (35¢–$1.25).

Shànghǎi Spas

In most people's minds, Shànghǎi may not be readily associated with the spa experience, but those addicted to their mud wraps, body polishes, and lomi lomi massages can now get their fix at a number of classy, brand-name spas in town. The world famous **Banyan Tree Spa,** located on the third floor of the Westin Hotel (Hénán Zhōng Lù 88; ℂ **021/6335-1888;** www.banyantreespa.com/shanghai), is beautifully designed using the theme of the Chinese five elements (wood, water, fire, earth, and metal). A host of beauty, hair-care, and massage treatments is available at steep international spa prices. Also from Thailand, the first **Mandara Spa** in China has set up shop at the JW Marriott Hotel (Nánjīng Xī Lù 399; ℂ **021/5359-4969;** www.mandaraspa.com), while the **Spa at the Hilton** (Huáshān Lù 250; ℂ **021/6248-0000,** ext. 2600) continues to dole out some of the city's best massages. The new **Evian Spa** at Three on the Bund (Zhōngshān Dōng Yī Lù 3; ℂ **021/ 6321-6622)** looks set to delivery luxury pampering at luxury prices.

For considerably less expensive (but still legitimate) massages *(àn mó),* try **Pǔrèn Táng** (Dōngfāng Lù 877, second floor; ℂ **021/5058-8182),** located just north of the St. Regis Hotel in Pǔdōng, which offers a variety of health and Chinese medical massages. The **Fùníng Point Pressure Massage Center of Blind People** (Fùxīng Lù 597; ℂ **021/6437-8378)** offers invigorating Chinese massages for less than ¥60 ($7.50) an hour. Little to no English is spoken at these local places, however.

GO-CARTING (KǍDĪNG CHĒ)   Best track for a Formula One drive in miniature is at the indoor arena at **Disc Kart** (Díshìkǎ Sàichēguǎn, Àomén Lù 326 at Jiāngníng Lù; ℂ **021/6277-5641),** where the timing system is high-tech, the carts have new Honda engines, and the driving goes on into the wee hours (Sun–Thurs 2pm–2am; Fri–Sat 2pm–4am). An outdoor alternative is the **Qūyáng Racing Cart Club,** Zhōngshān Běi Yī Lù 880 (ℂ **021/6531-6800;** Mon–Thurs 10am–8:30pm; Fri–Sun 9am–8:30pm).

GOLF (GĀO'ĚRFŪ QIÚ)   Greens fees at Shànghǎi's dozen or more golf courses run from ¥400 to ¥830 ($50–$100) on weekdays, ¥830 to ¥1,660 ($100–$200) on weekends. Caddies cost ¥83 to ¥166 ($10–$20) and club rental ¥250 to ¥415 ($30–$50). All courses require advance reservations; summer weekends are particularly crowded. Among the best courses are the world-class, Robert Trent Jones, Jr.–designed **Shànghǎi International Golf and Country Club** (Shànghǎi Guójì Gāo'ěrfū Xiāngcūn Jùlèbù), Xīnyáng Cūn, Zhūjiājiǎo (ℂ **021/5972-8111;** Wed–Mon 9am–5pm), an hour's drive west of Shànghǎi in Qīngpǔ County; the **Shànghǎi Riviera Golf Resort** (Shànghǎi Dōngfāng Bālí Gāo'ěrfū Jùlèbù), Yángzǐ Lù 277, Nánxiáng Town, Jiādìng County (ℂ **021/5912-6888;** Tues–Fri 9am–10pm; Sat–Sun 8am–10pm), a Bobby J. Martin–designed course with a driving range and year-round night golfing; the 18-hole Jack Nicklaus–designed **Shànghǎi Links Golf and Country Club** (Gāo'ěrfū Xiāngcūn Jùluèbù), Língbái Lù 1600 (ℂ **021/5897-5899;** Mon–Fri 8am–4pm), in the Pǔdōng region; the **Tomson Golf Club** (Tāngchén Gāo'ěrfū Jùlèbù), Lóngdōng Lù 1, also in Pǔdōng, with reservations available through the Inter-Continental Hotel Pǔdōng (℡ **021/5831-8888;** Mon 1–10pm, Tues–Sun 8am–10pm); and Shànghǎi's only 54-hole course, the **Shànghǎi Bīnhǎi Golf Club** (Bīnhǎi Gāo'ěrfū Jùlèbù), Bīnhǎi, Nánhuì, located near the Pǔdōng Airport (℡ **021/5805-8888** or 021/5047-6811; call for hours).

HEALTH & FITNESS CLUBS   Some hotels offer day rates to outsiders. The **Spa at the Hilton** (℡ **021/6248-0000,** ext. 2600; daily 6am–11pm), for example, charges ¥250 ($30) per day for use of its gym, pool, tennis and squash courts, sauna, Jacuzzi, locker rooms, and exercise room. The most complete range of fitness facilities in town is offered by the **Shànghǎi International Tennis Centre Club,** attached to the Regal International East Asia Hotel, Héngshān Lù 516, third floor, Xúhuì (℡ **021/6415-5588,** ext. 82), with its 25m (82-ft.) indoor lap pool, aerobics studio, exercise machines, simulated golf range, 12-lane bowling alley, and 10 of China's best indoor and outdoor tennis and squash courts (daily 6am–11pm). Among private fitness clubs, one of the best is **Fitness First** at Plaza 66, Nánjīng Xī Lù 1266, B/1; ℡ **0216288-0152;** www.fitnessfirst.com), which offers a vast array of state-of-the-art equipment; a full range of classes including pilates, step, yoga, boxing, and cycling; and excellent changing rooms with sauna and massage (Mon–Fri 6:30am–11pm; Sat–Sun 7am–10pm; day rate ¥150/$19).

KITE-FLYING (FÀNG FĒNGZHENG)   Chinese have been flying their invention for over 2,000 years. The best places to buy and to fly local Shànghǎi kites are in the public parks and in People's Square in front of the Shànghǎi Museum.

TAI CHI (TÀIJÍ QUÁN)   These venerable and graceful "shadow-boxing" exercises, which tens of thousands of Shanghainese practice every morning before work, and Wǔ Shù, the martial arts forms developed in China, can be learned at the **Shànghǎi Wǔshù Center (Wǔshù Yuàn),** Nánjīng Xī Lù 595, Huángpǔ (℡ **021/6215-3599**); or at the **Lóngwǔ International Kung Fu Center,** Shǎnxī Nán Lù 215 (℡ **13003252826** or 021/5465-0042; www. longwukungfu.com).

YOGA (YÚJIĀ)   You can now practice your sun salutations at a number of places, including the Shànghǎi International Tennis Centre (see above), and Y+ Yoga Centre (Fùxīng Lù, Lane 299, no. 2; ℡ **021/6433-4330;** www.yplus.com.cn). The latter offers ashtanga, bikram, and prenatal yoga as well as Pilates.

Formula One Fever

Formula One racing officially roared into China with the Shànghǎi Grand Prix in September 2004. Located in the northwestern suburb of Āntíng in Jiādìng County, about 40 minutes from People's Square, the Shànghǎi International Circuit (Shànghǎi Guójì Sàichēchǎng), which will host F1 races until 2010, features a stunning track in the contours of a Chinese character, and a 10-story glass and steel grandstand. Tickets range from ¥160 ($19) for practice sessions to ¥3,700 ($340) for top seats overlooking the finish line on the last day. Tourist bus line 6B (¥4/50¢) makes the run to Āntíng from the Shànghǎi Stadium (see "Getting Around: By Bus" in chapter 3). For more information, call ℡ **021/9682-6999** or 021/6330-5555; or visit www.icsh.sh.cn/en.

SPECTATOR SPORTS

Check local listings or your hotel desk for current sports in town. The **Chinese National Basketball League (CNBL)** has been building a strong following across China since its inception in 1994. Each team is allowed to hire two foreign players (usually Americans). The powerful Shànghǎi Sharks (home team of 2.26m/7 ft. 5 in. Yáo Míng, now playing for the Houston Rockets in the NBA) play most of their home basketball games November through April in Lúwān Stadium, Zhàojiābāng Lù 128 (*©* **021/6427-8673** or 021/6467-5358). Tickets are ¥30 to ¥200 ($3.60–$24). **Shànghǎi Stadium,** Tiānyáoqiáo Lù 666, Xúhuì (*©* **021/6426-6666** or 021/6426-6888, ext. 8268), is the usual venue for big sporting events (soccer, track, and field). **Shànghǎi Zhábeǐ Stadium,** Gònghé Xīn Lù 475, Chángníng (*©* **021/5690-8609**), is a popular venue for rugby tournaments.

7

Shànghǎi Strolls

Despite its immense and dense population, Shànghǎi is one of China's great cities for walking. Much of the street-level fascination comes from the European architecture left over from colonial days (1842–1949), when Shànghǎi was sliced up by the Western powers into foreign concessions. Shànghǎi's present cityscape is an amalgam of Art Deco mansions from that colonial period, *nòngtáng* (walled brick town house rows) with distinctive *shíkù mén* (stone frame gates) from the local Chinese tradition, and malls of towering glass and steel from international modernism.

Walking Shànghǎi is not without its obstacles. Sidewalks are often crowded not only with other pedestrians, but with bicycle parking lots, construction sites, vendors and their carts, card players, laundry strung between doors and trees, cars brazenly parked on walkways, and motorcycles and bicycles zooming up and down the sidewalks as though they were extensions of the streets. You'll also have to contend with the pollution and dust, occasional raw odors, and jarring sounds, so much so that a half-day's walk can sometimes leave you exhausted. But it is really only in walking that you'll get a chance to discover aspects of Shànghǎi you would otherwise miss from a speeding taxi or a tour bus: that faded colonial mansion hidden under years of grime, or that vegetable market teeming with local housewives—scenes that are themselves rapidly disappearing from today's Shànghǎi.

Walking just about anywhere in Shànghǎi requires vigilance. The basic rule of survival is that cars have the right of way even when they shouldn't. *Cars always have the right of way, even when you have a green light, so look both ways and always be prepared to yield.* At least at major roads and intersections, brown-clad, whistle-blowing traffic assistants now help direct pedestrian traffic. On smaller streets, simply follow the lead of locals. Above all, slow down and savor a walk through China's biggest, most densely packed city, where past and future, East and West, meet at every corner. The best way to see Shànghǎi, despite its hazards, is on foot.

WALKING TOUR 1   THE BUND & BEYOND

Start:	Wàibǎidù Bridge, Sūzhōu Creek (Metro: Hénán Zhōng Lù).
Finish:	Yán'ān Dōng Lù, south Bund.
Time:	3 to 4 hours.
Best Times:	Weekday mornings or late afternoons; nighttime for the lights, not the sights.
Worst Times:	Weekends bring out the crowds on the Bund Promenade. Evenings are pretty, with the lights on the Bund buildings and the river, but the architecture cannot be viewed well after dark.

Walking Tour 1: The Bund

1 Wàibáidù Qiáo (Wàibáidù Bridge)
外白渡桥

2 Huángpǔ Gōngyuán (Huángpǔ Park)
黄浦公园

3 Former British Consulate
英国领事馆旧址

4 Jardine Matheson Building (now the
Shànghǎi Foreign Trade Building)
上海外贸大楼

5 Bank of China (Zhōngguó Yínháng)
中国银行

6 Peace Hotel (Hépíng Fàndiàn)
和平饭店

7 Palace Hotel (Peace Hotel South Building)
和平饭店南楼

8 Russo-Chinese Bank Building (now the
China Foreign Exchange Trade System
Building)
(Zhōngguó Wàihuì Jiāoyì Zhōngxīn)
中国外汇交易中心

9 Shànghǎi Customs House
(Shànghǎi Hǎiguān)
上海海关

10 Hongkong and Shànghǎi Bank
(now the Shànghǎi Pǔdōng
Development Bank)
(Shànghǎi Pǔdōng Fāzhǎn Yínháng)
上海浦东发展银行

11 Intersection of Fúzhōu Lù and Jiāngxī Lù)

12 Hospital of the Shànghǎi Navigation
Company (now the Bangkok Bank and
the Thai Consulate)
(Màngǔ Yínháng)
曼谷银行

13 Three on the Bund (formerly the Union
Insurance Company Building)
(Wàitān Sān Hào)
外滩三号

14 Shànghǎi Club (Yīngguó Zǒng Huì)
英国总会

Defining the eastern boundary of downtown Shànghǎi, the Bund (Wài Tān) refers to both sides of the wide avenue (Zhōngshān Dōng Yī Lù) that runs north and south along the western shore of the Huángpǔ River. The **Bund Promenade** now occupies the east side of the street, affording terrific pedestrian-only walks along the river shore. Our stroll concentrates, however, on the colonial-era European-style architecture on the west side of the street.

The colonial era began in Shànghǎi after the Treaty of Nánjīng ended the First Opium War in 1842. The British and other Western nations moved in, establishing foreign enclaves (concessions) and opening up the city to trade. Consisting of mud flats and streams that were drained, the Bund (which means embankment) became the chief shipping, trading, and financial district of the colonialists. Shànghǎi's foreign population grew from 10,000 in 1910 to 60,000 by 1940, and it was during this period that the great buildings that still line the Bund were built. Many of the more notable buildings were designed by the architectural firm Palmer and Turner, including the Customs House, the former Hong Kong and Shànghǎi Bank, the Bank of China, and the Peace Hotel.

War with Japan signaled the end to the Bund's colonial heyday, the first bomb dropping on the Peace Hotel August 14, 1937. In January 1943, the Japanese occupation of Shànghǎi put an end to the city's foreign concessions. Shortly after the communist triumph of 1949, the last of the foreign trading houses abandoned the Bund. In the decades since, many of the buildings, occupied sporadically by local banks, organizations, and businesses, fell into disrepair, but since the late 1990s there has been a concerted effort to restore the Bund's architectural grandeur, to refurbish the colonial interiors, and to open them to a curious public, all of which makes for a fascinating walking tour.

Begin at the northern end of the Bund (Zhōngshān Dōng Yī Lù) on the southern shore of Sūzhōu Creek at:

❶ Wàibáidù Bridge

This steel span was built in 1907 to replace the wooden Garden Bridge that once connected the American Settlement north of the Sūzhōu Creek to the British Concession. On the north side of the bridge you can still see a number of colonial holdovers: to the left (west), the former **Broadway Mansions** (now Shànghǎi Mansions), an Art Deco apartment built in 1934 and which later housed the Foreign Correspondents Club after World War II; to the right on the north side of the street, the marvelous old **Astor House Hotel,** built in 1860 and reconstructed in 1906. The hotel was the first to use telephones and electric lights in China. Albert Einstein stayed here in 1921 and 1923 (and you can, too, in his former room, in today's Pǔjiāng Hotel, which serves primarily budget travelers). South of the Pǔjiāng is the former and again current **Russian Consulate,** built in 1917, which served as a seamen's hotel in intervening years.

From the bridge, head south down the east side of Zhōngshān Dōng Yī Lù past:

❷ Huángpǔ Gōngyuán (Huángpǔ Park)

Originally built by the British in 1868, this is the notorious park that in colonial days was reputed to have a sign posted forbidding entrance by dogs and Chinese. Actually, they were just 2 out of 10 park prohibitions, but the underlying attitude towards the Chinese was clear. Today, the park is dwarfed by the Bund Promenade, at the northern end of which is an obelisk, the **Monument to the People's Heroes.** This is a great spot to take in views of Pǔdōng across the river, as well as of the Bund buildings you'll soon be seeing up close. Underneath the monument is the Bund Historical Museum (Wàitān Lìshǐ Bówùguǎn; daily 9am–4:15pm; free admission), worth a quick tour if you want to see photos of the Bund's early days.

Cross to the west side of the Bund via the pedestrian underpass just south of Běijīng Dōng Lù. Take the right exit (heading north) and proceed north until the road starts to curve. To your left, you'll find the:

❸ Former British Consulate (No. 33–53)

This large sprawling compound with the two stately gray granite buildings was the former British Consulate, first established here in 1852 after the British victory in the Opium War of 1842, and rebuilt in 1873. From this perch at the top of the Bund, the British oversaw the growth and development of Shànghǎi into an economic powerhouse in the first half of the 20th century. Until early 2004, these two remaining buildings served as offices for the Shànghǎi Municipal Government, but the whole compound has now been slated for redevelopment. Details at press time were sketchy. South of here at no. 29 is the former **Banque de L'Indo-Chine,** a French classic structure built in 1911; and the **Glen Line Building** (no. 28), built in 1922, both now occupied by the Everbright Bank. The Glen Line Building had been the American Consulate for a brief spell after World War II.

If you're interested in seeing some well-preserved colonial architecture just behind the Bund, follow the road north as it curves to the left and becomes Sūzhōu Nán Lù. Take a left (south) at Yuánmíngyuán Lù, which has a row of remarkable Art Deco and classical buildings along its western edge. Take a left (east) at Běijīng Dōng Lù, which used to be dominated for a long time on the northern side by Shànghǎi's Friendship Store, since slated for demolition as part of a redevelopment program. At the southeastern corner of Běijīng Dōng Lù and the Bund, you'll find:

❹ Jardine Matheson Building (No. 27, now the Shànghǎi Foreign Trade Building)

Completed in 1922, this was one of the first and most powerful foreign trading companies to take root in Shànghǎi, their founders, Scotsmen William Jardine and James Matheson, having been some of the earliest profiteers from the opium trade. A sushi restaurant now occupies the ground floor. Next door is the former **Yangtze Insurance Building** (no. 26, now the Agricultural Bank of China), built in 1916 and possessed of a nicely restored lobby, worth a quick peek to whet your appetite for the splendors that lie ahead. The building at no. 25 Zhōngshān Dōng Yī Lù is now the **Industrial & Commercial Bank of China** (formerly the Yokohama Specie Bank). The last building on this block is the:

❺ Bank of China (No. 23) *pics*

Built in 1937 by the Chiang Kai-shek Nationalist government, this Art Deco building with a Chinese roof has always been and still is the **Bank of China.** During its construction, there was a competition between the bank director H. H. Kung (Chiang Kai-shek's brother-in-law) and Victor Sassoon, the owner of the Peace Hotel next door, for the claim to the tallest

building on the Bund. Sassoon won, barely, with the addition of a small tower on top of the Peace. Take a peek inside the bank for its grand interior.

Next door, on the corner of Nánjīng Lù, is a Bund landmark, the:

❻ Peace Hotel (No. 20) *closed!*

Built in 1929 as both the private residence of the Sassoon family and as a grand hotel, the **Cathay,** this is a living museum of Art Deco, capped by its famous pyramid roof. Walk through its romantic lobby and check out its rooftop views of the Bund (11th floor). The latter will now cost you ¥50 ($6) with a beverage. Noel Coward wrote his play *Private Lives* at the Peace in 1930, W. Somerset Maugham was a guest, and Steven Spielberg later filmed part of *Empire of the Sun* (based on J. G. Ballard's memoir of growing up as an expatriate during the Japanese occupation) here. Also take a look at the gorgeous gilded ballroom on the eighth floor (p. 166).

Immediately across Nánjīng Lù is the Peace's older sister, the:

❼ Palace Hotel (No. 19)

Built in 1906 by the Sassoons, this white and red brick hotel is now the South Building of the Peace Hotel. Its interiors are less extravagant than those of the Peace, but there is still plenty of grandeur in its marble lobby.

There are three more historic buildings in this first block south of Nánjīng Lù. The former **Chartered Bank of India, Australia, and China** (no. 18), with its two striking Ionic stone columns, built in 1923, is the latest building on the Bund slated for a complete renovation into a high-end commercial and restaurant complex. Next door, the former **North China Daily News Building** (no. 17, now the AIA Building), completed in 1921 in a late-Renaissance style, was originally home to the oldest English-language newspaper in China, the *North China Daily News,* where American writer Emily Hahn once worked. It now houses the American International Assurance Company. At the end of the block, the former **Bank of Taiwan Building** (no. 16, now the China Merchants Bank), with its simple classical lines, was built in 1924 and was actually a Japanese bank (Taiwan was occupied by Japan in 1895), despite its name.

In the next block of the Bund, across Jiŭjiāng Lù, is the:

⑧ Russo-Chinese Bank Building (No. 15, now the China Foreign Exchange Trade System Building)
Built in 1901, this was the first tile-faced construction in Shànghăi, a wide and squat edifice. Next door is the modernistic former **Bank of Communications Building** (no. 14, now the Bank of Shànghăi/Shànghăi Federation of Trade Unions), built in 1940, its large entrance framed in copper sheets.

Cross Hànkŏu Lù to a venerable landmark, the:

⑨ Shànghăi Customs House (No. 13)
Built in 1927, the classical-style Customs House is fronted by four massive granite Roman columns and topped by a rising bell tower (known as "Big Ching"). The low and dark lobby has beautiful mosaics of Chinese junks, but the rest of the building is run down and consists mostly of crowded offices and dank apartments in the back, where some family members of old Customs officials still live.

Next door is the even more spectacular:

⑩ Hong Kong and Shànghăi Bank (No. 12, now the Shànghăi Pŭdōng Development Bank)
This gorgeous classic European building with grand columns and archways, and capped by a huge dome, was built in 1923 (G. L. Wilson of Palmer and Turner was the chief architect). Inside the massive revolving doors, the restored dome and lobby are the most magnificent on the Bund. The foyer, supported by marble columns, is

decorated with eight gold-trimmed mosaic panels, each a salute to one of the world's financial capitals at that time (Bangkok, Hong Kong, Tokyo, New York, London, Paris, Calcutta, and of course Shànghăi). The bank's lobby is also stunning, restored in alabaster and polished wood. The English hailed it as the most spectacular building ever erected between the Suez Canal and the Bering Strait. Between 1955 and 1995, this building served as Shànghăi's city hall.

> **TAKE A BREAK**
> Stop for a coffee or a refresher at the **Bonomi Café** on the second floor of the Shànghăi Pŭdōng Development Bank (Room 226). This Italian-style cafe offers reasonably priced espressos, imported Italian juices, and light lunches, which you can linger over as you contemplate the splendid interior you've just seen.

When you are refreshed, head back out to the Bund and take a detour right (west) onto Fúzhōu Lù past a Tudor-style house (no. 44, Fúzhōu Lù), formerly the Calbeck, Macgregor and Company wine importers. Head to the:

⑪ Intersection of Fúzhōu Lù & Jiāngxī Lù
This intersection has four somewhat dilapidated but still grand colonial buildings. Notice the two identical Art Deco structures on the northeast (today's Metropole Hotel) and southeast (formerly the Hamilton House, an apartment complex) corners, both built by Palmer and Turner. In the building in the northwest corner lodged the Shànghăi Municipal Council—the governing body of the International Settlement. Just a bit further west at Fúzhōu Lù 209 is the former American Club, a classic red brick American Georgian-style building with marble columns. Today it's the Shànghăi's People Court. In the old days, Fúzhōu Lù was both the red light district and the location of Shànghăi's publishing

houses and bookstores, with many of the latter still located at the western end of the street.

Head back up (east) Fúzhōu Lù to the Bund and turn right. The building at no. 9 is currently the China Merchant Holdings Company; next to it stands the former:

⑫ Hospital of the Shànghǎi Navigation Company (No. 7, now the Bangkok Bank and the Thai Consulate) *cal design*

This handsome late French Renaissance building is one of the oldest buildings on the Bund, built in 1906. It was the site of China's first telephone switchboard. Next door, the English Gothic structure, the former **Commercial Bank of China** (no. 6, now empty) was built in 1906, but what you see today, though still intriguing, is a stripped-down version of the original, which had many more pillars, cornices, and chimneys. The narrower building next to it on the north corner of Guǎngdōng Lù is the former headquarters of the **Nishin Navigation Company** (no. 5, now the Huáxià Bank Building). Another modernistic, Western-style building, it was constructed in 1925 by its Japanese owners. Today, it's best known for its seventh-floor inhabitants, the restaurant and bar, M on the Bund.

On the south side of Guǎngdōng Lù is:

⑬ Three on the Bund (formerly the Union Insurance Company Building, No. 3)

Currently one of the toniest addresses in town, this newly restored Renaissance-style building from 1922 is the first of the traditional Bund buildings to be developed into a high-end retail and restaurant complex. Besides hosting world-renowned chefs like Jean Georges Vongerichten and David Laris, the building is home to the Evian Spa, luxury shops including Giorgio Armani's flagship store, and an art gallery showing the works of contemporary expatriate Chinese artists. Entrance is on Guǎngdōng Lù.

Next door to the south is one of the most famous buildings on the Bund, the former:

⑭ Shànghǎi Club (No. 2)

Built in 1910, this was the city's most extravagant private club, an English Renaissance structure with elaborate white columns and baroque attic windows. It housed the famous black-and-white granite **Long Bar,** at over 30m (100 ft.) reputedly the longest bar in the world; this was the watering hole for the "old boys' club" that ruled colonial Shànghǎi. For much of the late 20th century, this was the Dōng Fēng Hotel. Today, it is closed and gutted, awaiting yet another transformation. The last building on the block, at the corner of Yán'ān Dōng Lù, is the former **Asiatic Petroleum Building,** also known as the **McBain Building** (no. 1, now the China Pacific Insurance Company), built in 1916, a substantial structure employing the ubiquitous baroque pillars, Roman stone archway, and Greek columns.

You can conclude your walk at this point, or cross Zhōngshān Dōng Lù using the overpass just south of Jīnlíng Dōng Lù and head north on the Bund promenade for more views of the Bund skyline. You can also take a Huángpǔ River cruise (p. 147) from the docks along the promenade, or simply take a much-deserved break in one of the cafes or restaurants on the west side of the street.

WINDING DOWN
Head to the north side of Guǎngdōng Lù for the elevator to **M on the Bund** (seventh floor). M offers a splendid lounge, serves world-class Mediterranean cuisine, and offers a spacious balcony overlooking the Bund and the Huángpǔ River. Alternatively, **Three on the Bund** (south side of Guǎngdōng Lù opposite M) features top-notch French cuisine at **Jean Georges** (fourth floor), inventive Shanghainese dining at the **Whampoa Club** (fifth floor), creative "new world" cuisine at **Laris** (sixth floor), and inexpensive cafe food at **New Heights** (seventh-floor terrace). All are open for lunch and dinner.

Start:	Shànghǎi Centre (Metro: Jìng Ān).
Finish:	Peace Hotel, the Bund (Metro: Hénán Zhōng Lù).
Time:	2 to 3 hours (for the western half, from Shànghǎi Centre to People's Square/Xīzàng Lù); another 2 to 3 hours to tour the eastern half of Nánjīng Lù (from Xīzàng Zhōng Lù to the Bund). Those who want to see it all should allot a full day (7km/4½ miles).
Best Times:	Any weekday starting by 9:30am or 2:30pm (if you're only going to walk a portion), to avoid midday crowds.
Worst Times:	Weekends are impossibly crowded. Most stores aren't open before 9:30am, but they stay open late, often until 10pm.

Nánjīng Lù is the most famous shopping street in China, long celebrated for its large department stores, silk shops, and fashionable clothing stores. In colonial Shànghǎi, this was the main thoroughfare running through the International Settlement, built originally as a pathway to successive horse-race tracks, but which became dominated by silk shops, luxury hotels, and huge department stores. Today, this famous stretch is known as **Nánjīng Dōng Lù (Nánjīng Road East),** while the western portion, **Nánjīng Xī Lù,** is the current name for the former Bubbling Well Road, so named because of a now-displaced well located at the western end of the street (today's intersection with today's Huáshān Lù). **People's Park (Rénmín Gōngyuán)** is the halfway point, dividing the eastern and western sections. Today's Nánjīng Lù still has remnants of its past retail glories, but the department stores have been modernized and Western-style boutiques are rapidly cornering the fashion trade. There are still plenty of colonial period structures sandwiched in along the avenue (hotels, offices, department stores). If you're short on time or want to save your legs, begin your stroll at People's Park (at Xīzàng Zhōng Lù) and head east for the river along the **Nánjīng Lù Pedestrian Mall.** You can walk either the east or west half of Nánjīng Lù in a little more than an hour, if you don't stop—but you should.

To begin, take a taxi or walk straight east from the Jìng Ān Sì Metro station down Nánjīng Xī Lù to:

❶ Shànghǎi Centre (Shànghǎi Shāngchéng; No. 1376)

This premier all-in-one complex is home to the 42-floor Portman Ritz-Carlton Hotel, expensive residential apartments (mostly for foreign business families), the city's top business center, a medical clinic, a supermarket, ATMs, and a raft of upscale boutiques and restaurants. Starbucks is here, but if you need a more substantial breakfast, a light salad lunch, or a fresh fruit smoothie, pay a quick visit to the diner Element Fresh (Unit 112).

If you have plenty of time, cross the street south to the:

❷ Shànghǎi Exhibition Centre (Shànghǎi Zhánlǎn Zhōngxīn)

Built in 1955 with help from the Soviet Union (then a staunch communist ally), this somber, grandiose monument to socialist realism is yet another chapter in Shànghǎi's history of foreign architecture. Eye-catching on the outside, it's got a decaying air on the inside where there are regular uninteresting exhibits and a poorly displayed arts and crafts store. Before 1955, this was the site of the 10.5-hectare (26-acre) Hardoon Gardens, a colonial-era fantasy estate built by Jewish millionaire Silas Hardoon.

Continue east along the north side of Nánjīng Xī Lù across Xīkāng Lù and take a quick peek into:

Walking Tour 2: Nánjīng Lù

1 Shànghǎi Centre (Shànghǎi Shāngchéng)
上海商城

2 Shànghǎi Exhibition Centre
(Shànghǎi Zhǎnlǎn Zhōngxīn)
上海展览中心

3 Plaza 66 (Hénglóng Guǎngchǎng)
恒隆广场

4 Ohel Rachel Synagogue (Yóutài Jiàotáng)
犹太教堂

5 Shànghǎi Jǐngdé Zhèn Porcelain Artware
(Jǐngdé Zhèn Yìshù Cíqì)
景德镇艺术瓷器

6 Moller Villa (Mǎlè Biéshù)
马勒别墅

7 Westgate Mall (Méilóngzhèn Guǎngchǎng)
梅龙镇广场

8 Wújiāng Lù Měishí Jiē
吴江路美食街

9 Wángjiāshā Dumpling Restaurant
王家沙饺子馆

10 Léi Yǔn Shàng Pharmacy
雷允上药店

11 Tomorrow Square (Míngtiān Guǎngchǎng)
明天广场

12 Shànghǎi Art Museum
(Shànghǎi Měishù Guǎn)
上海美术馆

13 Grand Theatre
(Dàguāngmíng Yīngyuàn)
大光明影院

14 Park Hotel (Guójì Fàndiàn)
国际饭店

15 Pacific Hotel (Jīnmén Dàjiǔdiàn)
金门大酒店

16 People's Park (Rénmín Gōngyuán)
人民公园

17 Raffles City
(Láifúshì Guǎngchǎng)
莱佛士广场

18 Moore Church (Mù'ēn Táng)
沐恩堂

19 Nánjīng Lù Pedestrian Mall
(Nánjīng Lù Bùxíng Jiē)
南京路步行街

20 The No. 1 Department Store
(Shànghǎi Dìyī Bǎihuò Shāngdiàn)
上海第一百货商店

21 Shànghǎi No. 1 Provisions Store
(Shànghǎi Dìyī Shípǐn Shāngdiàn)
上海第一食品商店

22 Shànghǎi Fashion Company
(Shànghǎi Shízhuāng Gōngsī)
上海时装公司

23 Huálián Commercial Building
华联商厦

24 Century Square (Shìjì Guǎngchǎng)
世纪广场

25 Hénán Zhōng Lù Metro Station
河南中路站

26 Shàshì Lù Market (Shā Shì Lù Shìchǎng)
沙市路市场

❸ Plaza 66 (Hénglóng Guǎngchǎng, No. 1266)

This is as upscale and as Western a shopping mall as you'll find in Shànghǎi. A live pianist plays in the enormous glass atrium encircled by classy international shops on each floor (Hermes, Dior, Versace, Cartier). If no one actually seems to be shopping here, perhaps it's because of the high prices.

Head east 1 block and turn left (north) onto Shǎnxī Běi Lù for 1½ blocks, crossing Běijīng Xī Lù. Halfway up the block on the east side of the street is the former:

❹ Ohel Rachel Synagogue (Yóutài Jiàotáng, Shǎnxī Běi Lù, No. 1185)

Built in 1920 by Jacob Sassoon (uncle to Victor Sassoon who built the Peace Hotel) in memory of his wife Rachel, this vine-trellised synagogue served the wealthy Sephardic Jewish community until 1952. It was renovated and sanctified for the visit of Hillary Clinton in 1998, but otherwise belongs to the Shànghǎi Education Bureau and is not open to the public. It is also on the list of the hundred most endangered World Monuments.

Head back down (south) Shǎnxī Běi Lù and cross to the south side of Nánjīng Lù to:

❺ Shànghǎi Jǐngdé Zhèn Porcelain Artware (No. 1185)

This corner emporium carries a full array of classic Chinese pottery and porcelain, much of it from factories and artisans in Jǐngdé Zhèn, one of China's most celebrated pottery centers (located up the Yángzǐ River from Shànghǎi).

If you need a break from shopping, consider a detour 2 long blocks south along Shǎnxī Běi Lù to the intersection with Yán'ān Zhōng Lù. At the southwestern corner you'll find the:

❻ Moller Villa

garish but cool looking

This architectural fantasy of faux Gothic steeples and spires was once the residence of a Swedish shipping magnate but has recently been converted

into a hotel. Step inside for a look at the garish decor, a prime example of the excesses of colonial Shànghǎi (see "Museums & Mansions" in chapter 6 for more information).

Head back up Shǎnxī Běi and continue east on the north side of Nánjīng Xī Lù. The next block across Jiāngníng Lù is dominated on the north by:

❼ Westgate Mall (Méilóngzhèn Guǎngchǎng, No. 1038)

Yet another upscale shopping center, Westgate tenants include Burberry's, the Isetan Department Store, Zegna, and Givenchy; its atrium is frequently the site of retail exhibitions and sales. There's also a branch of the restaurant Méilóngzhèn in here; the original (p. 107) is across the street, as is a branch of **Kwun Kee** (no. 1079), a tailor shop that made its name in Hong Kong.

Continue east on the south side of the street past Màomíng Běi Lù. Running just south of and parallel to Nánjīng Xī Lù is:

❽ Wújiāng Lù Měishí Jiē

One of five food streets in Shànghǎi, this pedestrian lane is lined with restaurants, coffee shops, bars, and small retail stores.

You can walk all the way east on Wújiāng Lù until you end up back on Nánjīng Lù, or head north on Shímén Yī Lù past the entrance to the Metro (Line 2) which runs under Nánjīng Lù. At Nánjīng Lù, double back briefly on the south side of the street, if you're interested, to:

❾ Wáng Jiā Shā Dumpling Restaurant (No. 805)

One of Shànghǎi's oldest and most popular diners for cheap local eats. You can watch women wrapping *xiǎolóng bāo* dumplings through the glass windows. Just west of here is a **Silk Fabrics King** (no. 819; daily 10am–8:30pm), one of the many fabric stores that made Nánjīng Lù famous for fashions.

On the next block to the east, on the south side is:

⑩ Léi Yún Shàng Pharmacy (No. 719)

This Chinese apothecary claims to have been in business since 1662. All manner of exotic medicinal roots and herbs are dispensed on the second floor.

Continue east past the skyscraper complex (the Shànghǎi Broadcasting & Television International News Exchange Centre at no. 585) and cross the wide and very busy Chéngdū Běi Lù *very carefully.* **On the south side of the street is Gōngdélín (no. 445), Shànghǎi's most famous vegetarian restaurant (p. 96). In front of you is:**

⑪ Tomorrow Square (Míntiān Guǎngchǎng)

This architecturally intriguing rocket tower, which does a 90-degree horizontal shift at the 38th floor, is home to the new JW Marriott Hotel (the tallest hotel on the Bund side of the river) and the first Mandara Spa in China.

TAKE A BREAK
Stop for a cup of tea on the 38th floor **lobby lounge** of the **JW Marriott Hotel (Wànyí Jiǔdiàn)**, where you can choose from 40 different tea vintages while feasting on stunning panoramas of the city. There's no better place for a bird's-eye appreciation for how far you've come and how much further you have to go. Alternatively, you can jump straight to dessert and cappuccino at the **Kathleen's 5** (✆ 021/6327-0004) restaurant atop the upcoming Shànghǎi Art Museum.

Just east of Huángpí Běi Lù is:

⑫ Shànghǎi Art Museum (Shànghǎi Měishù Guǎn, No. 325)

This five-story landmark has been beautifully restored to its colonial splendor (p. 160). There's a lovely restaurant (Kathleen's 5) inside, too (and another Starbucks almost next door). At this point, you're at the northwestern edge of Rénmín Guǎngchǎng (People's Square; see p. 157).

Cross to the north side of Nánjīng Lù past the:

⑬ Grand Theatre (Dà Guǎngmíng Yǐngyuàn, No. 216)

This theatre built in 1933 used to show first-run Hollywood movies before 1949 and today still screens the occasional American blockbuster. The building was designed by prolific Hungarian architect Ladislaus Hudec (1893–1958), who also designed the building on the east side of **Huánghé Lù** (another restaurant street), the:

⑭ Park Hotel (Guójì Fàndiàn, No. 170)

This hotel, the tallest building outside North America when it was built in 1934, boasted the fastest elevators in Shànghǎi at the time. Young, fashionable Chinese came here in droves to party the night away. Don't miss its finely restored Art Deco interiors.

If colonial architecture excites you, take a look two doors down inside the:

⑮ Pacific Hotel (Jīnmén Dàjiǔdiàn, No. 108)

Built in 1926, serving first as the China United Assurance Company, then as the Overseas Chinese Hotel, this classic Italian-style hotel is a bit run down but still has a gorgeous Art Deco lobby of coffered ceilings and carved columns.

Legs need a break? Cross the street to the entrance of:

⑯ People's Park (Rénmín Gōngyuán, No. 231)

This is the city's biggest downtown green, which, together with People's Square, covers what was the Shànghǎi Race Track in colonial times. East of the park, one of Shànghǎi's main north-south thoroughfares Xīzàng Zhōng Lù marks the beginning of the eastern section of Nánjīng Lù.

Across the park on the east side of Xīzàng Zhōng Lù is:

⑰ Raffles City (Láifóshì Guǎngchǎng)

All gloss, this newest of Shànghǎi's megamalls has everything from a theatre multiplex to trendy shops (Guess, Swatch) and a diverse selection of restaurants.

Just to its north is:

⑱ Moore Church (Mù'ēn Táng)

This Protestant Church was established by American missionaries in 1887, and rebuilt in 1931 when it was designed by Czech architect Ladislaus Hudec. It was used as a middle school during the Cultural Revolution. In 1979, it was the first church to reopen in Shànghǎi (p. 153).

East of Xīzàng Zhōng Lù marks the beginning of Nánjīng Dōng Lù, and the wide, vehicle-free:

⑲ Nánjīng Lù Pedestrian Mall (Nánjīng Lù Bùxíng Jiē)

From here east to Hénán Zhōng Lù (which is 2 blocks from the Bund and the river), strollers can enjoy a pedestrian-only mall, paved in red brick and marble, designed by Arle Jean Marie Carpentier and Associates (France), and opened September 20, 1999. Here, new buildings dwarf the colonial-period landmarks of Nánjīng Lù, but there's still plenty of history along the way. *Caution: Although this is a pedestrian mall, the cross streets (north-south) still permit vehicular traffic, so look both ways at controlled intersections.* Alas, the circular overpass that used to stand at this intersection (affording some of the best photo ops of the chaotic shopping street) has been removed for good. The overpass once connected the modern **New World City** Shopping Center (Nánjīng Dōng Lù 830) on the northwest corner to:

⑳ The No. 1 Department Store (No. 800)

In the old days this emporium (now on the northeast corner of the pedestrian mall) was known as **The Sun,** one of Nánjīng Lù's "Big Four" department stores. The Sun's building was designed by Chinese architects, opened its doors in 1934, and was the first store in China to use an escalator. Later, renamed the No. 1 Department Store complex, it attracted over 150,000 shoppers daily; and it may be doing more business than ever these days with the addition of the 22-story tower on its East Building, its first 11 floors devoted to retailing.

Those too tired to walk the rest of the street can take a **sightseeing trolley,** a three-car electric train that weaves its way up and down the length of the pedestrian mall; tickets, purchased on board, cost ¥2 (25¢).

In the next block (across Guìzhōu Lù) on the north side is the:

㉑ Shànghǎi No. 1 Provisions Store (No. 700)

Formerly known as Sun Sun, another of Shànghǎi's "Big Four" department stores, this shop is still in its old building, where it opened in 1926. A Pizza Hut has attached itself to the old store. Just to the east is a stunning block-long gray Art Deco building, the:

㉒ Shànghǎi Fashion Company (No. 650)

The third of the "Big Four," this was the former Sincere Department Store. A hotel now occupies part of the premises. Across the street on the south side is the:

㉓ Huálián Commercial Building (No. 635)

The last of the "Big Four," this was the former **Wing On,** opened in 1918, a famous department store chain transplanted to Hong Kong after 1949.

At this point, the mall crosses a vast square at the busy intersection with Zhèjiāng Zhōng Lù and Húběi Lù. In the early colonial days, this intersection was the spot where electric trams heading west on Nánjīng Lù were rotated on a wooden plate so they could make the return journey eastward. Continuing east on the south side is:

Impressions

The Shànghǎinese were inordinately proud of Nanking Road, not only because of its shops overflowing with goods, but because there was truly nothing like it in the rest of China. It was so modern, and nothing enthralled the Shànghǎinese more than modernity. While the rest of the nation was still sunk in rusticity, here were young girls clacking about on Italian heels, photographic studios, department stores, special offers and seasonal sales, and publicity gimmicks which called for bands to play and even a dwarf got up in a top-hat to cry "Fantastic value! Fantastic value!" outside the shop.

—Pan Ling, *In Search of Old Shànghǎi*, 1982

㉔ Century Square (Shìjì Guǎngchǎng)

Still under construction at press time, this block-long square will eventually host open-air performances and exhibits.

To the north amidst all the shops are the usual suspects, **McDonald's** and an underground **KFC**, but a nicer option for a break or lunch is farther east, across Fújiàn Zhōng Lù, in the 30-story **Hotel Sofitel Hyland** (no. 505) or in the **Howard Johnson Hotel** just southwest of Century Square at Jiǔjiāng Lù 595.

TAKE A BREAK
Enjoy a coffee, tea, or ice cream in **Milano's Ice Cream**, located on the ground floor of the Sofitel. For a more substantial meal and beer brewed on the premises, try the **Brauhaus** upstairs (Hotel Sofitel Hyland, second floor), a Bavarian-style pub and eating hall with a fine view through a wall of windows on the Nánjīng Lù Pedestrian Mall. Alternatively, **San Rafael** in the Howard Johnson Plaza, just to the south at Jiǔjiāng Lù 595, offers light California fusion cuisine with Californian wine.

3 blocks east of Fújiàn Zhōng Lù lies the:

㉕ Hénán Zhōng Lù Metro Station

This subway station marks the end of the pedestrian mall, which is also the terminus for the sightseeing trolley. A plaque commemorates the building of the mall. This Metro station, equipped with restrooms and an elevator, is the last stop in Pǔxī for eastbound subways heading to Pǔdōng.

From Hénán Zhōng Lù, the eastern terminus of the pedestrian mall, you can continue 3 more blocks along Nánjīng Dōng Lù to the Bund. This pinched strip gives you an idea of what Nánjīng Lù was like before the mall was in place. The sidewalks are considerably narrower here, so watch out for vehicles. For those who haven't had enough shopping, walk 1 block east of Hénán Zhōng Lù to Jiāngxī Zhōng Lù, take a right (south), then a quick left (east) onto the small side street of Shāshì Èr Lù, where you'll find the cramped:

㉖ Shāshì Lù Market

Two small streets (including the Shāshì Yī Lù) of cramped makeshift stalls sell everything from fruits and vegetables to cheap clothing, knickknacks, and Buddhist statues. Items cheaper here than the glitzy stores on Nánjīng Lù. (Open daily from 8am to 6pm.)

WINDING DOWN
The nicest place to end this stroll is the landmark **Peace Hotel (Hépíng Fàndiàn, no. 20)**, at the intersection of Nánjīng Dōng Lù and the Bund, (described in detail on p.72). Take your pick of the gorgeous Art Deco lobby bar or the rooftop bar, where a cover charge of ¥50 ($6.25) buys you a soft drink and some unparalleled views of the Bund and Pǔdōng.

Start:	Shànghăi Lăo Jiē (Shànghăi Old Street), Nánshì District.
Finish:	Dàjìng Lù, Nánshì District.
Time:	2 to 4 hours.
Best Times:	Weekday mornings or early Sunday morning (for the Fúyòu antiques market).
Worst Times:	Weekends are packed with tourists and shoppers. If you must tour on the weekend, go early.

The Old Chinese City (Nánshì), located just southwest of the Bund, was the first part of Shànghăi to be settled. In the early days, Shànghăi had a city wall (which followed the course of today's Rénmín Lù and Zhōnghuá Lù) that came down when the last dynasty fell, in 1911. During the colonial era (1842–1949) when Westerners had their own enclaves (concessions), this was the main Chinese district, where foreigners almost never ventured. Considerably more frequented by foreigners these days (though mostly around the Yù Yuán Old Town Bazaar area), Nánshì, with its narrow winding streets and old houses, is still one of the least explored areas in town. Although this walk focuses mainly on the Old Town Bazaar (bounded by Rénmín Lù, Hénán Nán Lù, Fāngbāng Zhōng Lù, and Zhōnghuá Lù) with all its tourist attractions, hopefully you'll get from it as well a sense of traditional life around the old Chinese streets. Entire sections of the district are being torn down and replaced with new developments as quickly as this is being written, so hurry and get your walking shoes on.

There are many entry points into the maze of the Old Town Bazaar. Most tour buses enter from the north off Rénmín Lù, but to avoid congestion, begin your stroll at the intersection of Hénán Nán Lù and Fāngbāng Zhōng Lù on the southwest side of the Old Town Bazaar, where you'll pass through a traditional-style Chinese gate and enter:

❶ Shànghăi Lăo Jiē (Shànghăi Old Street)

This 825m (½-mile) stretch of Fāngbāng Zhōng Lù was renovated in 1999 as an Old Town theme street. The traditional shophouses, selling antiques, collectibles, ethnic crafts, and tea, reflect the architectural and cultural evolution of Shànghăi as you walk east, from the Míng Dynasty through the Qīng Dynasty into the Chinese Republican era. Just inside the entrance and immediately to your left is the irresistible:

❷ Fúyòu Antiques Market/ Cáng Băo Lóu

This is still the best and liveliest antiques market for browsing in

Shànghăi (especially early Sun morning), where four floors of vendors offer everything from coins and ceramics to jewelry and Russian cameras. Be prepared to stay a while; there's a lot of junk to sift through, but also the occasional real find.

Continuing east, in the second block after the Hòujiā Lù intersection, the two-story Old Shànghăi Teahouse (Fāngbāng Zhōng Lù 385) can provide a refreshing cup of tea or juice if you're already fatigued from shopping. Otherwise, continue your way east past the large Huábăo Building (Huábăo Lóu, Fāngbāng Zhōng Lù 265), with antiques on sale in the basement, to the stone arch entrance of:

❸ Chénghuáng Miào (Temple of the Town God)

This is also the southern entrance to the Old Town Bazaar. This Daoist temple, rebuilt many times since the early 15th century and most recently in the 1990s, can be quickly toured from 8:30am to 4pm daily (¥5/60¢ admission; see p. 150).

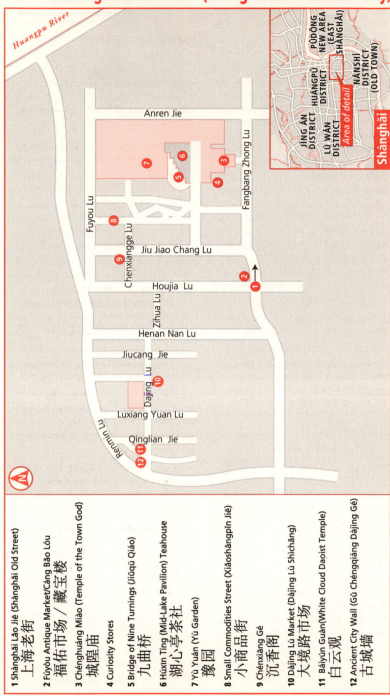

1 Shànghǎi Lǎo Jiē (Shànghǎi Old Street)
上海老街

2 Fúyòu Antique Market/Cáng Bǎo Lóu
福佑市场 / 藏宝楼

3 Chénghuáng Miào (Temple of the Town God)
城隍庙

4 Curiosity Stores

5 Bridge of Nine Turnings (Jiǔqū Qiáo)
九曲桥

6 Húxīn Tíng (Mid-Lake Pavilion) Teahouse
湖心亭茶社

7 Yù Yuán (Yù Garden)
豫园

8 Small Commodities Street (Xiǎoshāngpǐn Jiē)
小商品街

9 Chénxiāng Gé
沉香阁

10 Dàjìng Lù Market (Dàjìng Lù Shìchǎng)
大境路市场

11 Báiyún Guàn(White Cloud Daoist Temple)
白云观

12 Ancient City Wall (Gǔ Chéngqiáng Dàjìng Gé)
古城墙

Zigzag your way north by following the lane along the west side of the temple. Along the way you'll find a series of:

❹ Curiosity Stores

Here you'll find novelty stores such as the Pear Syrup Shop (selling old China's answer to cough drops), and the Five Flavor Bean Shop (selling a famous Shànghǎi snack, *wǔxiāng dòu* [five-flavor lima beans]) right next to a not-so-novel Starbucks. By now you should be in the main square with the teahouse floating on the artificial lake to your north. To get there, follow the:

❺ Bridge of Nine Turnings (Jiǔ Qū Qiáo)

This zigzag bridge is supposed to be propitious, as demons were believed to be afraid of corners. By contrast, camera-wielding tourists appear addicted to them. The bridge leads to the fine:

❻ Húxīn Tíng (Mid-Lake Pavilion) Teahouse

This is Shànghǎi's most famous place to drink tea (Yùyuán Lù 257). Step inside, take a look at the teas for sale on the first floor, and head upstairs for a cup and a Shànghǎi snack.

TAKE A BREAK
Pause for tea and snacks by an open window in the 200-year-old **Húxīngtíng Teahouse** (daily 8:30am–10pm). For a more substantial repast, lunch on a variety of Shànghǎi dumplings and noodle dishes at the **Nánxiáng Mántou Diàn** that lines the west shore of the lake.

The north side of the lake is the location of the main entrance to Shànghǎi's most complete classical garden:

❼ Yù Yuán (Yù Garden)

Completed in 1577, this pleasant private garden (Ānrén Lù 218) is a maze of ponds, bridges, pavilions, and small gardens, but it's impossible to get lost for long (p. 142). The garden is open daily from 8:30am to 5pm and usually quite crowded (admission ¥30/$3.75).

Exit at the southern Inner Garden (Nèi Yuán) and find your way back to the Húxīn Tíng Teahouse by walking west a block on Yùyuán Lù. If you haven't had your fill of shopping, the whole northwest part of the bazaar complex is chock-full of large and small stores offering everything from glittering gems to Chinese medicinal herbs.

Those seeking more curios can follow the lane outside the Nánxiáng Mántou Diàn as it winds north. Take a left onto:

❽ Small Commodities Street (Xiǎoshāngpǐn Jiē)

Along this street (Yùyuán Lǎo Lù) you'll find shops specializing in everything from musical instruments and chopsticks to scissors and bamboo crafts.

At the northern end of the street, if you haven't had enough shopping, take a peek inside the gargantuan Fúmín Commercial Building (Fúmín Shāngshà) to the right (east) on Fúyòu Lù, which seems to sell everything that's made in China. Otherwise, take a left onto Fúyòu Lù (west), passing the Shànghǎi Old Restaurant, then take another left (south) down Jiǔjiàochǎng Lù. West of the Tóng Hán Chuān Táng Chinese Medicine Store, take a right (west) onto Chénxiānggé Lù, where you'll find the temple:

❾ Chénxiāng Gé (Chénxiānggé Lù 29)

While Yù Yuán was built to honor Pān Yǔnduān's father, this small Buddhist temple was built for his mother (p. 151).

Continue west along Chénxiānggé Lù, take a left (south) onto Hòujiā Lù, then a right (west) onto Zǐhuá Lù, at the end of which is Hénán Nán Lù, marking the western boundary of the Old Town Bazaar. Cross Hénán Nán Lù, then jog slightly north and turn left (west) onto Dàjìng Lù. This area used to be full of old houses, many of which have been bulldozed to make way for the brand-new apartment complexes you see around you. About halfway down the street you'll find the:

❿ Dàjìng Lù Market (Dàjìng Lù Shìchǎng, Dàjìng Lù 150–160)

This delightful wet market is one of the city's largest, and a perfect place to catch a glimpse of daily life in the old

Chinese city as housewives and grand-mothers shop for everything from fresh fish and sea cucumbers to spices, tea, and tofu.

Further west on the north side of the street is:

⓫ Báiyún Guàn (White Cloud Daoist Temple)

At press time, the buildings that are to be the new home of this Daoist temple (p. 150) were still being constructed, but should be open and operational by the time you read this. Peek inside for a look at the hundreds of statues of Daoist deities and possibly even a Daoist service.

West of this temple on the same side of the street is the:

⓬ Ancient City Wall (Gǔchéngqiáng Dàjìng Gé, Dàjìnggé Lù 269)

Here is preserved the only remaining 50m (160 ft.) of Shànghǎi's old city wall, originally built in 1553 when it measured 8.1m (27 ft.) high and 4.8km (3 miles) around. There's a small exhibit on life in the old Chinese

city for those who can't find enough signs of it in today's streets.

Although this is the end of the walk, options abound for those who have energy to spare. About 20 minutes by foot to the south is the newly refurbished Wén Miào (Temple of Confucius), the Xiǎotáoyuán Qīngzhēn Sì (Peach Orchard Mosque), and more back streets and alleys for exploring. If more shopping is in order, Huáihǎi Zhōng Lù, the favorite modern shopping street of today's Shànghǎinese, is about a 30-minute stroll to the west, while the Dōngtái Lù Antique Market is an even closer 10-minute walk to the southwest. If vittles are all you can think about at this point, cross Rénmín Lù, then head north on Yúnnán Nán Lù.

WINDING DOWN

Yúnnán Lù Měishí Jiē (Yúnnán Lù Food St.), only a quick 2 blocks north of the old city wall, is packed with a host of bright and lively Chinese restaurants, though most places don't carry English menus. For Western fare, a 10-minute taxi ride west will land you at the super modern and chic Xīn Tiāndì, a contrasting bookend to a day begun in the old Chinese city.

WALKING TOUR 4   FRENCH CONCESSION

Start:	Huáihǎi Lù, Lúwān District (Metro: Huángpí Nán Lù).
Finish:	Héngshān Lù, Xúhuì District (Metro: Héngshān Lù).
Time:	4 to 6 hours.
Best Times:	Weekday mornings and mid-afternoons.
Worst Times:	On weekends (especially Sun) and evenings many of these streets are quite crowded with local shoppers and visitors. Lunchtime (11:30am–2pm) also brings out big crowds.

Shànghǎi's French Concession, consisting of a corridor running from the lower Bund between today's Yán'ān Lù and the Chinese Old Town west along Huáihǎi Lù, contains many of the city's most picturesque colonial mansions, parks, hotels, and town houses. The French arrived in 1846 and leased land just south of the British Concession's holdings. They established a series of fine residential neighborhoods west across today's Lúwān District, branching off Huáihǎi Lù, the main avenue known in colonial times as Avenue Joffre. The concession's northern border, today's Yán'ān Lù, was originally a creek named Yángjìngbāng, which was filled to become the street then known as Avenue Edouard VII. The streets in the long, sprawling settlement were lined with plane trees; the buildings, with their mansard roofs and shutters, resembled those of French towns of the time; and these neighborhoods, most now dating from the first 3 decades of the 1900s, remain much intact, although the modern construction boom has laid waste to considerable clusters of the French legacy. Still, especially in recent years, a concerted effort has been made to preserve and spruce up many charming blocks of the original French residences, open historic houses, and convert some of the surviving mansions and estates to fine restaurants and retail shops—all making for a delightful, if spread out, stroll through colonial Shànghăi. Refusing to join the International Concession formed in 1863 by the British and Americans, the French had their own electric power, bus system, and legal system within their 10-sq.-km (4-sq.-mile) quarter. It was a neighborhood that attracted not only the French, but international adventurers, Chinese gangsters, White Russian refugees, communist revolutionaries, and pimps and prostitutes as well. By the 1930s, the French were vastly outnumbered here, but their sense of style has endured.

Our walking tour of the old French Concession starts firmly in the 21st century, on one of Shànghăi's most modern shopping avenues, at Huáipí Nán Lù Station (Metro Line 1), on:

❶ Huáihăi Zhōng Lù

The former Avenue Joffre, this was the main street of the old French Concession, stocked with the latest fashions from Paris. Today, locals prefer this street to Nánjīng Lù for shopping, lined as it is with fashionable boutiques, modern shopping malls, and glittering department stores. Unlike Nánjīng Lù, this is no pedestrian mall. You may have to shoulder your way along the crowded sidewalk. If you take Exit no. 1 from the Huáipí Nán Lù Metro, it puts you on the south side of the street; head a short ways west, past the Shui On Center (no. 333), and at Mădāng Lù, go left (south) for a little over a block to:

❷ Xīn Tiāndì (New Heaven and Earth)

Beginning at Tàicàng Lù, this 2-square-block pedestrian mall of cafes and boutiques is the hottest venue in Shànghăi with its restored late colonial architecture known as *shíkù mén* (row houses with courtyards and stone frame gates). It's all very upscale and worth a stroll. In the evenings, you'll often see Chinese tour groups traipsing through. The **Site of the First National Congress of the**

Communist Party (Huángpí Nán Lù 374) anchors its southeast corner (p. 163).

Retrace your steps north to Huáihăi Zhōng Lù and head west, crossing the massive Chéngdū Běi Lù/Chóngqìng Nán Lù elevated overpass. Descend, and take the first major left, south on:

❸ Yándāng Lù

This is yet another cobblestone pedestrian food street lined with small cafes, bars, and shops in colonial-style buildings. If you need a pick-me-up, Da Marco Restaurant halfway down serves a bracing cup of cappuccino. Continue down Yándāng Lù 2 blocks to the entrance to:

❹ Fùxīng Park (on Nánchāng Lù)

Since the French established it as their park in 1909, it has been known locally as **French Park,** and it is still one of Shànghăi's loveliest urban green spots, famous for its rose gardens. Looking diagonally southeast from the southeastern entrance to the park, you can spy the former residence (southeastern corner of Fùxīng Zhōng Lù and Chóngqìng Nán Lù) of American journalist **Agnes Smedley.** At the statues of Karl Marx and Friedrich Engel (a favorite point for Shànghăi's ballroom dancers to practice), bear west for the upscale **Park 97** restaurant complex, and exit there on Gāolán Lù

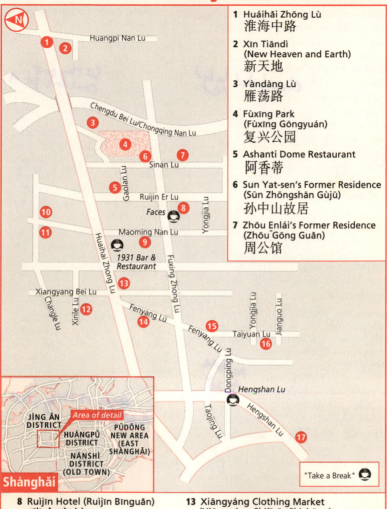

1 Huáihǎi Zhōng Lù
淮海中路

2 Xīn Tiāndì
(New Heaven and Earth)
新天地

3 Yàndàng Lù
雁荡路

4 Fùxīng Park
(Fùxīng Gōngyuán)
复兴公园

5 Ashanti Dome Restaurant
阿香蒂

6 Sun Yat-sen's Former Residence
(Sūn Zhōngshān Gùjū)
孙中山故居

7 Zhōu Enlái's Former Residence
(Zhōu Gōng Guǎn)
周公馆

8 Ruìjīn Hotel (Ruìjīn Bīnguǎn)
瑞金宾馆

9 Màomíng Nán Lù
茂名南路

10 Jǐnjiāng Hotel
(Jǐnjiāng Fàndiàn)
锦江饭店

11 Okura Garden Hotel
(Huāyuán Fàndiàn)
花园饭店

12 The Grape Restaurant
(Pútáo Yuán)
葡萄园

13 Xiāngyáng Clothing Market
(Xiāngyáng Shìlǐpǐn Shìchǎng)
襄阳饰礼品市场

14 Shànghǎi Conservatory of Music
(Shànghǎi Yīnyuè Xuéyuàn)
上海音乐学院

15 Shànghǎi Museum of Arts and Crafts
(Shànghǎi Gōngyì Měishù Bówùguǎn)
上海工艺美术博物馆

16 Tàiyuán Guesthouse (Tàiyuán Biéshù)
太原别墅

17 Héngshān Lù
衡山路

(the former Rue Corneille). Cross Sīnán Lù and continue 1 more block on Gāolán Lù to a decidedly strange sight at the:

❺ Ashanti Dome Restaurant (Gāolán Lù 16)

[handwritten: Closed but locked Next]

At press time, this former St. Nicholas Russian Orthodox Church was being renovated from its most recent incarnation as the Ashanti Dome French restaurant into a Spanish tapas bar (Boca) cum French restaurant. Built in 1933, the high-domed church is testimony to the bygone presence of White Russians in the French quarter. After 1949, it served for a time as a warehouse for washing machines. The church's icons, stained glass, and religious murals inside are lovely, the picture of Chairman Máo on the exterior façade less so.

After a gawk, retrace your steps east along this pretty lane, back to Sīnán Lù (the old Rue Masenet), and take it 1 block south to Xiāngshān Lù (Rue de Moliere), where you can enter:

❻ Sun Yat-sen's Former Residence (Sūn Zhōngshān Gùjū, Xiāngshān Lù 7)

[handwritten: no time to visit]

The founder of the Chinese Republic, Sun lived here with his famous wife, Soong Ching-ling, from 1918 to 1924, the year before his death. You can tour the house from 9am to 4:30pm. This is a typical small mansion of the French era (p. 164).

Continue south down Sīnán Lù past the busy Fùxīng Lù to: *[handwritten: Ny-carre]*

❼ Zhōu Ēnlái's Former Residence (Zhōu Gōng Guăn, Sīnán Lù 73)

Zhōu eventually became second in power to Chairman Máo, but as head of the Shànghăi branch of the Communist Party in the 1940s, he lived modestly in this French Concession house in 1946, whenever he was in town on party business (p. 165).

Return to Fùxīng Zhōng Lù (1 block north) and take it west to Ruìjīn Èr Lù (the former Rte. Pere Robert), the next major street. Turn left (south) for a block or so to the:

❽ Ruìjīn Hotel (Ruìjīn Bīnguăn, Ruìjīn Èr Lù 118)

[handwritten: Pretty but don't get in]

This beautiful estate on the west side of the street, now the grounds for a hotel and restaurant complex, was the **Morriss Estate** in colonial times. The owner of the villas that still stand in these spacious gardens built his fortune by running the *North China Daily News,* then the main English-language newspaper in Shànghăi; he also bred greyhounds which he would race at the 50,000-seat Canidrome just to the west (today's Cultural Square); the last Morriss descendent to live here died in the gatekeeper's house a few years after the communists took over in 1949. The wide green lawns and ornate villas with stained glass windows are exquisite relics of the privileged life wealthy foreigners led in old Shànghăi. The grand villa on the northwest edge of the property now houses a bar (Face) and two superb restaurants (one Thai, one Indian). *[handwritten: any nothing store Not here]*

☕ **TAKE A BREAK**
No place better to relax, have a drink, or eat a fine Asian meal than at **Face** on the Ruìjīn Hotel estate (Ruìjīn Èr Lù 118, Building 4). In the back is an Indian restaurant, **Hazara**; and upstairs, a superb Thai restaurant, **Lan Na Thai.** The setting is a 1930s colonial mansion with a large manicured lawn fit for a croquet match. If you prefer an old Chinese-Shànghăi setting, wait until you get to Màomíng Nán Lù (see below) for **1931 Bar and Restaurant** (Màomíng Nán Lù 112). *Qípáo*-clad waitresses will serve you teas, coffees, juices, wines, and classic Shànghăi dishes and snacks while Nat King Cole croons in Portuguese in the background. It's all very dreamy and nostalgic.

Retrace your steps through the Ruìjīn/Morriss estate to the entrance on Ruìjīn Èr Lù, turn right (south) 1 block to Yǒngjiā Lù (formerly Rte. Herve de Sieyes), and proceed to the corner, where you can cut through what's left of the Yǒngjiā Flower Market (it is being demolished) as you turn north on:

9 Màomíng Nán Lù

The most famous side street in the French Concession these days, Màomíng Lù was known in colonial days as Route Cardinal Mercier. Take it north, viewing the cafés, bars, and tiny shops on either side of this pinched but pretty and quaint tree-lined lane. (At night, the southern part of the street, flanked by some of Shànghǎi's hottest and loudest bars and clubs, becomes impossibly rowdy and not a little seedy.)

North up Màomíng you'll cross Fùxīng Zhōng Lù, Nánchāng Lù, passing the 1931 Bar and Restaurant along the way (see "Take a Break," above), and finally Huáihǎi Zhōng Lù, ultimately coming to another landmark, the:

10 Jǐn Jiāng Hotel (Jǐn Jiāng Fàndiàn, Màomíng Nán Lù 59)

The massive old hotel complex with its Art Deco buildings on the right (east) side of the street is most famous for being the site where Richard Nixon and Zhōu Ēnlái signed the Shànghǎi Communiqué in 1972, which opened China to the West for the first time since World War II. Originally built as exclusive apartments, the buildings became part of the Jǐn Jiāng Hotel in 1951. Since then, the various structures have been modernized, gaining in luxury but losing in character. No longer as lively as it was several years ago, the Jǐn Jiāng Shopping Lane (just inside the gate, parallel to Màomíng Lù) still has several restaurants and shops worth a browse, including the fine **Shànghǎi Tang** clothing and crafts store from Hong Kong. There is also a **bookstore** with a decent

collection geared to foreigners in the north building (Běi Lóu).

Re-emerging on Màomíng Lù and walking north to the corner, you can see the old Lyceum Theatre, built in 1931 by the British Consul for the Amateur Dramatic Society, across Chánglè Lù (formerly Rue Bourgeat). Margot Fonteyn danced here as a girl. Today, it serves as a theater primarily for large pop concerts. You can take a peek inside its restored lobby. Cross back to the west side of Màomíng Lù to the:

11 Okura Garden Hotel (Huāyuán Fàndiàn, Màomíng Nán Lù 58)

The towering Okura Garden Hotel, a Japanese-managed five-star property, opened in 1989 on the site of the 1926 **Cercle Sportif Française,** once the most luxurious private club in the French quarter, with its grand ballroom, swimming pool, lounges, and wicker sofas. For a look at its original Art Deco interiors now brilliantly restored, take a right inside the hotel lobby past the business center to the east wing. This was the original entrance to the Cercle Sportif's ballroom, complete with marble stairways and colonnades topped by nude female figures. The Grand Ballroom still bears its beautiful stained glass ceiling lights. This club served as Máo Zédōng's private quarters whenever he visited Shànghǎi, which perhaps explains the eight-room underground concrete bunker that connects to the Jǐn Jiāng Hotel across the street (the entrance near the fountain is usually locked, though).

Outside, head back north up Màomíng Nán Lù, turn left (west) on Chánglè Lù for 2 blocks (passing a row of shops that sell and tailor traditional *qípáo* dresses), then turn left (south) on Xiāngyáng Běi Lù (the former Rue L. Lorton). At the next intersection with Xīnlè Lù, you'll find in the southwest corner:

12 The Grape Restaurant (Xīnlè Lù 55)

This building with the gorgeous peacock-blue domes was the former

Russian Orthodox Cathedral of the Holy Mother of God, built in 1931, and then the most active church among Russians. The church recently housed a stock exchange with an electronic trading board, but is currently occupied by a restaurant, The Grape, popular with expatriates for its inexpensive and tasty Shànghǎi fare; and a bar, The Dome, which is still awaiting the crowds.

Continue south on Xiāngyáng Lù, passing on the east side of the street Xiāngyáng Gōngyuán, formerly a private garden in French Concession days famous for its cherry trees. Cross Huáihǎi Zhōng Lù to the south. To your immediate left (east) is the:

⑬ Xiāngyáng Clothing Market (Xiāngyáng Shì Lǐpǐng Shìchǎng, Huáihǎi Zhōng Lù 999)

This open-air market is the best place to pick up brand-name remainders and knock-offs, from North Face jackets to Prada bags. Bargain well. Shopaholics may never be heard from again if they disappear into this maze.

If you do emerge none the worse for wear, head west on Huáihǎi Lù, then left (southwest) down the slanting street of Fēnyáng Lù (the old Rte. Pichon). About halfway down the block on the right (west) you'll find the:

⑭ Shànghǎi Conservatory of Music (Shànghǎi Yīnyuè Xuéyuàn, Fēnyáng Lù 20)

The Oriental Music Instruments Museum (p. 161) located here is worth visiting for its collection of rare traditional and ethnic Chinese musical instruments. The lovely grounds also boast an old colonial mansion (the former Brazilian consulate).

Continue south on Fēnyáng Lù past Fùxīng Lù (or Rte. Lafayette, as it was once known) until you come to the intersection with

Tàiyuán Lù, where you'll find (on the eastern side of Fēnyáng Lù) hidden behind a tall wall the:

⑮ Shànghǎi Museum of Arts and Crafts (Shànghǎi Gōngyì Měishù Bówùguǎn, Fēnyáng Lù 79)

This marvelous 1905 French Renaissance–style marble and stone mansion (daily 8:30am–4:30pm) served as the private estate of the director of the French Municipal Council, a French general, and finally the first mayor of communist Shànghǎi, Chén Yì, before becoming the open workshops of some of China's most skilled artisans. This survivor of colonial Shànghǎi packs a triple punch: as a place to watch traditional arts and crafts being fashioned, as a museum of those works, and as an architectural masterpiece, resplendent with its unaltered interiors, sculptures, and marble fountains in its garden (p. 161).

At this point, you can take a quick detour south on Tàiyuán Lù past Yǒngjiā Lù to the:

⑯ Tàiyuán Guesthouse (Tàiyuán Biéshù, Tàiyuán Lù 160)

This lovely 1920s colonial mansion hosted American Gen. George Marshall in 1946 when he was attempting to mediate a truce between Chiang Kai-shek and Máo Zédōng (p. 79).

Head back up (north) Tàiyuán Lù, take a left (southwest) on Fēnyáng Lù until it ends at a four-way intersection of Fēnyáng Lù, Táojiāng Lù, Dōngpíng Lù, and south-running Yuèyáng Lù. The Pǔxījīn Monument located on the tiny island in the middle is dedicated to Russian poet Alexander Pushkin on his 200th birthday. From here, you can head west for your ultimate destination:

⑰ Héngshān Lù

Formerly Avenue Petain, a big tree-lined avenue with orange-tile sidewalks, wrought iron railings, and ivy-covered mansions, this is one of Shànghǎi's trendiest streets. End your walk here with a bit of shopping; or a look at the ivy-covered **International Community Church** (**Guójì Lǐbài Táng;** Héngshān Lù 53) established in 1925 and the former **Shànghǎi American School** (built 1923) across the street; or with a spot of people-watching at any of the cafes dotting the side streets. To get to Héngshān Lù, head west on Dōngpíng Lù with its row of quaint restaurants and shops. Don't miss the English-style villa with yellow walls at Dōngpíng Lù 9 where Chiang Kai-shek stayed with his wife Soong Mei-ling. Next door (west) at House no. 11 is another 1920s Soong family mansion (currently occupied by Sasha's).

WINDING DOWN
After this long jaunt through the old French quarters, there's no better reward than to enjoy some fine vittles in one of the many splendid colonial mansions around Héngshān Lù. If you fancy Continental dishes presented in a 1920s Soong family mansion, try **Sasha's** (Dōngpíng Lù 9, House no. 11 at Héngshān Lù). More Continental and Asian fare is served next door in the serene **Lapis Lazuli** (which also has lunch specials). For Irish ale, live Irish music, and Irish stew, served in an old courtyard house, try **O'Malley's** (Táojiāng Lù 42, west 1 block off Héngshān Lù). If just a leisurely cup of latte or tea will do, the "fragrant camphor" teahouse of **Harn Sheh** (Héngshān Lù 10 at Táojiāng Lù) is as undemanding a spot as any to wind down.

8

Shopping

Even before economic reforms in China kicked into high gear in the 1990s, Shànghǎi was a shopper's city. All across the country the Chinese dreamed of making one visit to the great port, not to sightsee, but to shop. Anything made and sold in Shànghǎi, it seems, had to be the best; non-Shànghǎi goods were by definition inferior—and this reputation for the best goods and great shopping persists today, with shoppers now able and willing to indulge in everything from uniquely Chinese products to international brand-name items, at venues ranging from modern department stores to open-air markets and sidewalk stalls. Even if you have no interest in doing your part for the Chinese economic miracle, it's still worth entering the fray (preferably with all your wits, commercial and otherwise, sharpened) to witness, if not join in, Shànghǎi's favorite pastime.

1 The Shopping Scene

Shànghǎi has long been an oasis of international shopping, so it is no surprise that Western-style malls are replacing traditional shop fronts, Chinese department stores, and alley markets across Shànghǎi. Some of the best buys, however, can be found in the tens of thousands of privately run shops that dot the city, from the unique one-offs to the fly-by-night outfits. Colorful open-air markets and street-side vendors also offer more traditional arts and crafts, collectibles, and clothing at low prices. If you're looking for souvenirs or Chinese treasures, check out the cost and selection at hotel shops, the Friendship Store, and modern shopping malls first; then see what's available in the streets and at markets. Most stores are open daily from about 10am to 10pm (especially in the summer). Weekends (especially Sun) are the most hectic days to shop.

SHÀNGHǍI'S BEST BUYS

Shànghǎi is no Hong Kong, but it has some of the best **antiques** shopping in mainland China. A red wax seal must be attached to any item created between 1795 and 1949 that is taken out of China; older items cannot be exported. Many hotel shops and modern department stores will send purchases to your home, and the Friendship Store has an efficient shipping department. **Furniture,** old or new, in traditional Chinese styles can be purchased or custom ordered at several antiques stores; prices are high but still lower than you'd pay at home; shipping, however, can add considerably to the bill.

Shànghǎi is also known for its selection and low prices in **silk** (both off the bolt and in finished garments). The Shanghainese being connoisseurs of fashion and style, shops selling **fashionable clothing** in cotton, wool, silk, and just about any imaginable material are a dime a dozen, and prices are low. **Traditional clothing** such as *qípáo* (mandarin collar dresses) and *mián ǎo* (padded jackets sometimes referred to as Máo jackets or Zhōngshān jackets) are once again fashionable purchases.

Jewelry can be a bargain, particularly **jade, gold, silver,** and **freshwater pearls,** but bargaining and a critical eye are required. **Electronics, cameras,** and other high-tech goods are not particularly good buys, but if you need anything replaced, you'll find a wide selection to choose from.

Among **arts and crafts,** there are also especially good buys in **ceramics,** hand-stitched **embroideries, teapots, painted fans,** and **chopsticks.** These are often sold in markets and on the sidewalks by itinerant vendors. Collectibles include **Máo buttons, posters of Old Shànghǎi** (covering everything from cigarette advertisements to talcum powder), old Chinese **coins, woodcarvings,** and **screens**—all priced lowest at markets and stands. Other popular crafts made in Shànghǎi are **handbags, carpets, lacquerware, painted snuff bottles,** and **peasant paintings.** Prices vary considerably. The best rule is to find something you truly like, then consider how much it is worth to you.

Designer-label **sportswear** and **stuffed toys** (such as Beanie Babies) are abundant in department stores and street markets alike. Another popular gift is a **chop** (also called a seal), which is a small, stone custom-engraved stamp with your name (in English, Chinese, or both), used with an ink pad to print your "signature" on paper. Chops can be created overnight, the same day, or sometimes even while you wait. Prices depend on the stone you select and the skill of the engraver.

THE ART OF BARGAINING

It helps to know the going prices for items you're interested in. The Friendship Store is worth scoping out with prices in mind because it sets the standard price for most items. Prices in hotel shops and at the new megamalls are usually your ceiling—you should be able to beat that price elsewhere. The street markets usually have the lowest prices. There, for example, you can buy porcelain chopstick rests for ¥5 (60¢), painted fans at ¥10 ($1.20), silk shirts at ¥100 ($12), quilts at ¥150 ($18), and ecru tablecloths at ¥200 ($24).

Haggling is not done at government-run stores, most hotel stalls, and modern shops, but it is expected on the street and in small private stores. A good rule of thumb is to offer no more than a quarter of the quoted price and not to accept the first counteroffer. Try to reach a compromise (no more than half the quoted price). Walking away with a firm but polite "No" often brings about a more favorable price. Smiling through the entire exchange (whatever the outcome) helps as well, as does negotiating alone with the vendor who will never give you the best price if he/she stands to lose face in front of other prying eyes. Remember that locals are demon shoppers who scrutinize each potential purchase and exercise mountains of patience before making a buy.

Tips Buyer Beware

A local saying goes, "Everything is fake, only the fake things are real." This is true of goods sold at many antiques markets, and especially the open-air markets that line the entrances to major tourist sites where, in general, you'll be charged extravagant prices for mass-produced kitsch of shoddy quality. **Jade** is particularly difficult to evaluate and prone to being fake, so buy only what you really like and don't pay much.

SHÀNGHĂI'S TOP SHOPPING AREAS

Shànghăi's top street to shop has always been **Nánjīng Lù,** enhanced recently by the creation of the **Nánjīng Lù Pedestrian Mall** on Nánjīng Dōng Lù downtown (described in chapter 7, "Shànghăi Strolls"), where the most modern and the most traditional modes of retailing commingle.

Even more popular among locals, however, is **Huáihăi Zhōng Lù,** the wide avenue south of Nánjīng Lù and parallel to it. The Huáihăi shopping area tends to run far west across the city, from the Huángpí Nán Lù Metro station to the Chángshú Lù station. The modern shopping malls here have better prices than you'll find on Nánjīng Lù, and there are plenty of boutiques featuring fashions and silks. Some of the most interesting shopping for fashion and accessories is concentrated in the **Màomíng Lù/Chánglè Lù** area, just off Huáihăi Lù. In the southern part of the concession, **Tàikàng Lù,** home to a bunch of art galleries and trendy clubs, also has some fashionable boutiques selling everything from designer handbags to pricey silks.

Another major shopping street is **Héngshān Lù,** which continues at the western end of Huáihăi Lù and runs south to the **Xújiāhuì** intersection and subway stop, where one of the city's largest collections of shopping centers is located.

Shànghăi's **Old Town Bazaar** (see chapter 7, "Shànghăi Strolls") is a fine place to shop for local arts and crafts and for antiques. In Pŭdōng, the shopping is concentrated mostly east of the riverfront and south of the Oriental Pearl TV Tower in the malls anchored by the massive **Nextage** department store on Zhāngyáng Lù and more recently the **Super Brand Mall** (Zhèngdà Guăngchăng) in Lùjiāzuĭ.

2 Markets & Bazaars

Some of Shànghăi's most interesting shopping experiences are provided by its colorful street markets and alley bazaars. Curios, crafts, collectibles, antiques, jewelry, and coins are all here for those who are willing to bargain hard, but perhaps the most common item you'll find in the markets these days is designer-label clothing, much of it knockoffs (copies) with upscale labels sewn in, although some items are factory seconds or overruns (sometimes smuggled out of legitimate brand-name factories). Many of the markets also sell fresh produce, seafood, spices, and other consumables to residents, along with snacks and drinks. At all such markets, cash is the only means of exchange, and pickpockets are plentiful, so keep all your valuables in a concealed pouch or money belt. If you're purchasing goods from an outdoor antiques market, be aware that not all older (pre-1949) items sold at such markets will have the red-wax seal attached. A stern Customs inspector, finding an old item without a seal, might confiscate it.

DŎNGJIĀDÙ FABRIC MARKET (DŎNGJIĀDÙ LÙ ZHĬPǏN SHÌCHĂNG) Located at Dŏngjiādù Lù and Zhōngshān Nán Lù in the southeastern corner of the old Chinese city, this gem of a market, a favorite with expatriates, features hundreds of stalls selling bales of fabric at ridiculously low prices, from traditional Chinese silk and Thai silk to cotton, linen, wool, and cashmere, though the heavier fabrics are only carried during the colder months. Many stalls have their own in-house tailors who can stitch you a suit, or anything else you want, at rates that are less than half what you'd pay at retail outlets like Silk King. Come with a pattern. Turnaround is usually a week or more. Open daily from 9am to 5pm.

Tips Vendors Behaving Badly

When visiting the Fúyòu Market, be very careful when navigating your way through the makeshift vendors on the third and especially fourth floors; many are itinerant peddlers here for the weekend who merely display their wares on the ground wherever they can find space. Shoppers with large bags or heavy bag packs should be especially vigilant, as a careless swing of an arm or even a tiny push from the crowd can cause bodies to topple and wares to go flying. This has happened before and will happen again (whether by accident or design). If you are the hapless soul who ends up damaging something (even if you were pushed by someone else), you will be held responsible. This is open season for vendors who, smelling blood, will claim that you've broken their precious Táng Dynasty vase (when it has just come from the factory backroom), and cite a ridiculously marked-up charge that you must pay. Fortunately, the Fúyòu Market now has a supervising manager familiar with the quality and price of the goods on sale to monitor and mediate precisely such incidents. Should you ever find yourself in such an unlucky situation, don't attempt to bargain your way out; immediately consult the supervisor *(jiāndū)* whose office is in the small alley just east of the building.

DŌNGTÁI LÙ ANTIQUES MARKET (DŌNGTÁI LÙ GǓWÁN SHÌCHǍNG) ★ This largest of Shànghǎi's antique markets has hundreds of stalls and many permanent shops along a short lane, located on Dōngtái Lù and Liúhé Lù, 1 block west of Xīzàng Nán Lù, Lúwān (about 3 blocks south of Huáihǎi Lù). Dealers specialize in antiques, curios, porcelain, furniture, jewelry, baskets, bamboo and woodcarvings, birds, flowers, goldfish, and nostalgic bric-a-brac from colonial and revolutionary days (especially Máo memorabilia). When it rains, most stalls aren't open, but the stores are. Open daily from 9am to 5pm.

FÚYÒU MARKET If you like rummaging through lots of junk for the chance to find the rare real nugget, this is still the best place to do it in Shànghǎi. This favorite for weekend antique and curio hunting, currently located in the Cángbǎo Lóu (building) at Fāngbāng Zhōng Lù 457 and Hénán Nán Lù (the western entrance to Shànghǎi Old St. in the Old Town Bazaar, Nánshì) is also called a "ghost market" because the traders—up to 800 of them—set out their wares before sunrise (when only ghosts can see what's for sale). Come as near to dawn as possible on Saturday or Sunday morning, preferably the latter, when vendors come in from the surrounding countryside. The goods are various and few are polished up; many of the items are from the attic or the farm, though increasingly also from some factory backroom that churns out modern pieces that are then scuffed up with mud to look old. Porcelains, old jade pendants, used furniture, Qīng Dynasty coins, Chairman Máo buttons and little red books, old Russian cameras, Buddhist statues, snuff bottles, and carved wooden screens are just a few of the treasures here, none with price tags. Three floors of the market building are open daily from 9am to 5pm, with the third floor specializing in concession-era relics; the weekend market (on the third and fourth floors) runs from 5am to 6pm, but tapers off by noon.

TEMPLE OF TOWN GOD MARKET (CHÉNGHUÁNG MIÀO SHÌCHǍNG)   This daily market starts out in the basement of the Huábǎo Building (Fāngbāng Lù 265, Old Town Bazaar, Nánshì), but on weekends it spills into the courtyards of the temple and nearby Yù Yuán pedestrian mall. It offers hundreds of vendors and hundreds of chances to bargain for curios, collectibles, and an occasional museum-quality relic. It's open daily from 8:30am to 9pm.

XIĀNGYÁNG CLOTHING MARKET (XIĀNGYÁNG LÙ FÚSHÌ SHÌCHǍNG) ✦   At the intersection of Huáihǎi Zhōng Lù and Xiāngyáng Lù, Xúhuì (between the Shǎnxī Nán Lù and Chángshú Lù Metro stations), you'll find Shànghǎi's version of Běijīng's famous Silk Alley—but with a broader range of goods. This outdoor market with many covered stalls has as its main draw designer-label clothing and accessories. The Western-branded merchandise (North Face jackets, Prada handbags, Nike shoes, and so on) sells for a fraction of retail, but of course the labels may not be genuine (that silk tie or scarf may prove to be synthetic, for example). Seconds and fakes abound, but some of the best deals are genuine, hustled out the back door of Shànghǎi factories. Haggling is expected. Do not, for example, pay more than ¥180 ($22) for a "North Fake" jacket or ¥100 ($13) for a pair of jeans. New rules imposed as a result of China entering the World Trade Organization have closed down some stalls, but the vendors are still there. Now they congregate at the entrance to the market and accost passers-by and tourists with their decrepit laminated photos of the Louis Vuitton handbags and the Rolex watches they have stashed away. *Do not* go with these vendors no matter how appealing the prices quoted. You can get similar items at plenty of stalls inside the market. Open daily from 8am to 9pm.

The Pearls of China

China's oyster beds remain among the world's most fertile grounds for pearls, of both the saltwater and freshwater variety. Seawater pearls are usually more expensive than the freshwater gems, but in both cases the qualities to look for are roundness, luster, and size. The bigger, rounder, and shinier the pearl, the better (and the more expensive). Here are a few ways to detect fakes, even if most shoppers don't bother:

- Nick the surface of the pearl with a sharp blade (the color should be uniform within and without).
- Rub the pearl along your teeth (you should hear a grating sound).
- Scrape the pearl on glass (real pearls leave a mark).
- Pass the pearl through a flame (fakes turn black, real pearls don't).

Try to pick a string of pearls that are of the same size, shape, and color. Here's a rough pricing guide, based on what's charged in Shànghǎi:

¥20 to ¥30 ($2.50–$3.80) for a string of small rice-shaped pearls.
¥30 to ¥50 ($3.80–$6) for a string of larger pearls of mixed or low luster.
¥50 to ¥120 ($6–$15) for a string of larger pearls of different colors.

A string of very large, perfectly round pearls of the same color sells for considerably more, ¥10,000 to ¥20,000 ($1,200–$2,400) and higher.

Tips What to Know about Knockoffs

The Customs services of many nations frown on the importation of knock-offs on trademark goods. The U.S. Customs Service allows U.S. residents to return with one trademark-protected item of each type; that is, one counterfeit watch, one knockoff purse, one camera with a questionable trademark, and so on. For instance, you may not bring back a dozen "Polo" shirts as gifts for friends. Even if the brand name is legitimate, you are not a licensed importer. Copyrighted products like CD-ROMs and books must have been manufactured under the copyright owner's authorization; otherwise, tourists may not import even one of these items—they are pirated. The U.S. Customs Service booklet *Know Before You Go* and the U.S. Customs website **www.customs.ustreas.gov** provide further guidelines.

3 Shopping A to Z

ANTIQUES & FURNITURE

The markets and bazaars (listed above) are a primary source of antiques, collectibles, and Chinese furniture and furnishings, as are some hotel shops; but there are also several private antiques stores worth checking out. Most of the warehouses are situated in west Shànghǎi's Chángníng District, near the Hóngqiáo Airport (no Metro). If you plan to make a day of shopping, have your hotel haggle with the taxi driver over a price for the trip. Half a day's shopping should cost no more than ¥250 (about $30).

Annly's Antique Warehouse (Ān Lì)   Annly Chan provides custom-made sofas, chairs, draperies, and cushions; picture framing; and pricey antique furniture. Daily 9am to 6pm. Zhōngchūn Lù 7611, no. 68 (by Hùsōng Lù), Mínháng Qū. ⓒ 021/6406-0242. No Metro.

Chine Antiques (Chúntiān Gé)   In business for the last 15 years, and noted for its high-end (and high-priced) antiques, mainly wooden pieces from the Qīng Dynasty, Chine will ship purchases overseas. The shop in the Dōngtái Market has pictures of what you can find in the warehouse showroom near the Hóngqiáo Airport. Daily 9am to 5pm. Shop: Liùhé Lù 38 (at Dōngtái Lù), Lúwān. ⓒ 021/6387-4100. Metro: Huángpí Nán Lù (about a mile away). Warehouse: Hóngqiáo Lù 1660, Chángníng. ⓒ 021/5914-4424 or 021/6270-1023.

Fúyòu Antique Market   Still the most fun place to scavenge for every imaginable antique and collectible, from Buddhist statuary to Qīng Dynasty coins (see above). Monday to Friday 9am to 5pm; Saturday to Sunday 5am to 5pm. Fāngbāng Lù 457 (at Hénán Lù), Nánshì. Metro: Hénán Zhōng Lù.

G-E-Tang Antique Co. Ltd. (Jíyì Táng Gǔwán)   Located in the antiques market west of Old Town, G-E-Tang sells top-of-the-line antique Míng and Qīng dynasties furniture, with overseas shipping available. Furniture finishes here tend to be lighter than in most shops. New pieces are made from parts of old pieces. Daily 9am to 6pm. Hù Qīng Píng Gōng Lù 8 (southwest of Hóngqiáo Airport), Chángníng. ⓒ 021/6384-6388. www.getang.com.

Henry Antique Warehouse (Hēnglì Gǔdiǎn Jiājù)   The English-speaking staff at this huge space show off antique Chinese furniture and furnishings, with a carved Chinese bed costing around ¥13,000 ($1,625). Overseas shipping provided. Daily 9am to 6pm. Hóngzhōng Lù 8 (off Wúzhōng Lù), Chángníng. ✆ 021/6401-0831. www.h-antique.com.

Huá Bǎo Lóu   The basement of this shopping center on "Shànghǎi Old Street" near the Temple of the Town God and Yù Garden has plenty of antiques and collectibles for sale, though not always at the best prices. Over 200 booths sell embroidery, calligraphy, jade, carvings, and porcelain pieces. Daily 9am to 9pm. Fāngbāng Zhōng Lù 265, Old Town, Nánshì. ✆ 021/6355-2272 or 021/6355-9999. Metro: Hénán Zhōng Lù.

Míng Qīng Antique Furniture (Míng Qīng Gǔwán)   Qīng and Míng Dynasty pieces and handcrafted reproductions are the specialty. Overseas shipping can be arranged. The showroom and workshop are open daily 9am to 6pm. Hù Qīng Píng Gōng Lù 1265 (west of Huáxiāng Lù), Chángníng. ✆ 021/6420-3364.

Shànghǎi Antique and Curio Store (Shànghǎi Wénwù Shāngdiàn)   The owners hope to make downtown Guǎngdōng Lù, which runs west off the south end of the Bund, into something of an antiques row for shoppers. One of the oldest and largest antiques stores, they have under their umbrella everything from calligraphy, old jades and porcelain, to antique furniture, woodcarvings, embroidery, and tapestries. Prices are even reasonable. Daily 9am to 5pm. Guǎngdōng Lù 192–246, Huángpǔ. ✆ 021/6321-4697, ext. 301. Metro: Hénán Zhōng Lù.

BOOKS

The **Foreign Language Bookstore** (below) offers a wide range of English-language material, but hotel kiosks and shops also have decent English-language guides to Shànghǎi attractions and books about China. The **Confucius Temple Book Market (Gǔshū Shìchǎng),** held every Sunday from 8am to 4pm at Wénmiào Lù 215 (east of Zhōnghuá Lù), traffics in secondhand and vintage books, including some foreign-language volumes.

Chinese Classics Bookstore (Shànghǎi Gǔjí Shūdiàn)   This antiquarian book dealer on Shànghǎi's book row (Fúzhōu Lù) specializes in old books published in or written about China. Most of the books are in Chinese. It also sells calligraphy supplies, including fine paper. Daily 10am to 9pm. Fúzhōu Lù 424, Huángpǔ. ✆ 021/6351-7745 or 021/6322-4984. Metro: Hénán Zhōng Lù.

Old China Hand Reading Room (Hànyuán Shūwū)   Shànghǎi's most charming coffeehouse, opened in 1996 by photographer Deke Erh, is also a bookstore, with hundreds of old and new, obscure and popular books and magazines on its shelves. Relax at a Qīng Dynasty antique table by the window as you peruse your possible purchases over green tea or cappuccino. This is the best place to purchase the series of books on colonial architecture in China put out by Deke Erh and Tess Johnston. Daily noon to midnight. Shàoxìng Lù 27 (between Ruìjīn Èr Lù and Shānxī Nán Lù), Lúwān. ✆ 021/6473-2526. Metro: Shānxī Nán Lù.

Shànghǎi Book Mall (Shànghǎi Shū Chéng)   Shànghǎi's state-of-the-art megamall for book lovers, this new store has eight floors of books, music, and DVDs. About 10% of its collection comprises English-language books. Daily 9am to 8pm. Fúzhōu Lù 465 (east of Húběi Lù), Huángpǔ. ✆ 021/6352-2222. Metro: Hénán Zhōng Lù.

Shànghǎi Foreign Language Bookstore (Wàiwén Shūdiàn)   The city's largest selection of English-language books and magazines (along with some maps, tapes, and CDs) can be found on the first and fourth floors of this big government-run store. They take credit cards and ship books overseas. Daily 9am to 6pm. Fúzhōu Lù 390 (east of Fújiàn Lù), Huángpǔ. ☏ 021/6322-3200. Metro: Hénán Zhōng Lù.

Shànghǎi Museum Bookshop   The gift shop on the museum's first floor carries a good selection of books in English on art, history, and culture, including coffee-table volumes. Daily 9am to 5pm (to 8pm on Sat). Rénmín Dà Dào 201 (People's Square), Huángpǔ District. ☏ 021/6372-3500. Metro: Rénmín Guǎngchǎng or Rénmín Gōngyuán.

Xīnhuá Shūdiàn (Xīnhuá Bookstore)   In most Chinese cities, this state-run bookstore is the only place to find English-language titles, but its relatively small collection of English-language material (mostly abridged translations of literary classics) in Shànghǎi stores is unimpressive. There are 133 locations across town. Daily 10am to 9pm. Nánjīng Xī Lù 777 (at Shímén Yī Lù). ☏ 021/6327-1914. Metro: Shímén Yī Lù.

CAMERAS & FILM

Kodak, Fuji, and other imported camera films can be purchased all over Shànghǎi, at hotel kiosks, department stores, and camera shops. Prices are about on par with those in the West. There are 1-hour and next-day film processing outlets in hotels and shopping centers, too. You can certainly purchase new cameras and accessories in Shànghǎi; prices are comparable to those in the West, perhaps slightly higher depending on the brand. Those looking for ancient Russian swing-lens cameras can sometimes find them in the Fúyòu Antique Market (p. 203).

Guànlóng Photographic Equipment Company (Guànlóng Zhàoxiàng Qìcái Yǒuxiàn Gōngsī)   This is a reputable firm on the Nánjīng Lù Pedestrian Mall selling top brand-name cameras, lenses, and all related accessories. There's a photo developing service as well, and they can handle camera repairs. Cameras range from ¥2,400 to ¥6,500 ($300–$800). Daily 9am to 9pm. Nánjīng Dōng Lù 180, Huángpǔ District. ☏ 021/6329-0414. V. Metro: Hénán Zhōng Lù.

Kodak (Kēdá)   This chain store has several locations around town where they can develop film and print ordinary and digital photos, the latter at ¥2 (25¢) per piece for a 4×6 print. Photo albums and digital camera accessories are also available. Daily 9am to 8pm. Wúníng Lù 280 (by Dōngxīng Lùm Pǔtuó). ☏ 021/5290-0325. Light Rail: Cáoyáng Lù. Huáihǎi Zhōng Lù 606–610 (by Chéngdū Nán Lù), Lúwān. ☏ 021/5306-8571. Metro: Huángpí Nán Lù.

CARPETS

Check over carpets carefully, with an eye to faded colors. Colors should be bright and the threads fine. A 1.8m×2.4m (6 ft.×8 ft.) silk carpet, tightly woven (300–400 stitches/in.), can cost ¥50,000 ($6,000) or more.

Bokhara Carpets   Excellent choice of new and old carpets from Iran, Pakistan, Afghanistan, India, and Uzbekistan. Daily 10am to 6:30pm. Xiānxiá Lù 679 (off Yán'ān Xī Lù, near Shuǐchéng Lù), Chángníng. ☏ 021/6290-1745. No credit cards. No Metro.

CLOTHING

A number of shops along Chánglè Lù and Màomíng Lù sell ready-made *qípáos* (mandarin-collar dresses with high slits), Táng jackets, and other traditional Chinese-style clothing, and can also tailor the same.

Huā Jiā Fúshì   One of several stores on this strip of Màomíng Lù selling traditional Chinese clothing, this one has been the haunt of several Chinese celebrities, so you know you're at least getting star-quality goods. *Qípáos* hover around ¥200 ($25). Daily 10am to 10pm. Màomíng Nán Lù 88 (south of Huáihǎi Zhōng Lù), Lúwān. ℂ **021/6467-2845.** Metro: Shǎnxī Nán Lù.

Shànghǎi Tang (Shànghǎi Tān)   This new (2003) store from Hong Kong fashion maven David Tang has finally opened in Shànghǎi. Besides his signature and pricey traditional Chinese shirts and *qípáo,* you can also pick up elegant scarves, photo frames, bags, and candles. Daily 10am to 10pm. Màomíng Nán Lù 59, Shop E, Jǐnjiāng Hotel Promenade, Lúwān Qū. ℂ **021/5466-3006.** Metro: Shǎnxī Nán Lù.

COMPUTERS

Cybermart (Sàibó Shùmǎ Guǎngchǎng)   This huge mall is a cyber geek's dream come true, with stores selling everything from laptops and printers to mobile phones and MD and DVD players. International brands such as Apple, IBM, Sony, and NEC also have outlets here. Repair services are also available. Daily 10am to 8pm. Huáihǎi Zhōng Lù 282 (by Huángpí Nán Lù), Lúwān. ℂ **021/6390-8008.** www.cybermartm.com.cn. Metro: Huángpí Nán Lù.

CRAFTS, CERAMICS & GIFTS

Liúlí Gōngfáng   With almost a dozen outlets around town, this chain started by former Taiwanese actress Yáng Huìshān features unique and unusual pieces of crystal and glassware, from Buddhist statues to ritual vessels and decorative tableware. International glass art techniques have been adapted to create gorgeous Chinese-themed pieces you're unlikely to come across elsewhere. Daily 10am to 10pm. Nánjīng Xī Lù 1266, Room 203, Hénglóng Guǎngchǎng (Plaza 66), Jìng Ān Qū. ℂ **021/6289-0892.** www.liuli.com. Metro: Shímén Yī Lù.

Madame Máo's Dowry (Máo Tài Shèjì)   This wonderful shop in the French Concession sells antique furniture, silk clothing, unusual housewares, ceramics, and art, with an emphasis on Cultural Revolution posters and propaganda art. Monday to Saturday 10am to 6pm; Sunday noon to 6pm. Fùxīng Xī Lù 70 (by Yǒngfú Lù), Xúhuì. ℂ **021/6437-1255.** Metro: Chángshú Lù.

Shànghǎi Arts & Crafts Museum (Shànghǎi Gōngyì Měishùguǎn)   What you see made in the open workshops of this French Concession mansion is for sale in the shops here, from embroideries and egg-shell porcelain to snuff bottles and kites. Daily 8:30am to 4:30pm. Fēnyáng Lù 79 (south of Fùxīng Zhōng Lù), Xújiāhuì. ℂ **021/6437-0509.** Metro: Chángshú Lù.

Shànghǎi Jǐngdé Zhèn Porcelain Artware (Shànghǎi Jǐngdé Zhèn Yìshù Cíqì Shāngdiàn)   An excellent selection of some of China's most prized ceramic creations, produced by factories and artisans in nearby Jǐngdé Zhèn. Vases, plates, cups, and artware are expensive here, but the quality is high and the reputation good. Daily 10am to 10pm. Nánjīng Xī Lù 1185 (at Shǎnxī Běi Lù), Jìng Ān. ℂ **021/6253-3178.** Metro: Jìng Ān Sì.

Simply Life (Yìjū Shēnghuó)   Tasteful gifts from China and throughout Asia are the hallmark of the new Simply Life stores, established in 2000. The vast foreigner-pleasing selection includes household decorations, painted bone china, tableware, crafts, linens, and silks. Alas, prices are simply sky-high. Open daily 9am to 9pm. Three branches: Xīntiāndì, Tàicāng Lù 181, North Block. ℂ **021/6387-5100.** www.simplylife-sh.com. Metro: Huángpí Nán Lù. Dōngpíng Lù 9, Xúhuì. ℂ **021/3406-0509.** Metro: Chángshú Lù. Huáihǎi Zhōng Lù 1312 (basement of Maison Mode), Xúhuì. ℂ **021/6431-0100,** ext. 022. Metro: Héngshān Lù.

Skylight (Tiān Lài)   Created by photographer Jones Wang, this stylish shop carries products handcrafted in Tibet (fabrics, religious artifacts, jewelry, shoes, housewares, musical instruments, furniture). Prices are high, but the merchandise is first-rate. Daily 10am to 9:30pm. Fùxīng Xī Lù 28 (by Wūlǔmùqí Zhōng Lù), Xúhuì. © 021/6473-5610. No credit cards. Metro: Chángshú Lù.

DEPARTMENT STORES

Shànghǎi has a large number of new, Western-style department stores that have almost completely replaced the traditional (but shoddy) Chinese version. Most of them are joint ventures with overseas retailing chains.

Friendship Store (Yǒuyì Shāngdiàn)   Friendship stores once catered exclusively to foreigners, but now compete freely (though not always successfully) with department stores and shopping plazas. For many visitors, this is the ultimate one-stop shop, containing a generous sampling of nearly everything worth hauling home: arts and crafts, jewelry, silk, books, souvenirs, antiques. Prices are relatively high (no bargaining allowed) but are generally still lower than in high-end hotel shops; and quality is decent. Recently moved here from its former Běijīng Dōng Lù address, this branch caters mostly to tour groups staying downtown. You can start here to get an overview of what's available in Shànghǎi at a fair price, shop the streets and malls, then return to make any last-minute purchases. There is another branch in the western part of town. The first branch is open daily 9:30am to 9:30pm. The western branch is open daily 10am to 10pm. Jīnlíng Dōng Lù 68, Huángpǔ. © 021/6337-3555. Metro: Hénán Zhōng Lù. Friendship Shopping Centre (Hóng Qiáo Yǒuyì Shāngchéng), Zūnyì Nán Lù 6, Chángníng. © 021/6270-0000. No Metro.

Isetan (Yīshìdān)   This Japanese department store puts high prices on its exceptional goods and fashions. It also offers its own bakery and an Esprit boutique in the heart of Huáihǎi Lù's most upscale shopping area. Daily 10am to 9pm. There's also a branch at the Westgate Shopping Mall, Nánjīng Xī Lù 1038 (© 021/6272-1111). Huáihǎi Zhōng Lù 527 (at Chéngdū Lù), Lúwān. © 021/5306-1111. Metro: Huángpí Nán Lù.

Jǐn Jiāng Dickson Centre (Jǐn Jiāng Díshēng Shāngshà)   Luxury clothing and housewares (as found in Hong Kong's best stores) are offered here in the heart of the French Concession next door to the five-star Jǐn Jiāng and Okura Garden hotels. This is the place to shop for Ralph Lauren (although why you've come all the way to Shànghǎi to do so is a bit of a mystery). Monday to Friday 11am to 9pm (to 10pm Sat and Sun). Chánglè Lù 400 (at Màomíng Nán Lù), Lúwān. © 021/6472-6888. Metro: Shǎnxī Nán Lù.

New World Department Store (Xīn Shìjiè Chéng)   Located on the northwest side of the intersection where Nánjīng Xī Lù ends and the pedestrian shopping mall begins, this flashy seven-story emporium is highlighted by name-brand Western fashions and cosmetics, but is also a decent place to shop for inexpensive generic items. Daily 10am to 10pm. Nánjīng Xī Lù 2–68 (at Xīzàng Zhōng Lù), Huángpǔ. © 021/6358-8888. Metro: Rénmín Gōngyuán.

Nextage Department Store (Shànghǎi Dìyī Bābǎibàn Xīnshìjì Shāngshà)   Touted as the second-largest department store on Earth (surpassed only by Macy's in New York), this megastore is 10 stories tall and a square block wide. It's chock-full of everything department stores ever carry (and some things they don't, such as automobiles). The Japanese supermarket Yaohan is also here. Daily 10am to 10pm. Directly across the street (south) is another big shopping mall, **Times Square** (**Shídài Guǎngchǎng;** ℂ 021/5836-8888), as if another were needed. Zhāngyáng Lù 501 (at Pǔdōng Nán Lù), Pǔdōng. ℂ 021/5830-1111. Metro: Dōngfāng Lù.

Parkson (Bǎishèng Gòuwù Zhōngxīn)   At one of the busiest junctures in town, this Malaysian-based French Concession department store is yet another upscale emporium of Western fashions and cosmetics, with a McDonald's and a Gino's Café next door and an excellent Park 'n Shop supermarket carrying foreign goods in the basement. Prices are lower than on Nánjīng Lù. Daily 10am to 10pm. Huáihǎi Zhōng Lù 918 (at Shǎnxī Nán Lù), Lúwān. ℂ 021/6415-6384. Metro: Shǎnxī Nán Lù.

Printemps-Shànghǎi (Shànghǎi Bālí Chūntiān Bǎihuò)   Carrying on the French Concession image of yesteryear, the Printemps is furnished in high Art Nouveau style (modeled after the 19th-c. mother store in Paris), down to its designer-label boutiques (Givenchy, Christian Lacroix) and Parisian cafes. Daily 10am to 10pm. Huáihǎi Zhōng Lù 939–947 (at Shǎnxī Nán Lù), Lúwān. ℂ 021/6431-0118. Metro: Shǎnxī Nán Lù.

Shànghǎi Downtown Duty Free Shop (Shànghǎi Shìnèi Miǎnshuì Diàn)   Restricting its sales to foreign visitors, this shop carries the sort of luxury international goods you find in airport duty-free shops, as well as Shànghǎi souvenirs and Chinese arts and crafts. You'll have to present your international airline ticket and passport if you make purchases, which can then be picked up at the airport when you leave. Daily 8:30am to 6pm. Tiānyáoqiáo Lù 666 (under no. 5 entrance of Shànghǎi Stadium), Xúhuì. ℂ 021/6426-6988. Metro: Shànghǎi Tǐyùguǎn.

Shànghǎi No. 1 Department Store (Shànghǎi Shì Dìyī Bǎihuò Shāngdiàn)   Shànghǎi's most famous department store, opened in 1934, has been thoroughly updated with the incorporation of a 22-story East Tower, the first 11 floors of which are devoted to retailing. All the usual suspects are here: clothing, shoes, children's wear, gifts, books, watches, toys, jewelry, cosmetics, housewares, sporting equipment, and electronic goods. The store has renown and volume, but not always the best prices. Daily 10am to 10pm. Nánjīng Dōng Lù 800–830 (at Xīzàng Zhōng Lù), Huángpǔ. ℂ 021/6322-3344. Metro: Rénmín Gōngyuán.

DRUGSTORES

Shànghǎi Number One Dispensary (Shànghǎi Dìyī Yīyào Shāngdiàn)
East meets West at this apothecary on the pedestrian mall that carries a considerable number of foreign medicines. Branches can be found all over town. Daily 9am to 10pm. Nánjīng Dōng Lù 616 (at Zhéjiāng Zhōng Lù), Huángpǔ. ℂ 021/6322-4567. www.dyyy.com.cn. Metro: Hénán Zhōng Lù.

Watson's (Qūchénshì)   Watson's is a large Western-style drugstore, with just about anything you might need, including a fairly wide range of imported beauty and health aids, from cosmetics to toothpaste. Daily 9:30am to 10pm. Huáihǎi Zhōng Lù 787–789 (west of Ruìjīn Èr Lù), Lúwān. ℂ 021/6431-8650. www.watsons.com.tw. Metro: Huángpí Nán Lù.

EMBROIDERIES

Zhang's Textiles   Here you'll find a superb collection of framed embroidery (from Qīng Dynasty royal costumes) and dynastic-era robes and skirts for purchase. These are genuine antique fabrics. Zhang's also carries jade bracelets, silk pillows, and silk pillow boxes. Items range from ¥60 to ¥200,000 ($7.20–$24,000).

Daily 10am to 9pm. Nánjīng Xī Lù 1376, Shànghǎi Centre 202A, Jìng Ān. ✆ **021/6279-8587.**
www.zhangstextiles.com. Metro: Jìng Ān Sì.

JEWELRY

Amy's Pearls (Àimǐnshì Zhūbǎo)   High-quality (and fairly high-priced)
pearls from China and Asia are sold by a knowledgeable and English-speaking
staff (with outlets in Běijīng as well). Daily 9am to 7pm. Gǔběi Lù 1445 (off Hóngqiáo
Lù, east a block from Carrefour), Gǔběi New Town, Chángníng. ✆ 021/6275-3954. www.amy-
pearl.com. No Metro. Xiāngyáng Nán Lù 77 (west entrance of Xiāngyáng Market), Xúhuì. Daily
9am–8:30pm. Metro: Chángshú Lù.

Angel Pearls   This is one of Shànghǎi's best shops for pearls (freshwater
pearls, South Sea pearls, Japanese cultured pearls). It also carries silk carpets and
embroideries. Daily 10am to 6:30pm. Xīnzhá Lù 1051, 17D (at Shǎnxī Lù), Jìng Ān.
✆ 021/6215-5031. Daily 9am–5:30pm. Metro: Jìng Ān Sì. Nánjīng Xī Lù 1376, Shànghǎi Centre,
Suite 605. ✆ 021/6279-8287. Metro: Jìng Ān Sì.

Lǎo Fèng Xiáng Jewelers (Lǎo Fèng Xiáng Yínlóu)   Located on the north
side of the Nánjīng Lù Pedestrian Mall, this jewelry store has long specialized
(since the Qīng Dynasty) in jade, pearls, and fine silver and gold ornaments.
Daily 9:30am to 10pm. Nánjīng Dōng Lù 432 (at Shǎnxī Nán Lù), Huángpǔ. ✆ 021/6322-
0033. Metro: Hénán Zhōng Lù.

Pearl Village (Zhēnzhū Cūn)   Located a few blocks west of the Temple of the
City God in the Yù Yuán Bazaar, Pearl Village has over 50 vendors representing
pearl dealers, pearl farms, and pearl factories from throughout China. Freshwater, seawater, inlaid, and black pearls are featured, often at reasonable whole-
sale prices. Daily 9am to 5:30pm. Fúyòu Lù 288, Yàyī Jīndiàn, 3rd Floor, Nánshì. ✆ 021/
6355-3418. Metro: Hénán Zhōng Lù.

MODERN ART

The nascent Chinese contemporary art scene is starting to flourish in Shànghǎi,
with galleries and showrooms cropping up all over town. Though contemporary
Chinese artists are slowly gaining more international recognition, they are still
relatively unknown and their works often sell below international prices, making them potential investments for those so inclined. **Tàikàng Lù 210** in the
southern part of the French Concession (Lúwān District), and **Mògān Shān Lù
50** just south of the Sūzhōu Creek in the northern part of town (Pǔtuó District)
are home to a series of industrial warehouses that have been converted to galleries and artists' studios, and are well worth a visit if you like modern art and
photography.

ShanghART Gallery (Xiānggénà Huàláng)   One of the earlier and more
interesting galleries to show the works of contemporary Chinese artists, this is
often recommended as the first stop for modern connoisseurs. Daily 10am to
7pm. There is a much larger warehouse at Mògānshān Lù 50 if you're interested.
Gāolán Lù 2A, Fùxīng Park, Lúwān. ✆ 021/6359-3923. www.shanghart.com. Metro: Huángpí
Nán Lù.

SHOPPING MALLS & PLAZAS

Shànghǎi has plenty of mammoth shopping plazas (consisting of scores of independent brand-name and designer-label outlets selling international merchandise under one roof), particularly along Huáihǎi Zhōng Lù and at Xújiāhuì.

D-Mall (Dǐměi Gòuwù Zhōngxīn)   Located underneath People's Square (Rénmín Guǎngchǎng) and accessible via the subway station entrance, this subterranean mall (courtesy of bomb shelters left over from the days of the Sino-Soviet split in the 1960s) has what seems like an infinite number of small shops trafficking in everything from tattoos and fashion accessories to books and local snacks. Prices are appropriately lower than those at aboveground establishments. Rénmín Dàdào 221 (underground of People's Square), Huángpǔ. Metro: Rénmín Guǎngchǎng/Rénmín Gōngyuán.

Grand Gateway Plaza (Gǎnghuì Guǎngchǎng)   The biggest and flashiest of the malls in the Xújiāhuì circle has a good mix of retail (clothing, books, accessories, electronic items), dining and entertainment outlets, a theatre (occasionally showing English-language movies) on the fifth floor, and a plethora of food court restaurants. Prices here are slightly lower than on Nánjīng Lù but still not the best in town. Daily 10am to 10pm. Hóngqiáo Lù 1 (at Huáshān Lù), Xúhuì. ✆ 021/6404-0111. Metro: Xújiāhuì.

Raffles City (Láifùshì Guǎngchǎng)   As the newest (2003) mall in a town that loves everything new, this ultramodern Singapore joint venture, aided by a prime location across from People's Square, is currently the biggest draw for hip mall rats. There's a cineplex showing Chinese and occasional Hollywood films, an IMAX theatre, a fitness center, and retail shops ranging from local outfits to international names like Nike, Guess, and Swatch, but it's the many dining establishments (Starbucks, Häagen-Dazs, a popular bakery called Bread Talk, and an excellent food court called Megabite) that have proven the biggest draw so far. Daily 10am to 10pm. Xīzàng Zhōng Lù 268, Huángpǔ. ✆ 021/6340-3600.

Shànghǎi Centre (Shànghǎi Shāngchéng)   With outlets like Starbucks, Mrs. Fields, and Tony Roma's dotting the landscape, this self-contained hub makes you feel like you've never left home. Also here are a deluxe hotel (Portman Ritz-Carlton Hotel), a medical and dental clinic, a grand theatre, ATMs, a supermarket with the city's widest selection of Western groceries, and offices for DHL, American Express, and half a dozen international airlines—all in the same complex. The shopping is among the most upscale in Shànghǎi, with such outlets as Cerruti, Louis Vuitton, a. testoni, and Cartier. Shop and office hours vary, but many are open daily from 10am to 6pm. Nánjīng Xī Lù, 1376, Jìng Ān. ✆ 021/6279-8600. www.shanghai-centre.com. Metro: Jìng Ān Sì.

Super Brand Mall (Zhèngdà Guǎngchǎng)   The latest, largest mall in Pǔdōng, this gargantuan 10-story edifice has only recently started to attract the crowds, and then mostly through its dining establishments. The anchor is a four-story department store with all the usual super goods. There's also a well-stocked Liánhuā supermarket and a Bank of China ATM in the basement, and scores of clothing, jewelry, and accessories stores competing for your attention. Daily 10am to 10pm. Lùjiāzuǐ Lù 168, Pǔdōng. ✆ 021/6887-7888. Metro: Lùjiāzuǐ.

Three on the Bund (Wàitān Sān Hào)   About as classy and pricey as you can get in Shànghǎi shopping, this new development on the Bund has a Giorgio Armani flagship store (✆ 021/6339-1133; daily 11am–1pm), and other not-too-shabby mouthfuls such as Ann Demeulemeester, Bottega Veneta, Vivienne Tam, Yves Saint Laurent, and more. Even if you are going to pick up that "Emporio Armani" watch at the Xiāngyáng Market for less than ¥200 ($25), it may be fun to come admire the real thing through the looking glass. Daily 10am to 10pm. Zhōngshān Dōng Yī Lù 3 (entrance on Guǎngdōng Lù), Huángpǔ. ✆ 021/6323-3355. Metro: Hénán Zhōng Lù.

Westgate Mall   Called **Méilóngzhèn** in Chinese (after the famous restaurant that's across the street and also occupies space here), this is one of Shànghǎi's top Western-style malls offering brand names at reasonable prices. Among its outlets are an Isetan department store (✆ **021/6272-1111**), the usual clothing shops, a six-plex cinema on the 10th floor, and frequent exhibitions and promotions in the first floor atrium. Daily 10am to 10pm. Nánjīng Xī Lù 1038 (at Jiāngníng Lù), Jìng Ān. ✆ 021/6218-7878. Metro: Shímén Yī Lù.

SILK, FABRICS & TAILORS

The **Dǒngjiādù Fabric Market** (p. 200) is the best place to shop for a variety of inexpensive fabrics, though you'd have to bargain hard; tailors here also generally do yeoman's work in churning out suits, dresses, and other garments.

Chinese Printed Blue Nankeen Exhibition Hall (Zhōngguó Lányìnhuā Bù Guǎn)   In business for over 20 years, this exhibition hall/shop started by Madam Kubo Mase revives the folk art of indigo batik dying. Bales of this *nankeen* (as indigo batik is known in China) cloth, so fashionable in ethnic restaurants and on fashion runways these days, are sold here, along with ready-made *nankeen* shirts, tablecloths, and craft souvenirs. Daily 9am to 5pm. Chánglè Lù 637, House 24 (by Chángshú Lù), Xúhuì. ✆ 021/5403-7947. Metro: Chángshú Lù.

Dave's Custom Tailoring   Specializing in men's fashion, with custom-made Saville Row three-piece suits starting from ¥3,500 ($438). Turnaround is normally 3 to 10 days but can be shorter for a hefty fee. Daily 10am to 8pm. Wǔyuán Lù, Lane 288, no. 6 (between Wūlǔmùqí Lù and Wǔkāng Lù), Xúhuì. ✆ 021/5404-0001. Metro: Chángshú Lù.

Silk King (Zhēnsī Dà Wáng)   Silk and wool yardage and a good selection of shirts, blouses, skirts, dresses, ties, sheets, and other finished silk goods have make Silk King one of the top silk retailers in Shànghǎi, and a favorite stop for visiting heads of state and other VIPs. Silk or wool suits can be custom tailored in as little as 24 hours. Silk starts around ¥100 ($13) per meter (3¼ ft.), while more delicate cashmere is almost 10 times that. Daily 9:30am to 10pm. There are several Silk King branches. Tianping Lù 139, Xújiahuì (headquarters; ✆ 021/6282-1533); Nánjīng Dōng Lù 66 (✆ 021/6321-2193; Metro: Hénán Zhōng Lù); Nánjīng Xī Lù 819 (✆ 021/6215-3114; Metro: Shímén Yī Lù); Huáihǎi Zhōng Lù 550 (✆ 021/5383-0561; Metro: Huángpí Nán Lù).

SUPERMARKETS

Shànghǎi's hotels might have a small shop with some Western snacks and bottled water, or a deli stand, but for a broad range of familiar groceries, try one of the large-scale supermarkets listed here. There is also a well-stocked Park 'n Shop in the basement of Parkson's (see "Department Stores" earlier in this chapter).

Carrefour (Jiālèfú)   This highly popular French commodities giant offers an extensive range of imported Western groceries, along with fresh fruits, vegetables, sporting goods, clothing, shoes, music, electronic items, books, bicycles, and film developing. Daily 8am to 10pm. Shuǐchéng Nán Lù 268, Gǔbèi Xīnqū, Chángníng. ✆ 021/6270-6829. No Metro.

City Supermarket (Chéngshì Chāoshì)   This small but comprehensive supermarket in the Shànghǎi Centre is among the best places in town to pick up those Western foodstuffs you've been missing. It's pricey, but there's a nice selection, with a fine deli in the back. Daily 8am to 10pm. Nánjīng Xī Lù 1376 (at Shànghǎi Centre), Jìng Ān. ✆ 021/6279-8018. Metro: Jìng Ān Sì.

Lotus Supermarket (Liánhuā Chāoshi)   Just one of the newer outlets of a huge modern Chinese grocery chain in Shànghǎi, Liánhuā carries plenty of local produce and Chinese brands, along with some imported goods at very reasonable prices. Clean, bright, and thoroughly up-to-date facilities make this the best local chain. Branches are located around town. Daily 8am to 10pm. Lùjiāzuǐ Xī Lù 168, Zhèngdà Guǎngchǎng, Basement (Super Brand Mall), Pǔdōng. ✆ 021/5047-0648. Metro: Lùjiāzuǐ.

TEA

Huángshān Tea Company (Huángshān Cháyè Diàn)   There's a wide assortment of classic Yíxīng teapots (made in the adjacent province) and loose Chinese teas sold by weight here. Daily 10am to 10pm. Huáihǎi Zhōng Lù 605 (west of Chéngdū Běi Lù), Lúwān. ✆ 021/5306-2258. Metro: Huángpí Nán Lù. Huáihǎi Zhōng Lù 868 (east of Màomíng Lù), Lúwān. ✆ 021/5403-5412.

9

Shànghǎi After Dark

Less than a century ago, Shànghǎi was the most notorious city in Asia, with a nightlife that rivaled that of Paris. Dubbed the "Whore of Asia," old Shànghǎi presented countless opportunities for debauchery in its gambling dens, opium joints, rowdy nightclubs, and glamorous theatres. After the communists came to power in 1949, Shànghǎi was cleaned up overnight; drugs and prostitution were ended by decree, and entertainment was reduced to a few politically acceptable plays and dances. Well in the 1990s, visitors retired to their hotels after dark unless they were part of a group tour going to see the Shànghǎi acrobats. In the last few years, however, the possibilities for an evening on the town have multiplied exponentially, and while Shànghǎi is still not in the same league as Hong Kong or Paris quite yet, it is fast becoming again a city that never sleeps.

Culture mavens can now find in Shànghǎi large-scale performances of acrobatics, musicals, opera, dance, theatre, and classical and contemporary music. New state-of-the-art theaters and auditoriums have attracted in recent years the likes of Yo-yo Ma, Luciano Pavarotti, Diana Krall, the Kirov Ballet, and touring companies of *Les Misérables* and *Cats,* among others. (Admittedly, large-scale pop and rock concerts are still few and far between, and when they do occur, are usually of a more benign Mando-pop or Canto-pop variety.)

Buying Tickets

Check the entertainment listings in *Shanghai Daily* or the free English-language monthly papers for tourists and expatriates such as *that's Shanghai* (www.thatsshanghai.com), *City Weekend* (www.cityweekend.com.cn), or *Shanghai Talk.* Tickets for all arts performances can be purchased at their individual venues, or at the Shànghǎi Cultural Information and Booking Centre, Fèngxián Lù 272 (℡ 021/6217-2426), northeast of the Shànghǎi Centre, behind the Westgate Mall. Tickets for the Grand Theatre can be purchased directly at their box office (Rénmín Dà Dào 200; ℡ 021/6372-8701), and movie tickets can be bought at the cinemas. If you don't wish to do it yourself, your hotel concierge may be able to secure tickets for a fee. The Jǐn Jiāng Optional Tours Center, Chánglè Lù 191, in the French Concession (℡ 021/6445-9525 or 021/6466-2828, ext. 231; fax 021/6472-0184), can secure tickets for the Peace Hotel Jazz Bar, acrobatics, and other performances at a number of theaters and concert halls.

Nightclubs and bars are also booming, with joints opening and closing faster than night can turn into day. Barflies now have a choice of everything from glamorous Art Deco lounges to the seediest watering hole; live rock and jazz can be heard into the wee hours (although 2am is the official closing hour); and the dance club scene now employs DJs, foreign and local, to keep the younger set raving.

With a return to the rollicking times has come the return of drugs and sexual exploitation, a phenomenon that periodically receives some government attention, but largely continues unchecked. Having converted some of its newly won wealth into so many venues for culture and entertainment, Shànghǎi, it seems, is not about to go gentle into that good night.

1 The Performing Arts

ACROBATICS

Chinese acrobats are justifiably world famous, their international reputation cemented in no small part by the Shànghǎi Acrobatic Troupe, formed in 1951. While the troupe, one of the world's best, frequently tours internationally, they also perform at home, and an acrobatic show has become one of the most popular evening entertainments for tourists. You can catch your share of gravity-defying contortionism, juggling, unicycling, chair-stacking, and plate-spinning acts at the following stages:

Great World (Dà Shìjiè)   This infamous vice den of the 1930s has been converted into an entertainment center for the entire family, with day (9am–6pm) and evening (7:30–9:30pm) shows of acrobatics and martial arts on the outdoor stage in back, and Chinese opera, magic, and comedy on the second-floor stage indoors. At press time, the Great World had been closed for renovations, so call ahead to check. Xīzàng Nán Lù 1 (southeast of People's Square), Huángpǔ. ✆ **021/6326-3760**, ext. 40, or 021/6374-6703. Metro: Rénmín Guǎngchǎng.

Shànghǎi Centre Theatre (Shànghǎi Shāngchéng Jùyuàn)   A favorite venue with foreign tour groups, this luxurious modern 1,000-seat auditorium at Shànghǎi Centre is equipped for a variety of performances but specializes in performances by the Shànghǎi Acrobatic Theater, which almost nightly gives a 2-hour variety show featuring about 30 standard and inventive acts, from plate-spinning and tightrope walking to clowns and magic. Shows are held most nights at 7:30pm with some seasonal variation. Nánjīng Xī Lù 1376, 4th Floor, Jìng Ān. ✆ **021/6279-8663** or 021/6279-7132. Tickets usually ¥50 and ¥100 ($6.25 and $12). Metro: Jìng Ān Sì.

Shànghǎi Circus World (Shànghǎi Mǎxìtuán)   The new home of the Shànghǎi Acrobatic Troupe, this glittering arena in the northern suburbs houses a 1,672-seat circus theater with computer-controlled lighting, state-of-the-art acoustics, and a motorized revolving stage, all the more to impress the already impressed crowd. Performances are usually held Wednesday, Friday, and Saturday at 7:30pm. Check with your hotel for the current schedule and tickets. Gònghé Xīn Lù 2266, Zháběi. ✆ **021/5665-6622**, ext. 2027. Tickets ¥50 – ¥150 ($6–$18); "VIP" seats ¥280 ($34). No Metro.

OPERA

Shànghǎi has its own troupe that performs Běijīng opera (*Jīng Xì*) regularly at the Yìfú Theatre. Běijīng opera is derived from 8 centuries of touring song and

Symphony Enters Its 3rd Century

The Shànghǎi Symphony was founded in 1879 to entertain the colonialists, taipans, and other Westerners in the city's International Settlement and French Concession. Known then as the Shànghǎi Municipal Band, it was the first such music group in China. Over the decades, the Shanghainese embraced it, and Shànghǎi has produced many world-class classical musicians. After 1900, German Rudolf Buck was its conductor; after World War I, the Italian Mario Paci took over; during World War II, the symphony suspended operations. In 1956, performances resumed—it has held more than 3,000 concerts, produced tapes and CDs, and performed across Europe and North America (including at Carnegie Hall in 1990). Often judged to be the best in China, the Shànghǎi Symphony has been on a 5-year, 100-city world tour since 2002.

dance troupes, but became institutionalized in its present form in the 1700s under the Qīng Dynasty. The stylized singing, costumes, acrobatics, music, and choreography of Chinese opera often strike uninitiated foreigners as rather screechy and incomprehensible. It helps to know the plot (usually a historical drama with a tragic outcome), which most Chinese do. Songs are performed on a five-note scale (not the eight-note scale familiar in the West), and gongs, cymbals, and string and wind instruments accompany the action on the stage. Faces are painted with colors symbolizing qualities such as valor or villainy, and masks and costumes announce the performer's role in society, from emperor to peasant. Most Běijīng opera these days consists of abridgements, lasting 2 hours or less (as opposed to 5 hr. or more in the old days). With martial arts choreography, spirited acrobatics, and brilliant costumes, these performances can be a delight even to the unaccustomed, untrained eye. Regional operas, including the Kūnjù form, are also performed in Shànghǎi. Regular venues for opera include:

Kūnjù Opera House Kūnjù, born near Shànghǎi in the old city of Kūnshān, is the oldest form of opera in China, and Shànghǎi has China's leading troupe. This opera tradition uses traditional stories and characters, as does Běijīng opera, but it is known for being more melodic. Performances are held Saturday at 1:30pm. Shàoxìng Lù 9 (south of Fùxīng Lù), Lúwān. ✆ 021/6437-1012. Tickets ¥20 – ¥50 ($2.50–$6.25). Metro: Shǎnxī Nán Lù.

Majestic Theater (Měiqí Dàxìyuàn) Opera in Chinese is performed by local and touring groups in one of Shànghǎi's oldest and most ornate theatres. The theatre is worth attending just for the traditional atmosphere. Jiāngníng Lù 66 (at Běijīng Xī Lù), Jìng Ān. ✆ 021/6217-4409. Metro: Shímén Yī Lù.

Yìfū Theatre (Yìfū Wǔtái) This is the premier venue for Shànghǎi's opera companies. The Shànghǎi Peking Opera House Troupe, featuring some of China's greatest opera stars, performs here regularly, as do the Shànghǎi Kūnjù Opera Troupe and other visiting companies. Performances most nights at 7:15pm; occasional matinees on weekends at 1:30pm. Fúzhōu Lù 701, Huángpǔ. ✆ 021/6351-4668 or 021/6322-5294. Tickets ¥30 – ¥300 ($3.80–$38). Metro: Hénán Zhōng Lù.

OTHER PERFORMANCE VENUES

Shànghăi is the site of major national and international music, drama, and dance performances nearly every day of the year. The most frequent venues are listed here. In addition, local and international dramatic productions are often mounted at the **Shànghăi Dramatic Arts Centre,** Ānfú Lù 288, Xúhuì (✆ **021/6433-5133**), and at the **Shànghăi Theatre Academy,** Huáshān Lù 630, Jìng Ān (✆ **021/6248-2920,** ext. 3040), where experimental plays are sometimes presented. At press time, the finishing touches were being put on the new **Oriental Art Centre (Dōngfāng Yìshù Zhōngxīn),** near Century Park in Pŭdōng. When complete, this Paul Andreu–designed (he also designed the Pŭdōng Airport) complex with a symphony hall, theatre, and cinema, is supposed to be Pŭdōng's answer to the Shànghăi Grand Theatre.

Jìng Ān Hotel (Jìng Ān Bīnguăn)   In the San Diego Room of this historic Art Deco hotel, delightful weekly chamber concerts feature performers from the Shànghăi Music Conservatory (Sun at 8pm). Huáshān Lù 370, Jìng Ān. ✆ **021/6248-1888,** ext. 687. Tickets ¥20 ($2.40). Metro: Jìng Ān Sì.

Shànghăi Concert Hall (Shànghăi Yīnyuè Tīng)   This is where the Shànghăi Symphony, the Shànghăi Broadcasting Symphony, and the Shànghăi Chinese Music Orchestra perform most. Tickets can sometimes be obtained at the Shànghăi Centre ticket office. Yán'ān Dōng Lù 523 (south of People's Square), Huángpŭ. ✆ **021/6460-4699** or 021/6386-9153. Metro: Rénmín Guăngchăng.

Shànghăi Grand Stage (Shànghăi Dà Wŭtái)   This stage, located inside the Shànghăi Sports Stadium, is mostly used for large rock and pop concerts. Cáoxī Bĕi Lù 1111 (inside Shànghăi Stadium), Xúhuì. ✆ **021/6438-5200** or 021/6438-4952, ext. 2567. Metro: Shànghăi Tĭyùguăn.

Shànghăi Grand Theatre (Dà Jùyuàn)   This stunning space-age complex with three theaters (the largest seating 1,800) has quickly become the city's premier venue for international performers and concerts. Prices are usually ¥80 ($10) or more, and can top ¥1,200 ($150) for the best seats to popular world-class groups. When Yo-Yo Ma performed here, for example, seats ran from ¥120 to ¥600 ($14–$72); when the local symphony performed, the range was ¥100 to ¥280 ($12–$34). Rénmín Dà Dào 300, People's Square, Huángpŭ. ✆ **021/6372-8701** or 021/6372-8702. Metro: Rénmín Guăngchăng.

2 Jazz Bars

Shànghăi's pre-revolutionary (before 1949) jazz legacy has been revived for the 21st century: Not only are the old standards being played once again at that most nostalgic of locales—the Peace Hotel bar—but more modern and improvisational sounds can now be heard around town, and there's a greater influx of international jazz artists to these shores than ever before. Hotel lounges and bars are the most obvious venues for jazz performances, though what you get here is mostly easy-listening jazz. Once a year, the jazz scene perks up with the Shànghăi International Jazz Concert Series, a spillover from the Bĕijīng Jazz Festival that has been held in the second week of November each year since 1996, and that draws headline groups from America, Europe, Japan, and Australia. During the rest of the year, live jazz can be heard at the following places:

CJW (Xuĕjiā Juéshì Hóngjiŭ)   Hoping to lure the affluent "cigar, jazz, wine" crowd, this newly opened (Oct 2003), darkly moody bar on the top floor of the

Bund Center is strictly for those with expense accounts (though even the company accountant may balk at a ¥90/$11 average glass of wine and a ¥330/$41 Cohiba). Continental cuisine is served nightly from 6 to 10pm, an international jazz band plays from 9pm to midnight, there's a small dance floor, but so far, there's not too many patrons. A more intimate branch at Xīn Tiāndì (Lane 123, House 2; ✆ 021/6385-6677) is a little more frequented. Yán'ān Dōng Lù 222, Wàitān Zhōng Xīn, 50th Floor, Huángpǔ (top floor of Bund Center). ✆ 021/6339-1777. Lounge 6pm–2am. Metro: Hénán Zhōng Lù.

Club JZ   Started by two musicians as a kind of informal jazz "living room," Shànghǎi's newest venue for live jazz is quickly garnering fans for its talented house band, good acoustics, and intimate environment. The crowd, largely other jazz musicians, is obviously here for the music, which tends towards more improvisational jams. Daily 11am to 2am; band plays 9:30pm to 1am. Huáihǎi Zhōng Lù 1111, Room 102–3 (by Fēnyáng Lù), Xúhuì. ✆ 021/6415-5255. Metro: Shǎnxī Nán Lù or Chángshú Lù.

Cotton Club (Miánhuā Jùlèbù)   Live jazz nightly is the hallmark of this local institution, Shànghǎi's longest running and still the best venue for live jazz and blues. The bands are skilled, the tunes are tight, and the informal, darkly atmospheric club often attracts standing-room only crowds on weekends. Open-mic night is Tuesday. Hours are Tuesday to Sunday 7pm to 2am. The band plays Sunday and Tuesday to Thursday 9:30pm to midnight (10:30pm–1:30am Fri–Sat). Fùxīng Xī Lù 8 (at Huáihǎi Zhōng Lù), Xúhuì. ✆ 021/6437-7110. ¥35 ($4.30) minimum drink charge. Metro: Chángshú Lù.

House of Blues and Jazz (Bùlǔsī Juéshì Zhī Wū)   Another consistently excellent spot to sing the blues, this intimate joint has a lovely, relaxed, unpretentious vibe. It's the music (international bands are the norm), not the crowd or the drinks (a bit pricey for mediocre brew), that takes center stage. Tuesday to Sunday 7pm to 2am; band plays 9:30pm to 1am. Màomíng Nán Lù 158 (at Fùxīng Nán Lù), Lǔwān. ✆ 021/6437-5280. Metro: Shǎnxī Nán Lù.

Peace Hotel Old Jazz Bar   This is an institution, with nearly continuous performances since the 1930s and an octogenarian member or two from pre-1949 days still playing. The drinks are predictably expensive and the music (old New Orleans standards) isn't always super, but the atmosphere is sheer nostalgia and no evening could be more Old Shànghǎi than this. Heads of state have dropped in here to hear Shànghǎi renditions of all the old standards. Performances start nightly at 8pm in the historic Art Deco jazz bar at the rear of the main lobby. Nánjīng Dōng Lù 20, Peace Hotel (on the Bund), Huángpǔ. ✆ 021/6321-6888. Cover ¥50 ($6) at door, ¥80 ($9.60) in advance, which will assure a table. Metro: Hénán Zhōng Lù.

3 Dance Clubs & Discos

Shànghǎi has some of the most sophisticated and elaborate dance clubs and discos in China. The bar scene is lively, too, but clubs and discos are for those who want to party on the dance floor as well as at the bar—or at least for those who want to observe Shànghǎi nightlife at a pitch it hasn't reached since the 1930s. Shànghǎi's dance club scene relies heavily on foreign DJs, whether superstars brought in on a short engagement or total unknowns, though most locals don't know the difference in any case. Here's a list of the top venues, which like all trends are subject to overnight revisions.

Babyface   Incredibly popular but ultrapretentious spot with black-clad, headset-wearing bouncers. A DJ spins pop music but the sleek, sophisticated crowd is usually more interested in sizing up all who walk through the door. Balcony seating, which can be reserved, only fuels the voyeurism. Daily 8:30pm to 3am. Màomíng Nán Lù 180 (just north of Yǒngjiā Lù), Lǔwān. 📞 021/6445-2330. Cover: ¥40 ($5) Fri–Sat. Metro: Shǎnxī Nán Lù.

B.Boss   This new spot in the Tàikàng Lù area tries awfully hard to be trendy, from its understated gray brick wall exterior to its raging red walls inside and its dark smoky booths in the back. The large stage holds a nightly live band (playing mostly pop), and leggy models on Wednesday nights present a Latin dance/fashion show (9pm) that will cost male oglers a ¥40 ($5) cover. Sunday to Thursday 9pm to 2am (to 3am Fri–Sat); live music 10pm to 12:30am. Tàikàng Lù 210 (between Sīnán Lù and Ruìjīn Èr Lù), Lǔwān. 📞 021/6467-0031. No Metro.

California Club (Jiāzhōu Jùlèbù)   Very upscale dance club with international DJs and brash red decor. Extremely popular with the stylish Hong Kong set, expatriates, and all who would emulate them, this is a place where appearance (and money) counts. Ogle and be ogled. Sunday to Thursday 9pm to 2am (to 4am Fri–Sat). Gāolán Lù 2, Lan Kwai Fong at Park 97, Fùxīng Gōngyuán, Lǔwān. 📞 021/5383-2328. Metro: Huángpí Nán Lù.

Guandii   A Táiwān import, this popular club located in the southern part of Fùxīng Gōngyuán attracts a Táiwān, Hong Kong, and hip local crowd. A small rock garden with a waterfall aims to distinguish this from all the other redwalled, strobe-lit clubs, though the music, ranging from house to hip-hop, rages just as loudly if not more so. The bar touts 30 brands of champagne; a beer chaser will set you back ¥50 ($6.25). Sunday to Thursday 8:30pm to 2:30am (to 4:30am Fri–Sat). Gāo'ān Lù 2 (inside Fùxīng Gōngyuán), Lǔwān. 📞 021/3308-0726. Metro: Húngpí Nán Lù or Shǎnxī Nán Lù.

Pu-J's Big Top

The Pǔdōng New Area on the east side of the Huángpǔ River, across from the Bund, has been the poor stepsister of old Shànghǎi when it comes to entertainment, but this late-night Cinderella suddenly stepped into the glass slipper with the opening of **Pu-J's Entertainment Centre**—Shànghǎi's most complete nightspot complex—in the Grand Hyatt Hotel. Located on Podium 3 at the base of the 88-story Jīn Máo Tower, it is divided into four continuous-action zones. There's a Music Room devoted to live jazz performances; a Tapas Bar with Mediterranean snacks; a Dance Zone with a raised disco stage encircled by glass barstools on the floor and a white alabaster mezzanine bar above; and the must-have KTV (karaoke) lounge. The preening crowd is all about looks, so make sure your ball gown doesn't turn into rags at the stroke of midnight. Open Sunday through Thursday from 7pm to 1am; Friday and Saturday from 7pm to 2am; ¥100 ($12) cover.

Podium 3, Jīn Máo Tower/Grand Hyatt Shànghǎi, Shìjì Dà Dào 88, Pǔdōng. 📞 021/5049-1234, ext. 8732. Metro: Lùjiāzuǐ.

Judy's Too (Jiédí Xīcāntīng) Flashing lights, sweaty bodies, and a crowded dance floor all make this longtime institution an extremely popular dance spot with expatriates. The carousing here starts early and often spills out into the streets on the weekends. There's a not very good Mexican diner, Taco Popo, upstairs, but it'll do if you have to load up for the night ahead. Doors open at 6pm, but the action doesn't start until much later. Sunday to Thursday 8pm to 2am (later on weekends). Màomíng Nán Lù 176, Lúwān. ✆ 021/6473-1417. Metro: Shǎnxī Nán Lù.

La Belle (Lèbēi'ěr) The Continental restaurant gives way by 10pm to moody red lighting, deep sofas, nightly DJs, and expensive cocktails in this renovated "Green House" gem designed by old Shànghǎi Czech architect Ladislau Hudec. Sunday to Thursday 11:30am to 1am (later Fri–Sat). Tóngrén Lù 333, 2nd Floor (just south of Běijīng Xī Lù), Jìng Ān. ✆ 021/6247-9666. Metro: Jìng Ān Sì.

M-Box (Yīnyuè Hé) A longtime favorite with local 20-somethings, M-box got a face-lift in March 2004. Local live bands kick things off at 9pm nightly, with reservations often required for good seats. Daily 6pm to 2am. Huáihǎi Zhōng Lù 1325, Peregrine Plaza, 3rd Floor (intersection of Bǎoqìng Lù), Xúhuì. ✆ 021/6467-8777 or 021/6445-1777. Metro: Chángshú Lù.

Pegasus One of Shànghǎi's most popular and sweaty dance and clubbing venues, Pegasus is still going strong (and loud) with Chinese rappers bringing it on Thursday nights. Daily 6pm to late. Huáihǎi Zhōng Lù 98, 2nd Floor, Jīn Zhōng Guǎngchǎng, Lùwān. ✆ 021/5385-8189. Metro: Huángpí Nán Lù.

Real Love (Zhēn Ài) Located on the second floor over a bowling alley, this is especially popular with the preternaturally young and moneyed local crowd. There are just enough red velvet sofas to go around. Nightly 8pm to 2am. Héngshān Lù 10 (near Gāo'ān Lù), Xúhuì. ✆ 021/6474-6830. Cover (includes 1 drink) ¥30 ($3.60) weekdays, ¥40 ($4.80) weekends. Metro: Héngshān Lù.

Rojam (Lóng Shù) This has a giant dance floor, with guest DJs, including Paul Oakenfold, spinning techno and trance music. It attracts a young crowd that really likes the laser lights. Daily 8:30pm to 2am. Huáihǎi Zhōng Lù 283, 4th Floor, Xiānggǎng Guǎngchǎng (by Sōngshān Lù), Lúwān. ✆ 021/6390-7181. Cover ¥40 ($5) weekdays, ¥50 ($6) weekends. Metro: Huángpí Nán Lù.

4 The Lounge & Bar Scene

The big hotels often have elegant lounges on their top floors and some of Shànghǎi's best bars in their lobbies. Independent spots outside the hotels run the gamut from upscale to down-and-dirty, but those listed here are frequented by plenty of English-speaking foreigners (residents and tourists alike) in addition to hip, well-to-do Shanghainese. At press time, Màomíng Lù laid claim to being the hippest and hottest bar street, with Tàikàng Lù on the rise, Héngshān Lù still in the mix, and Jùlù Lù all but abandoned save for the most wretched dives. Expect drink prices, especially for imports, to be the same as, if not more than, you'd pay in the bars of a large city in the West. Tipping is not necessary, although it does make the bartenders happy.

Gay-friendly nightspots (subject to change, as the scene shifts but never disappears) include **Eddy's**, Huáihǎi Zhōng Lù 1877, by Tiānpíng Lù (✆ 021/6282-0521; daily 7pm–2am); **Home**, Gāolán Lù 18, west of Sīnán Lù (✆ 021/5382-0373; Sun, Wed–Thurs 8pm–2am, Fri–Sat 8pm–3am); and the recently refurbished **Vogue in Kevin's,** Chánglè Lù 946, no. 40, at Wūlǔmùqí Běi Lù (© **021/6248-8985;** daily 8pm–2am).

Amber (Hēi Jiāng Guǒ)   A refreshingly sophisticated bar in the strip of otherwise seedy Màomíng Lù dives, this is a popular place for theme parties (a puppet party was just one of the many wacky ideas from the owners). There's an international DJ on hand, but before it gets too loud, it's actually possible to hear your partner in the upstairs lounge where the neon-lit lime green cube tables cast a wonderfully weird toxic glow. Sunday to Thursday 4pm to 2am (to 3am Fri–Sat). Màomíng Nán Lù 184 (north of Yǒngjiā Lù), Lǔwān. © **021/6466-5224.** Metro: Shǎxī Nán Lù.

B.A.T.S.   This "Bar At The Shangri-La" is a long-running top spot in Pǔdōng for lively drinking, dancing, and listening to international bands (Latin sounds, Top 40), but alas, it's still a hotel bar crowded with hotel guests. The dance floor has plenty of disco lights. Bring your own bellbottoms. Tuesday to Sunday 6pm to 1am; music starts about 9:30pm. Basement, Shangri-La Pǔdōng Hotel, Fùchéng Lù 33, Pǔdōng. © **021/6882-8888,** ext. 6425. Metro: Lùjiāzuǐ.

Blue Frog (Lán Wā)   Brought to you by Kathleen of the KABB American bistro fame, this is an unpretentious "just-the-drinks-ma'am" kind of place. At least the ¥25 ($3) draft beer is reasonably priced. The crowd starts off mostly foreign, which has a funny way of drawing in the locals. Daily 7pm to 2am. Màomíng Nán Lù 207–23, Lǔwān. © **021/6445-6634.** Metro: Shǎxī Nán Lù.

Cloud Nine and the Sky Lounge   A top reason to spend the evening on the other (east) side of the river, this lounge atop the Grand Hyatt Hotel is the highest hotel lounge in Asia. It takes three elevators just to reach Cloud Nine on the 87th floor; you then walk up yet another flight to the intimate Sky Lounge on the 88th floor. Extraordinary panoramas abound, and the spring rolls, roving magician, and champagnes shouldn't be missed either. Daily 5pm to 1am. Shìjì Dà Dào 88, Grand Hyatt Hotel (Jīn Mào Tower), 7th Floor, Pǔdōng. © **021/5049-1234,** ext. 8098. Metro: Lùjiāzuǐ.

Dublin Exchange (Dūbǎilín)   Irish pub grub and Guinness for those who don't want to venture west of the Huángpǔ River. Sister bar to the popular O'Malley's, the Pǔdōng-based Dublin Exchange is more upscale, with a handsome dark wooden Irish interior. On tap are Guinness and Kilkenny, darts, and TV sports. Live Irish music is played some nights, but the bar has yet to attract significant numbers of lads from the western shore. Monday to Friday 10am to 11pm, Saturday 5 to 11pm. Yínchéng Dōng Lù 101, HSBC Building, 2nd Floor (east of the Oriental Pearl TV Tower), Pǔdōng. © **021/6841-2052.** Metro: Lùjiāzuǐ.

Face   A perennial favorite for its setting inside an elegant colonial mansion (on the grounds of the Ruìjīn Hotel), Face has a cozy curving bar, but even more cozy opium beds you can curl up on. Drink prices are a little above average but the sophisticated locals and out-of-towners don't seem fazed. Faces serves the two superb restaurants in the mansion (Lan Na Thai and Hazara), and you can order Thai and Indian snacks in the bar as well. Daily noon to 2am. Ruìjīn Hotel, Building 4, Lúwān. © **021/6466-4328.** Metro: Shǎnxī Nán Lù.

Glamour Room   The glamorous bar in M on the Bund has romantic views of the Bund through its picture windows and a full range of creative cocktails to complement its Art Deco surroundings. There is live music as well to keep the well-heeled set happy. Daily 5:30pm to 2am. Guǎngdōng Lù 20, 7th Floor (off the Bund), Huángpǔ. ✆ 021/6350-9988. Metro: Hénán Zhōng Lù.

Long Bar   This bar in the Shànghǎi Centre, popular with foreign businessmen and residents, puts on fashion shows every Tuesday and Thursday at 9:30pm and daily happy hours from 5 to 8pm. The pizzas, sports TV, and jukebox are also worth a whirl. Daily 11am to 3am. Nánjīng Xī Lù 1376, Shànghǎi Centre, 2nd Floor, Jìng Ān. ✆ 021/6279-8268. Metro: Jìng Ān Sì.

Malone's (Mǎlóng Měishì Jiǔlóu)   A favorite of foreign residents in the area, Malone's is an informal American-style pub and restaurant with a dartboard, pool tables, and a slew of TV monitors beaming down Western sports events. Every night but Monday the house band rocks the place. Young waitstaff is a little inexperienced. Daily 11am to 2am. Tóngrén Lù 255 (northwest of Shànghǎi Centre), Jìng Ān. ✆ 021/6247-2400. Metro: Jìng Ān Sì.

Manifesto *Finds*   At press time, Manifesto's well-heeled customers were mostly diners headed next door to its sister restaurant Mesa (p. 107). The owners of both, formerly of the nightclub Face and the restaurant T-8, are hoping that this will be just your regular neighborhood bar where you'll feel free to kick up your heels and down a few Brazilian cocktails. The deep soft cushion banquettes that run down one wall certainly give you no choice but to doff the shoes and stretch out. Exposed ceiling pipes, long drapes, floor-to-ceiling windows, and a well-stocked bar lend this place a cool, trendy vibe. Best of all, you can order tapas and sinful chocolate desserts from the restaurant. Daily 5pm to 2am. Jùlù Lù 748 (east of Fùmín Lù), Jìng Ān. ✆ 021/6289-9108. Metro: Chángshú Lù.

O'Malley's Irish Pub (Ōumǎlì Cāntīng)   This very comfortable pub in a colonial villa is extremely popular with Shànghǎi's foreign residents (especially with its outdoor garden). Kilkenny and Guinness are on tap, and it's easy to quaff one too many here. The bartenders are tops, as is the live Irish music that gets cranking around 8:30pm every night except Sunday. Daily 11:30am to 2am. Táojiāng Lù 42 (1 block west of Héngshān Lù), Jìng Ān. ✆ 021/6437-0667 or 021/6474-4533. Metro: Chángshú Lù.

Ritz-Carlton Bar   Relaxed, sophisticated, and outfitted with Shànghǎi's largest selection of cigars and a walk-in humidor, this is a fine place to enjoy live jazz under the soothing fiber-optic lighting. Daily 5pm to 1:30am. Nánjīng Xī Lù 1376, Portman Ritz-Carlton Hotel, Mezzanine, Jìng Ān. ✆ 021/6279-8248, ext. 5777. Metro: Jìng Ān Sì.

Shànghǎi Sally's (Shànghǎi Gùxiāng Cāntīng)   Located in a fine old colonial mansion opposite the Sun Yat-sen residence, Sally's was one of the first Western bars in town. A friendly informal British-style pub filled with a rowdy, regular, mostly expatriate crowd, the ground floor sports a pool table, dartboard, and foosball. Downstairs is a nightclub and lounge that operates only on weekends. Guinness on tap drops from ¥65 ($8) to ¥45 ($5.50) during happy hour (daily 4–9pm), while other selected beers are half off. Ride, Sally, ride. Daily 11am to 2am. Xiāngshān Lù 4 (at Sīnán Lù), Lúwān. ✆ 021/5382-0738. Metro: Shǎnxī Nán Lù.

Upstairs at Park 97   A complement to the raging California Club downstairs, this red and purple lounge tries to tone it down just a mite with a live jazz band and terrace seating. Watch out for the tipples that would separate you from your wallet. Monday to Thursday 8pm to 2am (to 4am Fri–Sat). Gāolán Lù 2, Lan Kwai Fong at Park 97, Fùxīng Gōngyuán, Lǔwān. ✆ 021/5383-2328. Metro: Huángpí Nán Lù.

Heavenly Bars

Shànghǎi's trendiest upscale pedestrian mall Xīn Tiāndì (New Heaven and Earth), located just a short stroll south of Huángpí Nán Lù Metro station downtown, is famous for its upscale restaurants and international shops. But this impressive development comes truly alive only after dark when Shànghǎi's hip and wealthy spill out of its pretty bars and lounges. For now, the top nightspots here include:

Ark Live House   A lively rock, jazz, and pop music venue with balcony seating, bar, restaurant, and cover for special events. North Block, House 15. (✆ **021/6326-8008.** Daily 5:30pm–1am.

Dr Bar   Quietest place in Xīn Tiāndì for a chat and drink over candlelight. North Block, House 15. (✆ **021/6311-0358.** Daily 4pm–1am.

KABB   This American bar and cafe with candlelight in the evenings is the place for laid-back music and musings. North Block, House 5. (✆ **021/3307-0798.** Nightly 7pm–2am.

Le Club at La Maison   A large dance floor and creative DJs attract a mostly local crowd. North Block, House 23. (✆ **021/6326-0855.** Nightly 6:30pm–2am.

Soho Pub   A friendly amalgam of East-West decor, Hong Kong and Japanese tourists, and American and British food, drink, and prices. North Block, House 3, Unit 5. (✆ **021/3307-1000.** Daily 6pm to 2am.

Star East   Martial arts film star Jackie Chan is behind this flashy but informal cafe and bar with cinematic touches. North Block, House 17. (✆ **021/6311-4991.** Daily 11:30am to 2am.

TMSK   Here's a bar made entirely from colored glass, owned by a Taiwanese actress and glass entrepreneur. Even the wine and martini glasses are works of glass art. North Block, House 11. (✆ **021/6326-2223.** Sunday to Wednesday 2pm to midnight; Thursday to Saturday 2pm to 1am.

5 Cinema

Old Shànghǎi was the Hollywood of China. Many of its films were produced at the Shànghǎi Film Studios (located in Xújiāhuì on Cáoxī Běi Lù across from the Xújiāhuì Cathedral) during the 1930s and 1940s. A two-bit actress with the stage name Lán Píng was among thousands who never achieved a starring role then, but she had her revenge later, when she met and married the young revolutionary who would become Chairman Máo. Known as Jiāng Qīng after 1949 (and later punished as the leader of the Gang of Four), she helped dictate the nature of communist cinema, drama, and other arts during the 1950s, 1960s, and 1970s. She was a star on the political stage for decades, but her real dream remained Hollywood.

Today, Shànghǎi is no longer the center of Chinese filmmaking although the Shànghǎi Film Studio continues to churn out some movie and television projects and the occasional joint-venture film with foreign filmmakers. At the same time, China limits the release of new Hollywood films to just 20 a year. In the past, most of these movies were dubbed in Chinese, but recently, some have been shown in Shànghǎi in their original language with Chinese subtitles. In the last 2 decades, Chinese directors have made some of the best films in the world, but some of these still can't be officially shown in China. Of course, the pirated versions of these politically sensitive films and of hundreds of Hollywood movies are usually circulating on Shànghǎi streets within hours of (and even sometimes before) the film's world premiere, wherever it might be. Given this sad state of cinematic affairs in Shànghǎi, there isn't much here for the non-Chinese-speaking visitors hungering for a night at the pictures. The only exception is when the **Shànghǎi International Film Festival** comes to town every June. Originated in 1993, when Oliver Stone chaired the jury, the festival attracts over 250,000 viewers to the screenings.

In the long interval between festivals, cinephiles can also get their fix at regular screenings sponsored by the **Canadian Consulate** (✆ 021/6279-8400), **German Consulate** (✆ 021/6391-2068, ext. 602), and the **Cine-Club de l'Alliance Francaise** (✆ 021/6357-5388). The following are the best venues for flicks in Shànghǎi, which still has a long road to travel to regain its reputation as China's Hollywood. Tickets range from ¥30 to ¥80 ($3.80–$10) depending on the theatre and the movie shown. For up-to-date listings, consult the English-language monthlies, such as *that's Shanghai.*

Cathay Theatre (Guótài Diànyǐngyuàn)
Chinese and Hollywood movies are screened in this 1930s Art Deco theater. Huáihǎi Zhōng Lù 870 (at Màomíng Nán Lù), Lúwān. ✆ 021/5403-2980 or 021/6473-0415. Metro: Shǎnxī Nán Lù.

Golden Cinema Hǎixīng
This big multiplex with four big screens, DTS and Dolby sound systems, and all the up-to-date conveniences often shows Hollywood and foreign films. Ruìjīn Nán Lù, 4th Floor, Hǎixīng Plaza, Lúwān. ✆ 021/6418-7031, ext. 122. Metro: Shǎnxī Nán Lù.

Paradise Theatre (Yǒng Lè Gōng)
Many English-language films with Chinese subtitles are screened here (part of the Shànghǎi Drama Arts Centre complex). Ānfú Lù 308, Xúhuì. ✆ 021/6431-2961. Metro: Xújiāhuì.

Shànghǎi Film Art Center (Shànghǎi Yǐngchéng)
The leading venue during the Shànghǎi International Film Festival, this modern cinema complex with five spacious theaters features Hollywood releases on the big screen. Xīnhuá Lù 160 (next to Crowne Plaza Hotel), Chángníng. ✆ 021/6280-4088.

Studio City (Huányì Diànyǐngchéng)
One of Shànghǎi's top multiplex theaters with six cinemas, it features Dolby surround-sound system, seats with built-in cup holders, and popcorn from the concession in the lobby. Nánjīng Xī Lù 1038, 10th Floor, Westgate Mall, Jìng Ān. ✆ 021/6218-2173. Metro: Shímén Yī Lù.

UME International Cineplex
The latest, greatest multiplex in the Xīn Tiāndì complex, it's fully modern and screens Hollywood movies in their original language, just like you never left home. English schedule follows Chinese when you call. Xīngyè Lù, Lane 123, no. 6, 4th Floor. ✆ 021/6373-3333. Metro: Huángpí Nán Lù.

10

Sūzhōu, Hángzhōu & Other Side Trips from Shànghǎi

The over-quoted Chinese saying, "In heaven there is paradise, on earth there are Sūzhōu and Hángzhōu" *(shàng yǒu tiāntáng, xià yǒu sūháng),* promises more than today's reality can deliver, but it nevertheless calls deserved attention to two famous destinations within an easy day trip of Shànghǎi: Sūzhōu, to the northwest, with its famous gardens and canals; and Hángzhōu, to the southwest, renowned for beautiful West Lake and the surrounding tea plantations. Sandwiched in between are a host of water villages of the Yángzǐ River delta, with their arched bridges, narrow canals, and Chinese garden estates all spruced up for mass tourism. It's worth visiting at least one of these pastoral towns, though picking one can be difficult. The most famous, and perhaps most complete water village, Zhōu Zhuāng, has

unfortunately become a nightmarish tourist trap, and has been replaced in our recommendations by the villages of Nánxún and Tónglǐ, which are not only less commercial, but boast unique features not found elsewhere.

Many travelers to these destinations book a group tour with an English-speaking guide to smooth the way. The main drawback to such an arrangement is that you will have but a short time to explore the sites, the duration dictated by the tour company's schedule rather than your interest (or lack of it) at any point. Alternatives are to hire a driver and car yourself, with the assistance of your hotel concierge, or to use public transportation (trains and buses), which is more grueling, but is also the cheapest and most fun way to experience this beautiful corner of China.

1 Sūzhōu, City of Gardens

81km (50 miles) NW of Shànghǎi

Sūzhōu's interlocking canals—which once earned it the moniker of "Venice of the East"—its unparalleled collection of classic gardens, and its embroidery and silk factories are the chief surviving elements of a cultural center that dominated China's artistic scene for long periods during the Míng (1368–1644) and Qīng (1644–1911) dynasties. Rapid modernization in the last decade has robbed the city of much of its mystique, but enough beauty remains, especially in quiet corners of its celebrated gardens, to merit at least a day of your time.

ESSENTIALS

GETTING THERE   Sūzhōu can easily be visited on your own. There are frequent **trains** (1 hr.; ¥25/$3) from the Shànghǎi Train Station, with the most popular trains for day-trippers being Train no. K818 which leaves Shànghǎi at 7:40am and arrives at 8:38am; and Train no. 5068, which departs at 8:28am and arrives at 9:37am. Return trains to Shànghǎi in the afternoon include no. T731

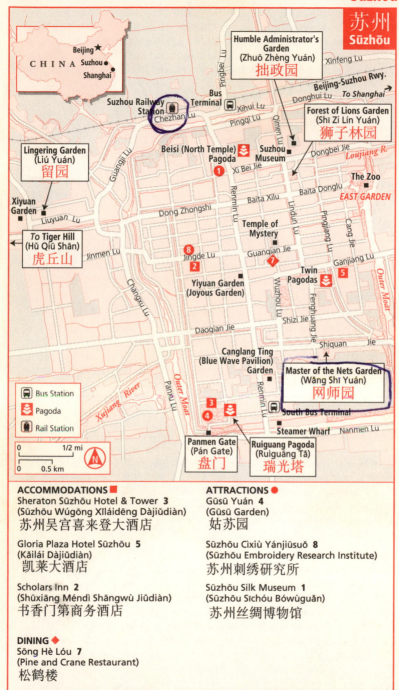

Sūzhōu
苏州
Sūzhōu

China inset: Beijing, Suzhou, Shanghai

Humble Administrator's Garden
(Zhuō Zhèng Yuán)
拙政园

Xinfeng Lu

Beijing-Suzhou Rwy.
To Shanghai

Bus Terminal

Donghui Lu

Suzhou Railway Station
Chezhan Lu

Xihui Lu

Pingqi Lu

Pingbei Lu

Qimen Lu

Forest of Lions Garden
(Shī Zi Lín Yuán)
狮子林园

Dongbei Jie

Loujiang R.

Lingering Garden
(Liú Yuán)
留园

Guangji Lu

Beisi (North Temple) Pagoda
❶

Suzhou Museum

Xi Bei Jie

Baita Xilu

Baita Donglu

The Zoo

EAST GARDEN

Xiyuan Garden

Liuyuan Lu

Dong Zhongshi

Renmin Lu

Lindun Lu

Pingjiang Lu

Cang Jie

To Tiger Hill
(Hǔ Qiū Shān)
虎丘山

Jinmen Lu

Changxu Lu

❽
Jingde Lu
❷

Temple of Mystery

Guanqian Jie
❼

Twin Pagodas
❺

Ganjiang Lu

Yiyuan Garden (Joyous Garden)

Wuzhou Lu

Fenghuang Jie

Shizi Jie

Outer Moat

Daoqian Jie

Shiquan Jie

Canglang Ting (Blue Wave Pavilion) Garden

Renmin Lu

Master of the Nets Garden
(Wǎng Shī Yuán)
网师园

Bus Station
Pagoda
Rail Station

Xujiang River

Outer Moat

Panyu Lu

❸
❹

South Bus Terminal

Steamer Wharf

Nanmen Lu

0 — 1/2 mi
0 — 0.5 km

N

Panmen Gate (Pán Gate)
盘门

Ruiguang Pagoda (Ruìguāng Tǎ)
瑞光塔

ACCOMMODATIONS ■

Sheraton Sūzhōu Hotel & Tower **3**
(Sūzhōu Wúgōng Xǐláidēng Dàjiǔdiàn)
苏州吴宫喜来登大酒店

Gloria Plaza Hotel Sūzhōu **5**
(Kǎilái Dàjiǔdiàn)
凯莱大酒店

Scholars Inn **2**
(Shūxiāng Méndì Shāngwù Jiǔdiàn)
书香门第商务酒店

DINING ◆

Sōng Hè Lóu **7**
(Pine and Crane Restaurant)
松鹤楼

ATTRACTIONS ●

Gūsū Yuán **4**
(Gūsū Garden)
姑苏园

Sūzhōu Cìxiù Yánjiūsuǒ **8**
(Sūzhōu Embroidery Research Institute)
苏州刺绣研究所

Sūzhōu Silk Museum **1**
(Sūzhōu Sīchóu Bówùguǎn)
苏州丝绸博物馆

(departs 5:07pm, arrives 6:30pm) and no. T715 (departs 5:54pm, arrives 6:42pm). The **Sūzhōu Train Station (Sūzhōu Zhàn; ℂ 0512/6753-2831)** is in the northern part of town on Chēzhàn Lù just west of the Rénmín Lù intersection. If you miss your train back, Sūzhōu is also well connected by **bus** to Shànghǎi. From Sūzhōu's **North Bus Station (Qìchē Běi Zhàn; ℂ 0512/6753-0686)**, buses depart for Shànghǎi (90 min.; ¥26–¥30/$3.25–$3.75) every 20 minutes from 7am to 6:20pm.

If you don't wish to visit on your own, check with your hotel tour desk to book a bus tour of Sūzhōu. The **Jǐn Jiāng Optional Tours Center,** Chánglè Lù 191 (ℂ **021/6445-9525**), offers a convenient 1-day group bus tour with an English-speaking guide and lunch, departing daily between 8:20am and 9am (from three pick-up points in town) and returning in the late afternoon. The price is ¥350 ($42) for adults, ¥175 ($21) for children 2 to 11, and free for children under 2. The same tour operator can also arrange a private tour with a guide, air-conditioned car, lunch, and door-to-door service (¥1,400/$168 for one person, ¥800/$96 each for two people, ¥600/$72 each for three or four people).

Sūzhōu is also linked to Hángzhōu to the south by overnight passenger **boats** on the Grand Canal. Tickets (¥60–¥130/$7.50–$16 per berth depending on class of service) can be bought at hotel tour desks and at the dock itself, Nánmén Lúnchuán Kèyùn Mǎtóu at Rénmín Lù 8 (ℂ **0512/6520-5720;** daily 6:30am–5:30pm) in the southern part of town.

VISITOR INFORMATION Sūzhōu has a tourist hot line (ℂ **0512/6522-3131**) that can help answer travelers' questions. **China International Travel Service (CITS),** at Dàjǐng Xiāng 18, off Guànqián Jiē (ℂ **0512/6522-3783** or 0512/6515-5805), offers a 1-day Panda Bus City Tour (¥350/$43 per person based on a two-person tour; cost per person can be reduced according to group size) with lunch and an English-speaking guide included. Or see the town on your own via **taxi,** with trips about town averaging between ¥10 and ¥20 ($1.25–$2.50).

EXPLORING SŪZHŌU

Central Sūzhōu, surrounded by remnants of a moat and canals linked to the Grand Canal in the west, has become a protected historical district, 3×5km (2×3 miles) across, in which little tampering and no skyscrapers are allowed. More than 170 bridges arch over the 32km (20 miles) of slim waterways within the town. The poetic private gardens number about 70, with a dozen of the finest open to public view. No other Chinese city contains such a concentration of canals and gardens.

CLASSIC GARDENS

Sūzhōu's magnificent formerly private gardens are small, exquisite jewels of landscaping art, often choked with visitors, making a slow, meditative tour difficult. Built primarily in the Míng and Qīng dynasties by retired scholars, generals, merchants, and government officials, these gardens, designed on different principles than those of the West, aimed to create the illusion of the universe in a limited setting by borrowing from nature and integrating such elements as water, plants, rocks, and buildings. Poetry and calligraphy were added as the final touches. Listed below are some classic gardens worth visiting.

FOREST OF LIONS GARDEN (SHĪZI LÍN YUÁN) ✦✦ Built in 1342 by a Buddhist monk to honor his teacher and reportedly last owned (privately) by relatives of renowned American architect I. M. Pei, this large garden consists of four small lakes, a multitude of buildings, and big chunks of tortured rockeries that are supposed to resemble lions. Many of these oddly shaped rocks, a standard feature of Chinese gardens, come from nearby Tài Hú (Lake Tài), where they've been submerged for a very long time to achieve the desired shapes and effects. During the Sòng Dynasty (A.D. 960–1126), rock appreciation reached such extremes that the expense in hauling stones from Tài Hú to the capital is said to have bankrupted the empire. Containing the largest rocks and most elaborate rockeries of any garden in Sūzhōu, Shīzi Lín can be a bit ponderous, but then again, you won't see anything like this anywhere else. The garden is located at Yuánlín Lù 23 (© **0512/6727-2428**). It's open daily from 7:30am to 5pm; admission is ¥15 ($1.90).

LINGERING GARDEN (LIÚ YUÁN) ★★ This garden in the northwest part of town is the setting for the finest Tài Hú rock in China, a 6m-high (20-ft.), 5-ton contorted castle of stone called Crown of Clouds Peak (Jùyún Fēng). Composed of four sections connected by a 700m-long (2,500-ft.) corridor, Liú Yuán is also notable for its viewing pavilions, particularly its **Mandarin Duck Hall,** which is divided into two sides: an ornate southern chamber for men, and a plain northern chamber for women. Lingering Garden is located at Liúyuán Lù 80 (© **0512/6533-7940**). It's open daily from 7:30am to 5pm; admission is ¥20 ($2.50).

HUMBLE ADMINISTRATOR'S GARDEN (ZHUŌ ZHÈNG YUÁN) ★★ Usually translated as "Humble Administrator's Garden," but also translatable tongue-in-cheek as "Garden of the Stupid Officials," this largest of Sūzhōu's gardens, which dates from 1513, makes complex use of the element of water. Linked by zigzag bridges, the maze of connected pools and islands seems endless. The creation of multiple vistas and the dividing of spaces into distinct segments are the garden artist's means of expanding the compressed spaces of the estate. As visitors stroll through the garden, new spaces and vistas open up at every turn. The garden is located at Dōng Běi Jiē 178 (© **0512/6751-0286**). It's open daily from 7:30am to 5pm; admission is ¥45 ($5.60).

MASTER OF THE NETS GARDEN (WǍNG SHĪ YUÁN) ★★★ Considered to be the most perfect, and also smallest, of Sūzhōu's gardens, the Master of the Nets Garden is a masterpiece of landscape compression. Hidden at the end of a blind alley, its tiny grounds have been cleverly expanded by the placement of walls, screens, and pavilion halls, producing a maze that seems endless. The eastern sector of the garden consists of the residence of the former owner and his family. At the center of the garden is a small pond encircled by verandas, pavilions, and covered corridors, and traversed by two arched stone bridges. Strategically placed windows afford different views of bamboo, rockeries, water, and inner courtyards, all helping to create an illusion of the universe in a garden. In the northwest of the garden, don't miss the lavish **Diànchūn Yí (Hall for Keeping the Spring),** the former owner's study furnished with lanterns and hanging scrolls. This was the model for Míng Xuān, the Astor Chinese Garden Court and Ming Furniture Room in the Metropolitan Museum of Art in New York City. Master of the Nets Garden is located at Kuotao Xiāng 11, off Shíquán Jiē (© **0512/6529-3190**). It's open daily from 8am to 4:30pm; admission is ¥15 ($1.90). In the summer, daily performances of traditional music and dance are staged in the garden (7:30pm; ¥60/$7.50).

TIGER HILL (HǓ QIŪ SHĀN) ★ This multipurpose theme park can be garishly tacky in parts, but it's also home to some local historic sights, chief among them the remarkable leaning **Yúnyán Tǎ (Cloud Rock Pagoda)** at the top of the hill. Now safely shored up by modern engineering (although it still leans), this seven-story octagonal pagoda dating from A.D. 961 is thought to be sitting on top of the legendary grave of Hé Lǔ, king of Wú during the Spring and Autumn period (770–464 B.C.), and also Sūzhōu's founder. Hé Lǔ was reportedly buried with his arsenal of 3,000 swords, his tomb guarded by a white tiger, which was said to have appeared 3 days after the king's death (hence the name of the hill).

Partway up Tiger Hill is a natural ledge of rocks, the **Ten Thousand People Rock (Wànrén Shí),** where according to legend a rebel delivered an oratory so fiery that the rocks lined up to listen. Another version claims they represent Hé Lǔ's followers who were buried along with him, as was the custom at that time. A deep stone cleavage, the **Pool of Swords (Jiàn Chí),** runs along one side of it, reputedly the remnants of a pit dug by order of the First Emperor (Qín Shǐ Huáng) 2,000 years ago in a search for the 3,000 swords. Tiger Hill is located 3km (2 miles) northwest of the city at Hǔqiū Shān 8 (② **0512/6732-2305**). It's open daily from 8am to 6pm; admission is ¥45 ($5.60).

WATER GATES & CANALS

Your best chance of catching what remains of Sūzhōu's once famous canal life is in the southern part of town in the scenic area just south of the Sheraton Hotel known as **Gūsū Yuán (Gūsū Garden).** Here you'll find in the southwestern corner **Pán Mén (Pán Gate),** built in A.D. 1351, and the only major piece of the Sūzhōu city wall to survive. **Pán Mén** once operated as a water gate and fortress when the Grand Canal was the most important route linking Sūzhōu to the rest of China. From here, you can still see a constant stream of canal traffic from motorized barges to hand-poled skiffs. To the south is a large arched bridge, **Wúmén Qiáo,** another fine place to view the ever-changing canal traffic. Near the main garden entrance in the east is **Ruìguāng Tǎ,** a seven-story, 37m-high (122-ft.) pagoda built in A.D. 1119 (admission ¥6/70¢ to climb) that affords some excellent views of the old city from its top floors. The rest of the grounds consist of a few lakes, gardens, various uninteresting newly built/restored temples and mansions, and an uninspiring amusement park. Gūsū Yuán is located at Dōng Dà Jiē 1 (② **0512/6826-7737**). It's open daily from 8am to 5pm; admission is ¥20 ($2.50).

SILK FACTORIES

Sūzhōu is synonymous not only with gardens and canals, but also with silk, which made Sūzhōu a city of importance in China. Since the Táng Dynasty (618–907), when sericulture began to develop here, Sūzhōu's silk fabrics have been among the most prized in China, and the art of silk embroidery is still practiced at the highest levels today. The **Sūzhōu Silk Museum (Sūzhōu Sīchóu Bówùguǎn),** Rénmín Lù 661 (② **0512/6753-6538**), just south of the railway station takes visitors through the history of silk in China, with an especially interesting section on sericulture complete with silkworms, cocoons, and mulberry leaves. Weavers demonstrate on traditional looms and there are lovely examples of silk embroidery. The museum is open daily from 9am to 5pm; admission is ¥7 (90¢).

The **Sūzhōu Cìxiù Yánjiūsuǒ (Sūzhōu Embroidery Research Institute),** Jǐngdé Lù 262 (② **0512/6522-2403**), is both a factory and sales outlet that has become a *de rigueur* stop on group tour itineraries. Here you can see artists hunched over, hand-stitching single and double-sided embroideries on silk gauze canvases. The finished embroidery, usually breathtaking, is mounted in a mahogany frame to be sold in the large store on the premises. Prices for these exquisite pieces are astronomical, of course, but you can purchase less expensive items as well, such as silk ties, scarves, pajamas, sweaters, and more (though prices here are still higher than in most retail stores). The institute is open daily from 9am to 5pm; admission is free.

WHERE TO STAY & DINE

If you plan to spend the night in Sūzhōu, the top hotel is the five-star **Sheraton Sūzhōu Hotel & Tower (Sūzhōu Wúgōng Xǐláidēng Dàjiǔdiàn),** Xīn Shì Lù 388, near Pán Mén in southwest Sūzhōu (② **800/325-3535** or 0512/6510-3388; fax 0512/6510-0888; www.sheraton.com/Sūzhōu). With 413 rooms starting at ¥1,660 ($200; usually no more than 10%–20% discount) for a double, this luxury hotel receives rave reviews from most visitors for its quality service and its Chinese-style buildings, which blend seamlessly with the landscape. Another good choice is the 296-unit Hong Kong–managed **Gloria Plaza Hotel Sūzhōu (Kǎilái Dàjiǔdiàn),** east of city center at Gànjiāng Dōng Lù 535 (② **0512/6521-8855;** fax 0512/6521-8533; www.gphSuzhou.com). Rooms (¥980–¥1,180/$118–$142 double; 30% discounts) were renovated in the last 2 years and have all the expected amenities as well as broadband access. A welcome option for those on a budget is the lovely 37-unit **Scholars Inn (Shūxiāng Méndì Shāngwù Jiǔdiàn),** newly opened in 2003 in the center of town at Jìngdé Lù 277 (② **0512/6521-7388;** fax 0512/6521-7326; www.sscholarsin@163.com). This modern three-star hotel with Chinese flourishes and books everywhere offers simple but clean doubles with air-conditioning, phone, TV, and showers for ¥300 to ¥520 ($38–$65).

Although hotel restaurants offer the most reliable fare and accept credit cards, Sūzhōu has a number of good restaurants that deserve to be tried, many of which are located on Tàijiān Nòng (Tàijiān Lane), also known as Gourmet Street, around the Guànqián Jiē area. One of the most famous local restaurants is the over 200-year-old **Sōng Hè Lóu (Pine and Crane Restaurant)** at Guànqián Jiē 141 (② **0512/6727-7006;** daily 8am–9pm), which serves Sūzhōu specialties such as Sōngshǔ Guìyú (Squirrel Shaped Mandarin Fish), Gūsū Lǔyā (Gūsū Marinated Duck), and Huángmèn Hémàn (Braised River Eel). Dinner for two ranges from ¥100 to ¥200 ($13–$25). Close by is **Wángshì Jiǔjiā** at Guànqián Tàijiān Nòng 23 (② **0512/6523-2967**), which also serves tasty local fare such as their house specialty, Jiàohuà Jī (Mud-baked Chicken) and Sōngzǐ Dōngpō Ròu (Dōngpō meat with pine nuts). Dinner for two averages ¥120 to ¥250 ($15–$31).

2 Hángzhōu & West Lake

185km (115 miles) SW of Shànghǎi

Seven centuries ago, Marco Polo pronounced Hángzhōu "the finest, most splendid city in the world . . . where so many pleasures may be found that one fancies oneself to be in Paradise." Hángzhōu's claim to paradise has always been centered on its famous **West Lake (Xī Hú),** surrounded on three sides by verdant hills. The islets and temples, pavilions and gardens, causeways and arched bridges of this small lake (about 5km/3 miles across and 14km/9 miles around) have constituted the supreme example of lakeside beauty in China ever since the

Hángzhōu

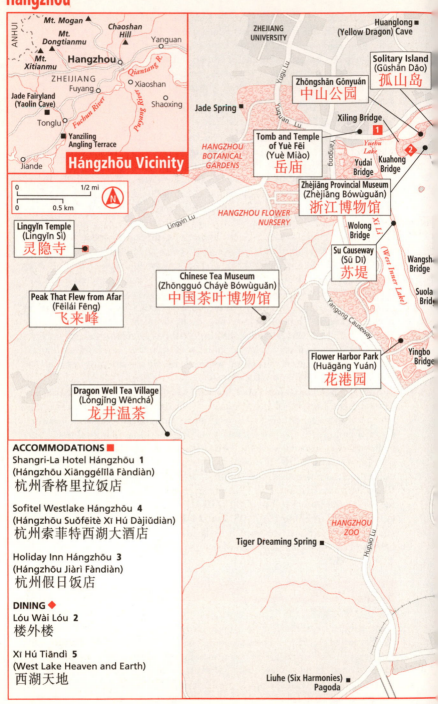

Hángzhōu Vicinity

ANHUI

ZHEIJIANG

Mt. Mogan ▲

Mt. Dongtianmu ▲

Chaoshan Hill ▲

Mt. Xitianmu ▲

Hangzhou

Yanguan

Qiantang R.

Xiaoshan

Fuyang

Shaoxing

Jade Fairyland (Yaolin Cave)

Fuchun River

Peyang River

Tonglu

Yanziling Angling Terrace

Jiande

0 ___ 1/2 mi
0 ___ 0.5 km

ZHEJIANG UNIVERSITY

Huanglong (Yellow Dragon) Cave ■

Solitary Island (Gūshān Dǎo) 孤山岛

Zhōngshān Gōnyuán 中山公园

Jade Spring ■

Yuquan Lu

Xiling Bridge **1**

Yuehu Lake

Tomb and Temple of Yuè Fēi (Yuè Miào) 岳庙

Yudai Bridge

Kuahong Bridge **2**

HANGZHOU BOTANICAL GARDENS

Yangong

Zhèjiāng Provincial Museum (Zhèjiāng Bówùguǎn) 浙江博物馆

HANGZHOU FLOWER NURSERY

Lingyin Lu

Wolong Bridge

Su Causeway (Sū Dī) 苏堤

Xi Li (West Inner Lake)

Wangsh Bridge

Lingyǐn Temple (Língyǐn Sì) 灵隐寺

Suola Brid

Peak That Flew from Afar (Fēilái Fēng) ▲ 飞来峰

Chinese Tea Museum (Zhōngguó Cháyè Bówùguǎn) 中国茶叶博物馆

Yangong Causeway

Flower Harbor Park (Huāgǎng Yuán) 花港园

Yingbo Bridge

Dragon Well Tea Village (Lóngjǐng Wēnchá) 龙井温茶

ACCOMMODATIONS ■

Shangri-La Hotel Hángzhōu **1**
(Hángzhōu Xiānggélǐlā Fàndiàn)
杭州香格里拉饭店

Sofitel Westlake Hángzhōu **4**
(Hángzhōu Suǒfēitè Xī Hú Dàjiǔdiàn)
杭州索菲特西湖大酒店

Holiday Inn Hángzhōu **3**
(Hángzhōu Jiàrì Fàndiàn)
杭州假日饭店

DINING ◆

Lóu Wài Lóu **2**
楼外楼

Xī Hú Tiāndì **5**
(West Lake Heaven and Earth)
西湖天地

HANGZHOU ZOO

Tiger Dreaming Spring ■

Hupao Lu

Liuhe (Six Harmonies) Pagoda ■

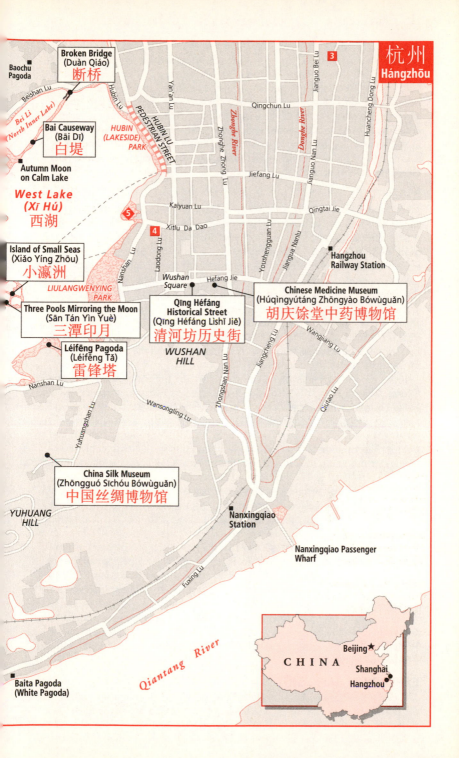

Broken Bridge
(Duàn Qiáo)
断桥

Baochu
Pagoda

Beishan Lu

Bei Li
North Inner Lake

Bai Causeway
(Bǎi Dī)
白堤

Autumn Moon
on Calm Lake

HUBIN
(LAKESIDE)
PARK

HUBIN LU PEDESTRIAN STREET

Hubin Lu

Yan'an Lu

Qingchun Lu

Jianguo Bei Lu

3

Huancheng Dong Lu

杭州
Hángzhōu

Zhonghe River

Donghe River

Zhonghe Zhong Lu

Jiefang Lu

Jianguo Nan Lu

West Lake
(Xī Hú)
西湖

Kaiyuan Lu

Qingtai Jie

5

Xitlu Da Dao

4

Hudong Lu

Nanshan Lu

Youshengguan Lu

Jianghua Namlu

Hangzhou
Railway Station

Island of Small Seas
(Xiǎo Yíng Zhōu)
小瀛洲

LIULANGWENYING
PARK

Wushan
Square

Hefang Jie

Chinese Medicine Museum
(Húqìngyútáng Zhōngyào Bówùguǎn)
胡庆馀堂中药博物馆

Three Pools Mirroring the Moon
(Sān Tán Yin Yuè)
三潭印月

Qing Héfáng
Historical Street
(Qīng Héfáng Lìshǐ Jiè)
清河坊历史街

Zhongshan Nan Lu

Jiangcheng Lu

Wangjiang Lu

Léifēng Pagoda
(Léifēng Tǎ)
雷锋塔

WUSHAN
HILL

Nanshan Lu

Wansongling Lu

Yuhuangshan Lu

Qiutao Lu

China Silk Museum
(Zhōngguó Sīchóu Bówùguǎn)
中国丝绸博物馆

YUHUANG
HILL

Nanxingqiao
Station

Nanxingqiao Passenger
Wharf

Fuxing Lu

Qiantang River

Baita Pagoda
(White Pagoda)

CHINA

Beijing ★

Shanghai

Hangzhou

Táng Dynasty when Hángzhōu came into its own with the completion of the Grand Canal (Dà Yùnhé) in 609. Hángzhōu reached its zenith during the Southern Sòng Dynasty (A.D. 1127–1279), when it served as China's capital. In 2003, much to the horror of purists, Xī Hú was enlarged in the western section with an additional causeway along its new western shoreline. New sights, shops, and restaurants were added to the eastern and southern shores. But the news is not all bad. Away from the commercial eastern edges of the lake, and especially in the surrounding hills and countryside, it's still possible to find pockets of peace and quiet. An overnight visit will allow you to appreciate more fully Hángzhōu's fabled beauty.

ESSENTIALS

Like Sūzhōu, Hángzhōu is perfectly tourist-friendly and is possible to see on your own. You can book a taxi for the day through your Shànghǎi hotel (Hángzhōu is a 2–3 hr. ride via the new Hú Háng Expwy.) or venture there completely on your own by frequent **trains** (2½ hr.). From Shànghǎi, the fastest train is the no. T701 leaving at 11:43am and arriving at 2pm. Soft-seat train tickets cost around ¥50 ($6) plus a typical ¥20 ($2.50) service charge if booked through hotel tour desks. Return train no. T706 departs Hángzhōu at 2:47pm and arrives in Shànghǎi at 4:47pm, while train no. K828 departs at 6:20pm and arrives at 8:09pm. The **Hángzhōu Train Station** (**Hángzhōu Huǒchē Zhàn;** ✆ **0571/5672-0222** or 0571/8782-9983) is in the eastern part of town. The no. 7 or no. K7 bus connects the station to downtown and the Shangri-La Hotel for ¥1 to ¥2 (12¢–25¢).

If you want to see Hángzhōu on a group tour, the **Jīn Jiāng Optional Tours Center,** Chánglè Lù 191 (✆ **021/6445-9525**), offers a somewhat rushed 1-day group bus tour with an English-speaking guide and lunch, departing at around 8am every day except Monday and Wednesday, and returning in the late afternoon. The price is ¥500 ($60) for adults, ¥250 ($30) for children 2 to 11, and free for children under 2. This tour can be extended to include overnight accommodations and a train back to Shànghǎi for an extra ¥350 ($42) for adults, ¥175 ($21) for children 2 to 11, and free for children under 2. The same tour operator can also arrange a private 1- or 2-day tour (on any day) with a guide, air-conditioned car, lunch, and door-to-door service for significantly more. If you're staying at the Shangri-La Hotel (see below) in Hángzhōu, their business center can also organize half- or full-day city tours.

Hángzhōu has an **airport** (✆ **0571/8666-1234**) about a 30-minute drive from downtown, with connections to Hong Kong, Macau, Běijīng, and other major Chinese cities, but not Shànghǎi. A taxi into town costs around ¥130 ($16) while an air-conditioned bus (¥20/$2.50) runs to the train station and the Marco Polo Hotel (nearest stop to the Shangri-La Hotel).

There are also overnight **boats** sailing the Grand Canal between Hángzhōu and Sūzhōu, with departures leaving from the Hángzhōu Wǔlín Mén Mǎtóu at 5:30pm and arriving in Sūzhōu around 7am. For information and bookings, call ✆ **0571/8515-3185.**

EXPLORING HÁNGZHŌU

The city surrounds the shores of West Lake, with modern Hángzhōu spread to the north and east. The lake is best explored on foot and by boat, while sights further afield will require a taxi or bus. Taxis cost ¥10 ($1.25) for 4km (2½ miles), then ¥2 (25¢) per kilometer. Add 20% after 8km (5 miles). Buses cost

¥1 to ¥2 (12¢–25¢) depending on whether they have air-conditioning. Bus no. K7 runs from the railway station to Língyǐn Sì via the northern shore of the lake (Běishān Lù) and the Shangri-La Hotel, while bus no. 27 runs along Běishān Lù to Lóngjǐng Cūn (Dragon Well Village), and bus no. Y1 makes a loop of the lake starting from Língyǐn Sì. Mountain bikes can be rented at the Shangri-La Hotel (see below) at ¥20 ($2.40) per hour and tandem bikes at ¥30 ($3.60) per hour.

XĪ HÚ (WEST LAKE)

Strolling the shores and causeways of West Lake and visiting the tiny islands by tour boat should not be missed. A **Lakeshore Promenade** 🎯—a combination walkway and roadway—encircles the lake, with the busiest parts along the eastern edge of the lake (or the western edge of downtown Hángzhōu). The once-busy thoroughfare Húbīn Lù has now become a rather pleasant tree-lined pedestrian walkway home to such outlets as Starbucks and Häagen-Dazs, while the area immediately to the south around Nánshān Lù and Xīhú Dà Dào is now known as Xī Hú Tiāndì (West Lake Heaven and Earth), a miniature version of Shànghǎi's Xīn Tiāndì (p. 168), right down to the *shíkù mén* (stone-frame) style housing and with some of the exact same restaurants. Following are the top attractions around the lake:

SOLITARY ISLAND (GŪSHĀN DǍO) 🎯   Situated just off the lake's northwest shore, this big island is accessible via the Xīlíng Bridge in the west and the Bái Causeway (Bái Dī) in the northeast. A roadway sweeps across the island, which is home to a number of minor sights, including the park **Zhōngshān Gōnyuán** (daily sunrise–sunset; free admission), which was once part of the old Southern Song imperial palace built in 1252, though nothing remains of it. A climb to the top of the hill affords views of the lake to the south. Also here is Hángzhōu's famous restaurant, Lóu Wài Lóu, and the large **Zhèjiāng Provincial Museum (Zhèjiāng Shěng Bówùguǎn;** ℰ **0571/8798-0281)**, which contains the oldest grains of cultivated rice in the world (developed 7,000 years ago in a nearby Hémǔdù village). The museum, with 12 exhibit halls containing ancient artifacts found in the province, is open Monday from noon to 4pm and Tuesday to Sunday from 9am to 4pm; admission is normally ¥15 ($1.90), though provincial and city museums in Zhèjiāng Province were granting free admission in 2004.

BÁI CAUSEWAY (BÁI DĪ) 🎯🎯   Solitary Island is connected in the east to downtown Hángzhōu by **Bái Dī,** a man-made causeway providing some of the finest walking around West Lake. Named after famous Táng Dynasty poet Bái Jūyì, who served as prefectural governor here in A.D. 822 to 824, the causeway was composed of silt dredged from the lake. It runs east for half a mile, rejoining the north shore road (Běishān Lù) at **Duàn Qiáo (Broken Bridge),** so named because when winter snows first melt, the bridge appears from a distance to be broken.

CRUISING WEST LAKE 🎯🎯   All along the lakeshore, but particularly on Húbīn Lù and near Gūshān Dǎo (northwest corner of the lake), there are boats for hire, from 3m (10-ft.), heavy wooden rowboats (where you take the oars) to small junks propelled by the owner's single oar to full-fledged ferries—flat-bottomed launches seating 20 under an awning. To tour the lake in a small junk, you have to bargain for the fare (usually about ¥60–¥80]/$7.50–$10 for an hour on the water). Individual rowboats cost roughly ¥20 ($2.50) with a ¥100 ($13) and passport deposit, while larger passenger ferries sell tickets for ¥35 to

¥45 ($4.40–$5.60), which includes entrance to the Island of Small Seas (below). There are ticket booths across the street from the Shangri-La Hotel and along the east side of the lake.

XIĂO YÍNG ZHŌU (ISLAND OF SMALL SEAS) ✸✸✸   Make sure your boat docks on this island at the center of West Lake. The **Island of Small Seas** was formed during a silt-dredging operation in 1607. As a Chinese saying goes, this is "an island within a lake, a lake within an island." Its form is that of a wheel with four spokes, its bridges and dikes creating four enclosed lotus-laden ponds. The main route into the hub of this wheel is the **Bridge of Nine-Turnings,** built in 1727. Occupying the center is the magnificent **Flower and Bird Pavilion,** an exceedingly graceful structure that is notable for its intricate wooden railings, lattices, and moon gates, though it only dates from 1959. It's open daily from 8am to 5pm; admission is ¥20 ($2.40).

SĀN TÁN YÌN YUÈ (THREE POOLS MIRRORING THE MOON) ✸✸   Located just off the southern shore of the Island of Small Seas are three little water pagodas, each about 2m (6 ft.) tall that have "floated" like buoys on the surface of West Lake since 1621. Each pagoda has five openings. On evenings when the full moon shines on the lake, candles are placed inside. The effect is of four moons shimmering on the waters. Even by daylight, the three floating pagodas are quite striking.

SŪ CAUSEWAY (SŪ DĪ) ✸✸   The best view from land of the Three Pools Mirroring the Moon is from the Sū Causeway (Sū Dī), the original great dike that connects the north and south shores along the western side of the lake. (A third causeway added in 2003, the Yánggōng Dī running parallel to Sū Dī in the west, is primarily for vehicles and is not as scenic.) Running nearly 3km (2 miles) and three times as long as Bái Dī, Sū Dī, named for Hángzhōu's poet-governor Sū Dōngpō (A.D. 1036–1101), is lined with weeping willows, peach trees, and shady nooks.

Sū Dī begins in the north across from the **Tomb and Temple of Yuè Fēi** (Yuè Miào; daily 7:30am–5:30pm; admission ¥25/$3), a 12th-century general famous in Chinese history for his unwavering patriotism. He was nevertheless accused of treason and executed, though later rehabilitated. Near the southern tip of Sū Dī is **Huāgǎng Yuán (Flower Harbor Park; ✆ 0571/8796-7386;** daily 8am–6pm; admission ¥12/$1.45), where there's a peony garden and ponds full of fat carp and goldfish.

LÉIFĒNG TĂ (LÉIFĒNG PAGODA) ✸ (Finds)   Completely rebuilt in 2003 on the south bank of West Lake, this totally modern octagonal steel and copper pagoda, reachable by escalator, would normally be a place to avoid were it not for the tremendous views of the lake it affords, as well as what lies beneath the modern construction. Discovered in 2001, and now safely preserved behind glass in the basement, are the brick foundations of the original Buddhist Léifēng Pagoda, which was built in 977 by Qiān Chū, the king of the Wǔyuè Kingdom, and which finally collapsed in 1924. The bricks you see were part of an underground vault used to store precious Buddhist relics, including a rare woodcut sutra, which was found among the ruins. The entrance fee of ¥40 ($5) is steep compared to Hángzhōu's other sights, but the panoramic views of West Lake in the north, the rolling hills of Lóngjǐng to the west, and the modern skyscrapers of new Hángzhōu to the east, are quite simply unbeatable. The pagoda and surrounding gardens (✆ 0571/8798-2111, ext.123) are open daily from 8am to 5:30pm (to 10pm July–Aug, and to 9pm in Sept for sunset and nighttime views).

OTHER ATTRACTIONS

LÍNGYǏN SÌ (LÍNGYǏN TEMPLE) ⭐   Located in the lush hills just west of West Lake, Língyǐn Sì (Temple of the Soul's Retreat) has been rebuilt a dozen times since its creation in A.D. 326. Don't expect to find any peace here, though, as the surrounding area seems to have been turned into one large amusement park. Entrance to the whole complex (open 7am–6pm) costs ¥25 ($3.10), while entrance to the temple itself is a separate ¥20 ($2.50).

The main attraction on the way to the temple is a limestone cliff, called **Fēilái Fēng (Peak That Flew from Afar),** so named because it resembles a holy mountain in India seemingly transported to China. The peak, nearly 150m high (500 ft.), contains four caves and about 380 Buddhist rock carvings, most of them created over 600 years ago. The most famous carving is of a Laughing Buddha from the year A.D. 1000. Scholars have deemed these stone carvings the most important of their kind in southern China.

The present temple buildings go back decades rather than centuries, but they are immense. The main Dàxióng Bǎodiàn (Great Hall) contains a gigantic statue of Buddha carved in 1956 from 24 sections of camphor and gilded with nearly 3,000 grams (104 oz.) of gold—not a bad modern re-creation.

LÓNGJǏNG WĒNCHÁ (DRAGON WELL TEA VILLAGE)   West of West Lake is the village of **Lóngjǐng (Dragon Well),** the source of Hángzhōu's famous **Lóngjǐng tea,** grown only on these hillsides and revered throughout China as a supreme vintage for its fine fragrance and smoothness. The best tea here is still picked and processed by hand. A popular stop near the village is the **Zhōngguó Cháyè Bówùguǎn (Chinese Tea Museum),** open daily from 8am to 5pm. Here you can comb through the extensive displays of Chinese teas, pots, cups, and ceremonial tea implements. The ¥10 ($1.25) admission includes a tea sampling and demonstration of the Chinese tea ceremony in a private tearoom.

Dragon Well Village itself, a few miles beyond the museum, is where much of the tea is grown and processed. Independent travelers are sometimes accosted by local farmers who will invite them into their homes, ply them with tea, and sell them a few pounds at inflated prices. This can actually be a good opportunity to buy this relatively expensive vintage at the source if you know how to bargain. The highest grade Xī Hú Lóngjǐng tea retails in Hángzhōu's stores for around ¥68 to ¥88 ($8.50–$11) per 50 grams (2 oz.), so aim for a price well below that.

ZHŌNGGUÓ SĪCHÓU BÓWÙGUǍN (CHINA SILK MUSEUM) Though Sūzhōu may be better known as a silk capital, Hángzhōu, too, produced its share of this much sought-after commodity. This large modern museum south of West Lake boasts a surprisingly comprehensive exhibit on the history and art of silk weaving and embroidery. Displays range from mulberry bushes and silkworms to traditional looms and exquisite pieces of damask brocades, all well annotated in English. There are demonstrations of traditional weaving techniques as well. The museum is located at Yùhuáng Shān Lù 73–1 and is open daily from 8:30am to 4pm; admission is ¥10 ($1.25).

QĪNG HÉFÁNG/HÚQÌNGYÚTÁNG ZHŌNGYÀO BÓWÙGUǍN (CHINESE MEDICINE MUSEUM)   Located east of West Lake in downtown Hángzhōu, **Qīng Héfáng Lìshǐ Jiē (Qīng Héfáng Historical Street)** has been the commercial center of Hángzhōu since the late 6th century. Restored in 2001 with Míng and Qīng dynasty–style buildings, this pedestrian mall has your usual quota of teahouses, restaurants, specialty stores, and also a few small museums. The most interesting of the lot is the **Húqìngyútáng Chinese Medicine**

Museum on Dàjǐng Xiāng. Established in 1874 by a rich merchant, Hú Xuěyán, the original apothecary, housed in a traditional courtyard mansion, has a striking dispensary hall with Chinese lanterns, and finely carved wooden pillars and brackets. Cubicle drawers along the walls contain an assortment of herbs, leaves, barks, seeds, and roots, much of which is on display in the many rooms that follow. There's also a large collection of stuffed animals valued for their particular curative properties such as leopard bone or the oil of the fur seal, this last section best avoided by animal lovers or PETA advocates. There are English explanations throughout. The museum is open daily from 8:45am to 3:45pm; admission is ¥18 ($2.25).

WHERE TO STAY & DINE

If you're spending the night, the best hotel is the very fine five-star, 384-unit **Shangri-La Hotel Hángzhōu (Hángzhōu Xiānggélǐlā Fàndiàn),** Běishān Lù 78, on the north shore of West Lake (✆ **800/942-5050** or 0571/8797-7951; fax 0571/8799-6637). Standard rooms with hillside or garden views cost ¥1,650 to ¥1,750 ($200–$210), while a room with a view of West Lake costs ¥2,250 ($270). You can expect 35% discounts off the rack rate. Another good option is the newly opened (2003) 200-unit **Sofitel Westlake Hángzhōu (Hángzhōu Suǒfēitè Xīhú Dàjiǔdiàn),** Xīhú Dà Dào 333, on the eastern shore of West Lake (✆ **800/221-4542** or 0571-8707-5858; fax 0571/8707-8383). Standard rooms start at ¥1,200 ($145), while lake-view rooms cost ¥1,736 ($210) before the average 40% discounts. The 294-unit **Holiday Inn Hángzhōu (Hángzhōu Jiàrì Fàndiàn),** Jiànguó Běi Lù 289, in the new central business district of northeast Hángzhōu (✆ **800/465-4329** or 0571/8527-1188; fax 0571/8527-1199), has doubles starting at ¥880 ($110).

For dining, try the Hángzhōu institution **Lóu Wài Lóu,** Gūshān Lù 30 (✆ **0571/8796-9023**), on Solitary Hill Island, between the Xīlíng Seal Engraving Society and the Zhèjiāng Library. Hours are daily from 11:30am to 2pm and from 5 to 8pm; specialties, such as Beggar's Chicken *(jiàohuà jī),* cost about ¥100 ($12) here, but a main course of local *dōngpō* pork costs half that. In the summer, this restaurant offers dinner cruises on West Lake. The Shangri-La Hotel's signature restaurant, **Shang Palace** (✆ **0571/8797-7951**), is more elegant and also more expensive, with a meal for two costing ¥200 ($25) and up. The international restaurants at the new development **Xī Hú Tiāndì (West Lake Heaven and Earth)** on the southeastern shore of the lake should provide plenty of comfort food.

3 Nánxún

123km (74 miles) W of Shànghǎi, 51km (31 miles) S of Sūzhōu, 125km (75 miles) NE of Hángzhōu

Of all the many water villages in the upper reaches of the Yǎngzǐ River, the Song Dynasty town of Nánxún is, for now, my favorite. Besides having it all—a charming mix of traditional houses that back right onto flowing streams, ancient stone arched bridges, narrow cobblestone lanes, friendly residents, and some of the most interesting mansions and estates to be found in any Yángzǐ water village (for their highly unusual mix of Chinese and Western architectural styles)— sleepy Nánxún was, at press time, still refreshingly free of the usual tourist glitter. The gauntlet of souvenir stands and the busloads of visitors had yet to make an appearance. But get here soon. At press time, space had been cleared for a gigantic parking lot. Located at the southern edge of Tài Hú (Lake Tài) on the boundary between Jiāngsū and Zhèjiāng provinces (it's officially in the

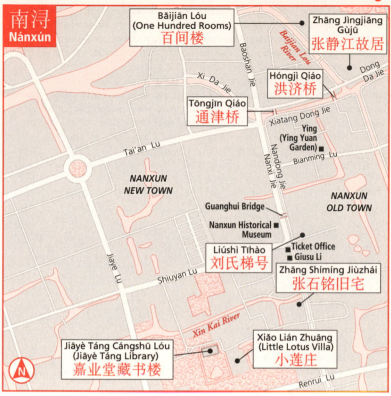

latter), it can be visited as a long day trip from Shànghǎi or combined with a longer trip to Sūzhōu or Hángzhōu.

ESSENTIALS

The easiest way to reach Nánxún (a 2–2½-hour ride from Shànghǎi) is by car, whether rented as part of an organized private tour, or separately arranged by your hotel concierge. Travel agencies can of course arrange private tours with the Jǐn Jiāng Optional Tours Center (Chánglè Lù 191; ✆ **021/6415-1188**) charging around ¥1,700 ($210) for one person, ¥1,000 ($125) each for two, and ¥700 ($88) each for three to four people. A cheaper alternative, though it's only available on the weekends, is the Nánxún tour bus (2½ hr.; ¥90/$12) round-trip, which includes the ¥45/$5.60 admission ticket) which leaves the Shànghǎi Sightseeing Bus Center (Gate 25 of the Shànghǎi Stadium/Shànghǎi Tǐyùguǎn) at 8:30am and returns at 5pm. For more information, call ✆ **021/6426-5555.**

Entry into the old town is free, but tickets to all the major sights cost ¥45 ($5.60) except for Liúshì Tīhào, which requires a separate ¥15 ($2) ticket. The main ticket office at Shíyuán Lù (✆ **0572/391-5115**) is open 8am to 3:30pm, though sights remain open until 4:30pm.

EXPLORING NÁNXÚN

Though a village existed here as early as 746, Nánxún was officially established around 1252 during the Southern Sòng Dynasty; the town reached its prominence only later in the Míng and Qīng dynasties. Today's town is made of a new

(1980) urban section to the west and the old town located in the east. Life in the old section, still a haven of relative peace and quiet, is largely clustered around the Gǔ Yùnhé canal in the north, and the small north-south tributary that flows from it. The main streets are Dōng Dàjiē in the north, and the north-south Nánxī Jiē and Nándōng Jiē.

The old town is best approached via Shìyuán Lù, at the eastern end of which is the ticket office. Because the worthwhile sights are scattered in opposite directions, one option would be to start from the southwest around Jiāyè Táng and Xiǎo Lián Zhuāng and slowly make your way to the northeast. Heading south, you can either walk along the canal or, better yet, take a **gondola** ride (¥60/$7.50 per boat for 30 min.). Watch for boats moored along the canal. (You can just as easily reverse the order by walking down and being poled back up.)

Many of Nánxún's traditional houses and garden estates are from the period between the late Míng and the late Qīng dynasties (1644–1911), when the town was a thriving center of trade, first in silk, then later in rice and salt. In fact, the town was so awash in wealth in the 19th century that it had its own list of the hundred richest residents, known as *sì xiàng bā gǔniú qīshíèr zhī huángjīnggǒu*, literally "4 elephants, 8 bulls, and 72 golden retrievers."

The richest animal of them all was a Qīng Dynasty merchant named Liú Yǒng (1826–99) who built his fortune from cotton, silk, salt, and real estate. His legacy is on view in Nánxún's most famous garden, the lovely **Xiǎo Lián Zhuāng (Little Lotus Villa),** which was built in 1885 as his private garden. The centerpiece here is an immense lotus pond that's especially beautiful in the summer (and underwhelming and scummy in winter). Anchoring the southeastern end of the pond is a Western-style two-story red brick house that was used as a retreat for the women of the house. To the southeast are two striking stone memorial archways *(páifáng)* built to honor Liú Yǒng's many charitable works as well as the chastity of the Liú womenfolk. Also here is the family ancestral hall.

In 1920, Liú Chénggān, Liú Yǒng's grandson, built the two-story courtyard-style **Jiāyè Táng Cángshū Lóu (Jiāyè Táng Library)** in the lot just west of Xiǎo Lián Zhuāng, where he reportedly spent a fortune accumulating up to 600,000 volumes of ancient books, among them rare finds such as the Sòng and Yuán Dynasty official histories, as well as block-printed books that were banned by the Qīng government. In the 1930s, the family was forced to sell much of its collection, and after 1949, what was left (of the books and the building) was given over to the Zhèjiāng Library. The rest of the compound is taken up by a sprawling garden with ponds, pavilions, and large clusters of rocks dredged up from Tài Hú (Lake Tài).

East of Xiǎo Lián Zhuāng is one of Nánxún's true treasures, the magnificent **Zhāng Shímíng Jiùzhái.** Built in 1905 by businessman Zhāng Shímíng (the grandson of one of the original four richest men in town), this unusual 4,000 sq. m (43,000 sq. ft.) estate features a front section done in a quintessentially Chinese style with beautifully carved stone frames, lattice windows and doors, and traditional Qīng Dynasty furniture. The buildings in the back, though, are distinctly Western in style (Zhāng did a great deal of business with the French): a rear courtyard, seemingly lifted right out of a New Orleans plantation, down to its abandoned, slightly decrepit air, sports a red and gray brick facade with French windows, wrought iron banisters, and Roman columns. Inside is an enormous ballroom with wainscoting, chandeliers, and a French mosaic floor.

You can almost hear the music and see the waltzing dancers, except, of course, this was during the time when female foot binding was still the norm, so there wouldn't have been many debutante balls. Don't miss the absolutely gorgeous blue and white flower-patterned stained glass windows on the second floor, which served as the women's quarters.

Across the main canal from here is another residence worth seeing: **Liúshì Tíhào** (separate ¥15/$2 admission). Built by Liú Ānshēng, third son of Liú Yǒng, this splendid **Hóng Fángzi (Red House),** designed in a similar Chinese-front/Western-back style, has a massive red brick rear facade with a second-floor balcony propped up by Greek columns, and deep-set arched French windows concealing dusty but still beautiful panes of stained glass. The building would look right at home in the West were it not for the unmistakably Chinese-style black tile roof.

Working your way north, cross the stone arched bridge **Tōngjīn Qiáo** (rebuilt in 1798) onto Dōng Dàjiē. Depending on the time of day, you should be able to get a pretty picture of the **Hóngjì Qiáo** (bridge) to the east. Dōng Dàjiē was one of the two busiest thoroughfares in Nánxún's heyday. At the eastern end of the street is **Zhāng Jìngjiāng Gùjū,** the former residence of Zhāng Jìngjiāng, a supporter of Sun Yat-sen's during the 1911 Republican revolution. Built in 1898, his house is much more traditionally Chinese with none of the Western flourishes found in the earlier mansions.

The real highlight in this northern section of town, however, is **Bǎijiān Lóu (One Hundred Rooms),** so named for the hundred or so houses that wind along both sides of the Bǎijiānlóu Hé (One Hundred Rooms River). These over 400-year-old row houses with white walls and black tiled roofs, attached to each other by a high white wall with a stepped crenellated roof, were reportedly built by Míng Dynasty official Dǒng Fèn for the servants of his female family members, though some find it hard to believe that such beautiful houses would be wasted on the help. Then again, it was a rich town. The front of each house typically has a covered walkway; lined up together, these walkways make for one long corridor running along each side of the canal. Bǎijiān Lóu offers one of the best photo opportunities in town—if you don't mind the modern-day wires, TV antennae, and hanging laundry, that is.

WHERE TO DINE

There are a number of informal restaurants and teahouses along Nánxī Jiē, Nándōng Jiē, and Dōng Dàjiē where you can take a break. The restaurants will serve inexpensive *jiācháng cài* (home-style Chinese cooking), with rice, noodles, and a variety of stir-fries such as *yúxiāng ròusī* (garlic pork) or *jiācháng dòufu* (home-style tofu). Local snacks include gelatinous candy like *júhóng gāo and gǔsǎo bǐng,* which some Westerners have likened to eating flavored chalk.

4 Tónglǐ

20km (12 miles) SE of Sūzhōu, 80km (49 miles) W of Shànghǎi

Surrounded by five lakes and crisscrossed by a skein of canals, the Sòng Dynasty town of Tónglǐ is more built up and commercialized than Nánxún, but it's still a pleasant enough water village with several impressive residences and gardens, and China's first and only official sex museum. It's not as if this picturesque town half an hour east of Sūzhōu needs any more publicity, having been a magnet for television and film crews since 1983. Try to visit on a weekday when you won't be overrun by the masses, though you just may find yourself in the midst of a film set.

ESSENTIALS

VISITOR INFORMATION   Entrance to Tónglǐ's old town is free but there is a ¥50 ($6.25) fee to visit the seven major sights listed below (not including the sex museum). Visiting hours are 8am to 5pm daily. There are introductory captions in English at the sights, but if you want greater detail, the **Tónglǐ Tourist Information Center** (✆ **0512/6349-3027** or 0512/6333-1145; daily 8am–5pm) southwest of Tuìsī Yuán offers English-speaking guides (¥160/$20 for sights in the old town as well as for the islet Luóxíng Zhōu; ¥120/$15 for Old Town sights; ¥60/$7.50 for Tuìsī Yuán).

GETTING THERE   Only a half hour away from Sūzhōu, Tónglǐ can just as easily be visited from there, especially if you decide to overnight in Sūzhōu. Your hotel tour desk in Shànghǎi or Sūzhōu can organize a day trip out here, as can any of the major travel agencies, but it's equally easy to do the trip on your own. From Shànghǎi, there is a Tónglǐ bus (2 hr., ¥110/$13 round-trip, includes ¥50/$6.25 entrance fee) which leaves the Shànghǎi Sightseeing Bus Center (Gate 25 of the Shànghǎi Stadium/Shànghǎi Tǐyùguǎn) daily at 9am and 10am and stops in Tónglǐ at a parking lot east of town on Huánzhèn Gōnglù, where there are free trams to shuttle visitors to the old town 2km (1¼ miles) away. Departure times may change so call ahead (✆ **021/5605-2581**) to confirm. From Tónglǐ, the 9am bus returns to Shànghǎi at 4pm and the 10am bus at 4:30pm. In general, you may not switch buses on the return trip unless prior arrangements are made, pending seat availability. Tónglǐ's public bus station (*qìchēzhàn*) is in the south in the new part of town on Sōngběi Gōnglù. From here, buses run to Sūzhōu (1 hr.; ¥12/$1.50) every hour between 7am and 5pm.

EXPLORING TÓNGLǏ

Buffeted in the south by new ugly concrete buildings, Tónglǐ's picturesque old town, located north of the Shàngyuán Canal (Shàngyuán Gǎng), is actually made up of seven islets connected to each other by over 40 arched stone bridges and fed by a network of some 15 canals. The town dates to the Sòng Dynasty (960–1279), though many of its surviving mansions are of later Míng and Qīng origin. As recently as 2 years ago, residents were still blithely going about their lives along the canals (it was not uncommon to see children bathing and women washing clothes in the streams), but all that messy living has now been largely cleaned up for tourists. The most common sight in the canals these days is a flotilla of tourist gondolas (and of course the inevitable trash that still results from hordes of visitors). You, too, can soak up the watery atmosphere by renting a **gondola** (¥60/$7.50 per boat for 30 min.) from various piers scattered along the canals.

Waterways aside, the rest of the old town is easily traversed on foot. The busiest street is **Míngqīng Jiē,** a winding lane flanked with Míng and Qīng dynasty–style wooden houses that have mostly been converted to shops and restaurants. The north end of this street leads to the old town's main attraction, **Tuìsī Yuán (Retreat and Reflection Garden).** Built in 1886 by a dismissed court official, this World Heritage garden is laid out from west to east in three sections, with the family's residences in the west, meeting and entertaining rooms in the center, and a small but cleverly designed landscaped garden in the

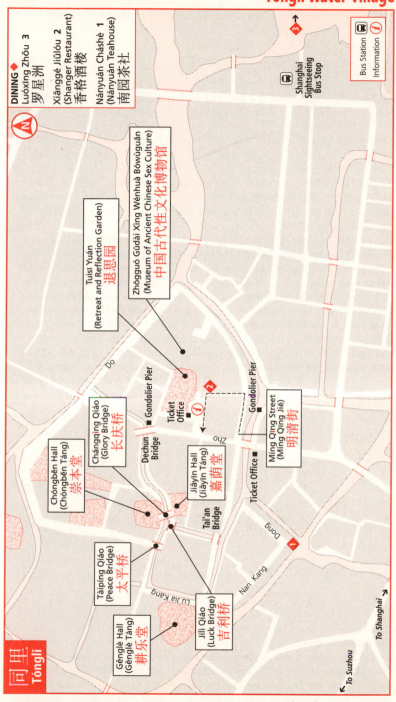

同里 Tónglǐ

DINING ◆
Luóxīng Zhōu **3**
罗星洲

Xiānggé Jiǔlóu **2**
(Shanger Restaurant)
香格酒楼

Nányuán Cháshè **1**
(Nányuán Teahouse)
南园茶社

Bus Station
Information

Shanghai
Sightseeing
Bus Stop

Tuìsī Yuán
(Retreat and Reflection Garden)
退思园

Zhōgguó Gǔdài Xìng Wénhuà Bówùguǎn
(Museum of Ancient Chinese Sex Culture)
中国古代性文化博物馆

Gondolier Pier

Chángqìng Qiáo
(Glory Bridge)
长庆桥

Chóngběn Hall
(Chóngběn Táng)
崇本堂

Ticket
Office

Dechun
Bridge

Jiāyìn Hall
(Jiāyìn Táng)
嘉荫堂

Gondolier Pier

Ming Qing Street
(Míng Qīng Jiē)
明清街

Tài'an
Bridge

Tàipíng Qiáo
(Peace Bridge)
太平桥

Ticket Office

Jílì Qiáo
(Luck Bridge)
吉利桥

Gēnglè Hall
(Gēnglè Táng)
耕乐堂

Lu Jia Kang

Nan Kang

Dong

To Shanghai

To Suzhou

east. The use of winding walkways with different shaped windows, jutting pavilions, and a reflecting pond make the garden appear larger than it is.

East of the garden is the former Lìzé Girls' School and the current home of the **Zhōgguó Gǔdài Xìng Wénhuà Bówùguǎn (Museum of Ancient Chinese Sex Culture; ℂ 0512/6332-2972)**. Relocated here from its two previous sites in Shànghǎi (see the box "China's Sex Museum" in chapter 6), the museum showcases the private collection of over 1,200 sex artifacts amassed through the years by Professor Liú Dálín of Shànghǎi University. Displays are divided into sections covering themes from sex and evolution to the sexual oppression of women, and sex in literature and the arts. The wide array of sexual relics includes ancient tomb paintings, statuary, and erotic devices, including a pottery penis with a woman's head dated 2000 B.C. There are also exhibits devoted to footbinding, furniture designed to enhance lovemaking, and "trunk bottoms" (explicit china figures placed at the bottom of dowry trunks by parents to instruct prospective brides). The museum is open daily from 8am to 5:30pm; admission is ¥15 ($1.90).

West of Tuìsī Yuán are three of the town's better-preserved traditional residences. The westernmost, **Gēnglè Hall (Gēnglè Táng),** which belonged to the Míng Dynasty nobleman Zhū Xiáng, is also the largest of the residences, with three major courtyards encompassing 41 rooms and a sprawling yard in the back. **Jiāyīn Hall (Jiāyīn Táng),** built in 1922 as the residence of famous local scholar Liǔ Yàzǐ, has high white walls and doorways fronted by upturned eaves—a style more reminiscent of the Southern Ānhuī Huīzhōu architecture. Here, the garden is in the center of the residence. The highlight at the 1912 **Chóngběn Hall (Chóngběn Táng),** with its four courtyards and three doorways, is the refined brick, stone, and wood carvings of scenes from Chinese literary classics, as well as of various propitious symbols such as cranes and vases (the Chinese word for vase, *píng,* is also a homonym for peace). Each row of buildings here is stepped increasingly higher than the previous, symbolizing the owner's wish that each subsequent generation in his family would attain greater success than the last.

The last two residences are connected by three bridges, **Tàipíng Qiáo (Peace Bridge), Jílì Qiáo (Luck Bridge),** and **Chángqìng Qiáo (Glory Bridge).** It was the custom in the old days to carry a bride in her sedan chair over all three bridges. Today, that custom has been resurrected for tourists who can don the proper red Chinese wedding finery and be carried in an old-fashioned sedan chair accompanied by a wailing *lúshēng* (wind musical instrument) and beating drums.

Also included in the price of the entrance ticket is **Luóxīng Zhōu (Luóxīng Islet),** located in the middle of Tónglǐ Hú (Tónglǐ Lake). Although there's been a temple here since the Yuán Dynasty (1206–1368), today's buildings are a strictly new (1996) mish-mash of Buddhist, Daoist, and Confucian influences. The boat ride over makes for a pleasant enough trip if you've exhausted the rest of the town's offerings.

WHERE TO DINE

As the official restaurant catering to foreign tour groups, **Xiānggé Jiǔlóu (Shanger Restaurant)** on Míngqīng Jiē (Míngqīng St.; ℂ 0512/6333-6988; daily 8:30am–8pm) has a handy English menu and serves local specialties and generic foreigner-friendly Chinese food. There are also many nondescript small restaurants along the same **Míngqīng Jiē** that serve basic *jiācháng cài* (Chinese home-style cooking) at reasonable prices, with a meal for two averaging ¥30 to ¥50 ($3.50–$6). The **Nányuán Cháshè (Nányuán Teahouse)** at the intersection of Dōngkāng Lù and Nánkāng Lù in the southern part of the old town is a restored Qīng Dynasty building where you can sip tea and nosh on local snacks as you look out over the canals from the second floor. Local specialties include the Tónglǐ version of braised pig's trotters, *zhuàngyuán tí, xiǎo xūnyú* (small smoked fish), and *mín bǐng* (a sweet glutinous rice pastry). Also look for the roasted chestnuts on sale in the streets.

Appendix A: Shànghǎi in Depth

1 Shànghǎi Today

No one knows quite how large China's largest city really is. Official figures for 2003 put the unofficial population at over 20 million, made up of an urban population of some 13.5 million registered residents, an additional 4 million registered migrants from the countryside, and an unregistered and uncounted floating population of at least another 3 million. At the same time, temporary foreign residents currently number around 70,000, not counting over 200,000 Taiwanese living in Shànghǎi while conducting business. The United Nations estimates that Shànghǎi's population will stand at 23.4 million by the year 2015. When Shànghǎi's unique architectural legacy and its recent economic transformation are factored in, it is easy to see why 7 of every 10 visitors to China come to Shànghǎi. This is China's economic, financial, and commercial center, its largest city, and the heart of China's future. No other super city in China, including Hong Kong and Běijīng, is more vibrant or fascinating.

Numbers, especially those put out by the Chinese government, seldom tell the full or realistic story, but in the case of Shànghǎi, even when the unverifiable, usually inflated numbers are taken with mountains of salt, they still point to the obviously formidable if unbalanced role Shànghǎi plays in China's economy. While the city has just 1.5% of China's population, Shànghǎi accounts for 5% of China's

Dateline

- **5000 B.C.** First evidence of settlements in the Shànghǎi area.
- **475–221 B.C.** Shànghǎi region is ruled by Chūnshēn, prime minister of the ancient Kingdom of Chǔ.
- **A.D. 5th–7th century** Shànghǎi is a small fishing village on the banks of the Wúsōng Jiāng (today's Sūzhōu Creek), which was known as Hù (for the crab traps in the river), and had its source in Tài Hú (Lake Tài). Later Shànghǎi would be known as Hù, and to this day, the name is still in use, as in the Hùníng Expressway connecting Shànghǎi to Nánjīng.
- **A.D. 751** During the Táng Dynasty, the Shànghǎi region is incorporated into the county of Huátíng.
- **1292** Shànghǎi benefits from its proximity to Hángzhōu, the capital of the Southern Sòng Dynasty (1127–1279), and quickly develops from a commercial town (*zhèn*) to a county seat (*xiàn*).
- **early 1400s** Míng Dynasty engineers dredge the Huángpǔ River (also known as *shēn*), making it the main tributary to serve Shànghǎi, and eventually eclipsing the Wúsōng Jiāng.
- **1553** City wall is built around what is today Shànghǎi's Old Town (Nánshì) as defense against Japanese pirates.
- **1603** Shànghǎi-born Xú Guāngqí is baptized Paul by Jesuit priest Matteo Ricci in Běijīng, and later deeds some of his land in Shànghǎi (today's Xújiāhuì, meaning Xú family village) to the Catholic Church, thus initiating Shànghǎi's first contact with the Jesuits.
- **1664** By the end of the Míng Dynasty, Shànghǎi has become a major cotton and textile center; its population will soon reach 200,000.

Gross Domestic Product (GDP), 11% of its financial services, 12% of China's total industrial output, and 25% of the country's trade. Textiles, steel, manufacturing, shipbuilding, and increasingly the retail sector, dominate the city's economy, which reports double-digit growth year after year. At the same time, Shànghăi accounts for around 10% of China's foreign investment, with firms from Volkswagen and Buick to Mary Kay, Amway, Hallmark, and Coca-Cola having invested billions in plants and personnel here. Not since colonial days (1846–1949), when Shànghăi was dominated by Western companies, has the port produced such an array of international investments.

At the beginning of a new millennium, then, Shànghăi has an air of prosperity and aggressive optimism that it has rediscovered from the heady days of the wealthy foreign concessions. Today's business, both domestic and foreign, has made Shànghăi quite wealthy by Chinese standards, with rising salaries creating an increasingly affluent middle class. The latter is comprised mostly of white-collar managers, many of whom earn upwards of ¥100,000 ($12,500) a year. As China's longtime center of shopping, there are also plenty of upscale places to dispose of the increased income. Residents are not only forward-looking and business-oriented, but fashionable. Shànghăi is a city of boutiques, malls, and up-to-date department stores. Year by year, it is catching up with Hong Kong as one of Asia's paradises for shoppers. Everything is writ large here. Shànghăi is not only home to China's first and largest stock exchange, it also contains over two dozen McDonald's, 50 KFCs, over 35 Starbucks, and over one million mobile phone users—not

1832 The British-based East India Company explores Shànghăi and the Yángzĭ River as a potential trading center for tea, silk, and opium, but is rebuffed by proud local officials.

1842 Following the First Opium War, the Treaty of Nánjīng opened five Chinese cities, including Shànghăi, to British consuls and merchants and their families. The British establish a consulate in Shànghăi to promote international trade; city population reaches 500,000.

1845 The British Concession is established. Miss Fay, the first unmarried American woman in China, arrives to help establish the Protestant Episcopal Mission.

1848 The American Concession is established in Hóngkŏu, north of the Sūzhōu Creek.

1849 The French establish their concession west of the old Chinese city and south of the British concession and are subject to direct French rule through the *Conseil d'Administration Municipale*.

1850 The first English-language newspaper in Shànghăi, the *North China Herald*, is launched, serving fewer than 200 readers.

1853–55 The Tàipíng rebels attempting to overthrow the Qīng government make Nánjīng their capital in 1853; the Small Sword Society, which claimed affiliation with the Tàipíngs, take over the old Chinese city, driving thousands of Chinese into the foreign concessions. Many Westerners become rich from building housing for the Chinese refugees. Small Sword Society eventually defeated by Qīng troops.

1854 Shànghăi Municipal Council is formed to rule the British Concession. British also form Chinese Maritime Customs to control trade.

1863 The International Settlement is formed from the merging of the British and American concessions, and is subject to rule by the Shànghăi Municipal Council.

continues

to mention the world's second largest department store and the tallest hotel on Earth. With prosperity, even sales of the venerable bicycle, formerly the chief means of transport in the city, have declined (from one million sales in Shànghǎi in 1990 to less than half that today). Meanwhile, the streets are crowded with some 600,000 vehicles (including 43,000 taxis) and 280,000 motorcycles.

Scratch the surface, however, and a slightly more complex picture emerges. The knock on Shànghǎi has always been that it is a city of appearances, a perception carried over from the early days when what seemed like a European city was in fact built on the backs of millions of Chinese, when its heyday prosperity and wealth masked a much crueler and more dire poverty for millions of Chinese. Today's detractors, often led by Shànghǎi's greatest competitor to the south, Hong Kong, like to claim that for all of Shànghǎi's glamorous exterior, there is no substance behind the flash. And indeed, a closer look beyond appearances shows that many of Shànghǎi's new handsome buildings remain empty, that your bathroom in the latest brand-new five-star hotel is already showing cracks, and that many more people are in fact window-shopping than plunking down cold cash.

The rosy numbers also mask the fact that while Shànghǎi has more than its share of overnight millionaires, ordinary Shanghainese must still be counted as residents of a developing rather than a developed nation. Even taking into account the highly inflated government figures, the city's average disposable income for 2003 was ¥14,867 ($1,858) per capita, one of the highest in the country, but still not high enough to keep up with Shànghǎi's soaring house prices (in 2004, the city's average housing price was over ¥5,000/$625 per sq. m, more than double the nation's average),

- **1871** The term "Shànghǎi," meaning to drug and forcibly kidnap hands for a departing ship, enters the English language; during this period, many sailors were literally "Shànghǎied," waking up at sea on clipper ships bound for China.
- **1895** The Treaty of Shimonoseki after Japan defeats China in the Sino-Japanese war allows Japanese to set up factories in Shànghǎi and other ports.
- **1912** Shànghǎi's old city wall is demolished following the downfall of the last imperial dynasty (the Qīng) and the establishment of the Republic of China under Sun Yat-sen, who lives from 1918 to 1924 in Shànghǎi. The foreign population in Shànghǎi tops 10,000.
- **1917** White Russians, fleeing the Russian Revolution, make Shànghǎi's international concessions their temporary home; by 1936, their population is 15,000.
- **1921** The Chinese Communist Party is founded in Shànghǎi, with Máo Zédōng in attendance.
- **1924** Triads make their presence felt as Dù Yuèshēng ("Big-eared Dù") takes power from Huáng Jīnróng ("Pockmark Huáng") as head of the Green Gang.
- **1925** A student protest on behalf of exploited Shànghǎi workers, known as the "May 30th Movement," leads to students being shot at by the Shànghǎi Municipal police, and paves the way for communist revolutionaries in China.
- **1927** On April 12, Chiang Kai-shek, the new leader of the Kuomintang (Nationalists), assisted by the Green Gang, round up and execute Communist leaders in Shànghǎi at today's Lónghuá Martyrs' Cemetery near Lónghuá Temple, thus initiating a protracted civil war.
- **1928** A greyhound racetrack (Canidrome) opens to 50,000 spectators in the French Concession.
- **1929** Shànghǎi millionaire Victor Sassoon opens the landmark Cathay Hotel (now the Peace Hotel) on the Bund; Noel Coward writes his play *Private Lives* here in 1930.
- **1931** Triad godfather "Big-Eared Dù" is elected to the governing council in the French Concession.

which have skyrocketed as a result of the large population influx and wealthy Chinese from around the country purchasing these units as investment properties. Little wonder, then, that living space is slim (under 140 sq. ft. per person); that many ordinary Shanghainese *(lǎobǎixìng)*, forcibly relocated to the outskirts of town because of mega-developments and downtown building projects, cannot afford even the smallest of homes; and that many others (including two million pensioners) must scrimp by on less than the official minimum wage (set at just above US$1 per day). At the same time, beggars can still be seen congregating at tourist sites, temples, and avenues where visitors are likely to appear. The unemployed, most arriving illegally without residence permits in Shànghǎi, can be sighted sleeping under bridges, awaiting work. The economic boom has brought other woes as well. Crime is on the rise (police arrested 5,000 pickpockets working just on buses in a recent 12-month period), prostitution is back in the bars and on the streets (after its complete eradication in the 1950s), and pollution is a major problem.

But Shànghǎi is nothing if not ambitious. This is a city of big dreams. Ever allergic to inactivity and resting on its laurels, Shànghǎi barely had time for the dust to settle from the massive modernization and reconstruction of the 1990s (which *New York Times* writer Ian Buruma hailed as "perhaps the greatest urban transformation since Baron Haussmann rebuilt Paris in the 19th century") before it won the bid in 2002 to host the 2010 World Expo, and is embarking on a new phase of building that will once again transform the city. City planners promise that Shànghǎi will soon be not only China's financial and manufacturing capital, but its "green" capital as well. Already, Shànghǎi has converted Nánjīng Lù to

■ **1935** Population reaches nearly four million, including 60,000 foreigners.

■ **1936** Lǔ Xùn, China's best-known modern author, dies at his residence in Shànghǎi's Hóngkǒu District.

■ **1937** Japan invades China, taking over Shànghǎi on August 13, initially leaving foreign concessions untouched. World War II in China is known primarily as the Anti-Japanese War. The Shànghǎi Municipal Council tallies 20,000 corpses of homeless people who have died in the streets during the year.

■ **1943** British and American forces relinquish their extraterritorial powers and concessions to the Chinese. In response to German requests to implement the Final Solution in Shànghǎi, the occupying Japanese army forces the stateless Jews escaping Nazism into a confined "Designated Area" in Hóngkǒu District.

■ **1945** World War II ends when Japan surrenders. American troops enter Shànghǎi.

■ **1949** Máo Zédōng proclaims the creation of the People's Republic of China on Oct 1, ending civil war; earlier, communists "liberate" Shànghǎi on May 25, without incident. Chiang Kai-shek, Soong Mei-ling, and the rest of the Soong family, except for Soong Ching-ling, escape to Táiwǎn. Chén Yì becomes Shànghǎi's first communist mayor. Remaining colonialists and foreign companies pull out within a year. CCP begins to shut down vice industries.

■ **1952** People's Park and People's Square are created on the former site of Shànghǎi's racetrack.

■ **1966–76** The Cultural Revolution, led by the Shànghǎi-based "Gang of Four," which includes Máo's wife, Jiāng Qīng, a former Shànghǎi actress, isolates and immobilizes China.

■ **1972** China reenters the world stage when Richard Nixon and Premier Zhōu Ēnlái sign the Shànghǎi Communiqué at the Jǐn Jiāng Hotel.

■ **1976** The Cultural Revolution ends with Máo's death.

■ **1978** A rehabilitated Dèng Xiǎopíng initiates "opening and reforms" *(gǎigé kāifàng)*.

continues

a pedestrian mall, remodeled the Bund and its promenade, revitalized many avenues and villas in the old French Concession, and created 1,800 hectares (4,500 acres) of greenway with trees and lawns (an area equivalent to 4,000 football fields). The latest environmental project is an ambitious one indeed: the Huángpǔ River Renovation Project, covering 20km (12 miles) of downtown riverfront on both shores, whereby the harbor will be transformed by green corridors, an elliptical canal, a maritime museum, marinas, riverside parks, and new housing estates.

If one can ignore the inevitable growing pains of any booming city, the present and the future look rosy indeed. The question of if and when the bubble will burst (consider, in addition to the high housing prices, that one now generally pays more for a cup of coffee in Shànghăi than back home), and other criticisms of superficiality, do not appear to have deterred Shànghăi's detractors and all others who would seek a better life from arriving in droves to stake out their share of the spoils. With an unprecedented degree of freedom (at least since the pre-revolutionary days) to express themselves, whether through their fashions or their purchases, just as long as it's not in the arena of politics, Shanghainese seem content, for the moment at least, to go along with their government's experiment of developing a country through economic but not political freedom. Love them or hate them, the Shanghainese—frank, efficient, chauvinistic, and progressive—are using their previous international exposure to create China's most outward-looking, modern, brash, and progressive metropolis. Simply put, no city on Earth seems more optimistic about its future than Shànghăi. A quick look through business and travel magazines and newspapers in the last year reveals that

- **1982** Shànghăi opens the Hóngqiáo Development Zone to attract foreign investors.
- **1985** Jiāng Zémín becomes mayor of Shànghăi.
- **1989** Weeks of student protest result in the Tiān'ānmén massacre in Běijīng; Shànghăi mayor Zhū Róngjī and predecessor Jiāng Zémín maintain calm in Shànghăi.
- **1990** Dèng Xiǎopíng designates Shànghăi to spearhead China's economic reform; the first (and largest) stock market opens; development of the Pǔdōng New Area on the east side of the Huángpǔ River begins.
- **1994** Jiāng Zémín, former Shànghăi mayor, becomes president. Metro Line 1, the second subway built in China, begins service.
- **1995** The Oriental Pearl TV Tower, the tallest such structure in Asia, opens in Pǔdōng, symbolizing the new Shànghăi.
- **1996** The new Shànghăi Museum, China's finest, opens on People's Square.
- **1997** Jiāng Zémín, Shànghăi's former mayor, becomes China's paramount leader after Dèng Xiǎopíng's death; Zhū Róngjī, former Shànghăi mayor, becomes the chief architect of China's economic revolution and China's premier in 1998.
- **1999** Nánjīng Lù Pedestrian Mall, Pǔdōng International Airport, the Yán'ān Elevated Expressway, and a second subway line open just in time to celebrate 50 years of communist rule. Fortune 500 Global Economic Forum takes place in Shànghăi.
- **2001** Shànghăi hosts the APEC Conference. China enters the World Trade Organization in December.
- **2002** Shànghăi wins the bid to host the World Expo of 2010; complete redevelopment of the Huángpǔ River and downtown riverfront launched.
- **2003** The world's fastest train, the Maglev, starts operating, connecting Pǔdōng Airport to the city.
- **2004** Shànghăi hosts the first Formula One Grand Prix race in China, and will continue to do so until 2010.

today's Shànghǎi is being hailed, once again, as the New York City or the Paris of China. Perhaps these comparisons are currently necessary to give foreigners a sense of the character and importance of the new Shànghǎi (and to entice visitors), but the pace and unique nature of Shànghǎi's current evolution suggest that one day in the not too distant future, Shànghǎi itself may well be the barometer city to which all others are compared.

2 Shànghǎi Ways & Manners

THE PEOPLE

Many of today's Shanghainese had ancestors who came from neighboring areas such as Sūzhōu, Níngbō, Hángzhōu, and even some from as far away as Guǎngdōng in the south. The Cantonese who came in with the British as their compradors, and the people from the southern seaport town of Níngbō, who were known as astute bankers, contributed greatly to Shànghǎi's development as a capital of business and trade. It used to be that Shànghǎi was welcoming to anyone who was smart, enterprising, and ambitious, and while that still holds true today, many of today's urban class-conscious Shanghainese tend to regard all non-native Shanghainese with some suspicion and condescension. Migrant peasants from poorer neighboring provinces such as Ānhuī and Jiāngxī who do much of the work Shanghainese deem too lowly, such as construction or trash collection, bear the greatest brunt of Shanghainese disdain. This chauvinism is not exclusive to the Shanghainese, of course; the term *wàidìrén* is used by Chinese throughout the country to refer to those not of their immediate native soil, and each group naturally tends to think itself superior to all *wàidìrén*. Still, the Shànghǎi brand of chauvinism is particularly strong, and while some of it may be slowly challenged with the increasing influx of educated and ambitious Chinese from other parts of the country, it's still alive and well in the Shanghainese preference for their own dialect whenever possible. Shanghainese is a sub-category of the Wú dialect, one of six major Chinese dialects not including Mandarin, but each dialect is so different from the others as to be considered by some experts as to be different languages entirely. Not surprisingly, the Shanghainese consider their dialect to be the most refined of all.

It's no exaggeration to say that there is little love lost between the Shanghainese and just about every other Chinese. The Shanghainese's biggest detractors are its main competitors to the north and south, the Beijingners and the Cantonese respectively, but the Shanghainese are regarded by almost all Chinese as superficial, arrogant, greedy, rude, ruthless, cunning, opportunistic, and unpatriotic. In the late 1990s, a popular refrain, *"Běijīng rén ài guó, Shànghǎi rén mài guó, Guǎngdōng rén chūguó,"* literally translated as "Beijingers love their country, the Shanghainese sell their country, while the Cantonese leave their country" (the Cantonese being historically the bulk of China's immigrants to foreign lands), captures the belief that the Shanghainese will sell anything and anyone down the river (the Huángpǔ perhaps) to make a quick buck, or *yuán*, as the case may be. Another Cantonese joke describes the Shanghainese as afraid, not of having his house burn down (because there's nothing inside), but of being caught in a rainstorm, which will make his clothes wet (the idea being that the outward appearance is all the Shanghainese has). Shanghainese are considered to be all bluster and no fight, as evident in the oft-cited examples of street arguments that may shatter the eardrums but never degenerate into fisticuffs. Shanghainese can also come across as being friendlier at the outset than the northern

Chinese, but the latter are widely viewed as being much more loyal once you get to know them, than are the fickle, shallow Shanghainese.

The Shanghainese themselves, too busy looking for the next money-making opportunity to disagree or bother with what they perceive as sour grapes, prefer to think of themselves as cosmopolitan, smart, shrewd, savvy, ambitious, open-minded, progressive, and enterprising, qualities they believe have allowed Shànghăi to lead the country's economic revolution and bull headlong into the 21st century. The Shanghainese are fashion setters and conspicuous consumers. That they enjoy a significantly higher standard of living than most other Chinese is, to them, both their entitlement and proof that they possess the necessary winning qualities. And indeed, foreign companies doing business in Shànghăi hail the locals as smart, eager, and hungry to learn. Some Chinese grouse that the Shanghainese are too slavish in their hurry to both please and ape Westerners, but the Shanghainese will just as quickly tell you that their historical exposure to foreigners has made them more open to Western ways, and therefore allowed them to succeed in today's global village. Whether in business (see below) or in social mores, the Shanghainese pride themselves on being pioneers willing to break old rules. Already, Shanghainese men, at least those of the post Cultural-Revolution (1966–76) generation, are considered to be a prime catch for young Chinese women, not necessarily because of their urbaneness or any putative business acumen, but because many younger Shanghainese husbands are known to do all the housework, the cooking, and the grocery shopping for their wives.

Even in China's most cosmopolitan and international city, however, there are still significant differences in customs and modes of behavior between the Shanghainese and foreign visitors. Though Shanghainese today have a remarkable amount of freedom in everything from fashions to critiquing corruption, politics is still a taboo subject for public discussion. If you broach any "embarrassing" topic—including questions about China's handling of political dissidents, the status of Tibet and Táiwān, restrictions on the media, abortion, prison labor, and the Tiānānmén Square protest—be prepared for stock answers from most people, but especially English-speaking tour guides. Some younger Shanghainese may seem eager to tackle such topics, but Western visitors sometimes find themselves surprised by the sincerely nationalistic responses to such questions. In general, feel free to ask the locals about anything, but remember that visitors can sometimes put their hosts—who may have government jobs—on the hot seat when posing politically sensitive questions. In return, visitors can expect some frank questions, not just from the Shanghainese but from the Chinese in general, about everything from your age and income to your marital status. You may answer such queries as you see fit, vaguely if you wish.

Another discernible difference in worldviews derives from the profound influence of Confucianism on Chinese society. Even though this uniquely Chinese philosophical tradition (dating to the 5th c. B.C when its founder, Confucius, 551 to 479 B.C., formulated a set of social and ethical precepts about the role of an individual in society, and Confucius's students later canonized his teachings which then became the state philosophy for almost 2,000 years) was completely repudiated during the Cultural Revolution (1966–76) and has never been rehabilitated since, aspects of Confucian philosophy continue to permeate Chinese life and culture to this day. Confucius's laying out of hierarchical relationships (between father and son, husband and wife, older and younger brothers, ruler and subject, and between friends) has led the Chinese to view the individual as part of greater wholes—of the family, foremost; of the workplace; and of the nation. The group has more power than the individual, and it must be consulted before decisions are made. In practical terms, this translates into a respect for hierarchies. Those of higher rank within any organization, be it a family or a business, hold the power over others and decide what those of lower rank may do. The individual often has far less autonomy and power in Chinese society than in Western societies—even when it comes to apparently insignificant matters. Many Westerners are often shocked to learn that until 2003, Chinese still had to seek permission from their assigned work unit *(dān wèi)* in order to get married. Other Confucian holdovers that generally still endure in modern Shànghăi are the respect for age, which is synonymous with wisdom and stature; the respect for higher education; and the respect for family matters, which are of more importance than those of work, politics, or world affairs. The importance of *guānxi* or connections in all aspects of Chinese life can arguably be traced back to the Confucian view of the individual as part of a larger nexus of social relationships.

While women are equal to men by law and by communist dogma, in fact women are often considered as they once were in traditional Chinese society: second best to men. Male children, who alone continue the family line, are still preferred over females by many couples. Even among foreigners, men are often treated with slightly more respect than women, although modern education and the influx of Western ideas have begun to erode such prejudices at the edges.

Where Confucianism, which stressed moral and ethical behavior, has been made a total mockery of is in the current exaggerated worship of money and the resultant corruption that now pervades every level of government, party, army, police, state, and private enterprise. Ever since Dèng Xiǎopíng told Chinese peasants that getting rich is glorious (part of his 1982 "opening and reform" *[gǎigé kāifàng]* programs—all but sounding the death knell of communism) this every-man-for-himself mentality has become the new *de facto* Chinese ideology. Of course, lip service is paid every now and then, usually on China's National Day (Oct 1), to communism, or at least to the Communist Party, but all savvy Chinese know to watch out for number one since neither the Party nor anyone else is watching out for them. Periodically, some egregious offender unlucky enough to be caught is given a capital sentence and made an example of, but by and large, corruption continues at every level, even as some in the government are doing their best to curb it. Prices are marked up so high not because one person or party is raking in all the spoils (though sometimes that happens, too), but because everyone along the way is skimming his or her share. These days, even when the *lǎobǎixìng* (ordinary Chinese) complain about corruption and graft, it is usually not out of any true moral or ethical outrage, but from their own failure to get a piece of the pie as well.

DOING BUSINESS

The vision of one billion consumers for their products has driven countless foreign companies to do business and set up factories in China in the last decade. However, as almost all foreign companies have discovered, some of who have pulled out, the consumers have not materialized as envisioned, and government red tape, inertia, corruption, false financial information filed by companies, and "mysterious" Chinese business practices, such as they are, have proven to be significantly more challenging than expected.

Like the rest of Chinese society, Chinese business relies greatly on connections or *guānxi*. Blood ties (however thin, even if it's the fourth uncle of your father's second aunt) and who you know will often get you in the door where a solid business proposal may not. The idea that business deals are often closed not in the boardroom, but indirectly over the umpteenth cup of *máotái* (a potent Chinese spirit) at a Chinese banquet, followed by a night of karaoke singing and more, and that the outcome is sometimes dependent less on the merits of the deal than on the willingness to play the game, can take foreigners (not to mention their livers, vocal chords, and other body parts) some getting used to. What is at play here, though, is the building of a relationship. Chinese business practices tend to emphasize building a strong relationship before closing a deal and it is ultimately the quality of the business *relationship* that will determine the success of the venture. Even when a deal is closed, however, there is no guarantee that it will be honored. Any reneging, though, is usually never direct, for that would entail a loss of face (see box below); instead, some important element or condition of the deal, which is always out of the control of the Chinese partner, will somehow fall through. As a result, contracts and agreements cannot necessarily be counted on to be worth more than the paper they're printed on. In fact, it is quite common that the Chinese will continue to press for a better deal even after the contract is signed. While the government has tried to establish something resembling an integrated legal system with enforceable pro-business laws, at present the Chinese court system is still such a quagmire that most foreign companies usually just write off the losses.

Saving Face

In social or business settings, the Chinese often take great pains to preserve "face," which involves maintaining one's self-respect while deferring important decisions to those of higher rank within a group. "Losing face" means to suffer embarrassment before others. To be criticized roughly by a visitor, for example, or to be asked to do something that is impossible, puts a Chinese person in a difficult position. "Saving face" is achieved by compromising, or sometimes by ignoring a problem altogether. You will seldom be told a direct "no" in response to a difficult or impossible request; instead you may get some more ambivalent answers such as "Maybe" or "I'm not sure" or "We'll see," which is usually tantamount to "No." Many Chinese will go to extremes to avoid settling a dispute or handling a complaint, because any loss of face in "kowtowing" to another could reflect badly upon their family and China, as well as upon themselves.

What visitors need to do when making requests or issuing complaints in Shànghǎi, then, is to control their tempers, avoid assigning personal blame, seek compromise when possible, and practice patience. A polite approach has a better chance of success than a more aggressive, brutally frank, or simply angry outburst. In a nation renowned for the size and inertia of its bureaucracy, some things are slow to be done, and some things are never done at all. It often helps to ask a person to relay your complaint or demand to a superior, remembering that a response may not be immediate.

As China's economic, financial, and commercial center, and gateway to the international business community, Shànghăi's business environment is better regulated and business practices are slightly more codified here than elsewhere in the country, though many of the same challenges exist. The Shanghainese believe that it is their previous exposure to foreigners that allows them today to be the quickest to adapt to international business practices and ways. But lest the foreigner think the Shanghainese are pushovers in their eagerness to do business, the Shanghainese are some of the shrewdest business and trades people you will likely encounter anywhere. Attitudes towards "getting mine" are just as prevalent (if not more so) here as elsewhere. Many foreign businessmen have discovered, much to their chagrin, that while the Shanghainese may be openly welcoming of foreign expertise and know-how, the hospitality sometimes extends only until they've received all the help they need to make a run of their own enterprises and become competitors to the foreigners who helped them in the first place. Still, the business opportunities are here for the taking, and those who can approach the process with some humility, massive doses of patience (delays are inevitable and you must expect to make several trips to China to solidify your business relationship before even cementing the deal), and as much knowledge as possible about China, the Chinese, and their culture (learning some of the language will also be greatly appreciated) will stand a greater chance of success. See "Etiquette & Customs" in chapter 3 for more information.

3 The Shànghăi Menu

Food plays such an important role in Chinese culture that when people meet, they often greet each other with the words, "Have you eaten" *(Chī le ma?)*. For the visitor to China, food will (or should) be one of the highlights of your trip. If you're traveling on a group tour, you'll likely be fed fare that is fairly ordinary and generic, and above all inexpensive. Try to sneak out for an independent Chinese meal if possible. Mealtimes are practically sacred, and you'll find, especially if you are on an organized tour, that visits and events are often scheduled around meals, which are usually taken early (11:30am–noon for lunch and 5:30–6pm for dinner). In a city such as Shànghăi, few businesses or tourist attractions close for the lunch hour, though this is more common in smaller Chinese towns.

Following Daoist principles, Chinese cooking aims for a balance of flavors, textures, and ingredients. Certain foods are thought to have *yáng* (warming) or *yīn* (cooling) properties, and the presence of one should ideally be offset by the presence of its opposite. Seldom is one ingredient used exclusively, and meals should reflect that harmonious blend of meat and vegetables, spicy and bland, and so forth. China has a staggering variety of regional cuisines (see box in chapter 5, p. 91), which reflect the different ingredients available in a particular environment, and also emphasize different cooking methods, and you are encouraged to try as many of these as possible while you are in the country. Chances are that little of it will taste like the food from the neighborhood Chinese restaurant back home; if anything, it'll taste better.

While you can sample almost any of the diverse Chinese cuisines in Shànghăi (though admittedly, few ethnic Chinese cuisines make it here entirely intact, as the local preference for sweet invariably finds its way onto most menus), the emphasis here is on Shànghăi's traditional cuisine, also known locally as *běnbāng cài*. Considered a branch of the Huáiyáng style of cooking, Shànghăi cooking favors sugar, soy sauce, and oil, and seafood is featured prominently. While it is true, as some critics allege, that traditional Shànghăi cooking does tend towards the oily and the over-sweet, many typical Shànghăi dishes are simply delicious and deserve to be tried, as it's likely you won't find much like it back home. You can find the following typical Shànghăi dishes in any local restaurant serving *bĕnbāng cài:* cold appetizers such as *xūnyú* (smoked fish), *kăofū* (braised gluten), *zuì jī* (drunken chicken marinated in Shàoxīng wine), and *pídàn dòufu* (tofu with "thousand year" eggs); snacks like *xiăolóng bāo* (steamed pork dumplings with gelatinous broth), *shēngjiān bāo* (pork-stuffed fried bread dumplings), and *jiŭcài hézi* (leek pie); traditional dishes such as *chăo niángāo* (fried rice cakes), *Shànghăi cū chăomiàn* (Shànghăi fried thick noodles), *shīzĭ tóu* (braised "lion's head" meatballs), *típáng* (braised pig trotters), *méicài kòuròu* (braised pork with preserved vegetables), *yóumèn sŭn* (braised fresh winter shoots), *jiāobái* (wild rice stems), *shuĭjīng xiārén* (crystal prawns), *dàzhá xiè* (hairy crab), *xuĕcài máodòu băiyè* (bean-curd sheets with soy beans and salted winter greens), and the soup *yīdŭxiān;* and desserts including *bābăofàn* (eight treasure glutinous rice) and *dòushā sūbĭng* (red bean paste in flaky pastry).

Regional differences notwithstanding, Chinese food is usually eaten family style, with a number of dishes to be shared by all. If you find yourself dining solo, you can ask for *xiăo pán* (small portions), usually about 70% of the full dish and the full cost, though not all restaurants will accommodate this request. Dishes can arrive in random order, though most meals usually begin with cold appetizers *(liáng cài),* then move on to seafood, meat, and vegetable main dishes. Except in Cantonese cuisine when it's taken as one of the first courses, soup is usually served last. Plain rice is typically eaten as an accompaniment in your average proletarian setting, but is seldom voluntarily offered in finer dining, where the emphasis is supposed to be on the subtle flavors of each dish and ingredient, and rice is considered a mere filler. (You can always request rice if it's not automatically offered.) Outside of the more sophisticated restaurants, the food in many places throughout the country can be a bit oilier than foreigners are used to; if this is a cause for concern, you can specify beforehand *shăo yóu* ("less oil"), though don't expect this request always to be honored. In your average Chinese restaurant, dessert, if it exists, usually consists of a few orange wedges and not much else, though Shànghăi and Cantonese cuisines feature a slightly wider choice of sweets such as red bean pastries *(dòushā sūbĭng),* and sesame seed paste *(zhīma hú).* Tea is usually served free, though if you're asked what kind of tea you want, you'll probably be charged for it. A vintage like *lóngjĭng* tea (from the Hángzhōu) is considerably more expensive than something like your average chrysanthemum *(júhuā chá)* or jasmine tea *(mòlihuā chá).* Napkins and chopsticks should be free, though if you're given a pre-wrapped package of tissues, you'll likely be charged for opening it, and possibly for the peanuts as well. In general, there is no tipping, though a few restaurants outside the major hotels may add on a service charge, which usually guarantees you won't get much in the way of service.

The following glossary of Chinese dishes is listed in alphabetical order in pīnyīn with Chinese characters. The first section is a list of snacks and dishes (also called *jiācháng cài* or "home-style" cooking) widely available in most restaurants in any given Chinese city, while the second is a list of typical Shànghăi dishes as well as specialized dishes recommended in the restaurant reviews in chapter 5.

WIDELY AVAILABLE DISHES & SNACKS

PINYIN	ENGLISH	CHINESE
bābǎo zhōu	rice porridge with nuts and berries	八宝粥
bāozi	stuffed steamed buns	包子
bīngqílín	ice cream	冰淇淋
chǎofàn	fried rice	炒饭
chǎo miàn	fried noodles	炒面
chūnjuǎn	spring rolls	春卷
diǎnxin	dim sum (snacks)	点心
dòujiāng	soy bean milk	豆浆
gānbiān sìjìdòu	sautéed string beans	干煸四季豆
gōngbào jīdīng	spicy diced chicken with cashews	宫爆鸡丁
guōtiē	fried dumplings/ potstickers	锅贴
huíguō ròu	twice-cooked pork	回锅肉
húntun	wonton (dumpling soup)	馄饨
huǒguō	hot pot	火锅
jiācháng dòufu	homestyle tofu	家常豆腐
jiāoyán páigǔ	salt-and-pepper pork ribs	椒盐排骨
jiǎozi	dumplings/ Chinese ravioli	饺子
jīngjiàng ròusī	shredded pork in soy sauce	京酱肉丝
júhuā chá	chrysanthemum tea	菊花茶
lā miàn	hand-pulled noodles	拉面
lóngjǐng chá	Lóngjǐng Tea (from Hángzhōu)	龙井茶
mápó dòufu	spicy tofu with chopped meat	麻婆豆腐
miàntiáo	noodles	面条
mǐfàn	rice	米饭
mòlihuā chá	jasmine tea	茉莉花茶
mù xū ròu	sliced pork with fungus (mushu pork)	木须肉
niúròu miàn	beef noodles	牛肉面
ròu chuàn	kabobs	肉串
sānxiān	"three flavors" (usually prawn, mushroom, pork)	三鲜
shuǐjiǎo	boiled dumplings	水饺
suānlà tāng	hot-and-sour soup	酸辣汤
sù miàn	vegetarian noodles	素面
sù shíjǐn	mixed vegetables	素什锦
xiàn bǐng	pork- or vegetable-stuffed fried pancake	馅饼
xiānggū càibāo	vegetable steamed buns	香菇菜包
xīhóngshì chǎo jīdàn	tomatoes with eggs	西红柿炒鸡蛋
yángròu chuàn	barbecued lamb skewers with ground cumin and chili powder	羊肉串

PINYIN	ENGLISH	CHINESE
yóutiáo	fried salty doughnut	油条
yúxiāng qiézi	eggplant in garlic sauce	鱼香茄子
yúxiāng ròusī	shredded pork in garlic sauce	鱼香肉丝
zhēngjiǎo	steamed dumplings	蒸饺
zhōu	rice porridge	粥

SPECIALTY DISHES (FROM SHÀNGHĂI & ELSEWHERE) RECOMMENDED IN RESTAURANT REVIEWS

PINYIN	ENGLISH	CHINESE
bābǎo fàn	sweet glutinous rice with nuts and berries	八宝饭
bābǎo jiàng	spicy paste of soya beans, nuts, and berries	八宝酱
báopí yángròu juǎn	minced lamb wrapped in pancakes	薄皮羊肉卷
càixīn xièhuángyóu	vegetarian crab (carrot, mushroom, bamboo)	菜心蟹黄油
chǎo niángāo	stir-fried glutinous rice cakes with meat and vegetables	炒年糕
chénpí sùyā	orange peel vegetarian duck	陈皮素鸭
cōngyóu bǐng	scallion pancakes	葱油饼
dàjiùjià	rice-flour pastry stir-fried with ham, mushrooms, and vegetables	大救架
dāndān miàn	noodles in spicy peanut sauce	担担面
dàzhá xiè	hairy crab	大闸蟹
dōngpō ròu	braised fatty pork in small clay pot	东坡肉
dòushā sūbǐng	crispy pastry with mashed bean filling	豆沙酥饼
duòjiāo yútóu	fish head steamed with red chili	剁椒鱼头
fūqī fèipiàn	beef and tongue doused in chili oil and peanuts	夫妻肺片
gānbiān tǔdòu bā	fried potato pancake	干煸土豆粑
gānguōjī guōzi	spicy chicken with peppers	干锅鸡锅子
guòqiáo mǐxiàn	crossing-the-bridge noodles	过桥米线
gūsū lǔyā	marinated duck	姑苏卤鸭
Hángzhōu jiàohuà jī	"beggar's chicken"— baked in clay	杭州叫化鸡
hóngshāo típǎng	braised pig thighs	红烧蹄膀
huángmèn hémàn	braised river eel	黄焖河鳗
huíguō ròu jiā bǐng	twice-cooked lamb wrapped in pancakes	回锅肉夹饼
huōyàn niúròu	beef with red and green peppers	火焰牛肉

PINYIN	ENGLISH	CHINESE
jiāobái	wild rice stems	茭白
jiǔcài hézi	leek pie	韭菜盒子
kǎofū	braised wheat gluten	烤麸
kǎo quányáng	roast lamb	烤全羊
kǎo yángròu	barbecue lamb skewers	烤羊肉
kòu sān sī	julienne strips of tofu skin, ham, and bamboo	扣三丝
lǎohǔ cài	Xīnjiāng salad	老虎菜
làzi jīdīng	spicy chicken nuggets	辣子鸡丁
liǎngmiàn huáng	panfried noodles	两面黄
lóngjǐng xiārén	shelled shrimp sprinkled with lóngjǐng tea	龙井虾仁
méicài kòuròu	braised pork with mustard greens	梅菜扣肉
mín bǐng	sweet glutinous rice pastry	闵饼
mìzhī chāshāo fàn	barbecue pork rice	蜜汁叉烧饭
mìzhī huǒfǎng	pork and taro in candied sauce	蜜汁火舫
Nánxiáng xiǎolóng bāo	Nánxiáng crabmeat and pork dumplings	南翔小龙包
pídàn dòufu	tofu with "thousand year" eggs	皮蛋豆腐
qícài dōngsǔn	winter shoots with local greens	荠菜冬笋
qìguō jī	steamed chicken	汽锅鸡
qīngzhēng dòuní	creamy mashed beans	青蒸豆泥
rìběn jièmo chǎo niúliǔlì	*wasabi* stir-fried beef	日本芥末炒牛柳粒
sānsī méimáo sū	pork, bamboo, and mushroom-stuffed crisp	三丝眉毛酥
shèngguā chǎo zhūjǐngròu	crispy-skinned pork	胜瓜炒猪颈肉
shēngjiān baōzi	pork-stuffed fried bread dumplings	生煎包子
shīzi tóu	lion's head meatballs	狮子头
shuǐjīng xiārén	stir-fried shrimp	水晶虾仁
shuǐzhǔ yú	fish slices and vegetables in spicy broth	水煮鱼
sōngshǔ guìyú	sweet-and-sour deep-fried fish	松鼠桂鱼
sōngshǔ lúyú	sweet-and-sour fried perch	松鼠鲈鱼
sōngzǐ dōngpō ròu	braised meat with pine nuts	松子东坡肉
suān dòujiǎo ròuní	diced sour beans with minced pork	酸豆角肉泥
suān jiāngdòu làròu	sour long beans with chilies and bacon	酸豇豆腊肉
sùjī	vegetarian chicken	素鸡
sùyā	vegetarian duck	素鸭

PINYIN	ENGLISH	CHINESE
xiānggū miànjīn miàn	noodle soup with gluten and mushrooms	香菇面筋面
xiāngwèi hóngshǔ bō	fragrant sweet potato in monk's pot	香味红薯钵
xiānxiā yúntūn miàn	shrimp wonton noodles in soup	鲜虾云吞面
xiǎolóng bāozi	pork-stuffed steamed bread dumplings	小笼包
xiǎo xūnyú	smoked fish	小熏鱼
xiāròu xiǎohúntūn	soup wontons with shrimp filling	虾肉小馄饨
xiāròu xiǎolóng	steamed shrimp and pork dumplings	虾肉小笼
xièfěn huì zhēnjūn	braised mushroom with crabmeat	蟹粉烩珍菌
xièfěn shēngjiān	crabmeat and pork buns steamed in oil	蟹粉生煎
xièfěn xiǎolóng	pork and powdered crabmeat dumplings	蟹粉小笼
Xīnjiāng píjiǔ	Xīnjiāng black beer	
XO jiàng chǎo sìjìdòu	stir-fried string beans in XO sauce	XO 酱炒四季豆
xūnyú	cold smoked fish	熏鱼
yángròu chuàn	spicy mutton skewers with cumin	羊肉串
yóumèn sǔn	braised bamboo shoots	油焖笋
yóutiáo niúròu	sliced beef with fried dough in savory sauce	油条牛肉
zhāngchá yā	crispy smoked duck with plum sauce	樟茶鸭
zhuàngyuán tí	braised pig's trotters	猪油捞饭
zhūyóu lāofàn	rice with lard and soya sauce	状元蹄

Appendix B:
The Chinese Language

by Peter Neville-Hadley

Chinese is not as difficult a language to learn as it may first appear to be—at least not once you've decided what kind of Chinese to learn. There are six major languages called Chinese. Speakers of each are unintelligible to each other, and there are, in addition, a host of dialects. The Chinese you are likely to hear spoken in your local Chinatown or Chinese restaurant, or used by your friends of Chinese descent when they speak to their parents, is more than likely to be Cantonese, which is the version of Chinese used in Hong Kong and in much of southern China. Shanghainese is a sub-dialect of the Wú language group. But the official national language of China is **Mandarin** (**Pǔtōnghuà**—"common speech"), sometimes called Modern Standard Chinese, and viewed in mainland China as the language of administration, of the classics, and of the educated. While throughout much of mainland China people speak their own local flavor of Chinese for everyday communication, they've all been educated in Mandarin which, in general terms, is the language of Běijīng and the north. Mandarin is less well known in Hong Kong and Macau, but it is also spoken in Táiwān and Singapore, and among growing communities of recent immigrants to North America and Europe. Although the Shanghainese are conversant in *pǔtōnghuà,* you're just as, if not more, likely to hear Shanghainese spoken wherever locals gather.

Dialects notwithstanding, Chinese grammar is considerably more straightforward than those of English or other European languages, even Spanish or Italian. There are no genders, so there is no need to remember long lists of endings for adjectives and to make them agree, with variations according to case. There are no equivalents for the definite and indefinite articles ("the," "a," "an"), so there is no need to make those agree either. Singular and plural nouns are the same. Best of all, verbs cannot be declined. The verb "to be" is *shì.* The same sound also covers "am," "are," "is," "was," "will be," and so on, since there are also no tenses. Instead of past, present, and future, Chinese is more concerned with whether an action is continuing or has been completed, and with the order in which events take place. To make matters of time clear, Chinese depends on simple expressions such as "yesterday," "before," "originally," "next year," and the like. "Tomorrow I go New York," is clear enough, as is "Yesterday I go New York." It's a little more complicated than these brief notes can suggest, but not much.

There are a few sounds in Mandarin that are not used in English (see the rough pronunciation guide below), but the main difficulty for foreigners lies in tones. Most sounds in Mandarin begin with a consonant and end in a vowel (or -n, or -ng), which leaves the language with very few distinct noises compared to English. Originally, one sound equaled one idea and one word. Even now, each of these monosyllables is represented by a single character, but often words have been made by putting two characters together, sometimes both with the same meaning, thus reinforcing one another. The solution to this phonetic poverty is to multiply the available sounds by making them tonal—speaking them at different pitches, thereby giving them different meanings. *Mā* spoken on a high level tone (1st tone) offers a set of possible meanings different from those of *má* spoken with a rising tone (2nd tone), *mǎ* with a dipping then rising tone (3rd tone), or *mà* with an abruptly falling tone (4th tone). There's also a different meaning for the neutral, toneless *ma*.

In the average sentence, context is your friend (there are not many occasions in which the 3rd-tone *mǎ* or "horse" might be mistaken for the 4th-tone *mà* or "grasshopper," for instance), but without tone, there is essentially no meaning. The novice best sing his or her Mandarin very clearly, as Chinese children do— a chanted sing-song can be heard emerging from the windows of primary schools across China. With experience, the student learns to give particular emphasis to the tones on words essential to a sentence's meaning, and to treat the others more lightly. Sadly, most books using modern Romanized Chinese, called *Hànyǔ pīnyīn* ("Hàn language spell-the-sounds"), do not mark the tones, nor do these appear on **pīnyīn** signs in China. But in this book, the authors, most of whom speak Mandarin, have added tones to every Mandarin expression, so you can have a go at saying them for yourself. Where tones do not appear, that's usually because the name of a person or place is already familiar to many readers in an older form of Romanized Chinese such as Wade-Giles or Post Office (in which Běijīng was written misleadingly as Peking); or because it is better known in Cantonese: Sun Yat-sen, or Canton, for instance.

Cantonese has *eight* tones plus the neutral, but its grammatical structure is largely the same, as is that of all versions of Chinese. Even Chinese people who can barely understand each other's speech can at least write to each other, since written forms are similar. Mainland China, with the aim of increasing literacy (or perhaps of distancing the supposedly now thoroughly modern and socialist population from its Confucian heritage), instituted a ham-fisted simplification program in the 1950s, which reduced some characters originally taking 14 strokes of the brush, for instance, to as few as three strokes. Hong Kong, separated from the mainland and under British control until 1997, went its own way, kept the original full-form characters, and invented lots of new ones, too. Nevertheless, many characters remain the same, and some of the simplified forms are merely familiar shorthands for the full-form ones. But however many different meanings for each tone of *ma* there may be, for each meaning there's a different character. This makes the written form a far more successful communication medium than the spoken one, which leads to misunderstandings even between native speakers, who can often be seen sketching characters on their palms during conversation to confirm which one is meant.

The thought of learning 3,000 to 5,000 individual characters (at least 2,500 are needed to read a newspaper) also daunts many beginners. But look carefully at the ones below, and you'll notice many common elements. In fact, a rather limited number of smaller shapes are combined in different ways, much as we combine letters to make words. Admittedly, the characters only offer general hints as to their pronunciation, and that's often misleading—the system is not a phonetic one, so each new Mandarin word has to be learned as both a sound and a shape (or a group of them). But soon it's the similarities among the characters, not their differences, which begin to bother the student. English, a far more subtle language with a far larger vocabulary, and with so many pointless inconsistencies and exceptions to what are laughingly called its rules, is much more of a struggle for the Chinese than Mandarin should be for us.

But no knowledge of the language is needed to get around China, and it's almost of assistance that Chinese take it for granted that outlandish foreigners (that's you and me unless of Chinese descent) can speak not a word (poor things) and must use whatever other limited means we have to communicate—this book and a phrase book, for instance. For help with navigation to sights, simply point to the characters in this book's map keys. When leaving your hotel, take one of its cards with you, and show it to the taxi driver when you want to return. In section 2, below, is a limited list of useful words and phrases that is best supplemented with a proper phrase book. If you have a Mandarin-speaking friend from the north (Cantonese speakers who know Mandarin as a 2nd language tend to have fairly heavy accents), ask him or her to pronounce the greetings and words of thanks from the list below, so you can repeat after him and practice. While you are as much likely to be laughed *at* as *with* in China, such efforts are always appreciated.

1 A Guide to Pīnyīn Pronunciation

Letters in pīnyīn mostly have the values any English speaker would expect, with the following exceptions:

c *ts* as in bi*ts*

q *ch* as in *ch*in, but much harder and more forward, made with tongue and teeth

r has no true equivalent in English, but the *r* of *r*eed is close, although the tip of the tongue should be near the top of the mouth, and the teeth together

x also has no true equivalent, but is nearest to the *sh* of *sh*eep, although the tongue should be parallel to the roof of the mouth and the teeth together

zh is a soft j, like the *dge* in ju*dge*

The vowels are pronounced roughly as follows:

a as in f*a*ther

e as in *e*rr (*leng* is pronounced as English "lung")

i is pronounced *ee* after most consonants, but after c, ch, r, s, sh, z, and zh is a buzz at the front of the mouth behind closed teeth

o as in s*o*ng

u as in t*oo*

ü is the purer, lips-pursed u of French t*u* and German *ü*. Confusingly, **u** after j, x, q, and y is always ü, but in these cases the accent over "ü" does not appear.

ai sounds like *eye*

ao as in *ou*ch

ei as in h*ay*

ia as in *ya*k

ian sounds like *yen*

iang sounds like *yang*

iu sounds like *you*

ou as in t*oe*

ua as in g*ua*va

ui sounds like *way*

uo sounds like *or,* but is more abrupt

Note that when two or more third-tone "ˇ" sounds follow one another, they should all, except the last, be pronounced as second-tone "ˊ."

2 Mandarin Bare Essentials

GREETINGS & INTRODUCTIONS

ENGLISH	PINYIN	CHINESE
Hello	Nǐ hǎo	你好
How are you?	Nǐ hǎo ma?	你好吗？
Fine. And you?	Wǒ hěn hǎo. Nǐ ne?	我很好你呢？
I'm not too well/things aren't going well	Bù hǎo	不好
What is your name? (very polite)	Nín guì xìng?	您贵姓
My (family) name is . . .	Wǒ xìng . . .	我姓。。。
I'm known as (family, then given name)	Wǒ jiào . . .	我叫。。。
I'm [American]	Wǒ shì [Měiguó] rén	我是美国人
[Australian]	[Àodàlìyà]	澳大利亚
[British]	[Yīngguó]	英国
[Canadian]	[Jiānádà]	加拿大
[Irish]	[Àiěrlán]	爱尔兰
[New Zealander]	[Xīnxīlán]	新西兰
I'm from [America]	Wǒ shì cóng [Měiguó] lái de	我是从美国来的
Excuse me/I'm sorry	Duìbùqǐ	对不起
I don't understand	Wǒ tǐng bù dǒng	我听不懂
Thank you	Xièxie nǐ	谢谢你
Correct (yes)	Duì	对
Not correct	Bú duì	不对
No, I don't want	Wǒ bú yào	我不要
Not acceptable	Bù xíng	不行

BASIC QUESTIONS & PROBLEMS

ENGLISH	PINYIN	CHINESE
Excuse me/I'd like to ask	Qǐng wènyíxià	请问一下
Where is . . . ?	. . . zài nǎr?	。。。在哪儿？
How much is . . . ?	. . . duōshǎo qián?	。。。多少钱？
. . . this one?	Zhèi/Zhè ge . . .	这个。。。
. . . that one?	Nèi/Nà ge . . .	那个。。。
Do you have . . . ?	Nǐ yǒu méi yǒu	你有没有。。。？
What time does/is . . . ?	. . . jǐ diǎn?	。。。几点？
What time is it now?	Xiànzài jǐ diǎn?	现在几点？
When is . . . ?	. . . shénme shíhou?	。。。什么时候？
Why?	Wèishénme?	为什么？
Who?	Shéi?	谁？
Is that okay?	Xíng bù xíng?	行不行？
I'm feeling ill	Wǒ shēng bìng le	我生病了

TRAVEL

ENGLISH	PINYIN	CHINESE
luxury (bus, hotel rooms)	háohuá	豪华
high speed (buses, expressways)	gāosù	高速
air-conditioned	kōngtiáo	空调

NUMBERS

Note that more complicated forms of numbers are often used on official documents and receipts to prevent fraud—see how easily one can be changed to two, three, or even ten. Familiar Arabic numerals appear on bank notes, most signs, taxi meters, and other places. Be particularly careful with *four* and *ten*, which sound very alike in many regions—hold up fingers to make sure. Note, too, that *yī*, meaning "one," tends to change its tone all the time depending on what it precedes. Don't worry about this—once you've started talking about money, almost any kind of squeak for "one" will do. Finally note that "two" alters when being used with expressions of quantity.

ENGLISH	PINYIN	CHINESE
zero	líng	零
one	yī	一
two	èr	二
two (of them)	liǎng ge	两个
three	sān	三
four	sì	四
five	wǔ	五
six	liù	六
seven	qī	七
eight	bā	八
nine	jiǔ	九
10	shí	十
11	shí yī	十一
12	shí èr	十二
21	èr shí yī	二十一
22	èr shí èr	二十二
51	wǔ shí yī	五十一
100	yì bǎi	一百
101	yì bǎi líng yī	一百零一
110	yì bǎi yī (shí)	一百一（十）
111	yì bǎi yī shí yī	一百一十一
1,000	yì qiān	一千
1,500	yì qiān wǔ (bǎi)	一千五百
5,678	wǔ qiān liù bǎi qī shí bāi	五千六百七十八
10,000	yí wàn	一万

MONEY

The word *yuán* (¥) is rarely spoken, nor is *jiǎo*, the written form for ¹⁄₁₀ of a *yuán*, equivalent to 10 *fēn* (there are 100 *fēn* in a *yuán*). Instead, the Chinese speak of "pieces of money," *kuài qián*, usually abbreviated just to *kuài*, and they speak of *máo* for ¹⁄₁₀ of a *kuài*. *Fēn* have been overtaken by inflation and are almost useless. Often all zeros after the last whole number are simply omitted, along with *kuài qián*, which is taken as read, especially in direct reply to the question *duōshǎo qián*—"How much?"

ENGLISH	PINYIN	CHINESE
¥1	yí kuài qián	一块钱
¥2	liǎng kuài qián	两块钱
¥0.30	sān máo qián	三毛钱

ENGLISH	PINYIN	CHINESE
¥5.05	wǔ kuài líng wǔ fēn	五块零五分
¥5.50	wǔ kuài wǔ	五块五
¥550	wǔ bǎi wǔ shí kuài	五百五十块
¥5,500	wǔ qiān wǔ bǎi kuài	五千五百块
Small change	língqián	零钱

BANKING & SHOPPING

ENGLISH	PINYIN	CHINESE
I want to change money (foreign exchange)	Wǒ xiǎng huàn qián	我想换钱
credit card	Xìnyòng kǎ	信用卡
traveler's check	lǚxíng zhīpiào	旅行支票
department store	bǎihuò shāngdiàn	百货商店
	gòuwù zhōngxīn	购物中心
convenience store	xiǎomàibù	小卖部
market	shìchǎng	市场
May I have a look?	Wǒ Kànyíxia, hǎo ma?	我看一下，好吗？
I want to buy . . .	Wǒ xiǎng mǎi . . .	我想买。。。
How many do you want?	Nǐ yào jǐ ge?	你要几个？
Two of them	liǎng ge	两个
Three of them	sān ge	三个
1 kilo (2.2 lb.)	yì gōngjǐn	一公斤
Half a kilo	yì jǐn	一斤
or	bàn gōngjǐn	公斤
1 meter (3¼ ft.)	yì mǐ	一米
Too expensive!	Tài guì le!	太贵了
Do you have change?	Yǒu língqián ma?	有零钱吗

TIME

ENGLISH	PINYIN	CHINESE
morning	shàngwǔ	上午
afternoon	xiàwǔ	下午
evening	wǎnshang	晚上
8:20am	shàngwǔ bā diǎn èr shí fēn	上午八点二十分
9:30am	shàngwǔ jiǔ diǎn bàn	上午九点半
noon	zhōngwǔ	中午
4:15pm	xiàwǔ sì diǎn yí kè	下午四点一刻
midnight	wǔ yè	午夜
1 hour	yí ge xiǎoshí	一个小时
8 hours	bā ge xiǎoshí	八个小时
today	jīntiān	今天
yesterday	zuótiān	昨天
tomorrow	míngtiān	明天
Monday	Xīngqī yī	星期一
Tuesday	Xīngqī èr	星期二
Wednesday	Xīngqī sān	星期三
Thursday	Xīngqī sì	星期四
Friday	Xīngqī wǔ	星期五
Saturday	Xīngqī liù	星期六
Sunday	Xīngqī tiān	星期天

TRANSPORT

ENGLISH	PINYIN	CHINESE
I want to go to . . .	Wǒ xiǎng qù . . .	我想去。。。
plane	fēijī	飞机
train	huǒchē	火车
bus	gōnggòng qìchē	公共汽车
long-distance bus	chángtú qìchē	长途汽车
taxi	chūzū chē	出租车
airport	fēijīchǎng	飞机场
stop or station (bus or train)	zhàn	站
(plane/train/bus) ticket	piào	票

NAVIGATION

ENGLISH	PINYIN	CHINESE
North	Běi	北
South	Nán	南
East	Dōng	东
West	Xī	西
Turn left	zuǒ guǎi	左拐
Turn right	yòu guǎi	右拐
Go straight on	yìzhí zǒu	一直走
crossroads	shízì lùkǒu	十字路口
10 kilometers	shí gōnglǐ	十公里
I'm lost	Wǒ diū le	我丢了

HOTEL

ENGLISH	PINYIN	CHINESE
How many days?	Zhù jǐ tiān?	住几天？
standard room (twin or double with private bathroom)	biāozhǔn jiān	标准间
passport	hùzhào	护照
deposit	yājīn	押金
I want to check out	Wǒ tuì fáng	我退房

RESTAURANT

ENGLISH	PINYIN	CHINESE
How many people?	Jǐ wèi?	几位
waiter/waitress	fúwùyuán	服务员
menu	càidān	菜单
I'm vegetarian	Wǒ shì chī sù de	我是吃素的
Do you have . . . ?	Yǒu méi yǒu . . . ?	有没有。。。？
Please bring a portion of . . .	Qǐng lái yí fènr . . .	请来一份儿。。。
beer	píjiǔ	啤酒
mineral water	kuàngquán shuǐ	矿泉水
Bill, please	jiézhàng	结帐

SIGNS

Here's a list of common signs and notices to help you identify what you are look-ing for, from restaurants to condiments, and to help you choose the right door at the public toilets. These are the simplified characters in everyday use in China, but note that it's increasingly fashionable for larger businesses, and those with a long history, to use more complicated traditional characters, so not all may match what's below. Hong Kong and Macau also use traditional characters, and sometimes use different terms altogether, especially for modern inventions. Also, very old restau-rants and temples across China tend to write their signs from right to left.

ENGLISH	PINYIN	CHINESE
hotel	bīnguǎn	宾馆
	dàjiǔdiàn	大酒店
	jiǔdiàn	酒店
	fàndiàn	饭店
restaurant	fànguǎn	饭馆
	jiǔdiàn	酒店
	jiǔjiā	酒家
vinegar	cù	醋
soya sauce	Jiàngyóu	酱油
bar	jiǔbā	酒吧
Internet bar	wǎngbā	网吧
cafe	kāfē[il]iguǎn	咖啡馆
teahouse	cháguǎn	茶馆
department store	bǎihuò shāngdiàn	百货商店
	gòuwù zhōngxǐn	购物中心
market	shìchǎng	市场
bookstore	shūdiàn	书店
police (Public Security Bureau)	gōng'ānjú	公安局
Bank of China	Zhōngguó Yínháng	中国银行
public telephone	gōngyòng diànhuà	公用电话
public toilet	gōngyòng cèsuǒ	公用厕所
male	nán	男
female	nǚ	女
entrance	rùkǒu	入口
exit	chūkǒu	出口
bus stop/station	qìchē zhàn	汽车站
long-distance bus station	chángtú qìchē zhàn	长途汽车站
luxury	háohuá	豪华
using highway	gāosù	高速
railway station	huǒchē zhàn	火车站
hard seat	yìng zuò	硬座
soft seat	ruǎn zuò	软座
hard sleeper	yìng wò	硬卧
soft sleeper	ruǎn wò	软卧
metro/subway station	dìtiě zhàn	地铁站
airport	fēijīchǎng	飞机场

ENGLISH	PINYIN	CHINESE
dock/wharf	mǎtóu	码头
passenger terminal (bus, boat, and so on)	kèyùn zhàn	客运站
up/get on	shàng	上
down/get off	xià	下
ticket hall	shòupiào tīng	售票厅
ticket office	shòupiào chù	售票处
left-luggage office	xíngli jìcún chù	行李寄存处
temple	sì	寺
	miào	庙
museum	bówùguǎn	博物馆
memorial hall	jìniànguǎn	纪念馆
park	gōngyuán	公园
hospital	yīyuàn	医院
clinic	zhěnsuǒ	诊所
pharmacy	yàofáng/yàodiàn	药房/药店
travel agency	lǚxíngshè	旅行社

[Handwritten annotations:]

DAY 0: plane ride, long taxi ride, massage, gym on TV

DAY 1 walk to Bund, People Square/Fuxing rd, Old town visit, Baiyunguan temple, Pudong, lunch at noodle place in Raffles.

DAY 2 we got lost on way to subway (French Quarter walk, then People's Square meet for dinner at Cantonese rest. strange old man in park (Fuxing) 2 Xi'an students in Renmin

DAY 3: Fitness Center at Hotel, laundry, Shanghai Museum, noodle restaurant (silver ware) walk home in rain (Renmin, Nanjing, Bund) internet, got sick from room service :(couple from plane

DAY 4: Jing An Si + park, taxi to airport, menu's, she, Fuxing bookstore, lost (use compass from battery pack) walk to Bund, check out lobbies back to Jing An Si, check out Moller Villa, acrobat show, dinner at Pizza Hut, nighttime walk

DAY 5: get up early, packed train station

Index

See also Accommodations and Restaurant indexes, below.

ACCOMMODATIONS

RESTAURANTS

FROMMER'S® NATIONAL PARK GUIDES

Algonquin Provincial Park
Banff & Jasper
Family Vacations in the National
  Parks

Grand Canyon
National Parks of the American
  West
Rocky Mountain

Yellowstone & Grand Teton
Yosemite & Sequoia/Kings
  Canyon
Zion & Bryce Canyon

FROMMER'S® MEMORABLE WALKS

Chicago
London

New York
Paris

San Francisco

FROMMER'S® WITH KIDS GUIDES

Chicago
Las Vegas
New York City

Ottawa
San Francisco
Toronto

Vancouver
Walt Disney World® & Orlando
Washington, D.C.

SUZY GERSHMAN'S BORN TO SHOP GUIDES

Born to Shop: France
Born to Shop: Hong Kong,
  Shanghai & Beijing

Born to Shop: Italy
Born to Shop: London

Born to Shop: New York
Born to Shop: Paris

FROMMER'S® IRREVERENT GUIDES

Amsterdam
Boston
Chicago
Las Vegas
London

Los Angeles
Manhattan
New Orleans
Paris
Rome

San Francisco
Seattle & Portland
Vancouver
Walt Disney World®
Washington, D.C.

FROMMER'S® BEST-LOVED DRIVING TOURS

Austria
Britain
California
France

Germany
Ireland
Italy
New England

Northern Italy
Scotland
Spain
Tuscany & Umbria

THE UNOFFICIAL GUIDES®

Beyond Disney
California with Kids
Central Italy
Chicago
Cruises
Disneyland®
England
Florida
Florida with Kids
Inside Disney

Hawaii
Las Vegas
London
Maui
Mexico's Best Beach Resorts
Mini Las Vegas
Mini Mickey
New Orleans
New York City
Paris

San Francisco
Skiing & Snowboarding in the
  West
South Florida including Miami &
  the Keys
Walt Disney World®
Walt Disney World® for
  Grown-ups
Walt Disney World® with Kids
Washington, D.C.

SPECIAL-INTEREST TITLES

Athens Past & Present
Cities Ranked & Rated
Frommer's Best Day Trips from London
Frommer's Best RV & Tent Campgrounds
  in the U.S.A.
Frommer's Caribbean Hideaways
Frommer's China: The 50 Most Memorable Trips
Frommer's Exploring America by RV
Frommer's Gay & Lesbian Europe
Frommer's NYC Free & Dirt Cheap

Frommer's Road Atlas Europe
Frommer's Road Atlas France
Frommer's Road Atlas Ireland
Frommer's Wonderful Weekends from
  New York City
The New York Times' Guide to Unforgettable
  Weekends
Retirement Places Rated
Rome Past & Present

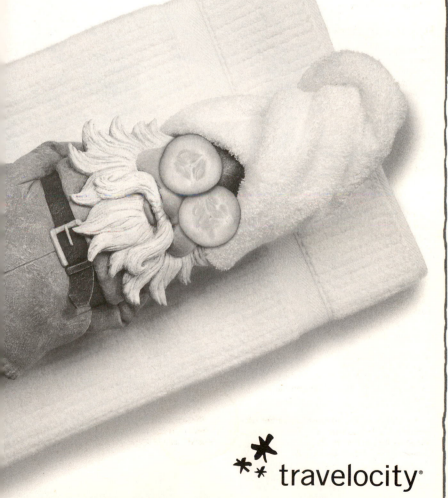

Travel Tip: He who finds the best hotel deal has more to spend on facials involving knobbly vegetables.

Hello, the Roaming Gnome here. I've been nabbed from the garden and taken round the world. The people who took me are so terribly clever. They find the best offerings on Travelocity. For very little cha-ching. And that means I get to be pampered and exfoliated till I'm pink as a bunny's doodah.

*** travelocity®

-888-TRAVELOCITY / travelocity.com / America Online Keyword: Travel

Travel Tip: Make sure there's customer service for any change of plans — involving friendly natives, for example.

One can plan and plan, but if you don't book with the right people you can't seize le moment and canoodle with the poodle named Pansy. I, for one, am all for fraternizing with the locals. Better yet, if I need to extend my stay and my gnome nappers are willing, it can all be arranged through the 800 number at, oh look, how convenient, the lovely company coat of arms.

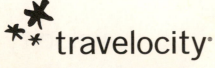

travelocity®

1-888-TRAVELOCITY | travelocity.com | America Online Keyword: Travel